EDWARD BOREIN: COWBOY ARTIST

EDWARD BOREIN: COWBOY ARTIST

July 21–September 11, 2000
Gerald Peters Gallery, 1011 Paseo de Peralta, Santa Fe, NM 87501
Tel 505 954-5700 Fax 505 954-5754

ISBN: 0-935037-63-2

Exhibition & Catalogue Direction: Brady Roberts
Catalogue Design: Laura McCurdy
Editor: Jo Ann Baldinger
Photography: Joe D'Alessandro
Printing & Binding: Advanced Litho Printing, Great Falls, MT

Front cover: *Roping Wild Horses* (detail). Watercolor and gouache on paper. 13 3/4 x 18 5/8 inches. Signed lower right: *EDWARD BOREIN.*

EDWARD BOREIN: COWBOY ARTIST
(1872–1945)

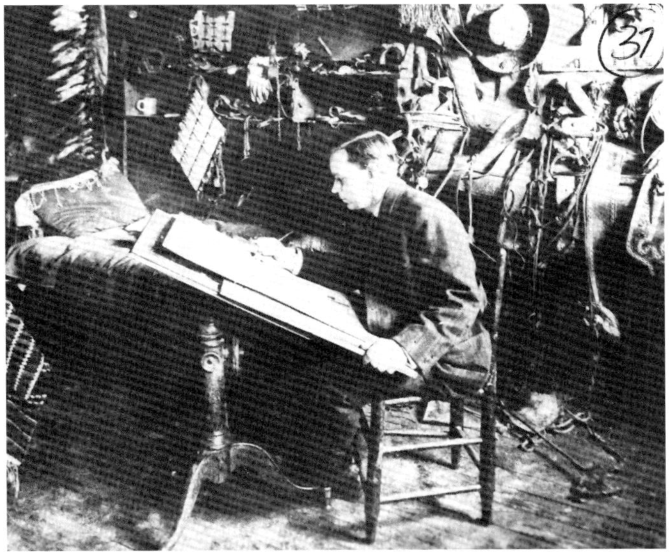

Edward Borein in his New York studio (ca. 1912).
Photograph courtesy of Harold G. Davidson.

GERALD GP PETERS GALLERY

1011 PASEO DE PERALTA, SANTA FE, NEW MEXICO 87501

TEL 505 954-5700 FAX 505 954-5754 WWW.GPGALLERY.COM

SANTA FE • NEW YORK • DALLAS

FOREWORD

The Gerald Peters Gallery is pleased to present this comprehensive survey of works by one of the great artists of the American West, Edward Borein. Like his friend Charles Russell, Borein portrayed cowboy life from direct experience. He began drawing western scenes at an early age, and by the 1890s was working on drives and ranches from Oregon to the Baja peninsula. Although Edward Borein was one of the finest draftsmen of his generation, it is surprising that he is only now beginning to receive the national recognition he deserves.

One of Borein's greatest admirers was Dr. Otey Johnson, who built the finest private collection of works by the artist which forms the core of this show. Additional works from several other private collections help round out the exhibition. For many years, it was my pleasure to help Otey Johnson develop his collection, and it is a pleasure now to be re-associated with these works. Otey was a collector of unique vision and dedication, and an old friend who will be missed.

Much of what we know about Edward Borein comes through the tireless efforts of Harold G. Davidson. Mr. Davidson has been investigating and writing about Borein for over three decades. We are indebted to Hal for his work, and in particular for the marvelous essay that follows.

An exhibition of this scale could not be accomplished without the hard work of the staff at the Gerald Peters Gallery. My thanks to Brady Roberts for coordinating the exhibition; Doniece Pitts, Otey Johnson's Curator for fourteen years, for her invaluable insight; Meredith Nix, Registrar, for documenting the works; Joe D'Alessandro and his assistant, Therese Williams, for the excellent photography; Laura McCurdy for designing the catalogue; and Jay Nelson, Mark Rivera and Steve Zolin for preparing and installing the works. I would also like to thank our colleague Marlene Miller at the Arlington Gallery for her research assistance.

For over two decades, the Gerald Peters Gallery has been dedicated to presenting and interpreting the finest examples of Western American art. It is my hope that this exhibition and catalogue will help to clearly establish Edward Borein as a key figure of this great genre.

Gerald P. Peters

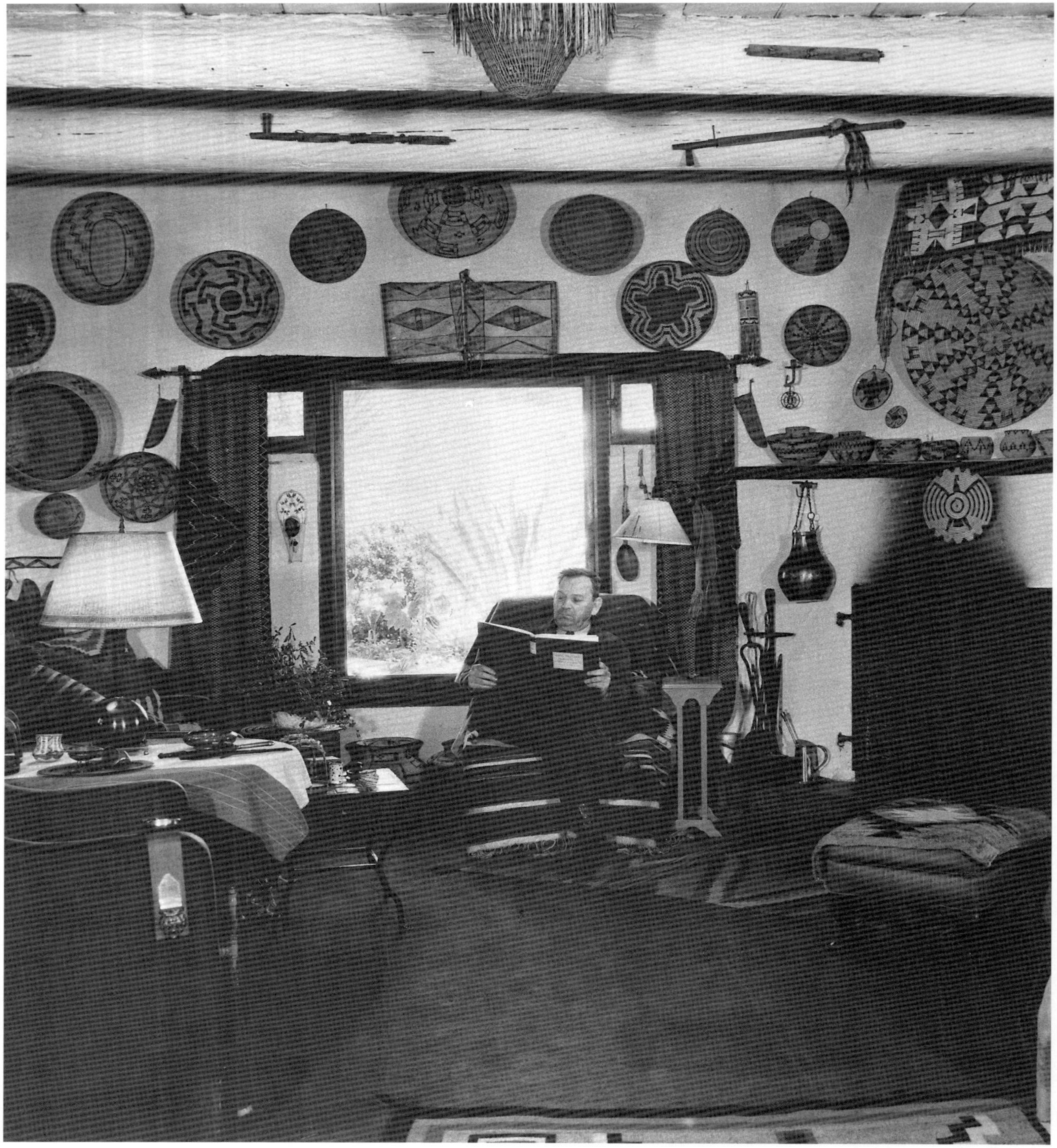

Edward Borein in his living room surrounded by some of his collection of artifacts.
Photograph courtesy of Harold G. Davidson.

EDWARD BOREIN: COWBOY ARTIST (1872–1945)

by Harold G. Davidson

On a sunny morning in June 1914, in the sleepy Bosnian town of Sarajevo, Archduke Francis Ferdinand was killed by an assassin's bullet; the armies of Europe mobilized, and World War I had begun. The Panama Canal was opened to traffic the same year, while back in New York, John Phillip Sousa's band played in concert at the Hippodrome, Robert Henri had a one-man show at the Macbeth Galleries, and Childe Hassam exhibited his new paintings at the Montross Galleries. In a building over on West 42nd Street, a forty-two-year-old cowboy artist from California was producing the first of his prodigious output of etchings of the West, which would eventually total over four hundred different subjects.

John Edward Borein had reached New York by a circuitous route. He was born in San Leandro, California, on October 21, 1872, and thus was one of the few western artists actually born in the West. His father, Peter R. Borein, was a deputy sheriff in that city and had met and wooed Miss Annie Blake. Peter and Annie were married on December 9, 1871.

San Leandro was a western cow town on the main trail between the South and the stockyards and slaughterhouse pens a few miles north at Emeryville. As a result, there was an almost daily passage of cattle and colorful vaqueros, and this constant exposure impressed Edward, the oldest of five Borein children. At the age of five, he commenced to sketch the men and animals that he observed on the streets of the town. His parents encouraged his drawing, and after a grade school education, he enrolled at the

San Francisco Art Association Art School in 1891, where his fellow students included Maynard Dixon, Jimmy Swinnerton, Homer Davenport, and the wild and unpredictable Xavier Martinez. But Ed grew restless and, after one month's instruction, left the school, having made the decision to become a working cowboy.

He had earlier learned to sit a horse and rope and drive cattle, and soon found work on ranches in the area. He left San Leandro in 1893 and drifted down the West Coast, working as a cowboy on several ranches and sketching the daily activities of routine ranch life. He soon dropped his first name, John, and thereafter was known as Edward, or more frequently, Ed.

He eventually arrived at the vast old Spanish cattle ranch of Jésus Maria in Santa Barbara County, which was situated on the present site of Vandenberg Air Force Base. He signed on as a cowboy, resumed his after-hours sketching, and eventually wrapped up some of his drawings and mailed them to *The Land of Sunshine,* a Los Angeles magazine. To his amazement, he received a check for fifteen dollars.

Borein traveled farther south and obtained employment at the Rancho Malibu, just north of Los Angeles. Here he met Leo Carrillo, a precocious descendant of early Spanish families; their subsequent friendship lasted throughout their lifetimes. Carrillo later achieved fame in his role of Pancho on television's "Cisco Kid." Borein soon had the bunkhouse walls covered with his sketches, which prompted Francisco Ruiz, the range boss, to snort, "He draws peechers, peechers all day long. If thees fellow work hard he might be a good vaquero, but no, he draws peechers all day."

Frederick Rindge, the ranch owner, became interested in the artist and later financed Borein's first trip to Mexico in 1897. The early California Spanish period was on the wane, the roving Indian bands were now on reservations, and the picturesque Mexican longhorns were being slowly replaced by other breeds. The open range was being fenced by new owners, and the California types and subjects that filled Borein's sketchbooks were disappearing from the scene. The artist was unaware of it, but he was documenting the gradual transition from Spanish to American influence in California.

Borein reasoned that Old Mexico would still have the glamour and color of the frontier. The Mexican border was 160 miles away from Rancho Malibu, the sun was warm, and he was young and had a good horse. With Rindge's encouragement, Borein decided to make the move.

One day in 1897, he asked for his time, packed his belongings, and rode across the border into Mexico.

He soon found what he was looking for. The fierce heat, bright colors, and the dry and desolate landscape of Mexico, along with the hard-working natives and their lifestyle, were made to order for his sketchbooks. He traveled and sketched, and when funds ran low, he would get work as a cowboy. This first Mexican trip produced a virtual torrent of drawings of the places he visited and the people he met, and many of them were later used as source material for his drawings, paintings, and etchings.

In June 1900, Borein returned to Oakland where his family now lived, and after setting up a studio at his parents' home, found a job as staff artist on the old *San Francisco Call*. His pay was eight dollars week, and this short newspaper apprenticeship paid dividends in the quality of his later work. Many of his Mexican drawings were used for full-page feature articles, including several with interesting texts written by the artist.

Borein was working mostly with pencil, India ink, and occasionally watercolor, and sold many of his drawings to *Sunset Magazine* for use as story illustrations and commercial advertisements. During his first Oakland period (1900–1907), Borein painted numerous oil paintings. He worked rapidly and turned out dozens of paintings — more than he is usually credited with. He also fashioned a few wax and clay models but was not particularly interested in sculpture.

Borein had met Maynard Dixon during his short stay at the San Francisco Art School in 1891. The pair had gone their separate ways until they met again in spring 1901, when they made plans for a sketching trip by horse and pack animal through the Sierras and into the Northwest. They left on May 6 and returned to San Francisco in late fall, after traveling through California, Oregon and Idaho. Dixon came home with many sketches and notes, but there appear to have been few Borein drawings from this journey. Upon his return home, Borein remarked: "My next trip will be to Mexico, where you don't have to go 847 miles to see nothing."

Borein could not overcome his urge to return to Mexico. As he was about to leave Oakland, he met Leo Carrillo, then working as an illustrator on the *San Francisco Examiner*, and asked him to come with him. The practical Carrillo asked, "Have you got any money?" "Sure," said Ed. "I've got two dollars, and I've already shipped my saddle down, so all we have to do is catch a freight." Carrillo declined. Borein found another friend, Owen O'Neill of Santa Barbara, and the pair arrived in Mexico in early 1903. After working and sketching for several months, Borein parted company with O'Neill and hired on as a cowboy at the Hearst-owned Babicora Ranch in Chihuahua. Toward the end of the year, he helped drive a herd of 3,800 head of Babicora cattle north into the United States at Columbus, New Mexico. He was paid off and started a long trip home through the Pueblo Indian country of the Southwest. He visited and sketched at Laguna, Acoma, and Taos in New Mexico, and at Oraibi and Walpi in Arizona. Many drawings from this trip were later used as source materials for his etchings.

Borein arrived in Oakland in June 1904. He was flat broke, but managed to rent a studio and living quarters in the downtown area of the city. He supplied illustrations for *Sunset Magazine* and developed a sideline of display and show-card writing. It kept him going, as he said, "Until I get good. Someday I will be better than Remington, but never as good as Charlie Russell."

The San Francisco earthquake of 1906 gave Oakland, and Borein's studio, a bad shaking. Articles were knocked from tables, and pictures fell from the walls. Several of his drawings and paintings were completely destroyed, but the artist and a friend, Walt Fieberling, cleaned up the debris and salvaged most of the pictures.

Borein's friends and critics had for many years told him that he would have to go to New York, the art capital of America, and meet other artists, visit the galleries, and learn new methods. Fortunately, Ed took their advice, left Oakland and arrived in New York in December 1907.

His friends proved to be right. He did as they had advised, and by 1910–11 his work had improved dramatically. Under the guidance of Edwin Emerson, a friend and successful journalist, Borein made the rounds of art editors of New York's magazines and newspapers and received many commissions for his work. It was the heyday of the illustrators, and the exciting western subjects that Borein and other artists provided were in demand by eager eastern readers. It is not generally known that Borein became a successful illustrator during his New York period (1907–1919), and it is this author's opinion that these years were his finest and most productive.

He met Charlie and Nancy Russell when they came to the city during the winter of 1908, and the two artists soon found they had much in common. The Russells were in the same

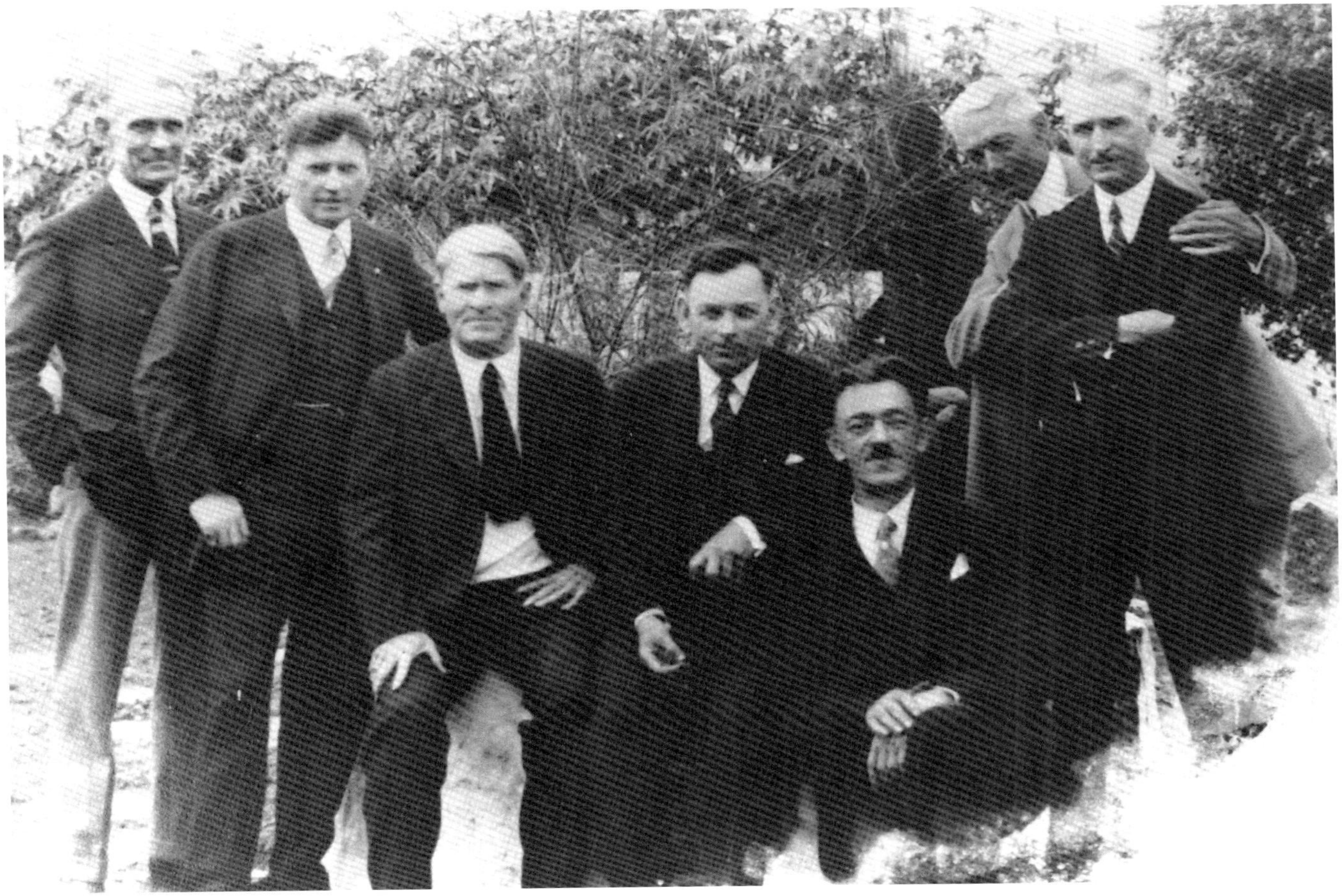

Artists, from left to right: Max Wieczorek, Frank Tenney Johnson, Charles M. Russell, Edward Borein, Alexis Podchernikoff, William L. Otte, and Jack W. Smith in Beverly Hills, California, 1923.
Photograph courtesy of Harold G. Davidson.

circumstances as Borein, scurrying around New York selling a few pictures, and trying to get commissions from editors for commercial illustrations.

Borein became convinced that by means of etching he could get his work into the hands of the greatest number of collectors. Accordingly, he enrolled in etching classes at the New York Art Students League in 1914 and received instruction from Voitjtech Preissig. He also got good advice and encouragement from Childe Hassam and Ernest David Roth. His direct type of sketching was readily adaptable to the etching medium, and he required little apprenticeship before producing first-class etchings.

Many of Borein's greatest etchings were done in New York, and by the time he returned West in

1919, he was an established etcher. A visitor to his New York studio at 138 West 42nd Street noted that he cleaned his etching plates in the bathtub, which rendered it unfit for human use. None of this bothered the artist or his visitors, who included Teddy Roosevelt, Charlie Russell, Will Rogers, Jimmy Swinnerton, Maynard Dixon, Fred Stone, Leo Carrillo and a host of displaced and homesick westerners. West 42nd Street was then in the heart of the old theatrical district, where the hurly-burly of show biz and the noise and excitement of New York sharply contrasted with Borein's former leisurely life in California and Mexico.

His commercial illustrations were mainly large, dry brush drawings; dozens of them depicted exciting western subjects. Probably his best were the series of posters he did to advertise the Calgary Stampede and the Sheepshead Bay Stampede in New York, held August 5–12, 1916.

There was also time for fun. Borein and a friend one day decided to have an old-fashioned barbecue in Central Park. They bought the thickest steaks they could afford, some bread and coffee, and set off. They found a secluded spot and had their steaks ready to come off the fire, their aroma filling the air, when one of New York's "Finest" — a mounted policeman — rode up and interrupted the preparations. He was in a mood to put the pair in jail, but Borein invited him to share their feast. The policeman tied his horse behind some trees and joined them. He hadn't had barbecued steak in years. The story made the newspapers the next day, but there was no mention of the fate of the hungry patrolman.

Borein headed back to the West in 1919, and after a trip to Great Falls to see his old friend Charlie Russell, he returned to Oakland. There he met a widow, Lucile Maxwell, and after a short romance, they were married on June 27, 1921. The Boreins made their home in Santa Barbara, where Ed opened the first of his eventual four studios and soon became a popular addition to the artistic community. Santa Barbara in the twenties had a flourishing art colony, with such artists as Thomas Moran, Carl Oscar Borg, Frank Tenney Johnson, Fernand Lungren, Joe De Yong and many others who appreciated the Channel City's bucolic climate.

The Boreins built a Hopi-style home and studio on the Santa Barbara Mesa overlooking the Pacific Ocean and moved in just in time for the great Santa Barbara earthquake of 1925. The house was badly damaged and Lucile was injured.

She recovered after several months and helped her husband rebuild their home.

After the earthquake, the artist moved into a new studio in El Paseo — a Spanish-style shopping plaza — where there was a daily flow of tourists and townspeople. He continued to work on his etchings, and sales were good, at prices ranging from $5 to $35. One of the best stories about Edward Borein which bears repeating, concerns a little old lady looking over the etchings in his shop, finally selecting one and asking Borein, "How much?" He replied, "Thirty-five," and the lady rummaged in her purse, produced thirty-five cents, and handed it to the artist. Borein, with a twinkle in his eyes, wrapped the print, thanked her, and handed her the parcel.

Will Rogers was probably Borein's closest friend and came to visit whenever he could get away from his heavy Hollywood schedule. The two had met in New York when they were both struggling, and their warm friendship lasted until Rogers' tragic death in 1935. Other celebrities who came to see Borein at his studio in El Paseo included the humorist Irvin S. Cobb, Fred Stone, Charlie Russell, and Jimmy Swinnerton, creator of the cartoon strips "Little Jimmy" and "The Canyon Kiddies," and later an outstanding painter of the Grand Canyon and the Southwest.

Old Spanish Days in Santa Barbara is an annual event held during the full of the August moon, and Borein helped organize the first Fiesta Parade in 1924. He arranged to have his friends Will Rogers, Leo Carrillo and Irvin S. Cobb come to Santa Barbara to give shows during Fiesta.

Borein also helped to organize Los Rancheros Vistadores in 1930, a riding group that meets each year. Come the first of May, more than five hundred men from all parts of North America arrive in Santa Barbara to ride over the hills and enjoy good companionship and outdoor living for six days. Borein rode with the group for many years.

Borein had first experimented with watercolors during his travels in Mexico (1897–1903) but practically abandoned it during his New York period (1907–1919). In Santa Barbara he commenced his serious work in watercolor, and the results of his efforts quickly became popular. Spencer Bagdatopoulos, a Greek-born artist who came to Santa Barbara in 1932, gave him practical advice and encouragement, and by the mid-1930s Borein was reaching his peak as a watercolorist. His watercolors are eagerly sought

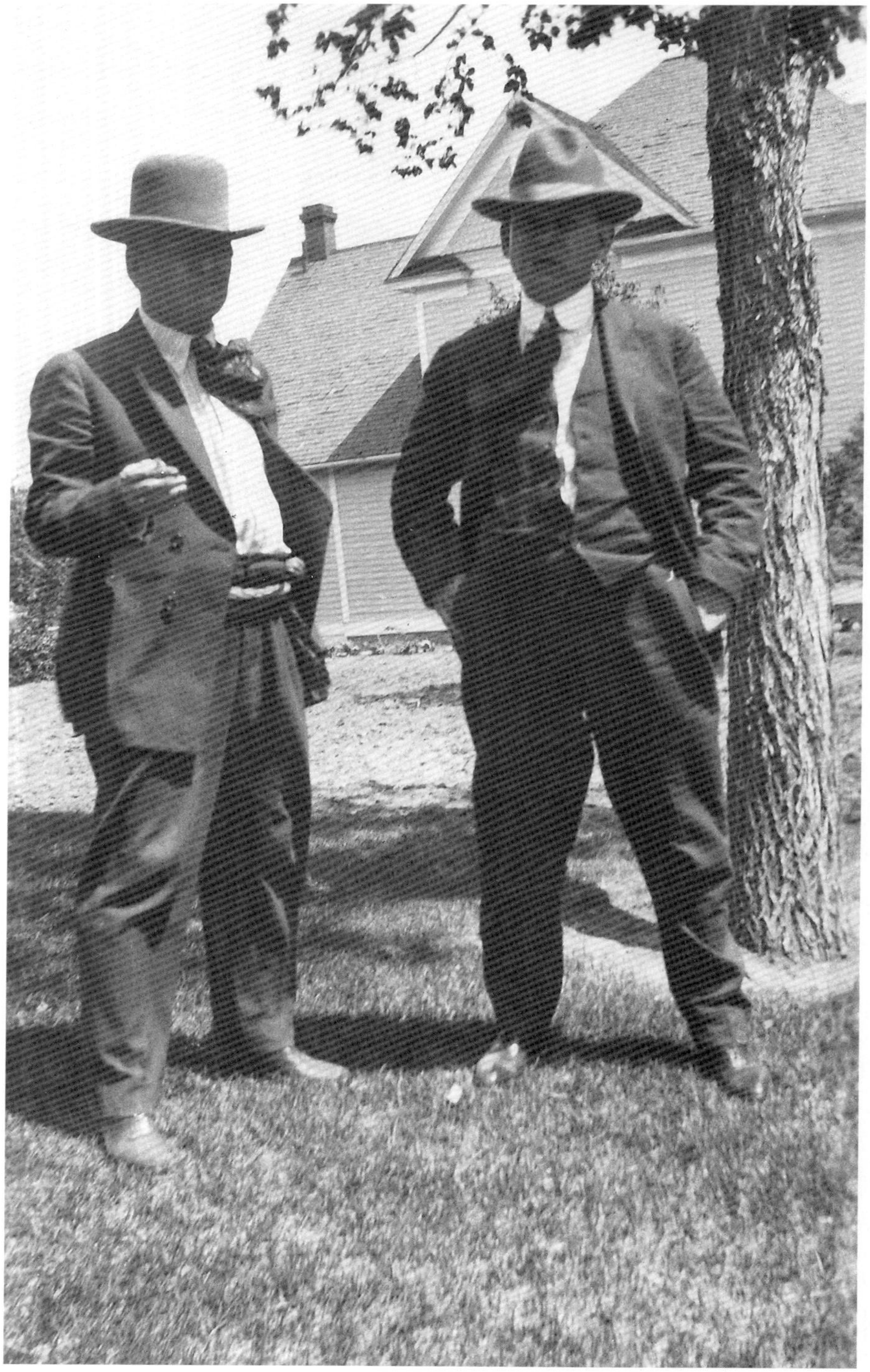

Charles M. Russell and Edward Borein in Great Falls, Montana, June 1919.
Photograph courtesy of Harold G. Davidson.

by collectors of western art, and good quality examples bring the highest prices of all his work.

Edward Borein, in company with every painter of note, had his bad days. No artist who ever lived produced a ceaseless flow of flawless masterworks, but for a self-taught artist in this most demanding of mediums, Borein achieved wonders. He can claim his rightful place among the pioneer watercolorists of the West.

The artist had served a short apprenticeship in a saddlery shop in San Leandro during his youth, and later in Santa Barbara. He occasionally made his own saddles, tooling the leather with beautiful designs. He would hand craft miniature saddles of leather, authentic to the last detail, and was constantly braiding rawhide into intricate patterns. He felt this would keep his fingers supple and help him avoid a disease all artists dread —arthritis. He also produced a few plaster and clay sculptures that were later bronzed.

Edward Borein lived and worked in Santa Barbara until his death in 1945, and during this period, he produced thousands of etchings, watercolors, india ink sketches, and pencil drawings. He was a master of the quick, direct sketch. A few short lines with the pen or pencil, and a horse would quickly appear on the paper, followed quickly by the rider. His economy of line is equaled by few artists, and he did hundreds of these sketches, which he considered his "practice." Mrs. Borein would sit in the evening reading the newspaper to Ed, while he sketched. When he went to bed, the floor would be littered with sketches, and he would tell his wife to "throw them in the fire," but fortunately she gathered and collected them instead.

Edward Borein was one of the most prolific artists the West has ever seen and has to his credit numerous magnificent watercolors and drawings. His place in the annals of American art is, however, assured by virtue of his etchings of the West. They are intellectually honest documents of how he lived and what he saw.

COLOR PLATES

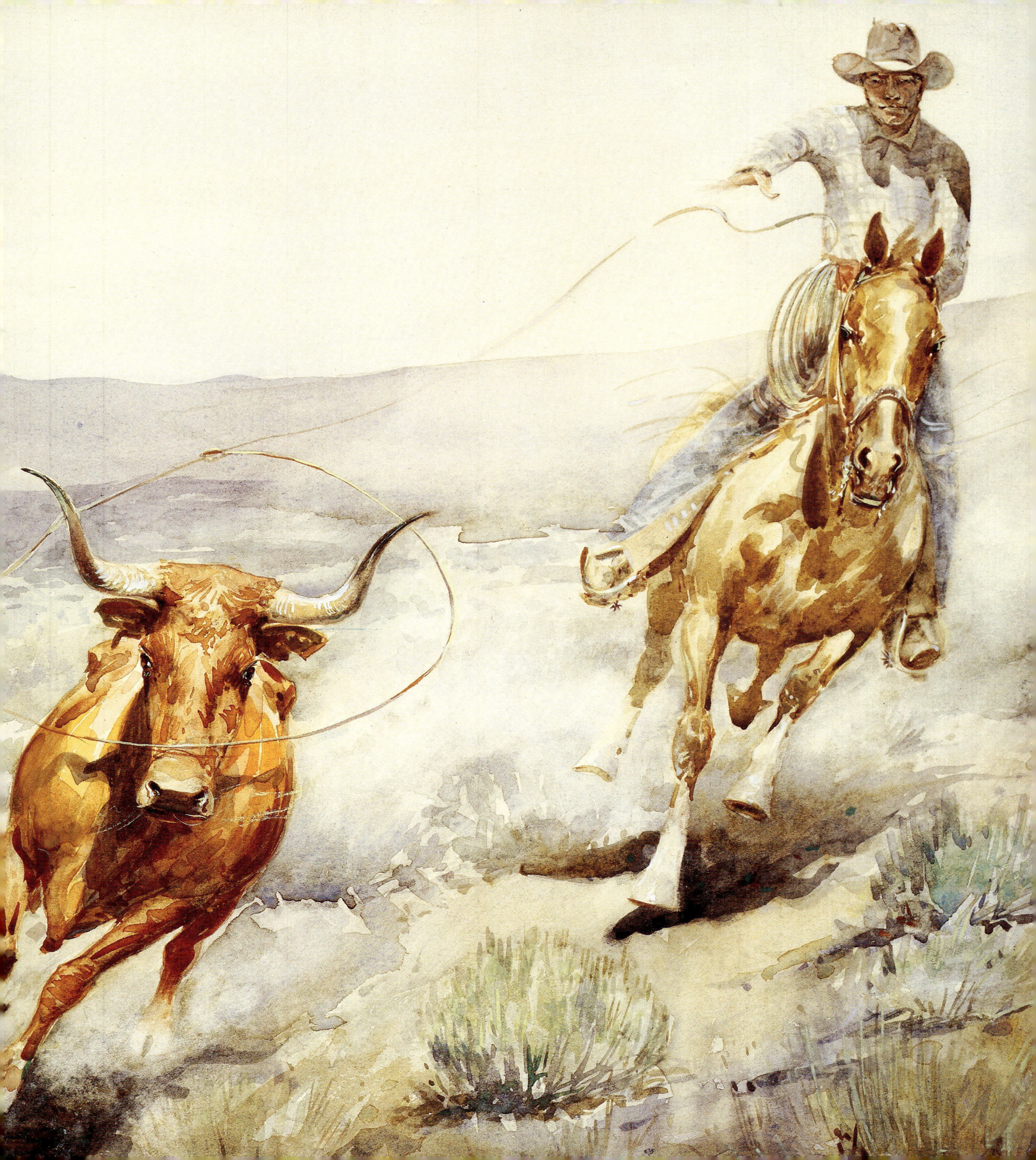

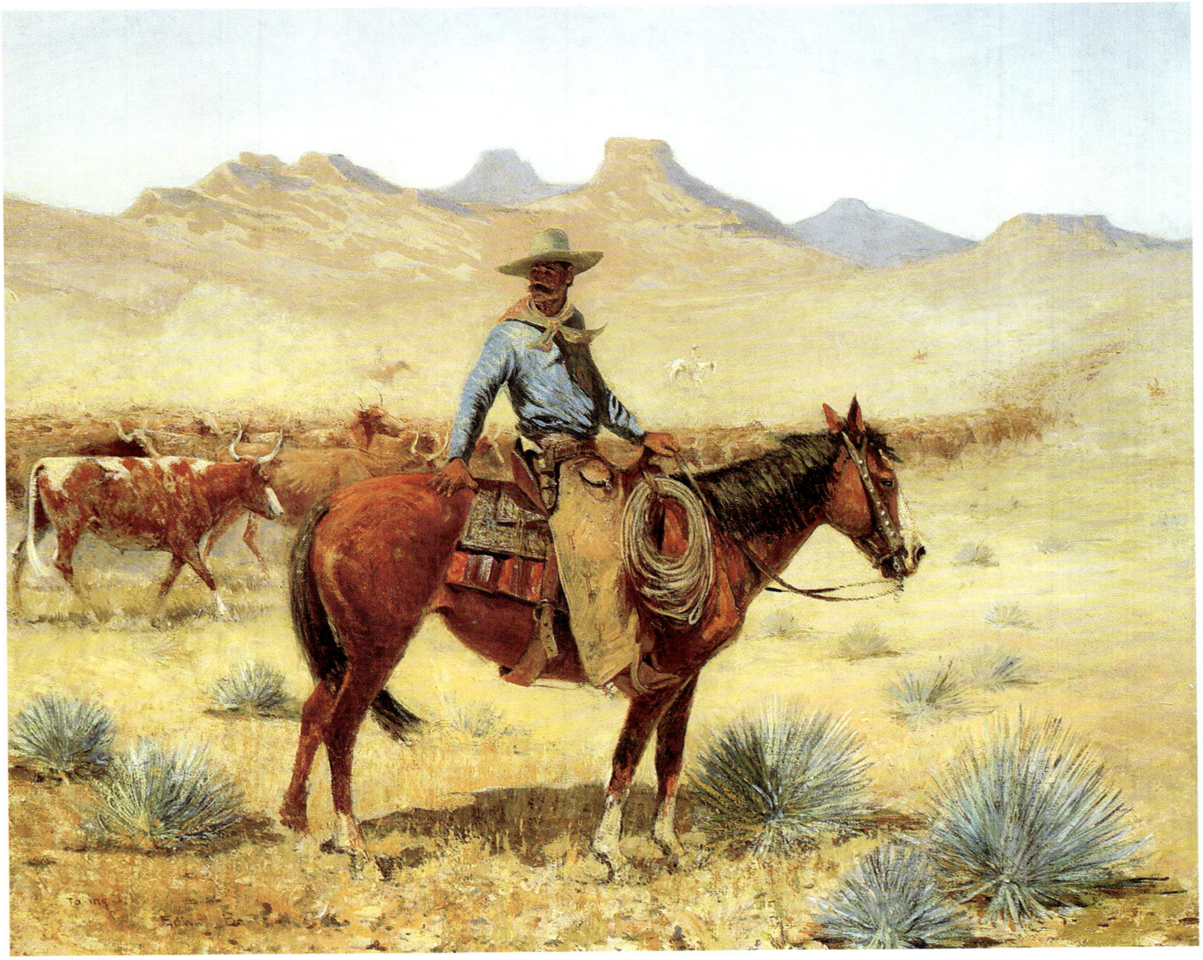

Vaqueros on the Range. Oil on canvas. 20 x 24 inches.

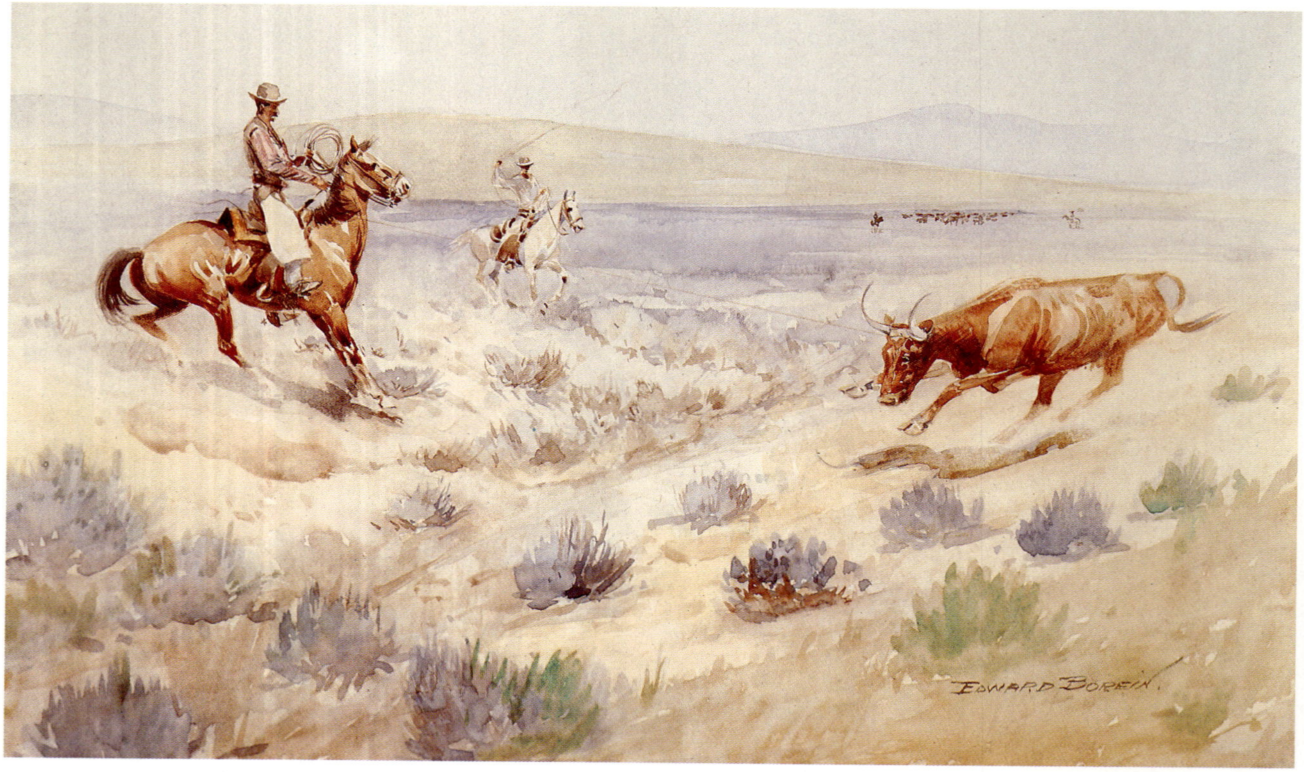

Roping the Steer. Watercolor on paper. 8 5/8 x 14 1/2 inches. Signed lower right: *EDWARD BOREIN.*

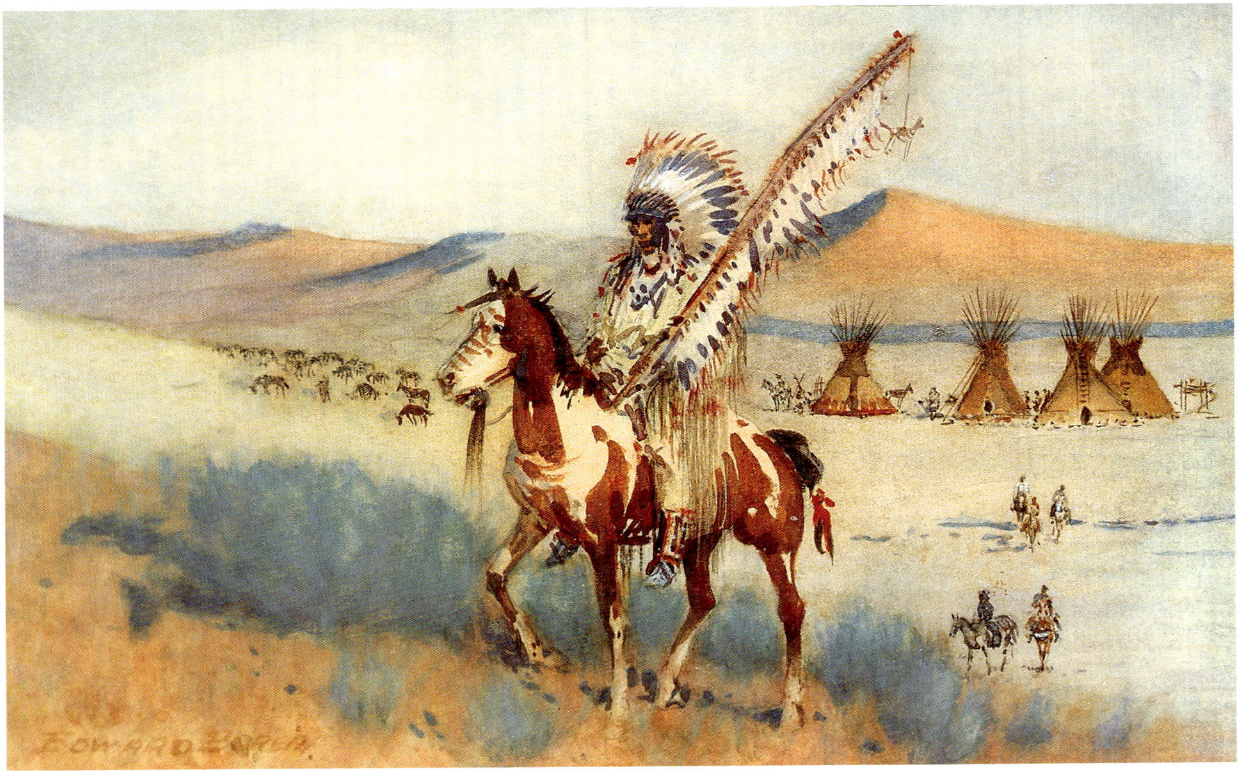

Indian Chief Leaving Village. Watercolor on paper. 6 x 9 1/4 inches (sight). Signed lower left: *EDWARD BOREIN.*

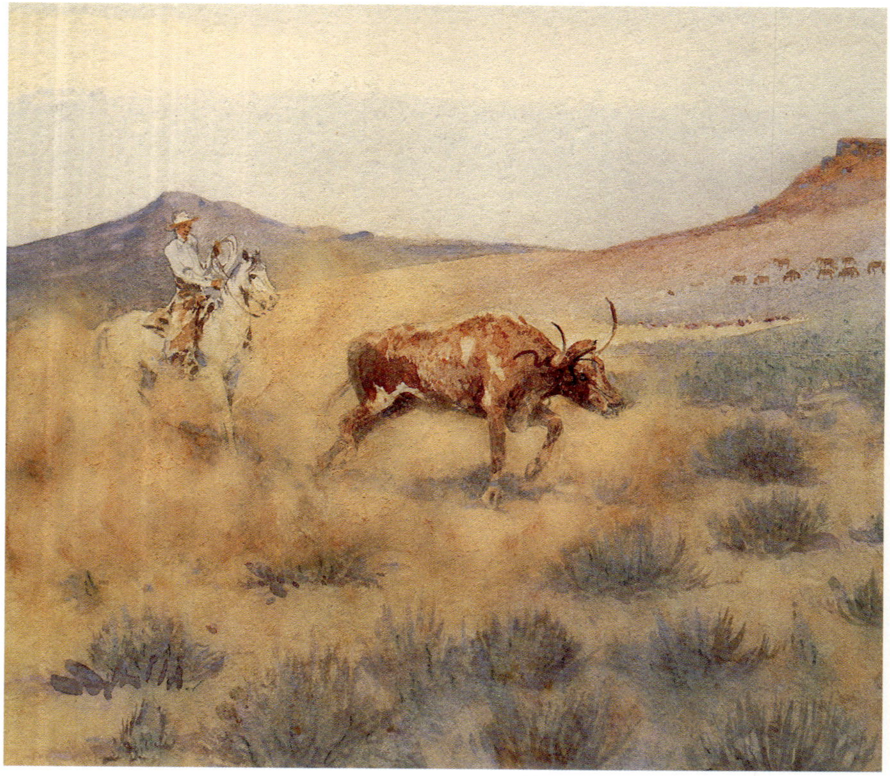

Roping a Steer. Watercolor on paper. 9 5/8 x 9 3/4 inches (sight). Signed lower right: *EDWARD BOREIN*

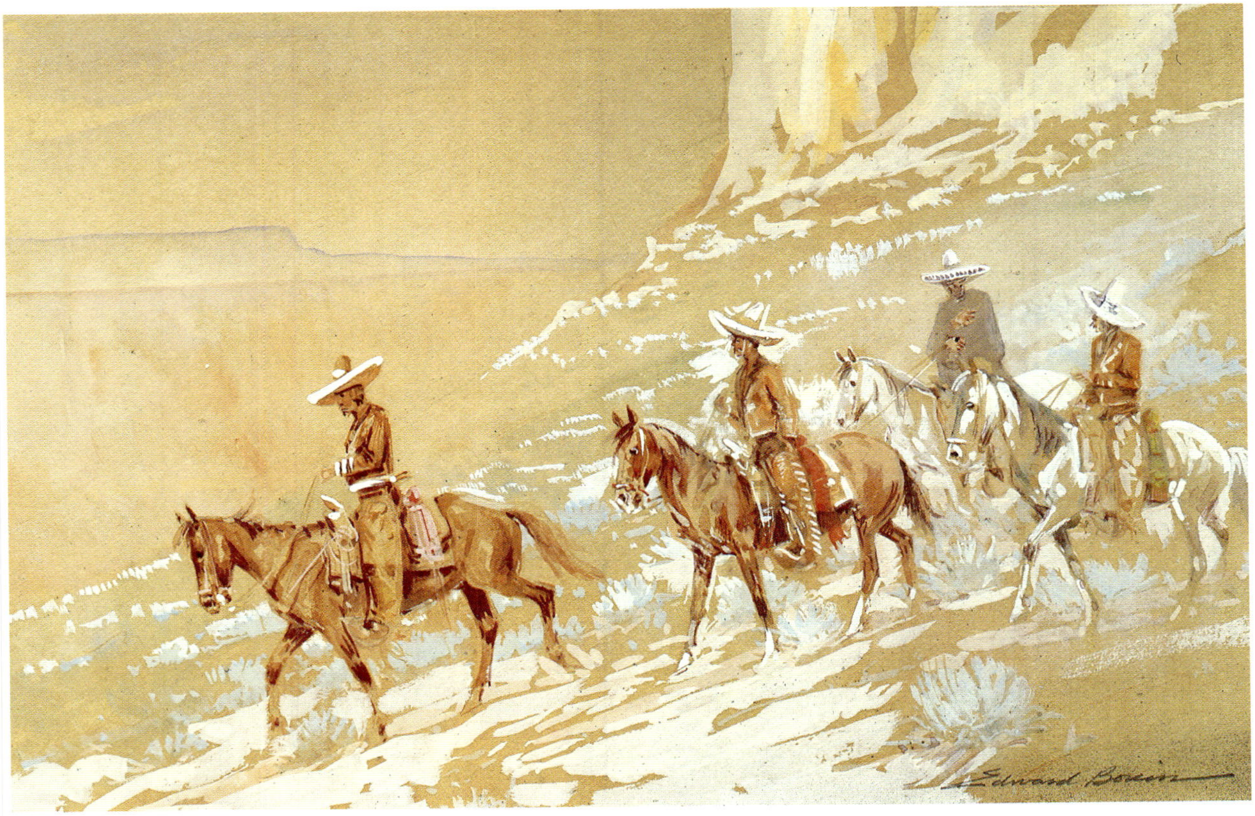

Vaquero Band. Watercolor and gouache on paper. 7 3/4 x 11 3/4 inches (sight). Signed lower right: *Edward Borein*.

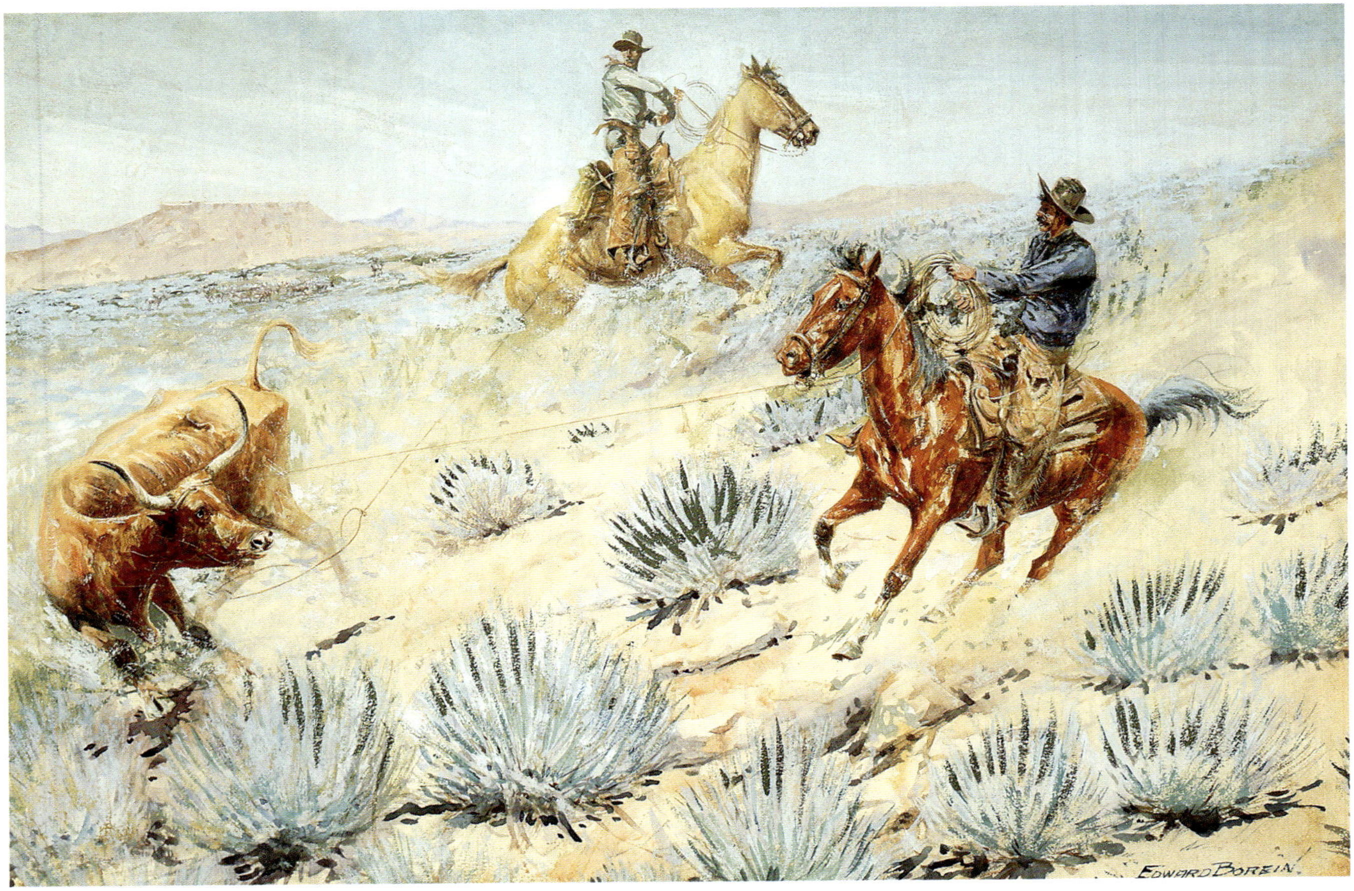

The Renegade. Watercolor and gouache on paper. 13 1/4 x 20 inches (sight). Signed lower right: *EDWARD BOREIN.*

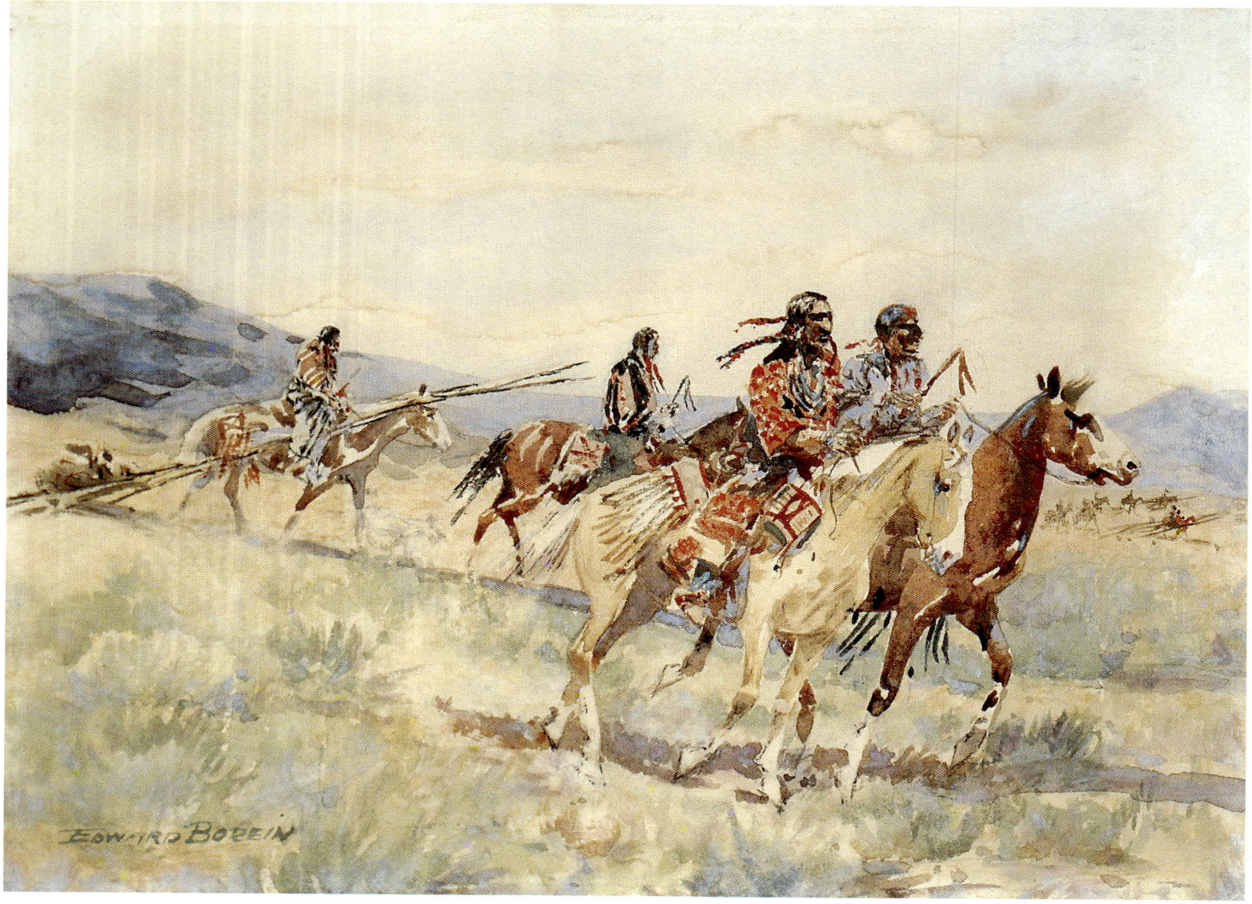

Crow Women. Watercolor on paper. 7 1/4 x 9 3/4 inches (sight). Signed lower left: *EDWARD BOREIN*.

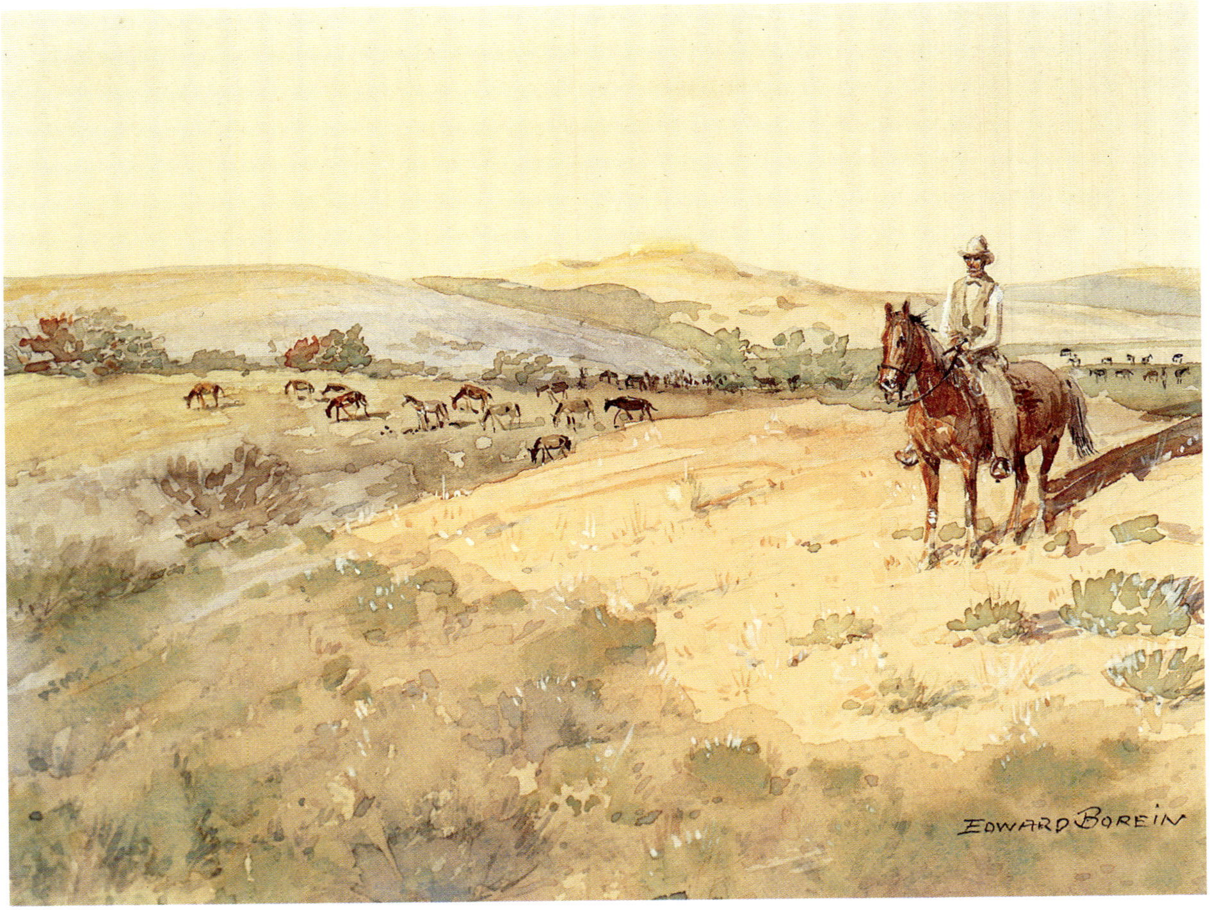

Checking the Remuda. Watercolor on paper. 7 1/8 x 9 1/4 inches (sight). Signed lower right: *EDWARD BOREIN.*

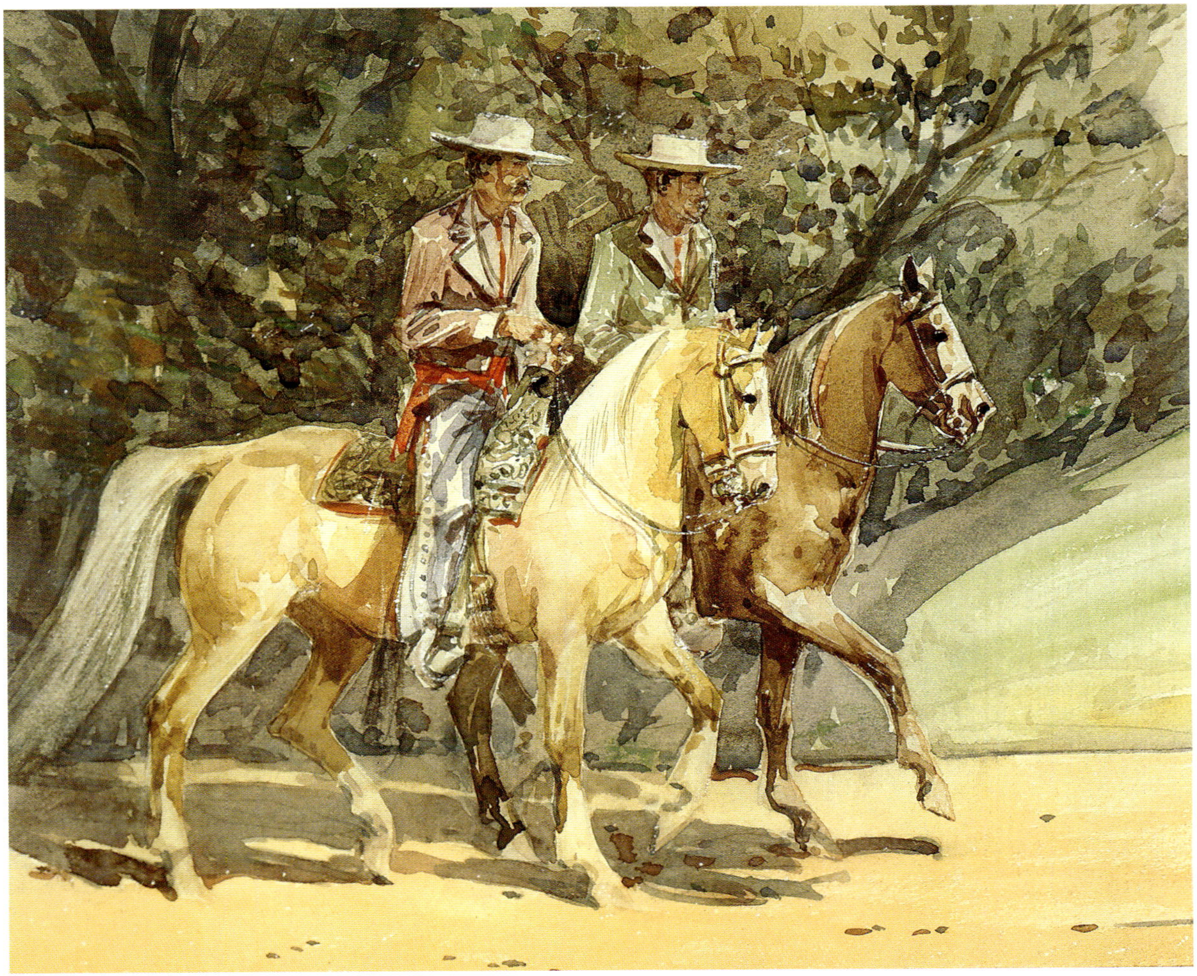

Two Caballeros. Watercolor on paper. 9 1/4 x 11 inches (sight).

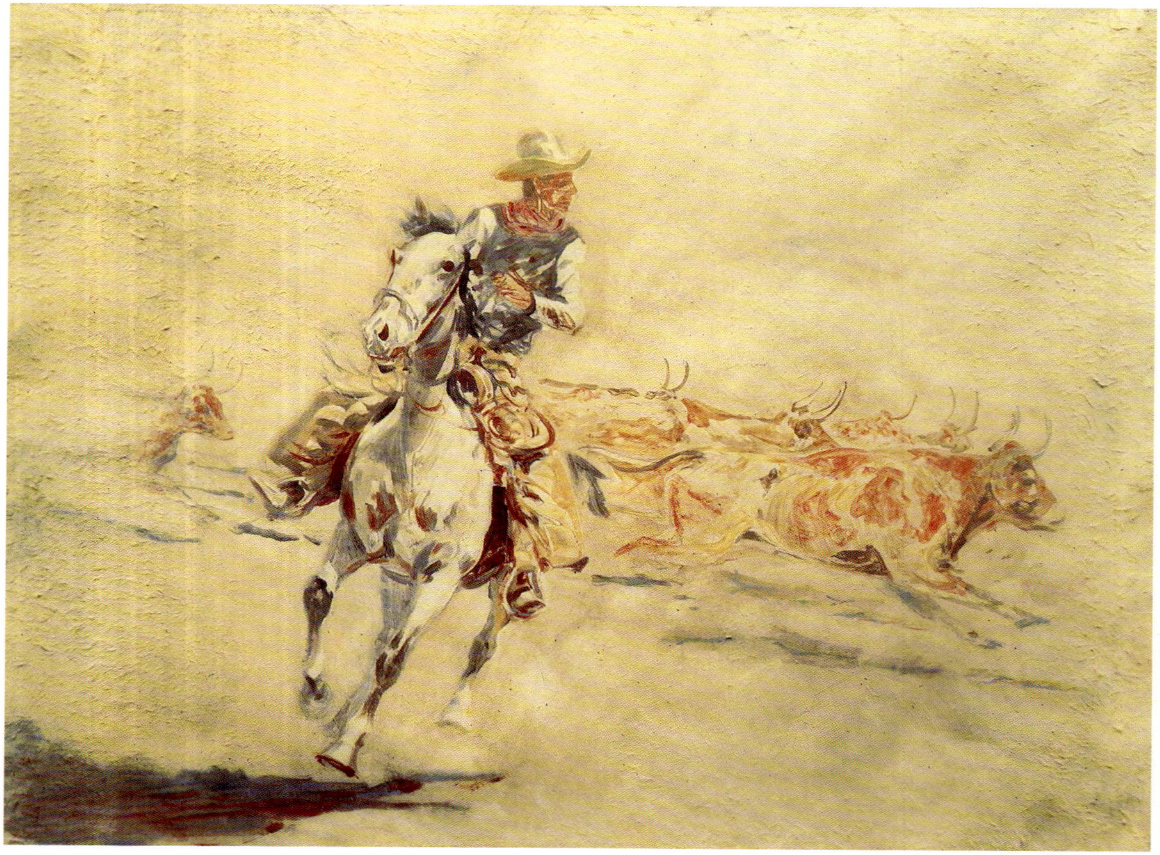

Cowboy in Stampede. Monotype. 12 x 14 1/8 inches (sight).

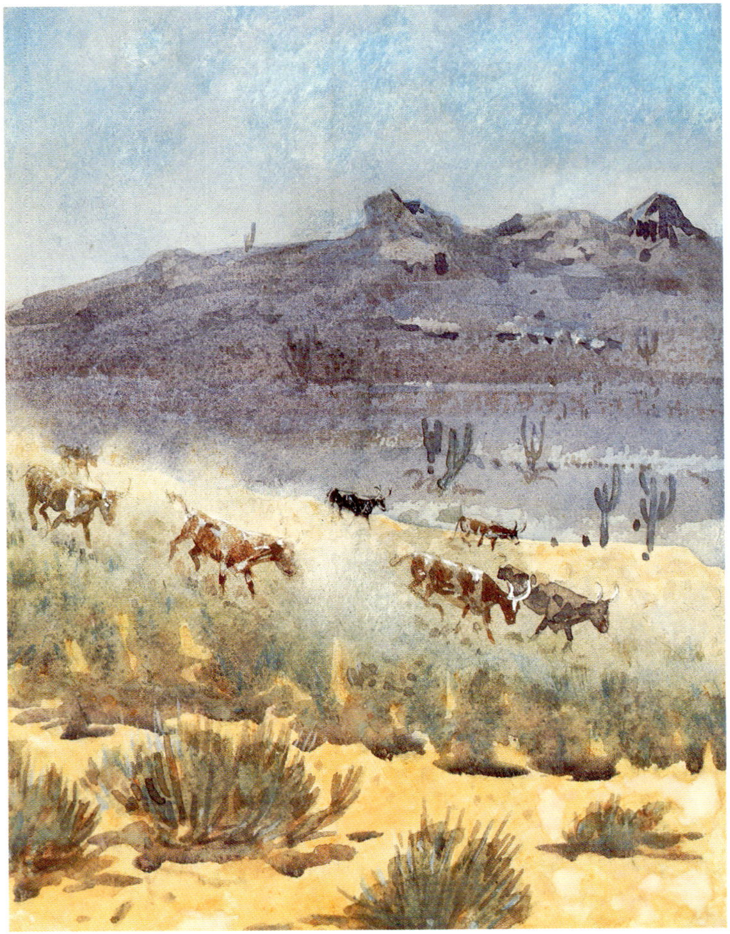

Cattle on a Trail. Watercolor on paper. 8 1/2 x 6 3/8 inches (sight).

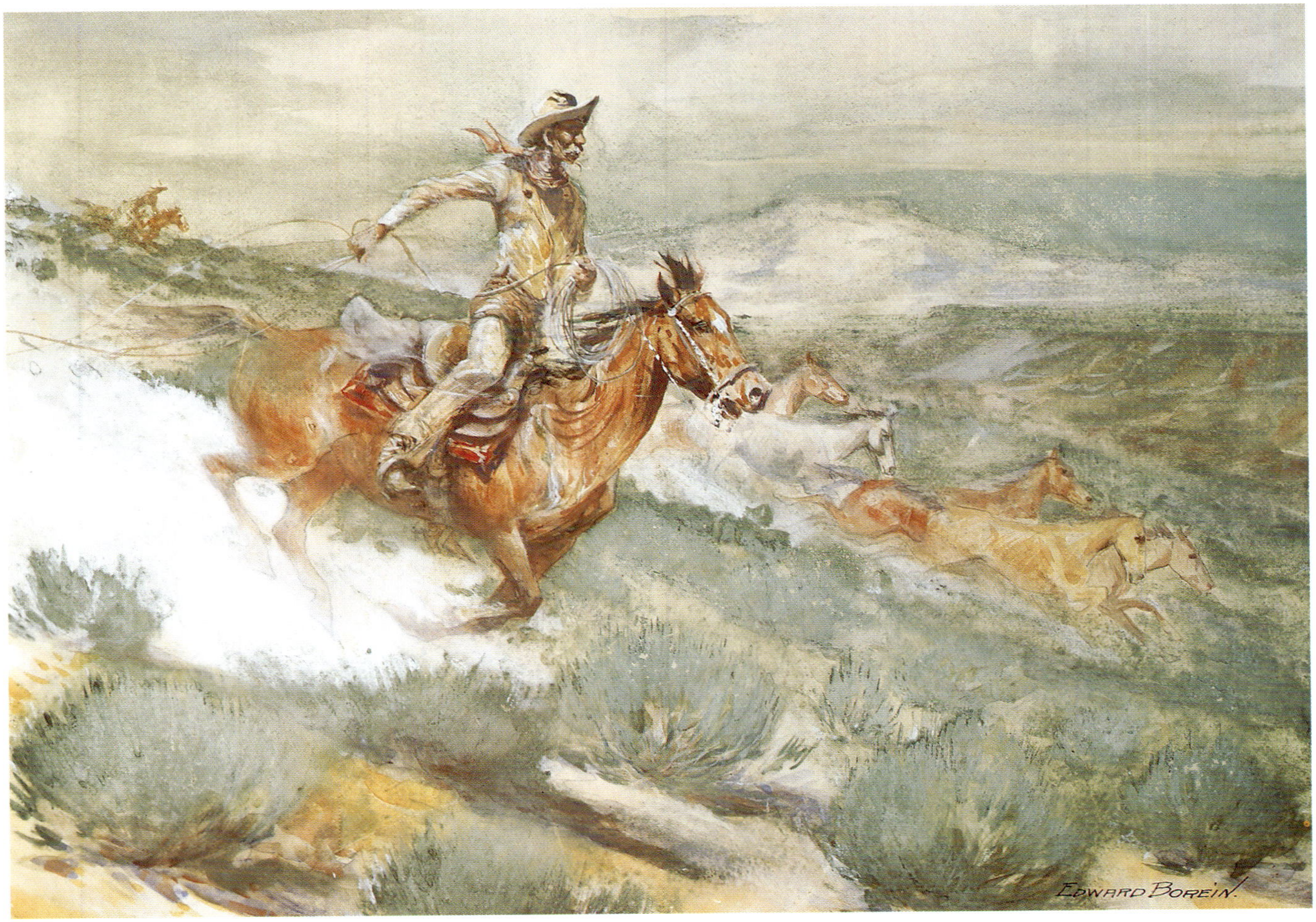

Roping Wild Horses. Watercolor and gouache on paper. 13 3/4 x 18 5/8 inches (sight).
Signed lower right: *EDWARD BOREIN.*

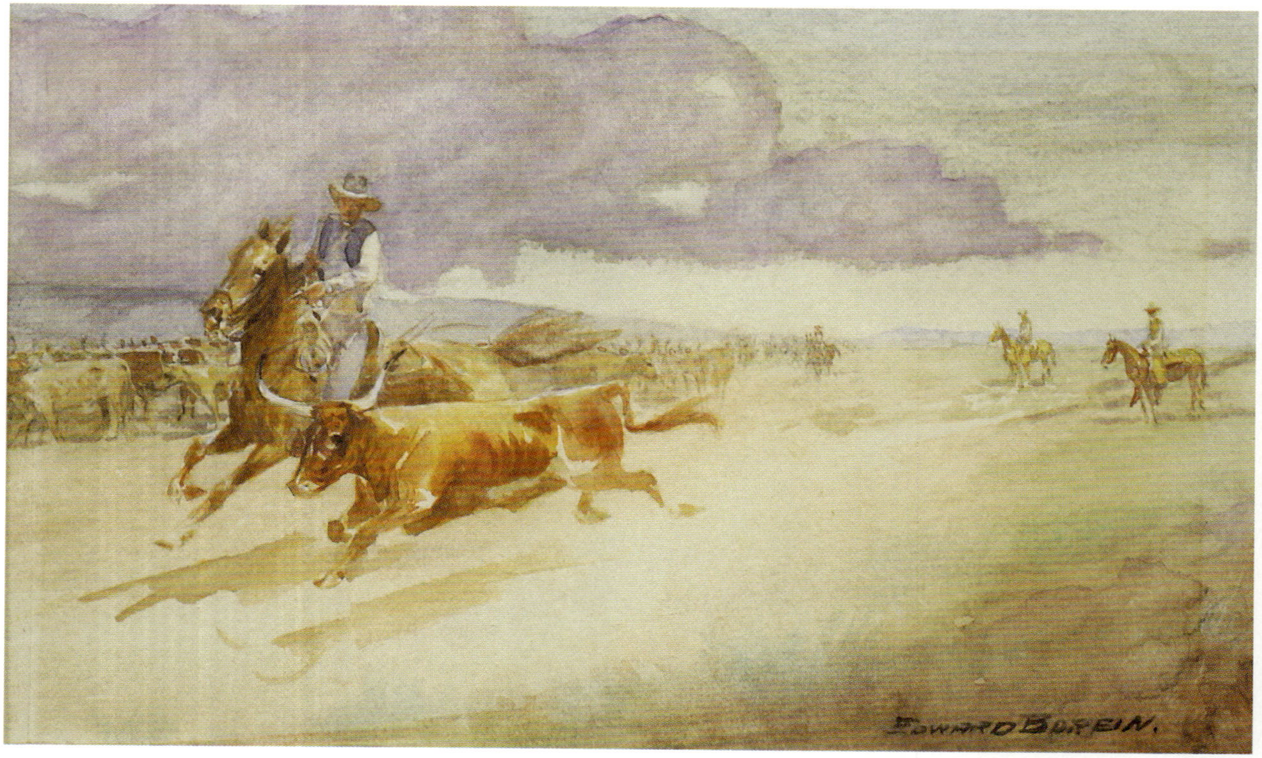

Cutting Out a Steer. Watercolor on paper. 5 3/4 x 9 inches (sight). Signed lower right: *EDWARD BOREIN.*

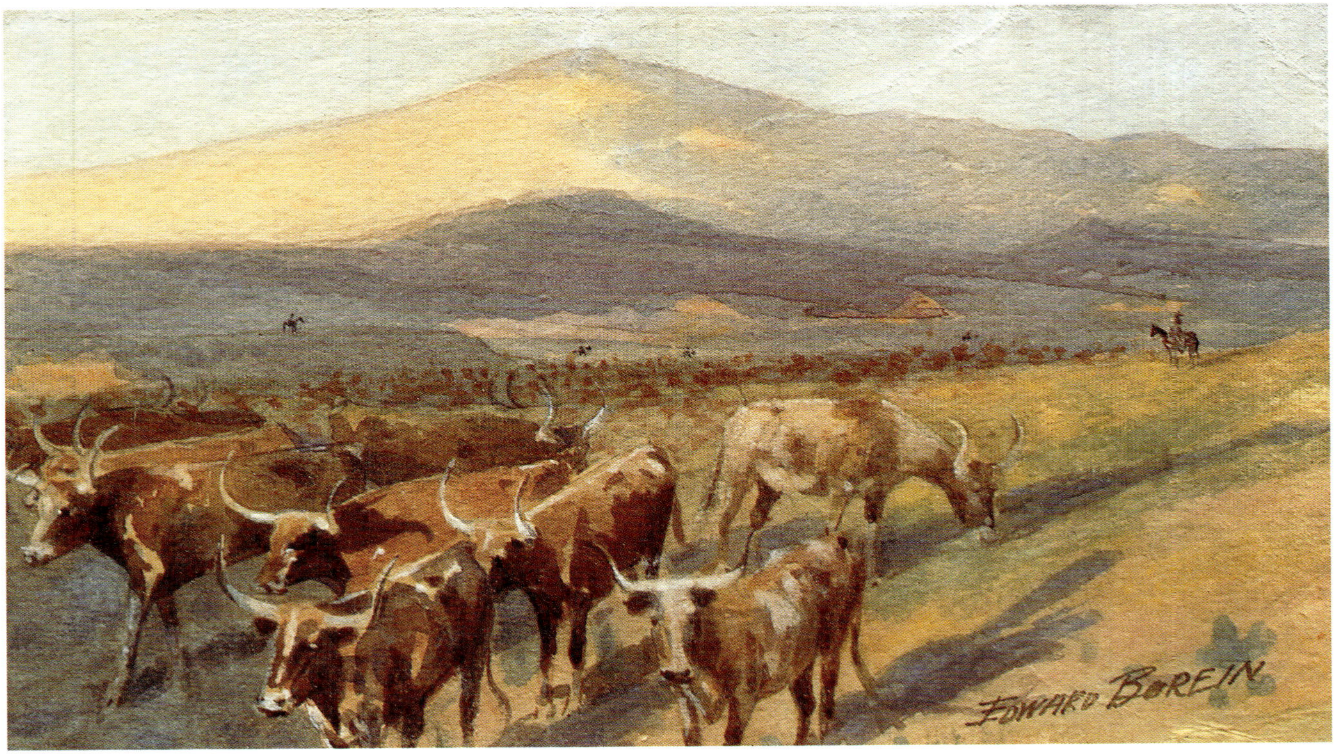

Grazing Steers. Watercolor on paper. 4 1/8 x 7 3/8 inches (sight). Signed lower right: *EDWARD BOREIN*.

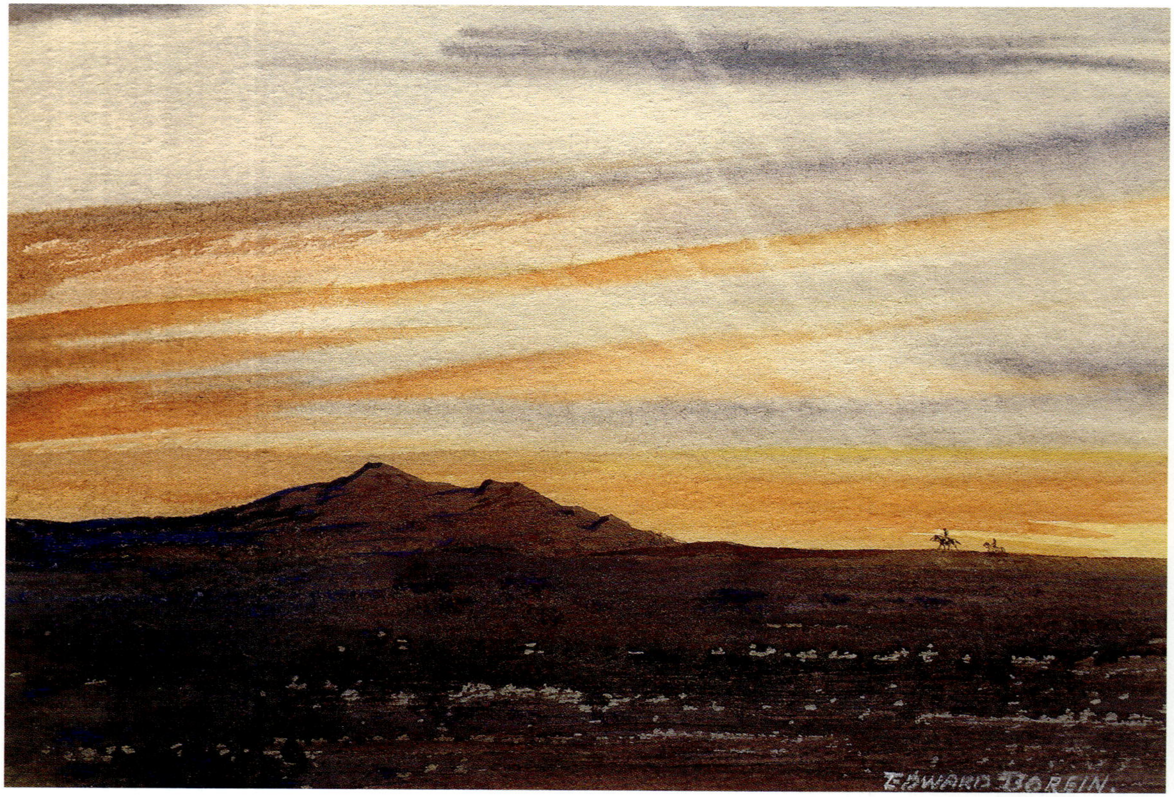

Early Riders. Watercolor on paper. 6 3/8 x 9 1/8 inches (sight). Signed lower right: *EDWARD BOREIN*.

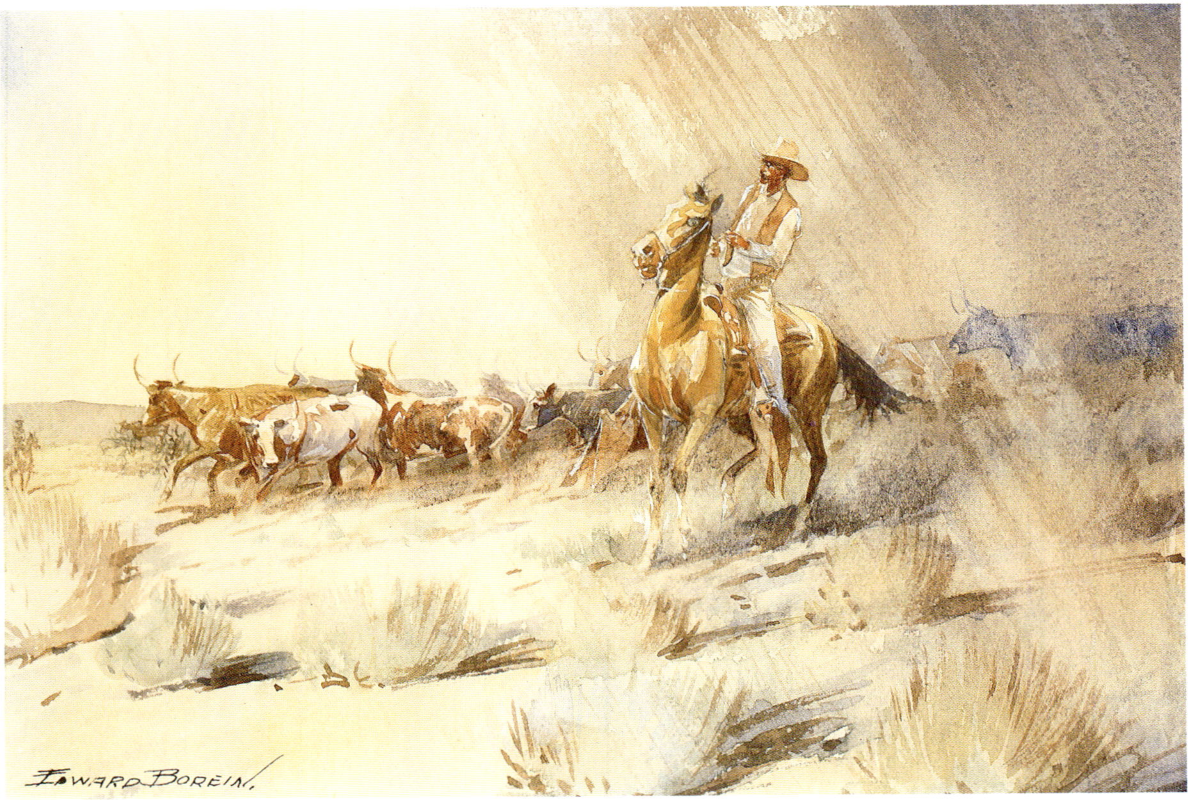

The Shower. Watercolor on paper. 6 3/4 x 10 inches (sight). Signed lower left: *EDWARD BOREIN.*

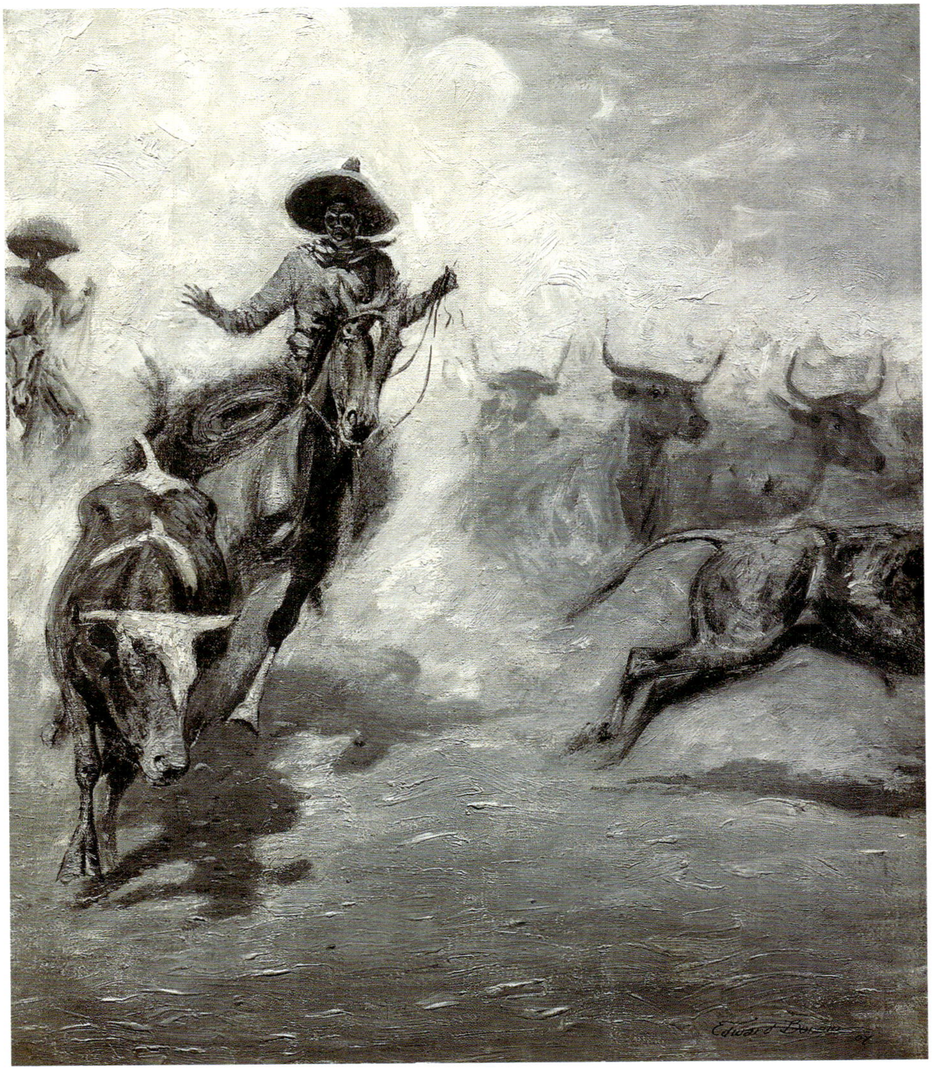

A Mexican Rodeo. 1907. Oil on canvas. 22 x 18 1/4 inches. Signed and dated lower right: *Edward Borein / 07*.

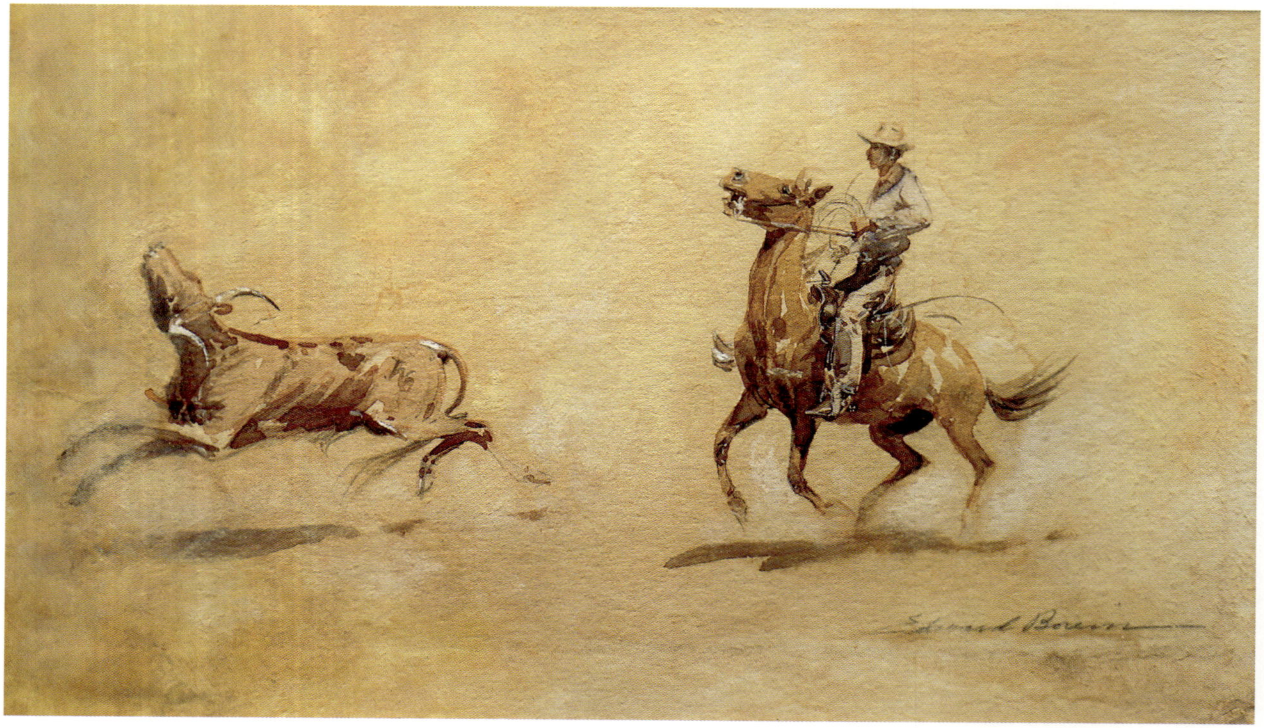

Roping a Steer. Watercolor on paper. 5 1/8 x 8 3/4 inches (sight). Signed lower right: *Edward Borein.*

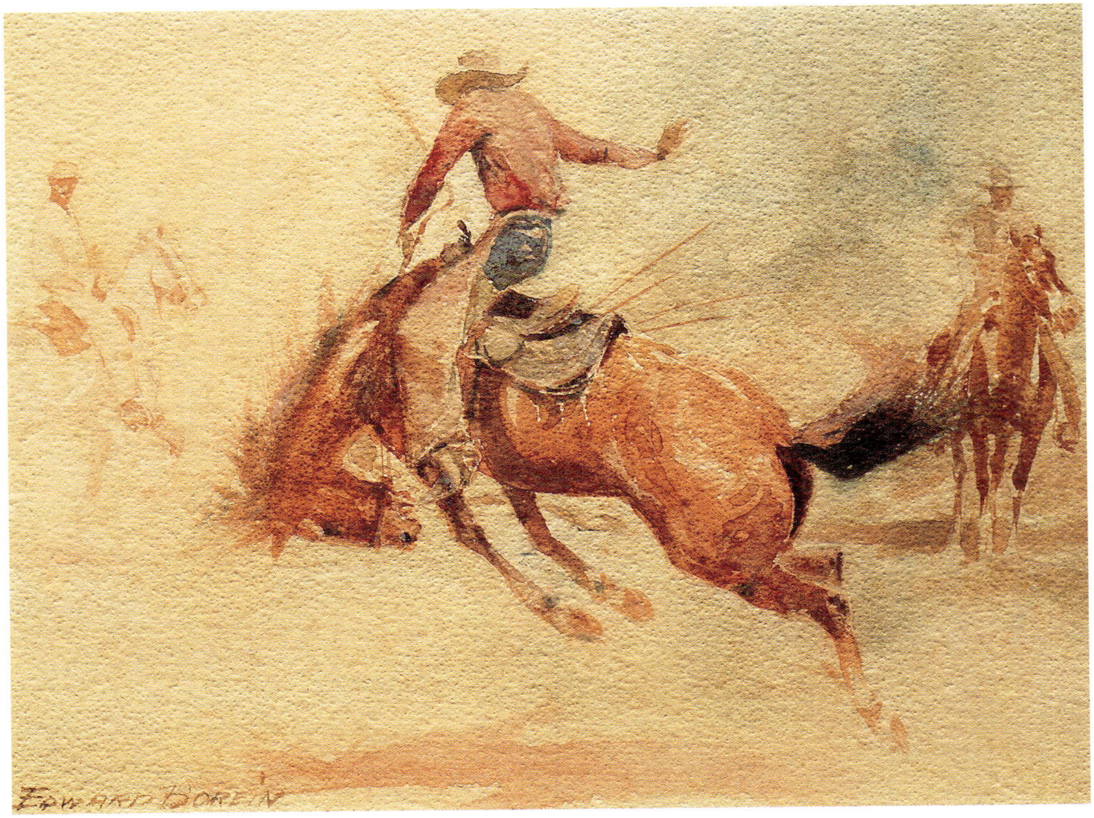

Bucking Horse. Watercolor and graphite on paper. 6 1/4 x 8 1/8 inches (sight). Signed lower left: *EDWARD BOREIN*.

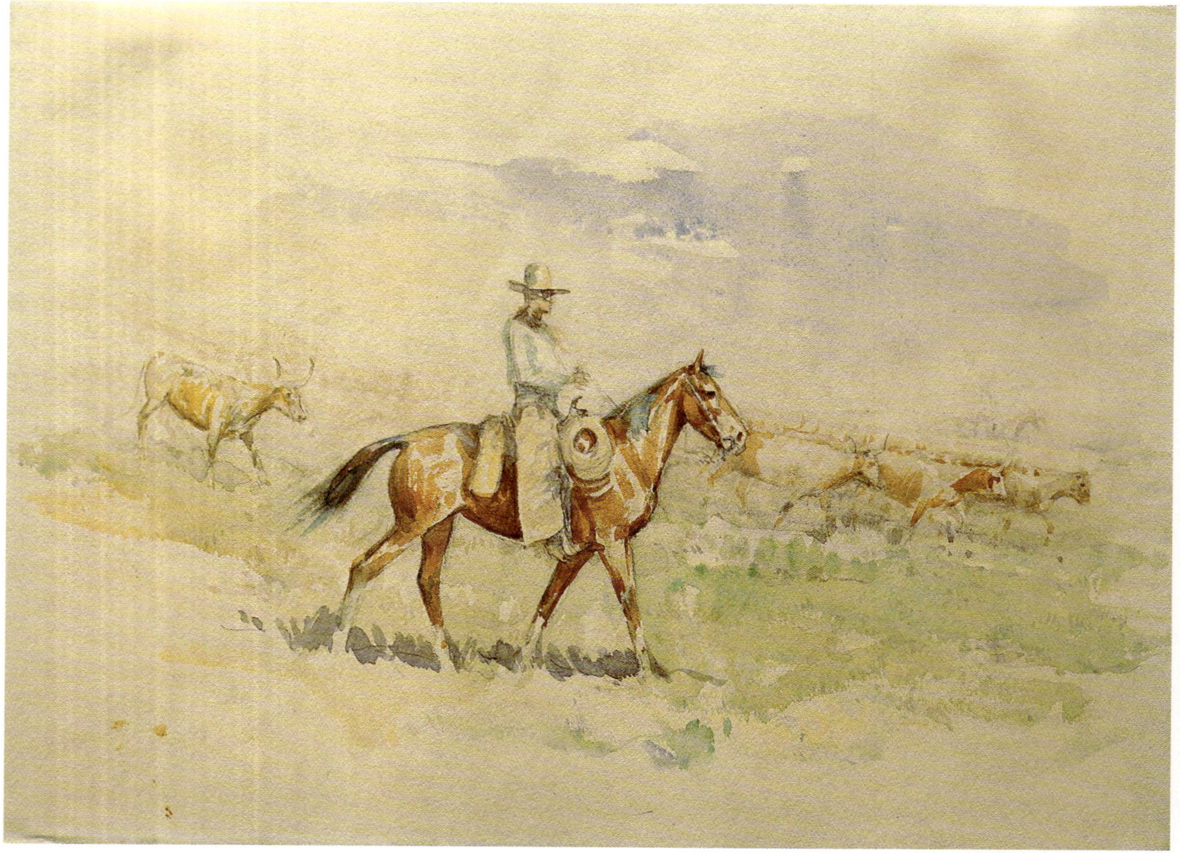

Cowboy on the Range, Riding Herd. Watercolor on paper. 6 3/4 x 11 1/4 inches (sight).

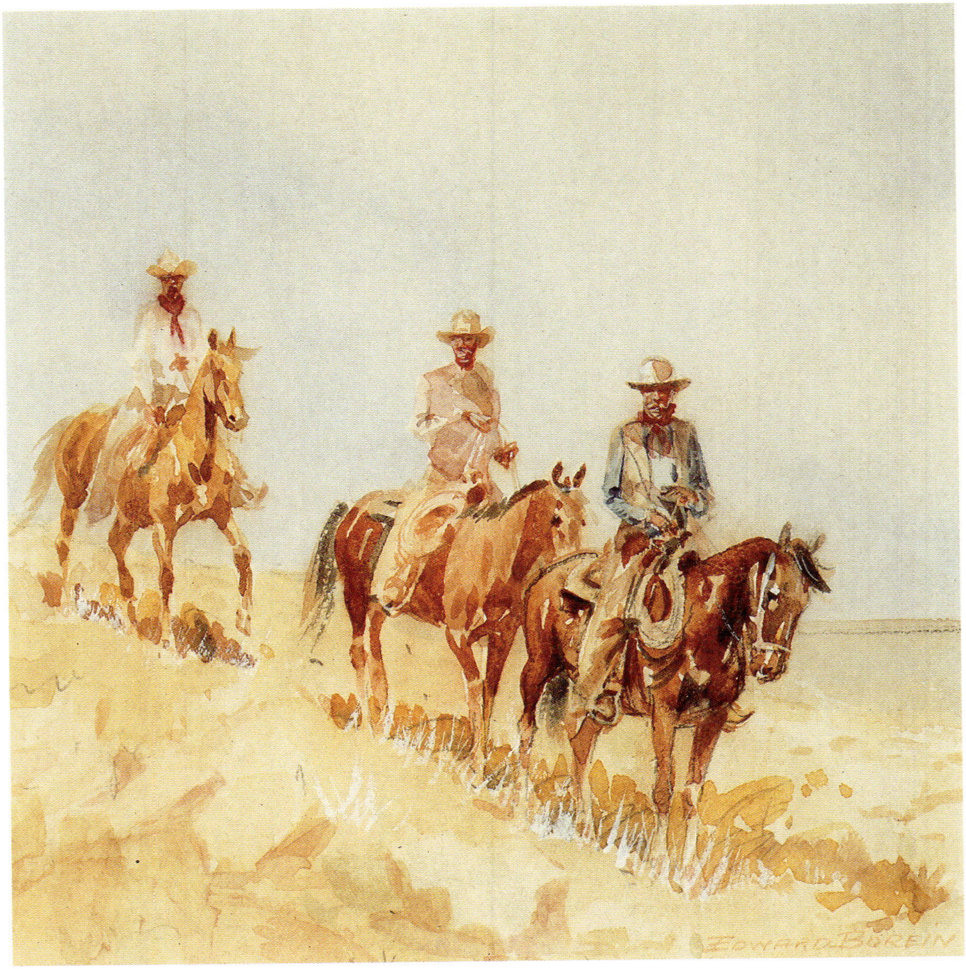

Three Cowboys on Horseback. Watercolor and graphite on paper. 6 1/8 x 5 7/8 inches (sight).
Signed lower right: *EDWARD BOREIN*.

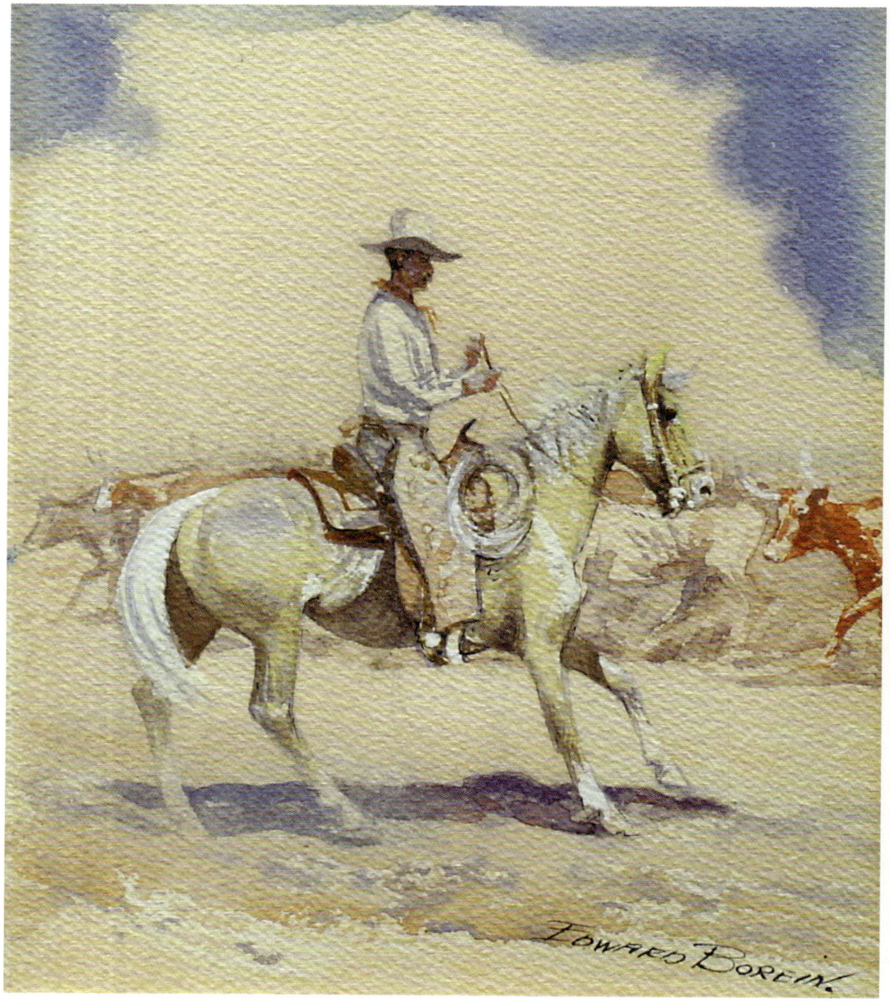

Cowboy on Palomino. Watercolor, gouache and india ink on paper. 7 1/8 x 6 inches (sight).
Signed lower right: *EDWARD BOREIN.*

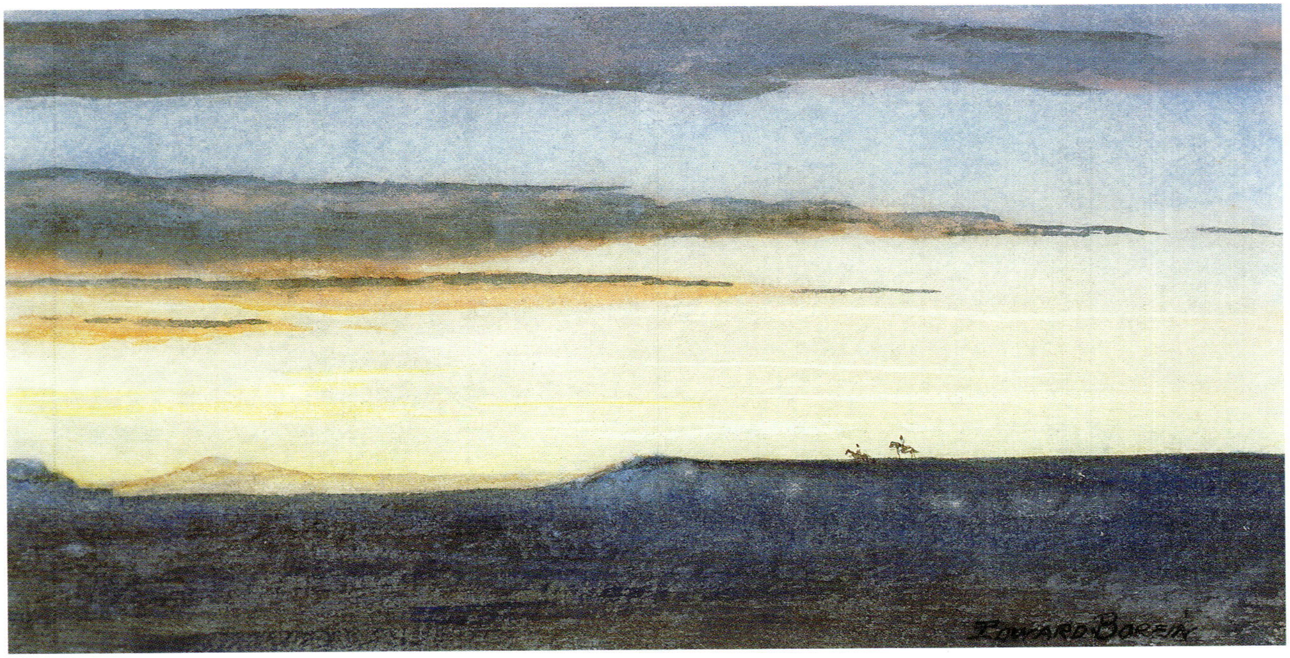

Two Cowhands at Dusk. Watercolor on paper. 4 7/8 x 9 3/8 inches (sight). Signed lower right: *EDWARD BOREIN.*

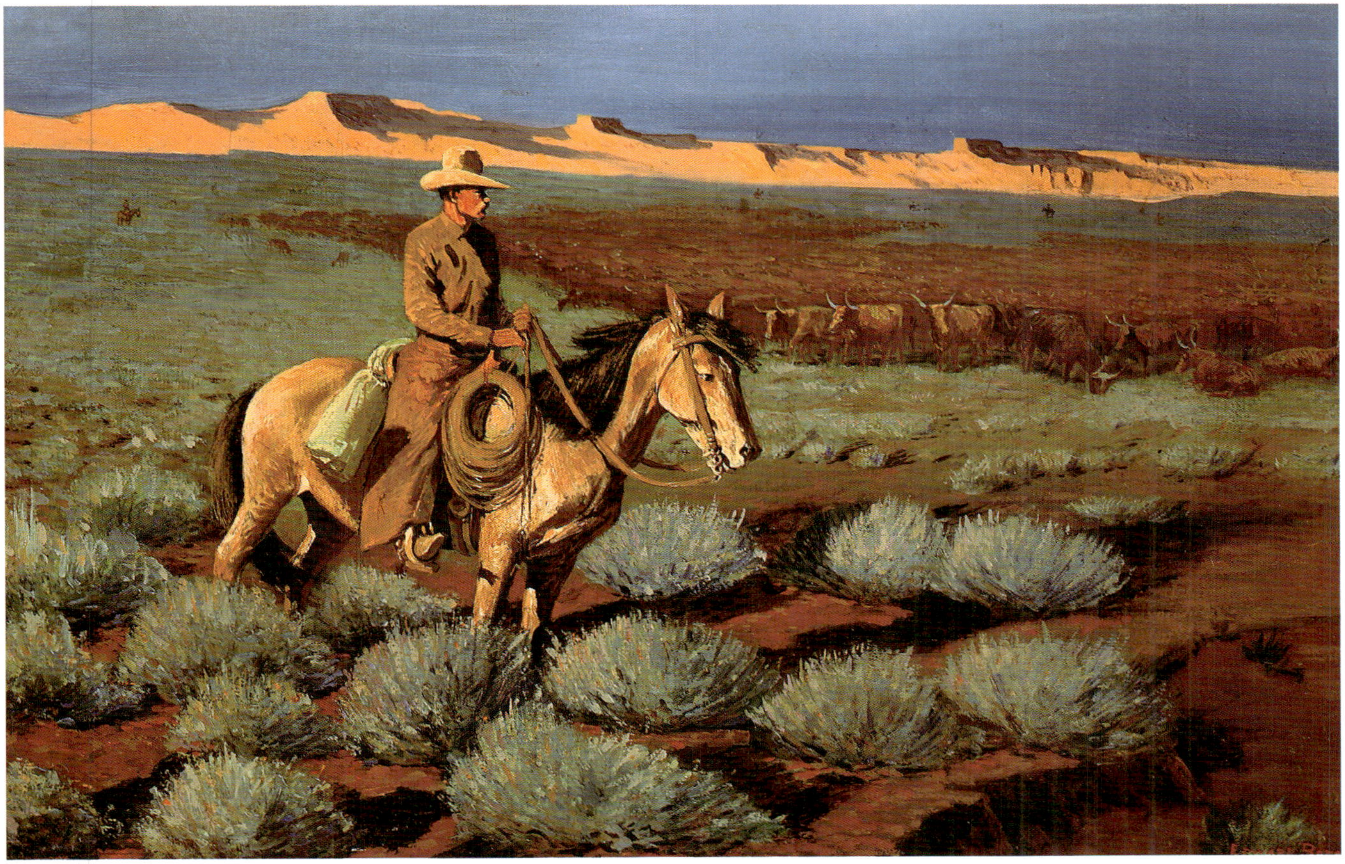

The Trail Boss. Oil on canvas mounted on panel. 19 x 28 1/2 inches. Signed lower right: *EDWARD BOREIN.*

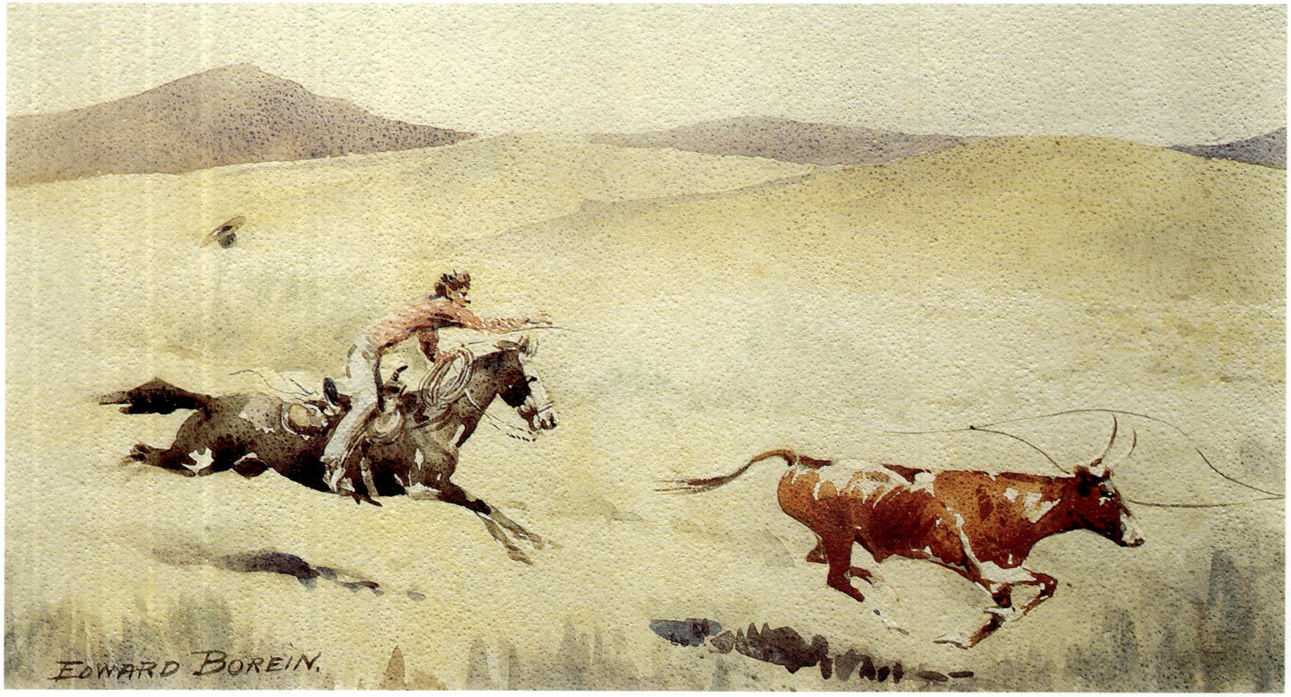

Roping a Steer. Watercolor on paper. 5 7/8 x 10 5/8 inches (sight). Signed lower left: *EDWARD BOREIN.*

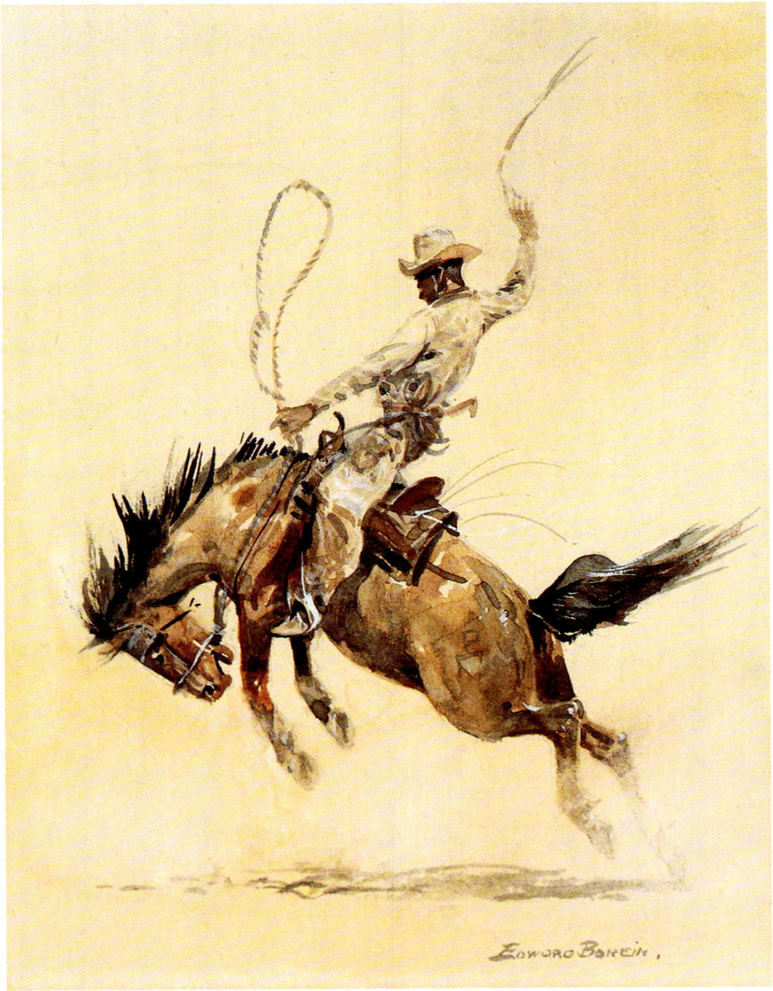

Bucking Bronc with Rider. Watercolor and gouache on paper. 8 x 6 inches (sight). Signed lower right: *EDWARD BOREIN.*

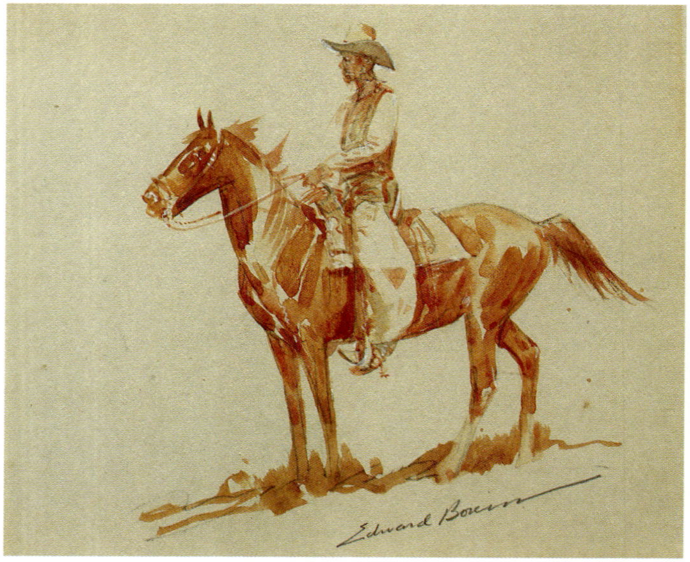

Horse and Rider. Watercolor on paper. 4 3/4 x 5 1/2 inches (sight). Signed lower right: *Edward Borein.*

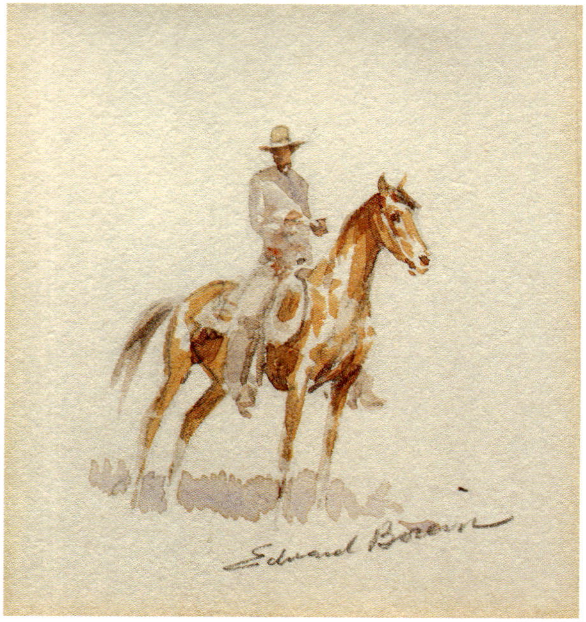

Lone Rider on Horse. Watercolor on paper. 3 1/8 x 2 3/4 inches (sight). Signed lower right: *Edward Borein.*

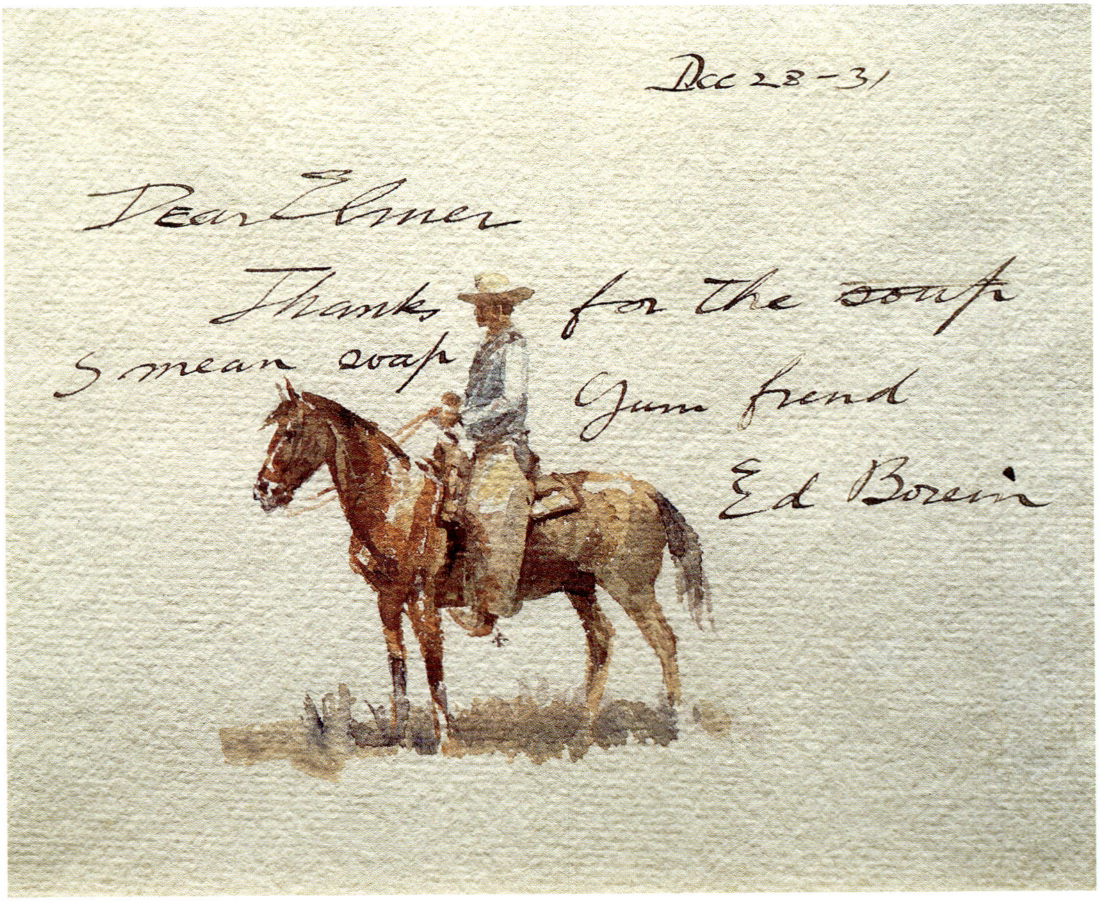

Illustrated Letter to Dear Elmer [Awl], December 28, 1931. Watercolor and ink on paper. 5 1/2 x 6 1/2 inches (sight).
Signed center right: *Ed Borein.*

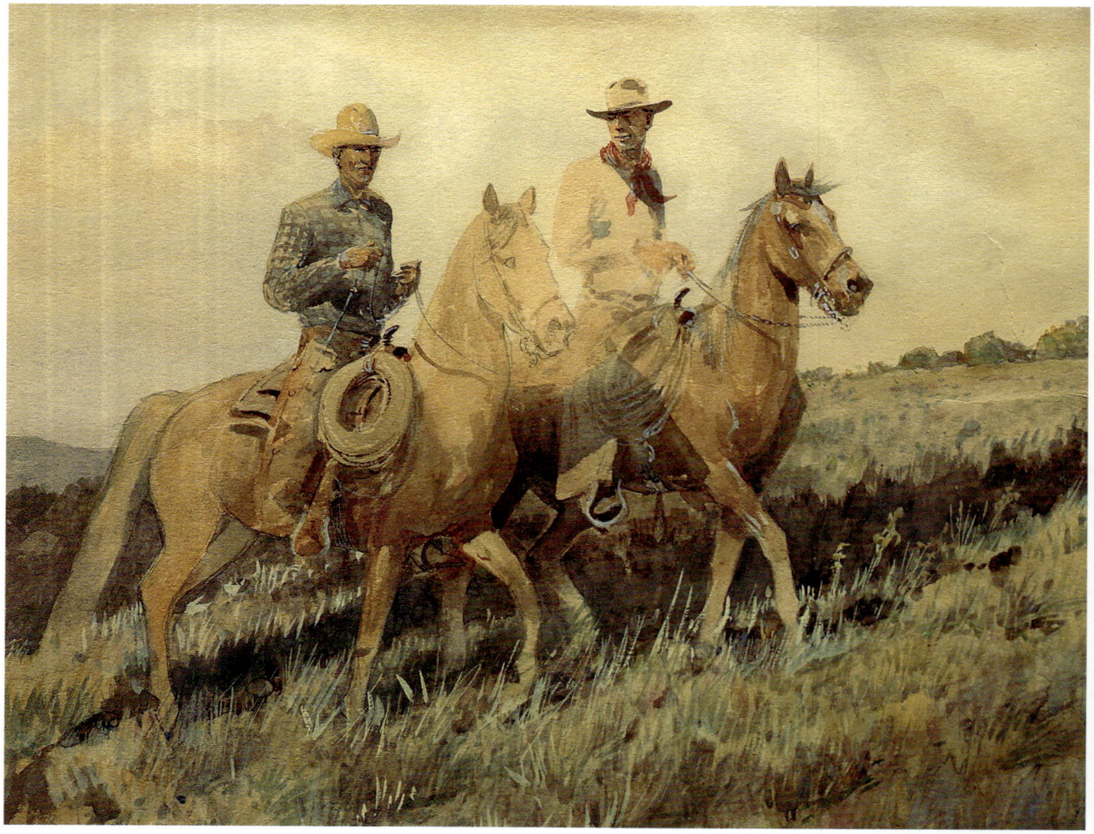

Two Mounted Cowboys. Watercolor on paper. 13 3/4 x 17 5/8 inches (sight).

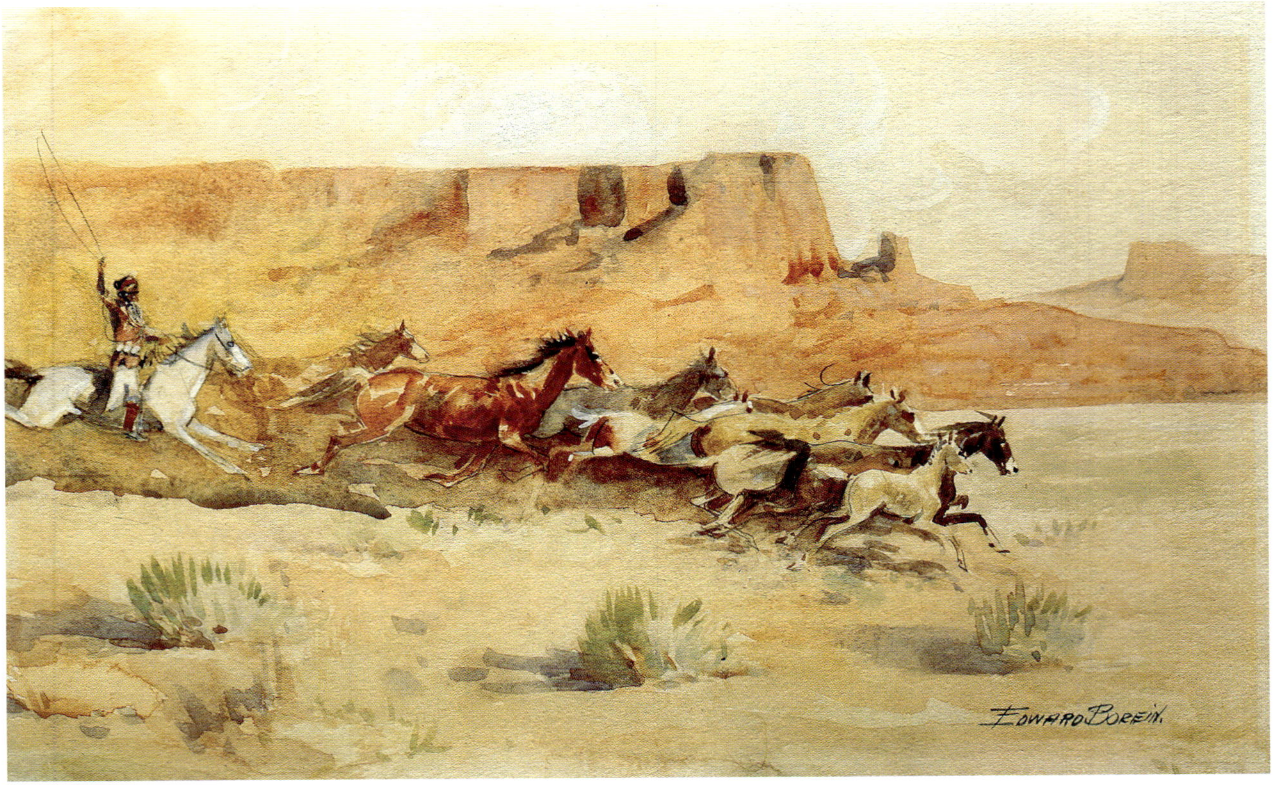

Indian Chasing Wild Horses. Watercolor on paper. 6 1/2 x 11 inches (sight). Signed lower right: *EDWARD BOREIN.*

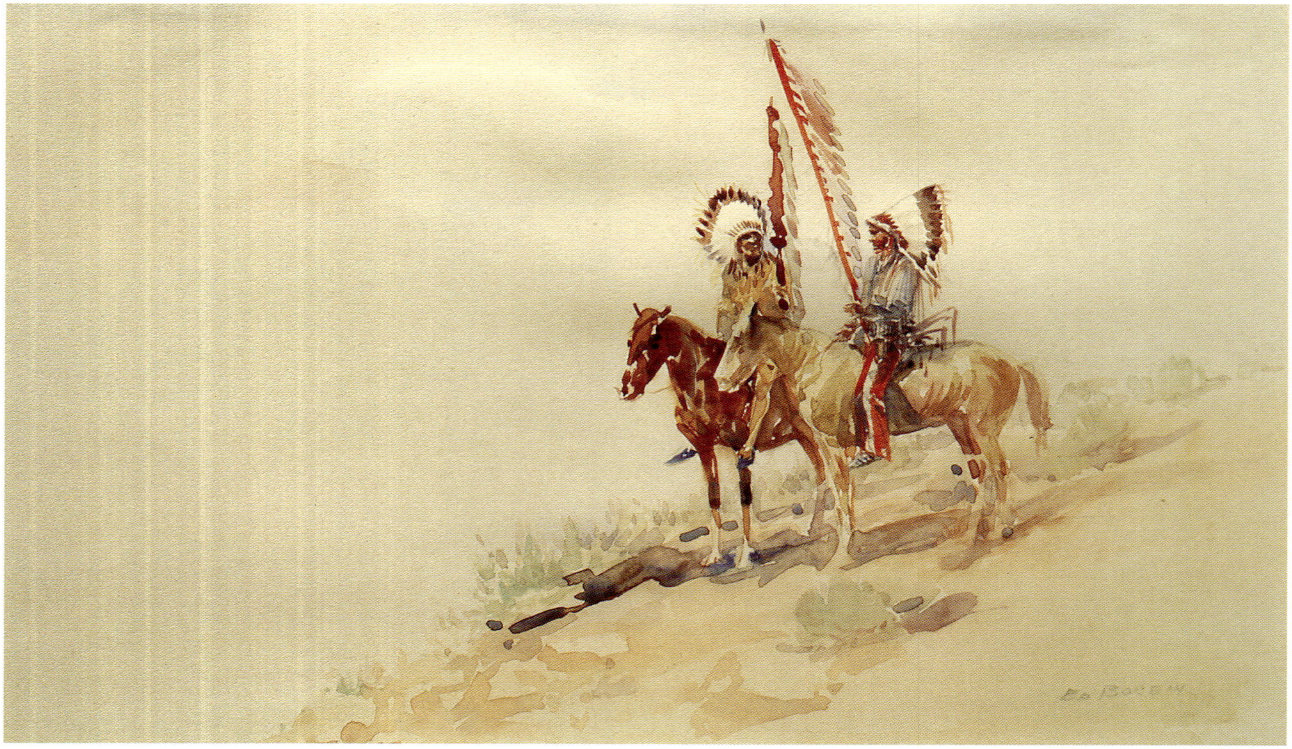

Two Indians with Lances. Watercolor on paper. 6 1/8 x 10 1/8 inches (sight). Signed lower right: *ED BOREIN*.

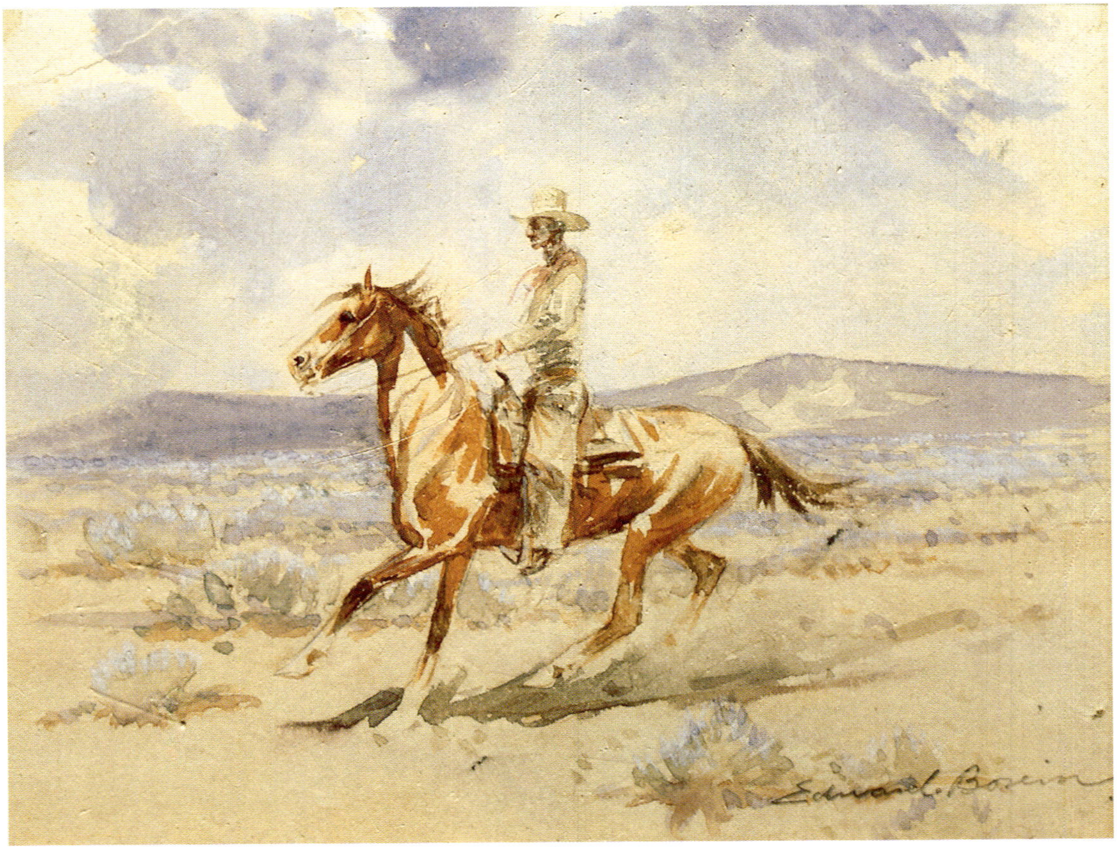

Cowboy on Horse. Watercolor and gouache on paper. 5 3/8 x 6 3/4 inches (sight). Signed lower right: *Edward Borein*.

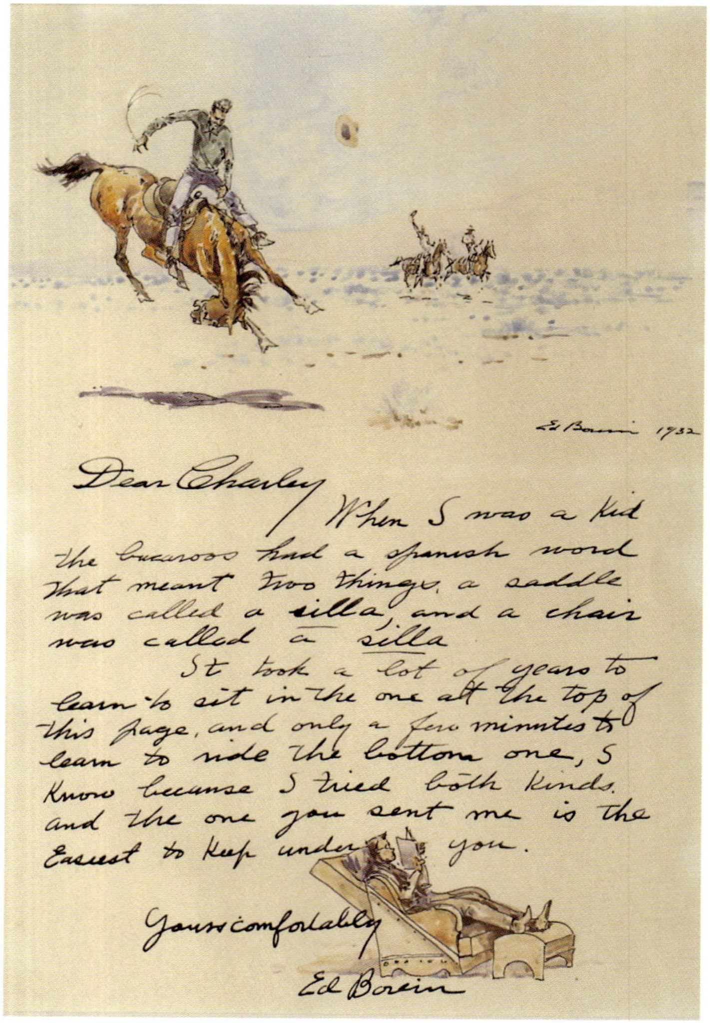

Ed Borein 1932

Dear Charley

When I was a kid
the buckaroos had a spanish word
that meant two things, a saddle
was called a silla, and a chair
was called a silla

It took a lot of years to
learn to sit in the one at the top of
this page, and only a few minutes to
learn to ride the bottom one, I
know because I tried both kinds.
and the one you sent me is the
Easiest to keep under you.

Yours comfortably

Ed Borein

Illustrated Letter to Charley, 1932. Ink, watercolor and graphite on paper. 11 3/4 x 8 1/8 inches (sight).
Signed and dated below upper image: *Ed Borein 1932.*

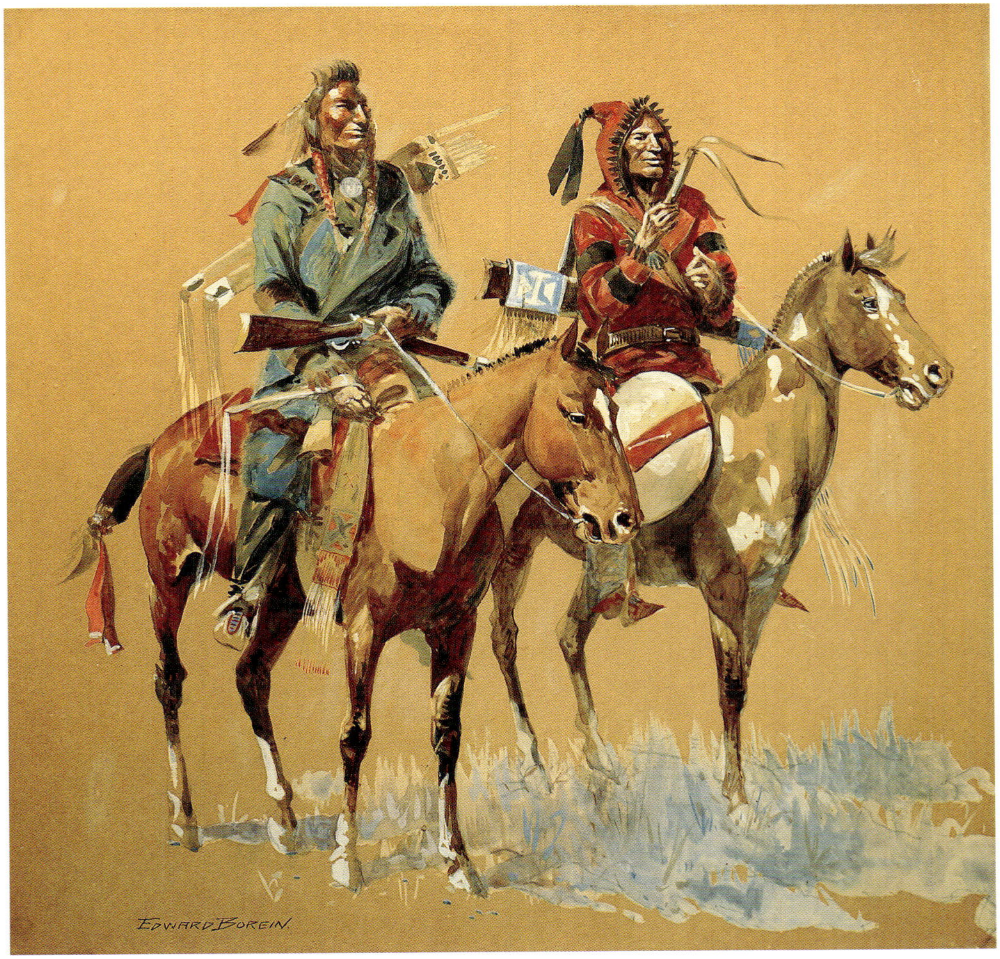

The Sentinels. Watercolor and gouache on paper. 18 1/4 x 18 5/8 inches. Signed lower left: *EDWARD BOREIN.*

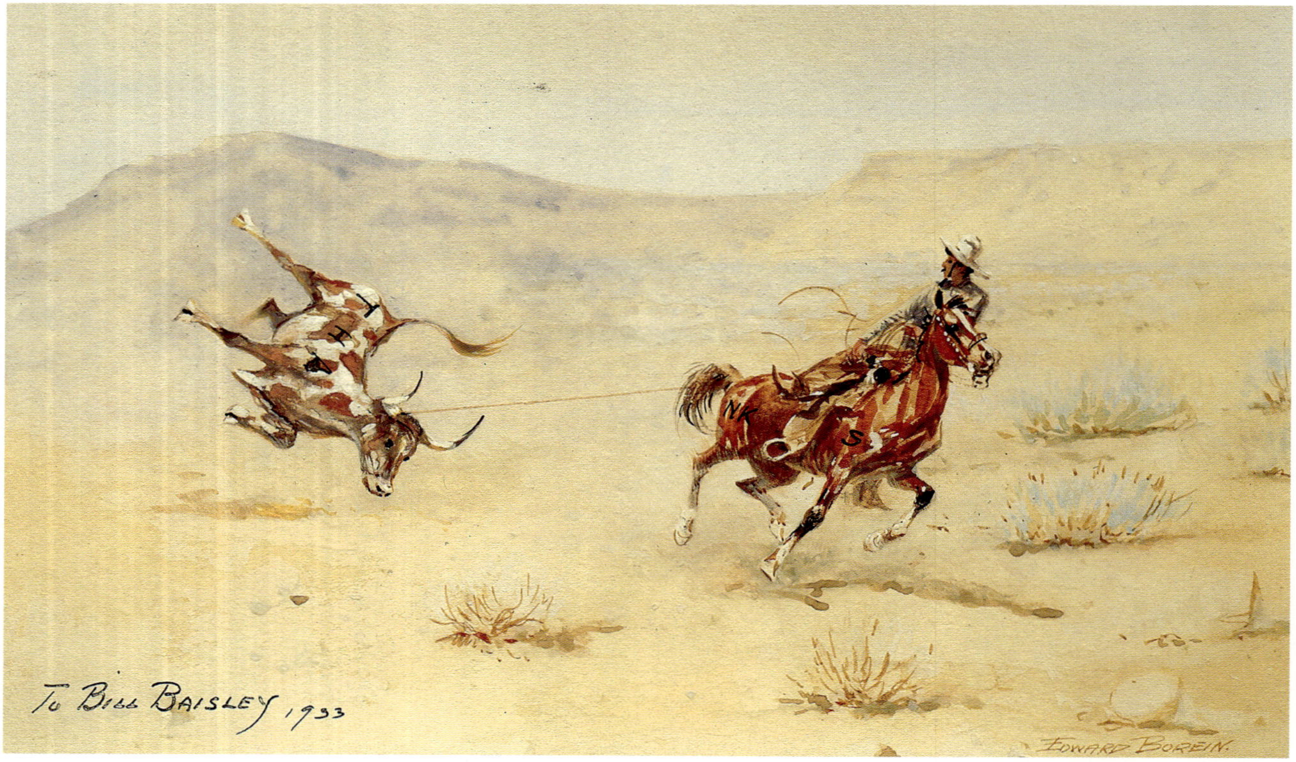

Breaking a Steer (Thanks), 1933. Watercolor and ink on paper. 5 7/8 x 9 3/4 inches (sight).
Signed lower right: *EDWARD BOREIN*. Inscribed and dated lower left: *TO BILL BAISLEY 1933*.

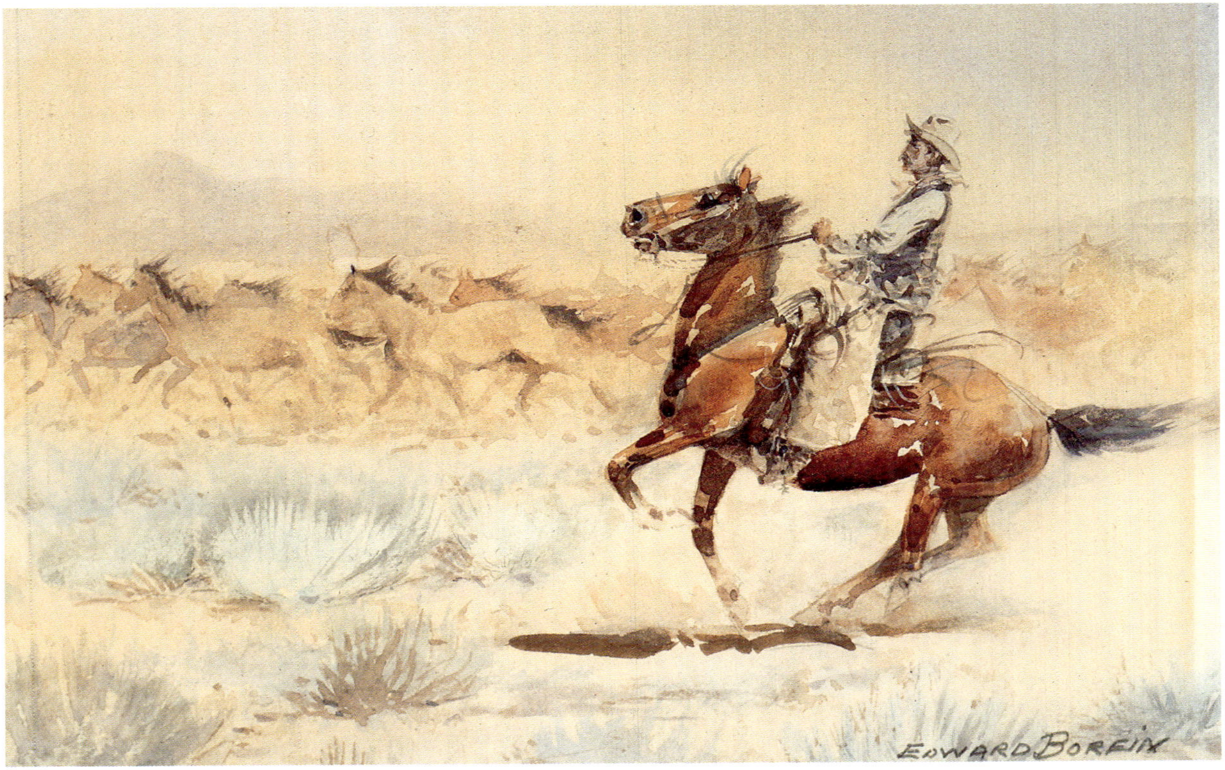

The Roundup. Watercolor on paper. 6 5/8 x 9 1/4 inches (sight). Signed lower right: EDWARD BOREIN.

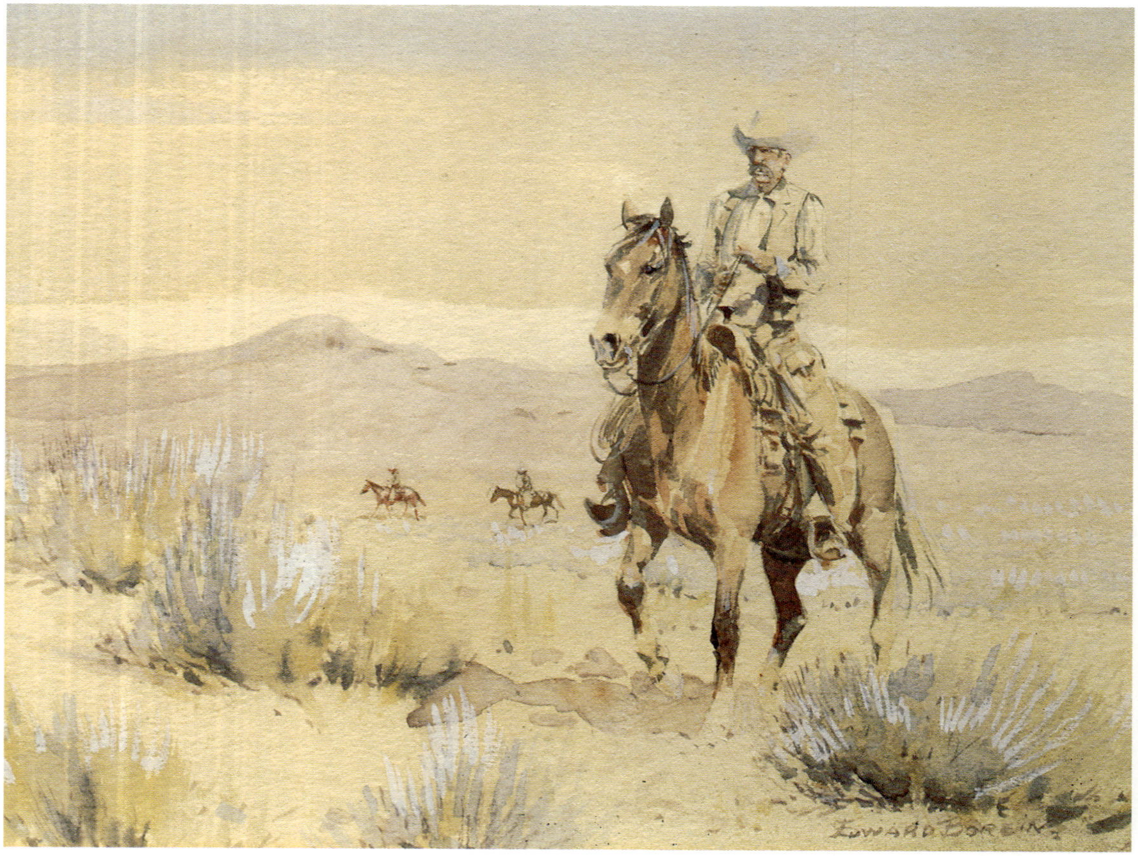

Cowboy on Horse. Watercolor and gouache on paper. 7 1/2 x 9 1/2 inches (sight). Signed lower right: *EDWARD BOREIN.*

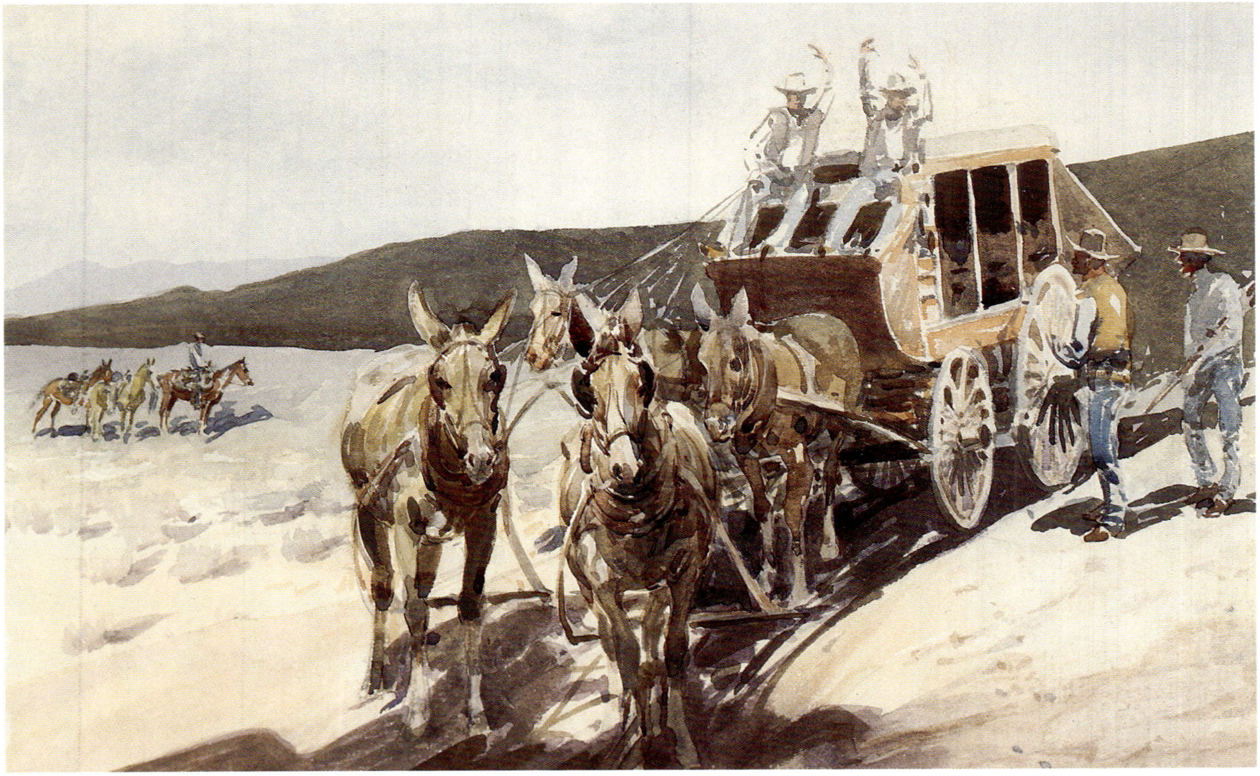

Stagecoach Holdup. Watercolor on paper. 10 x 15 3/4 inches (sight).

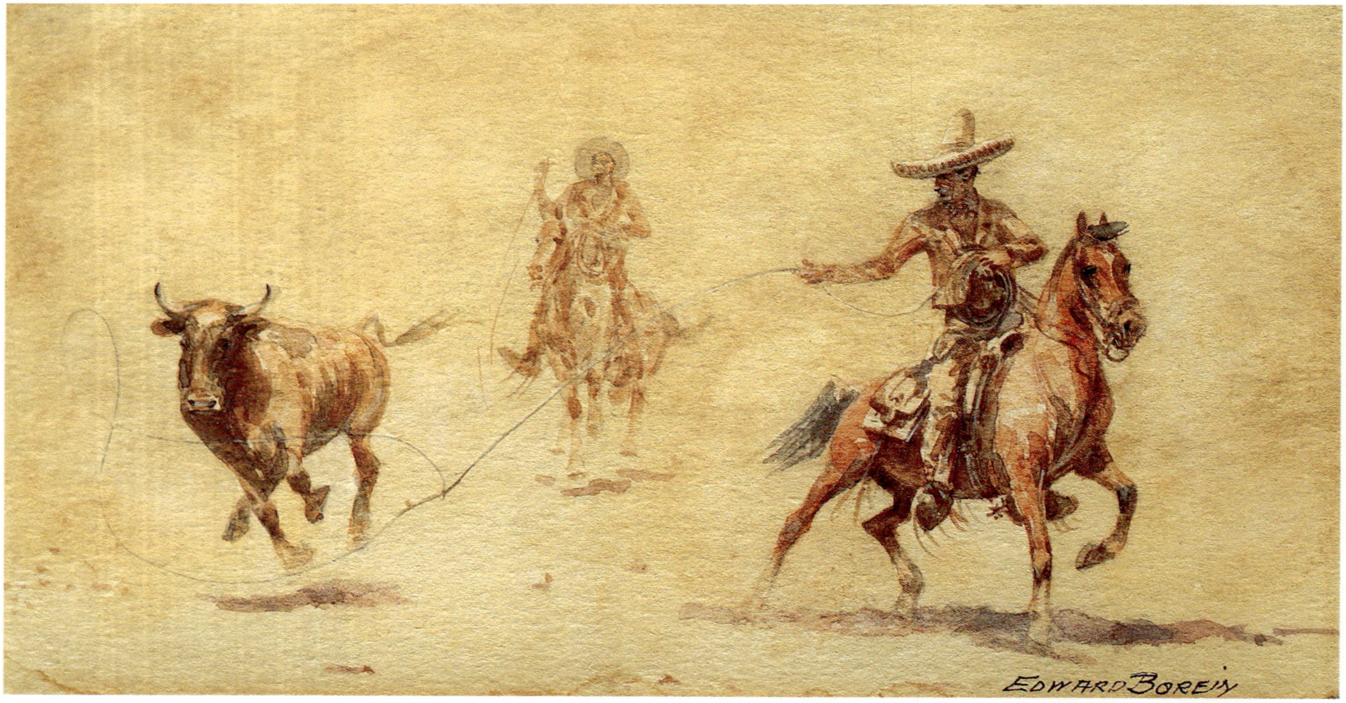

Lassoing a Steer. Watercolor and graphite on paper. 4 3/4 x 8 1/2 inches (sight). Signed lower right: *EDWARD BOREIN.*

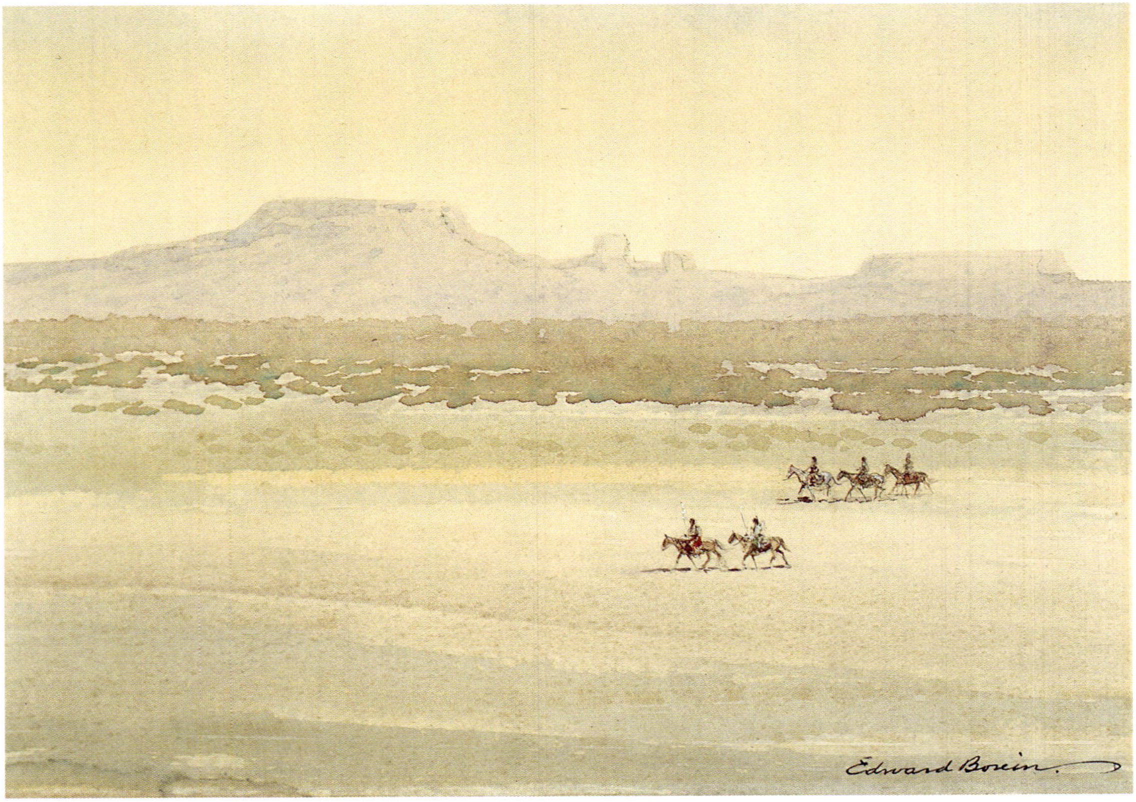

Pahutes. Watercolor on paper. 7 x 9 1/4 inches (sight). Signed lower right: *Edward Borein*.

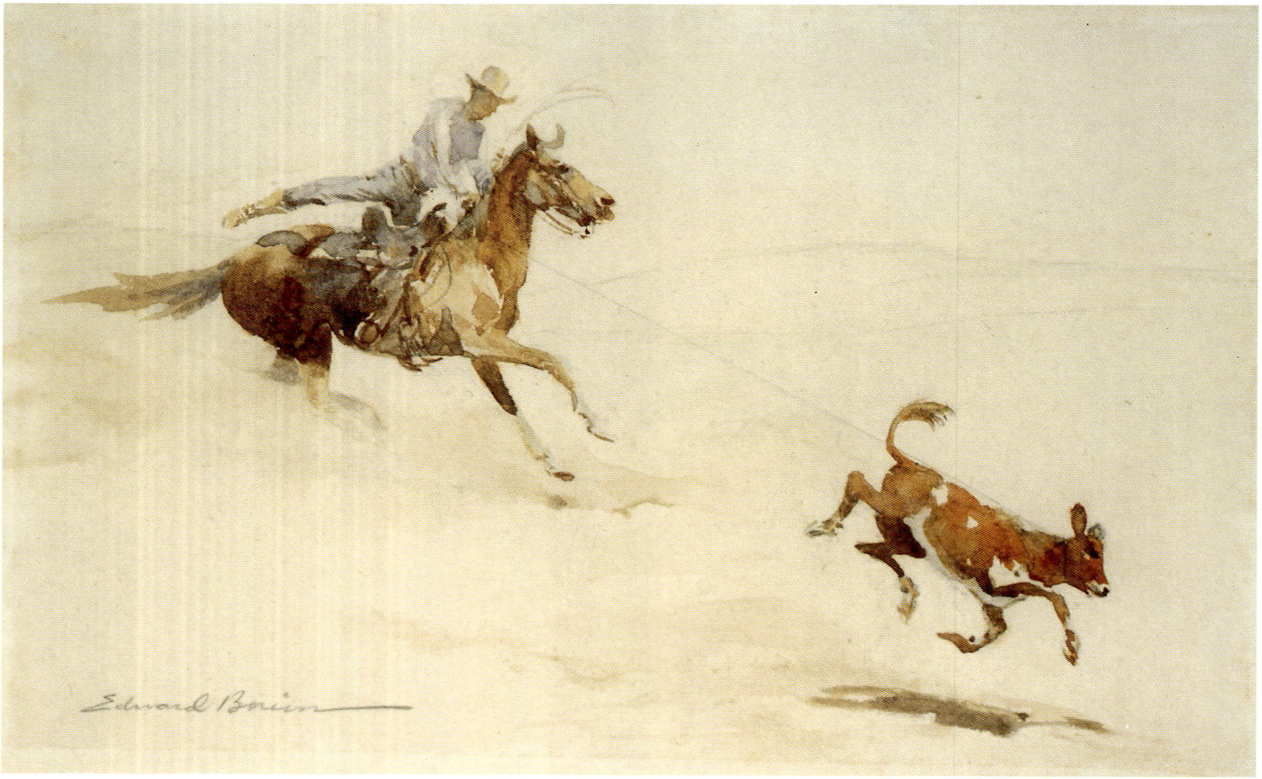

Roping a Calf (recto illustrated) / *Mounted Cowboy and Cattle* (verso). Watercolor on paper. 5 x 8 inches (sight).
Signed lower left of recto: *Edward Borein*.

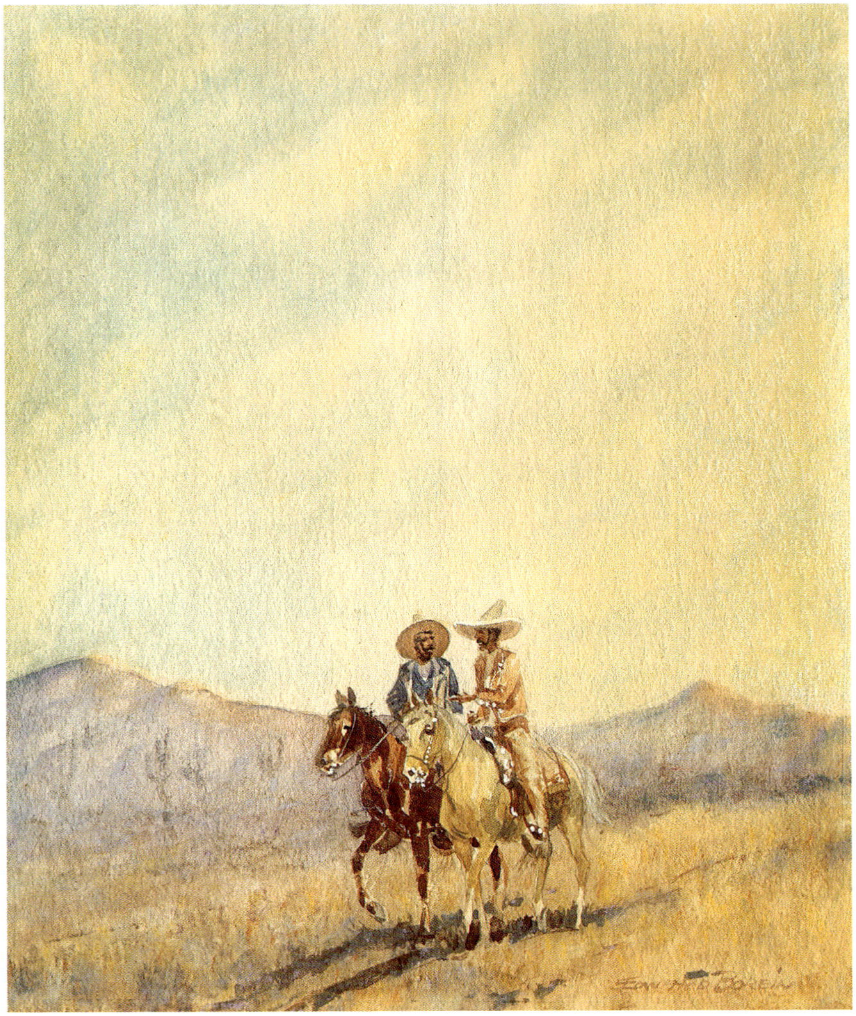

Two Mexicans on Horseback. Watercolor on paper. 8 5/8 x 7 1/8 inches (sight). Signed lower right: EDWARD BOREIN.

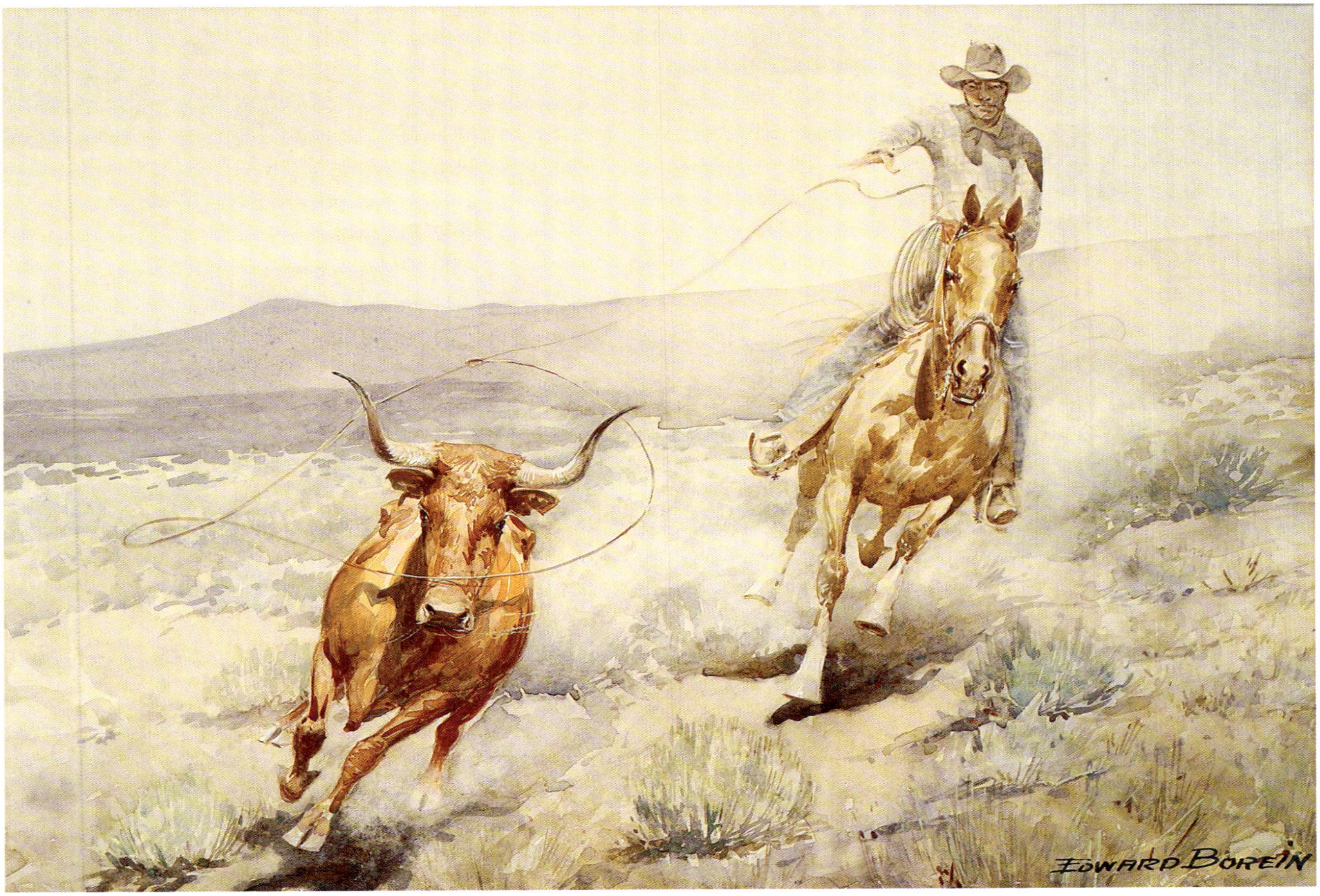

Roping a Steer. Watercolor on paper. 14 1/4 x 20 1/2 inches (sight). Signed lower right: *EDWARD BOREIN.*

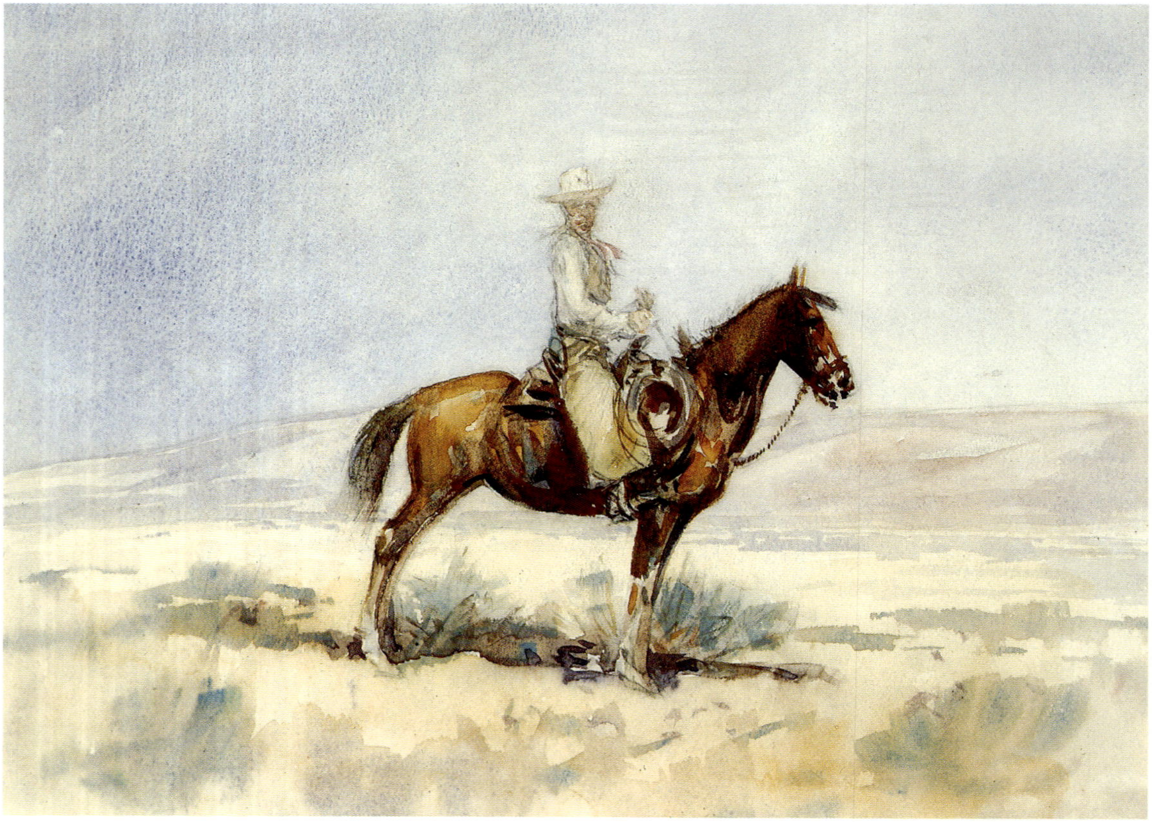

Rosenstock Cowboy. Watercolor on paper. 8 3/8 x 11 3/8 inches (sight).

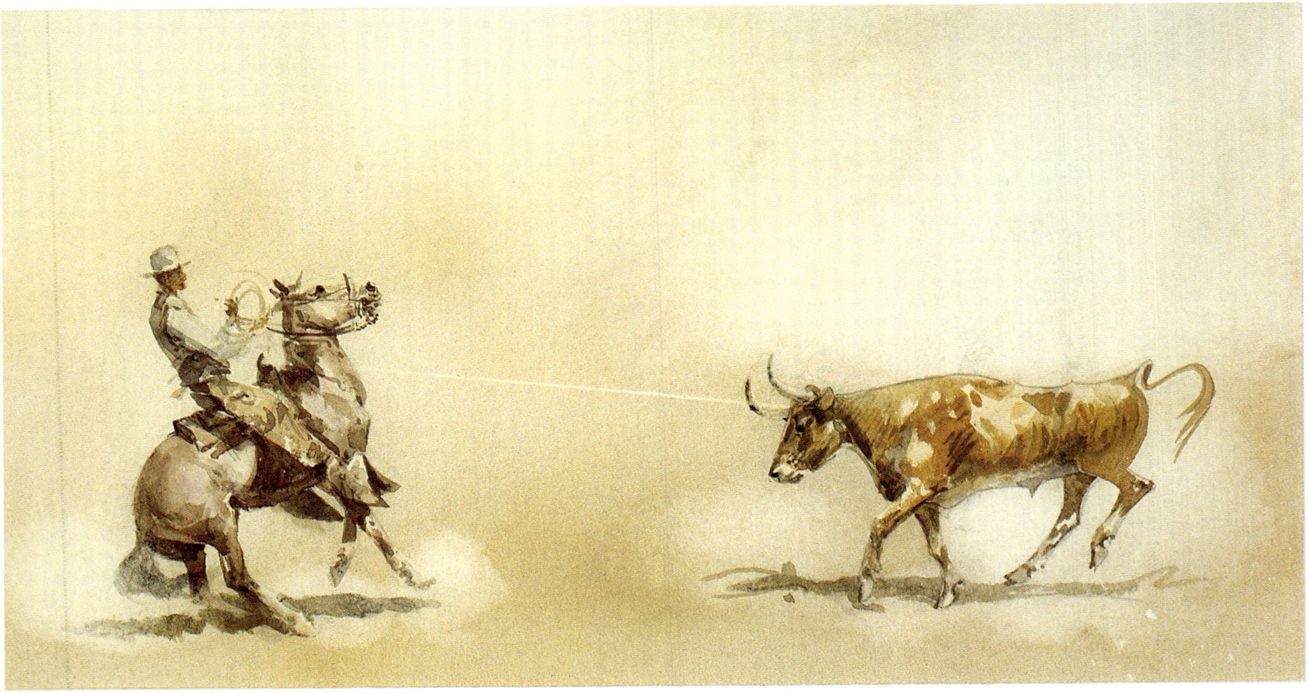

Cowboy and Lassoed Steer. Watercolor on paper. 7 1/8 x 13 1/4 inches (sight).

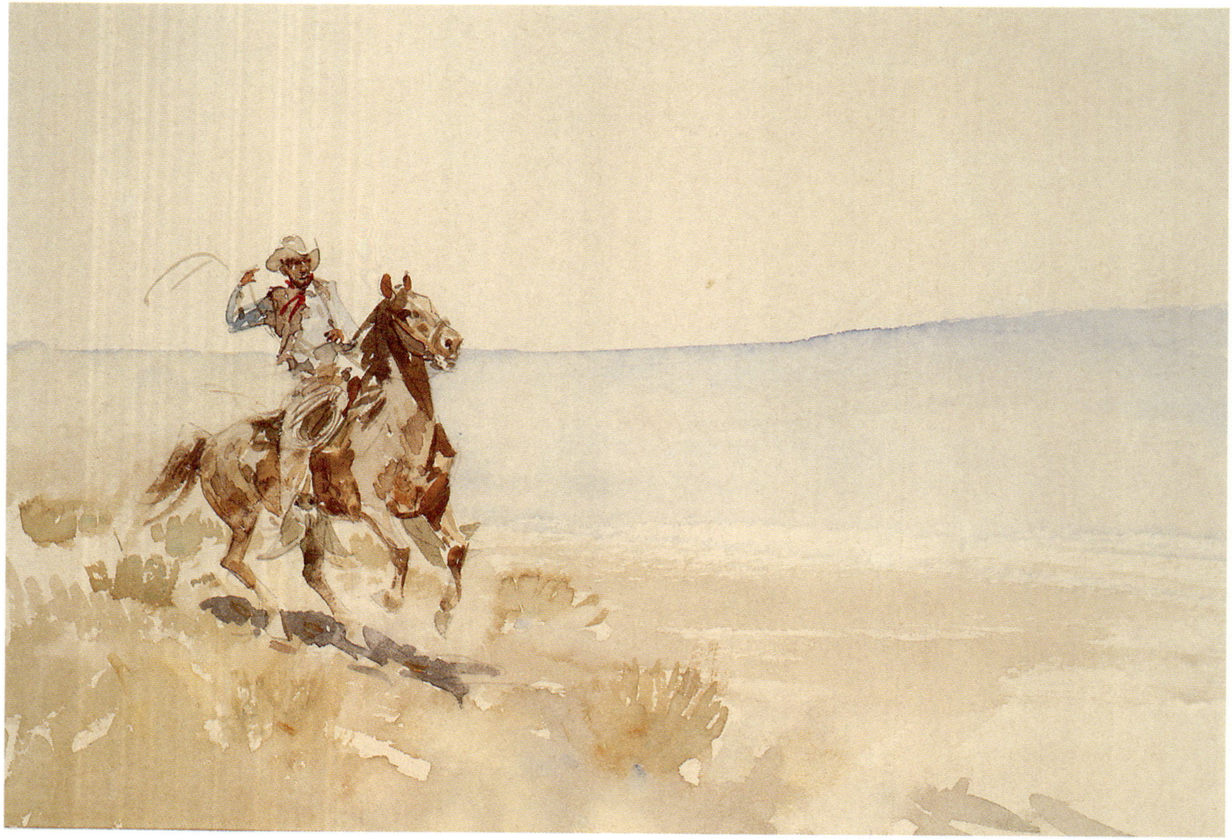

Cowhand on Horseback with a Rope. Watercolor on paper. 6 3/8 x 9 1/8 inches (sight).

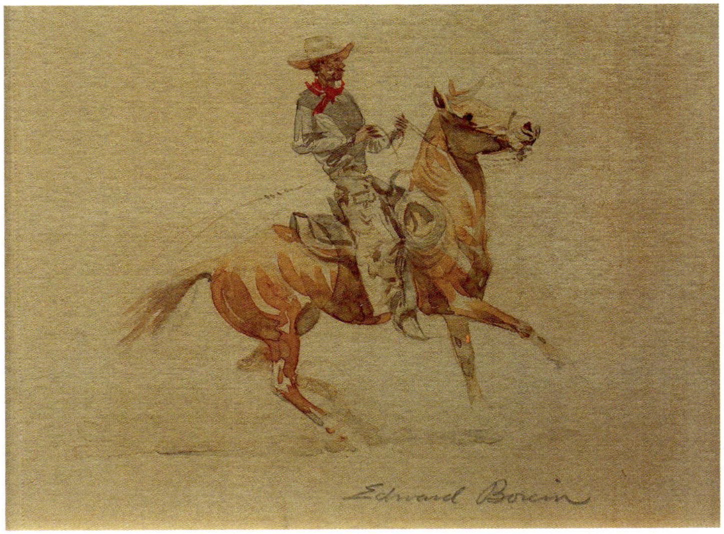

Rider on Brown Horse. Watercolor on paper. 4 1/2 x 5 3/4 inches (sight). Signed lower right: *Edward Borein*.

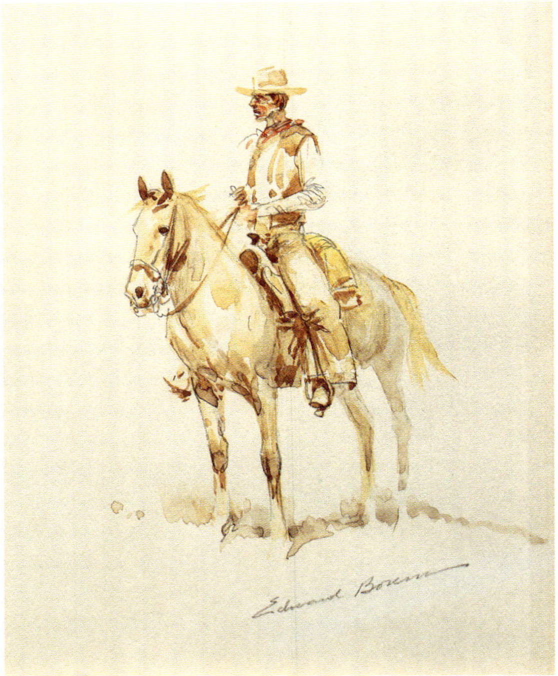

Rider on Horse. Watercolor and graphite on paper. 7 x 5 1/4 inches (sight). Signed lower right: *Edward Borein*.

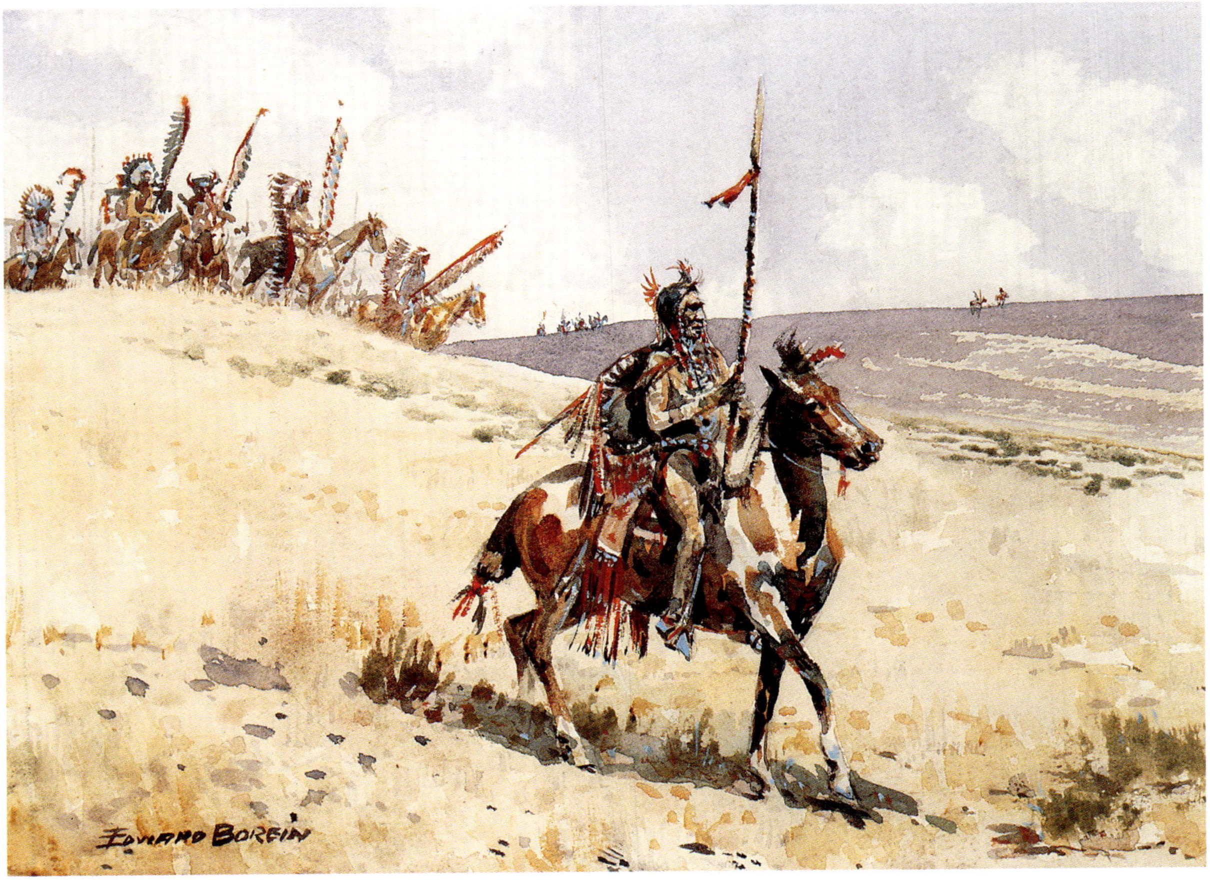

Indian Chiefs. Watercolor on paper. 7 x 9 1/2 inches. Signed lower left: *EDWARD BOREIN*.

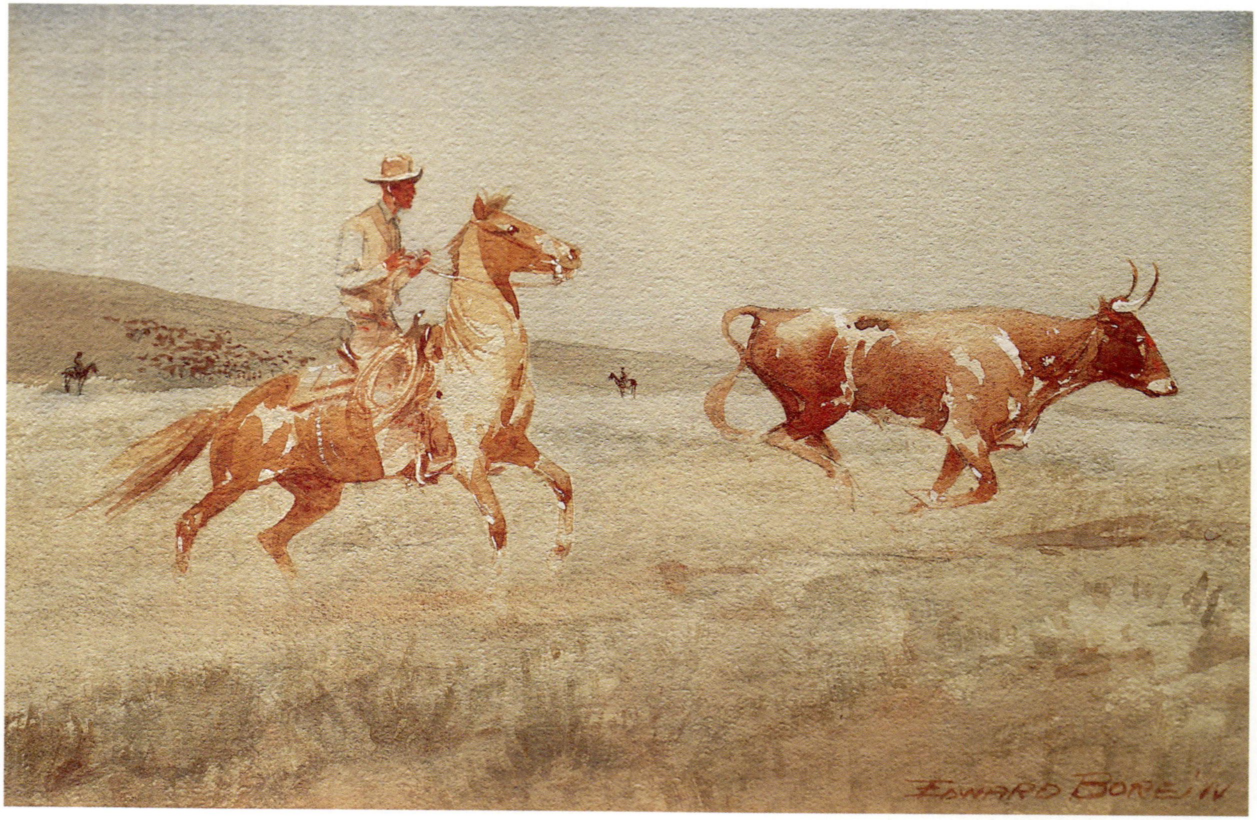

Cowboy Chasing Steer. Watercolor on paper. 6 1/4 x 9 inches (sight). Signed lower right: *EDWARD BOREIN.*

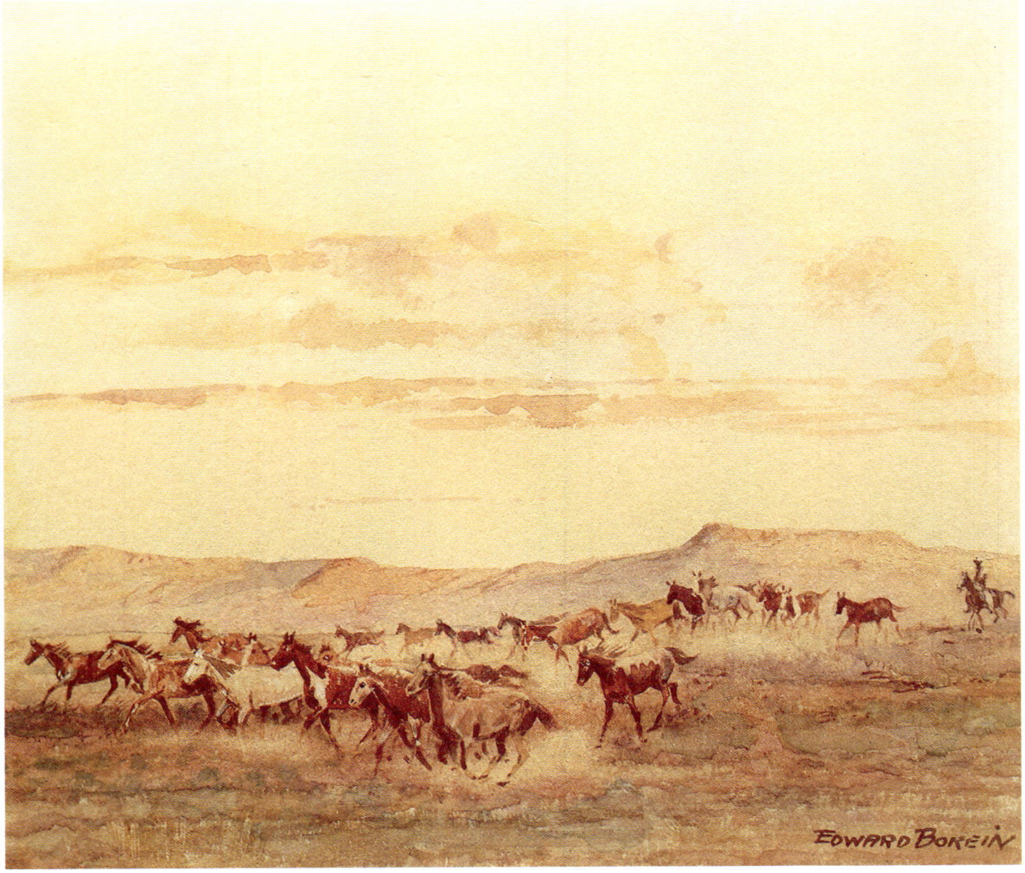

Herding Horses. Watercolor on paper. 8 1/2 x 9 3/4 inches (sight). Signed lower right: *EDWARD BOREIN*.

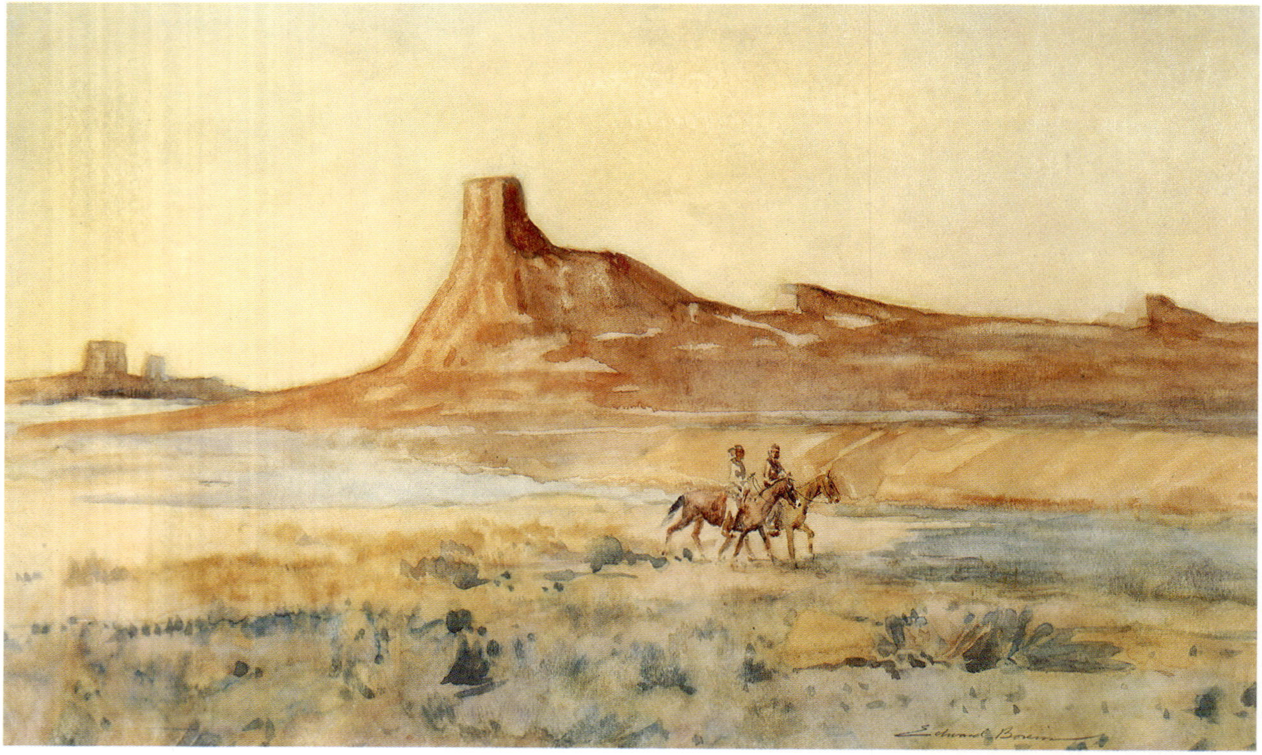

Navajos in the Desert. Watercolor on paper. 9 x 14 3/4 inches (sight). Signed lower right: *Edward Borein.*

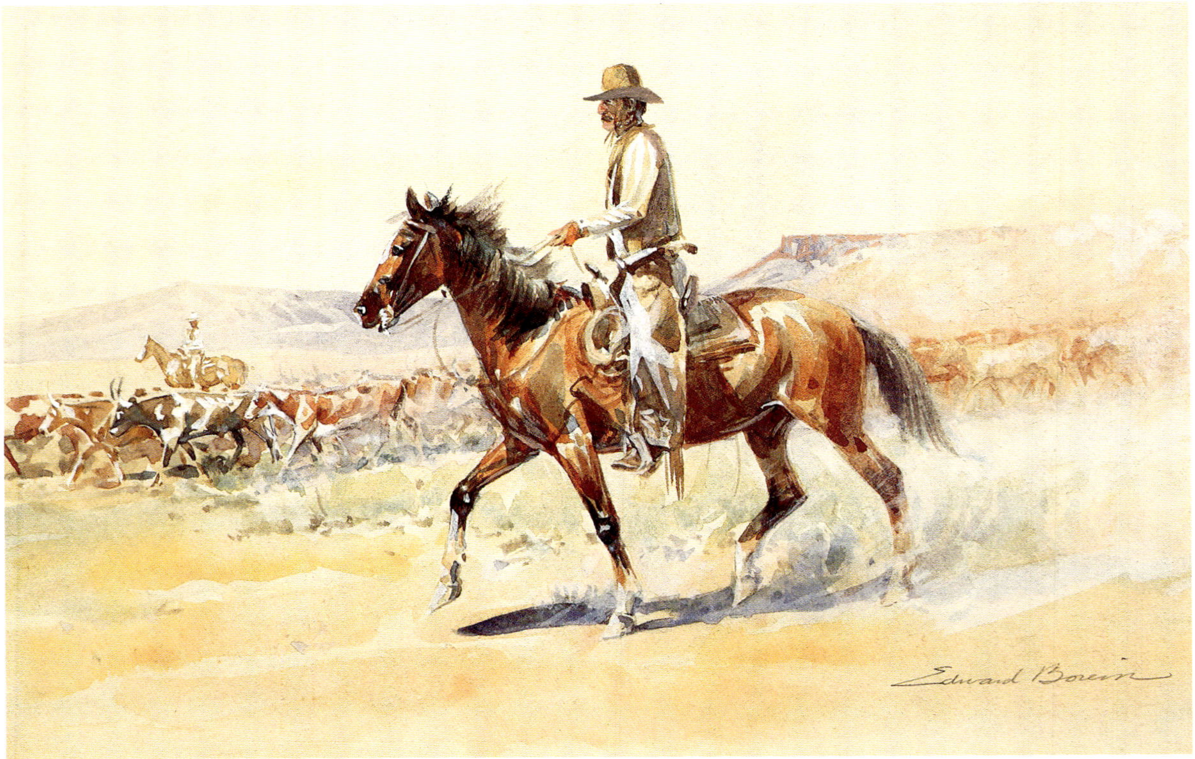

Cowboys Herding Cattle (recto illustrated) / *Cowboy on Horseback* (verso). Watercolor on paper. 6 7/8 x 10 1/4 inches (sight) (recto). Signed lower right of recto: *Edward Borein*.

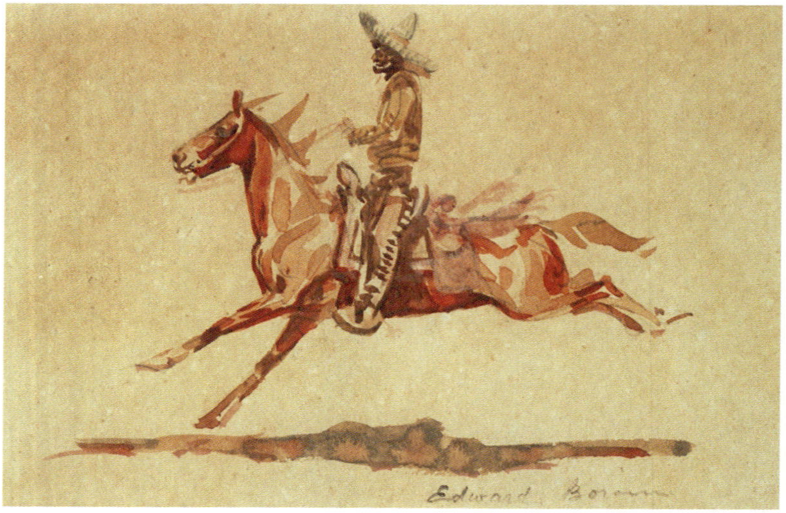

Untitled (Galloping Vaquero). Watercolor on paper. 2 7/8 x 4 1/8 inches (sight). Signed lower right: *Edward Borein.*

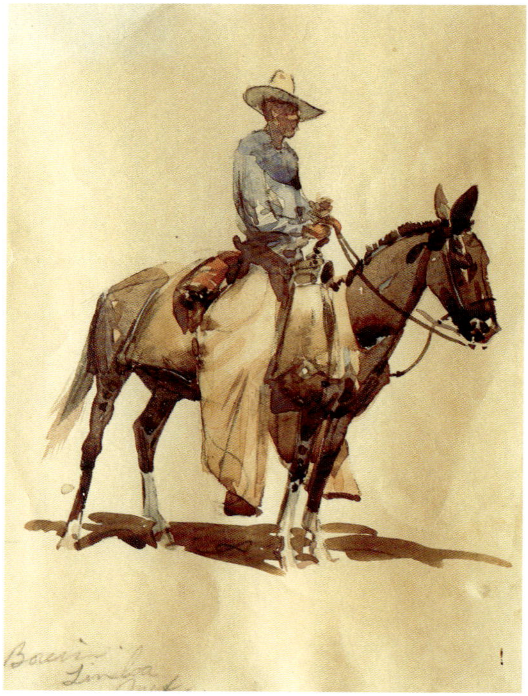

Cowboy on Mule. Watercolor and graphite on paper. 6 3/8 x 4 5/8 inches.
Signed and placed lower left: *Borein / Sinaloa / Mex.*

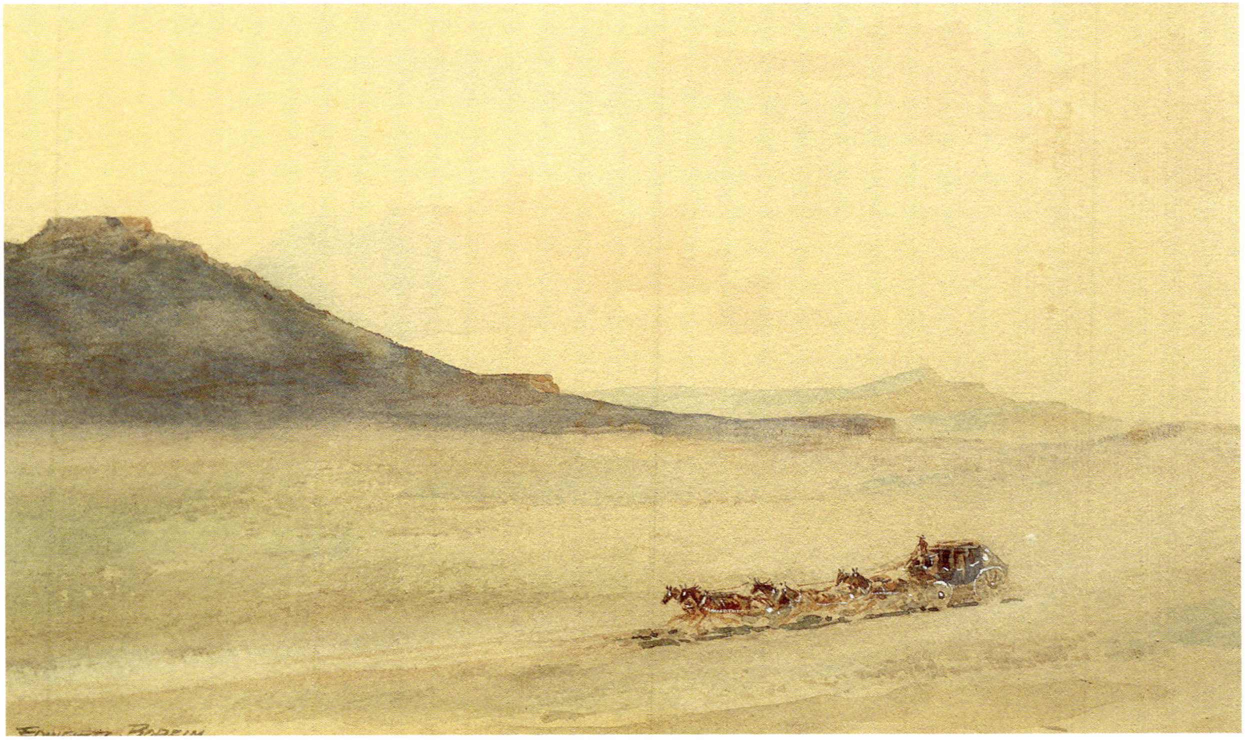

Stagecoach Crossing the Desert. Watercolor on paper. 6 1/2 x 10 3/4 inches (sight).
Signed lower left: *EDWARD BOREIN*.

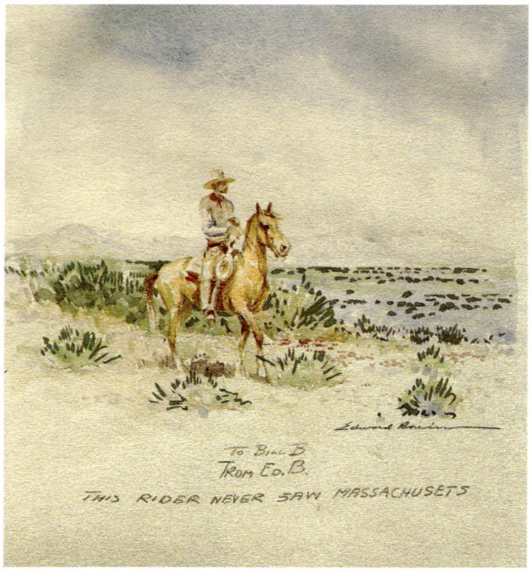

This Rider Never Saw Massachusetts. Watercolor on paper. 6 3/4 x 6 1/2 inches (sight). Signed lower right: *Edward Borein*. Inscribed lower center: *TO BILL B / FROM ED B / THIS RIDER NEVER SAW MASSACHUSETTS*.

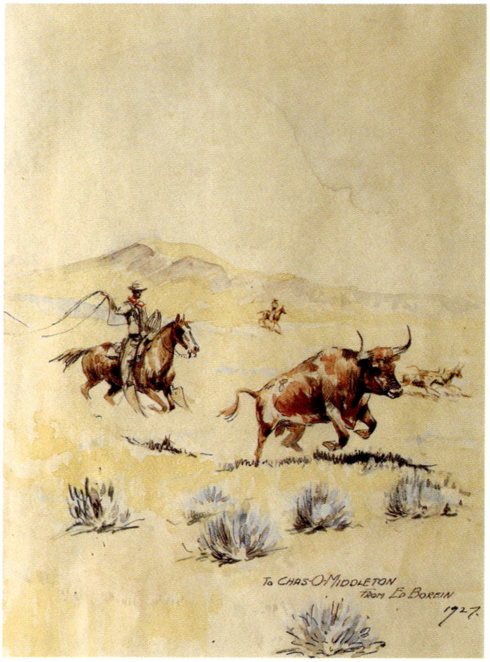

Roping the Bull, 1927. Watercolor and ink on paper. 9 x 6 3/8 inches (sight). Signed, inscribed and dated lower right: *TO CHAS-O-MIDDLETON / FROM ED BOREIN / 1927*.

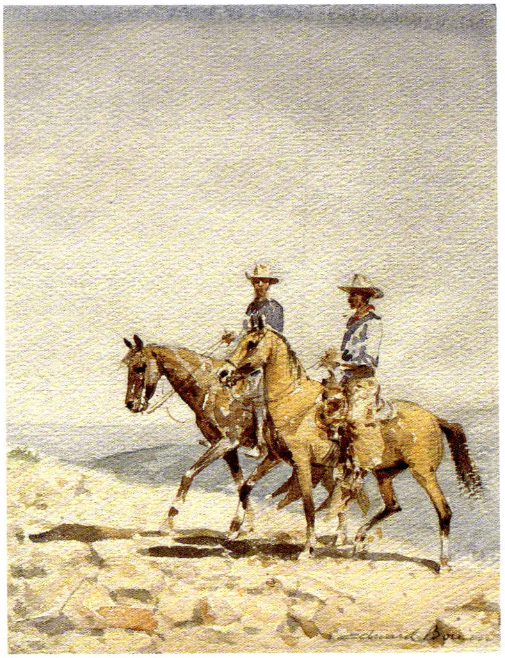

Pards (Two Riders on Horseback). Watercolor on paper. 7 5/8 x 5 7/8 inches (sight).
Signed lower right: *Edward Borein.*

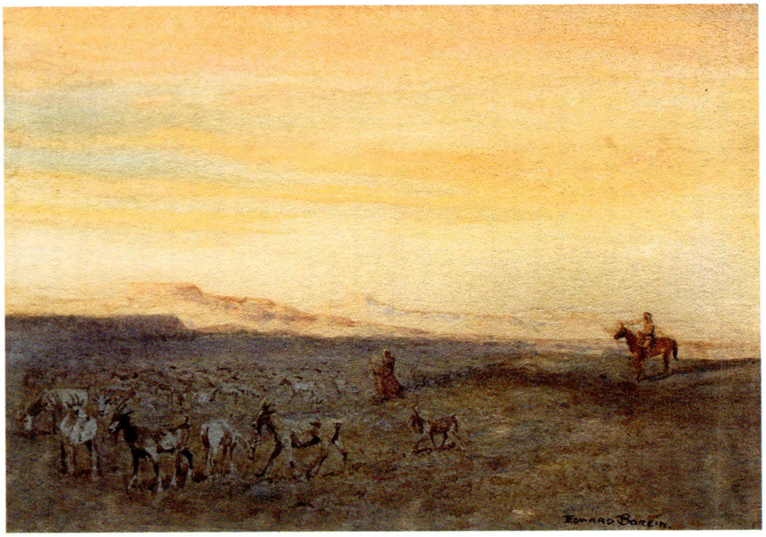

Navajo Shepherds and Their Flocks. Watercolor and graphite on paper. 7 x 9 5/8 inches (sight).
Signed lower right: *EDWARD BOREIN.*

DRAWINGS

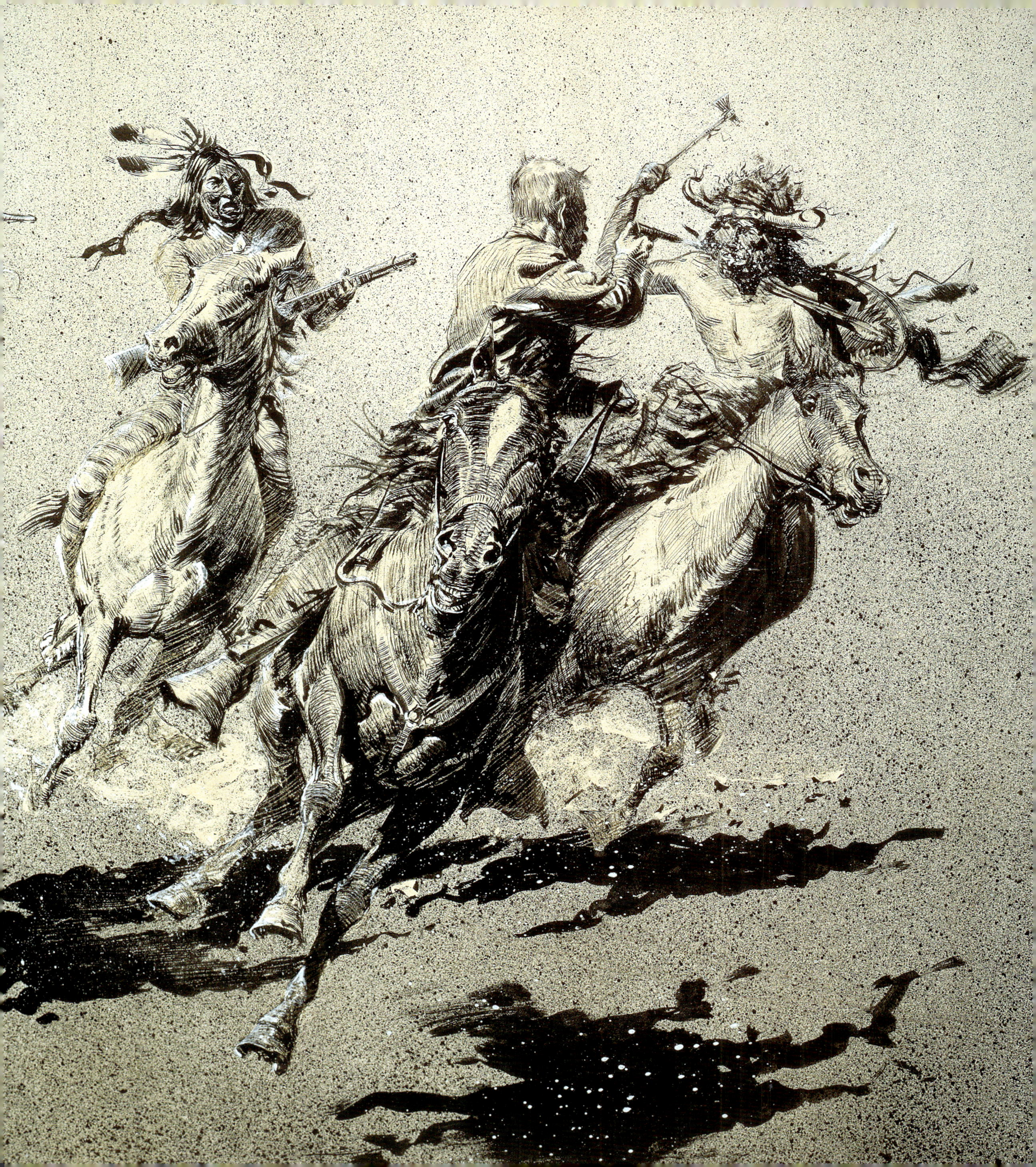

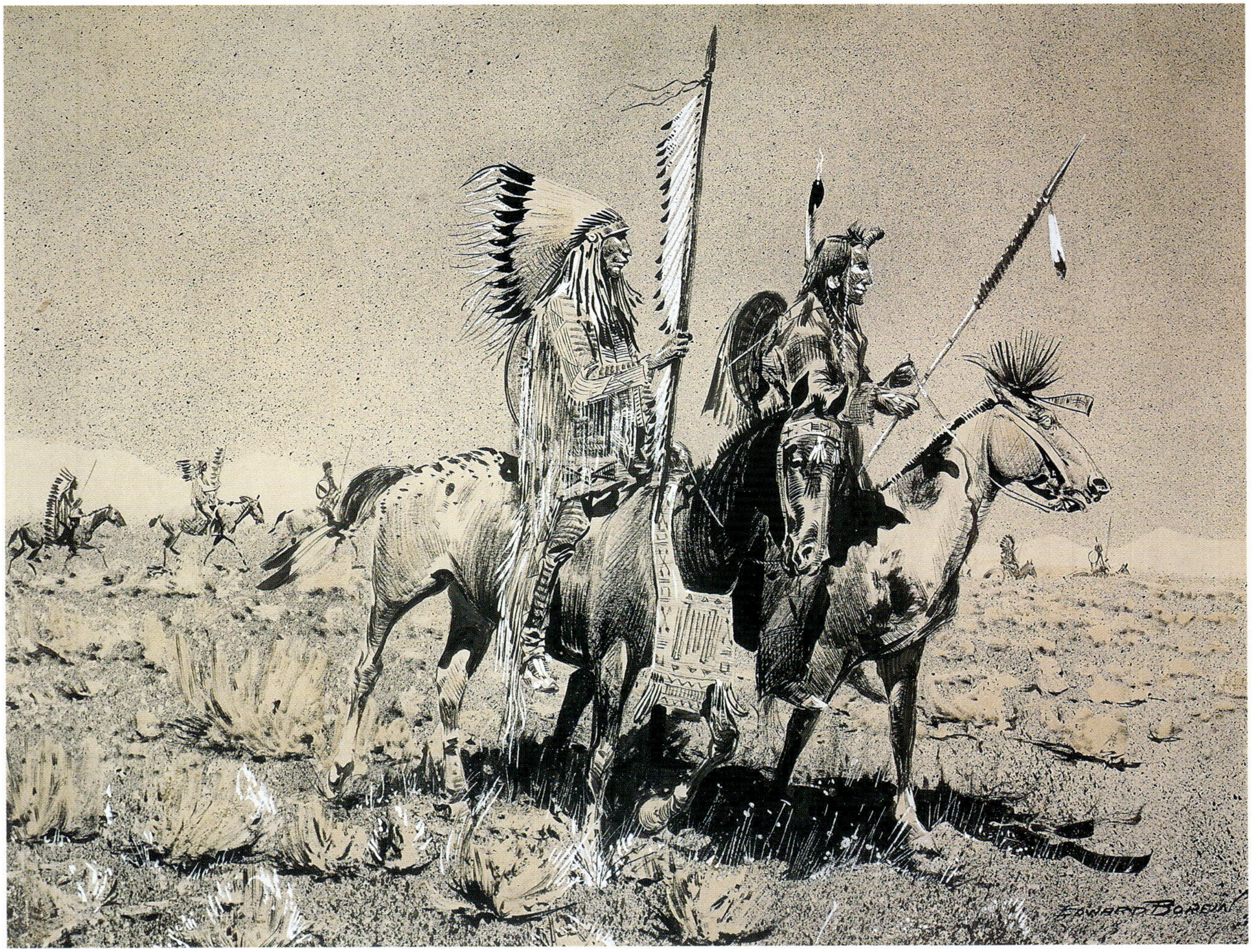

Indian War Party. Ink and gouache on paper. 21 1/4 x 27 inches (sight). Signed lower right: *EDWARD BOREIN*.

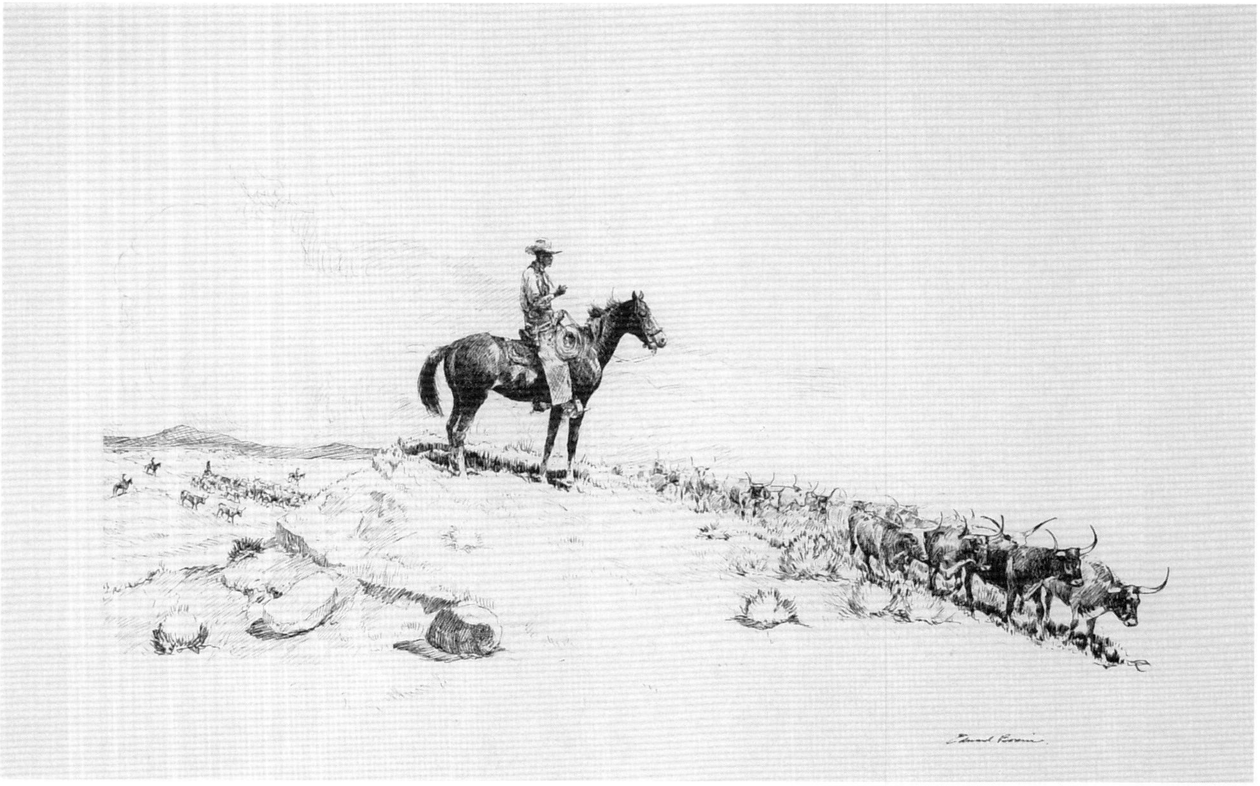

Trail Drive. Ink on paper. 15 x 23 inches (sheet). Signed lower right: *Edward Borein.*

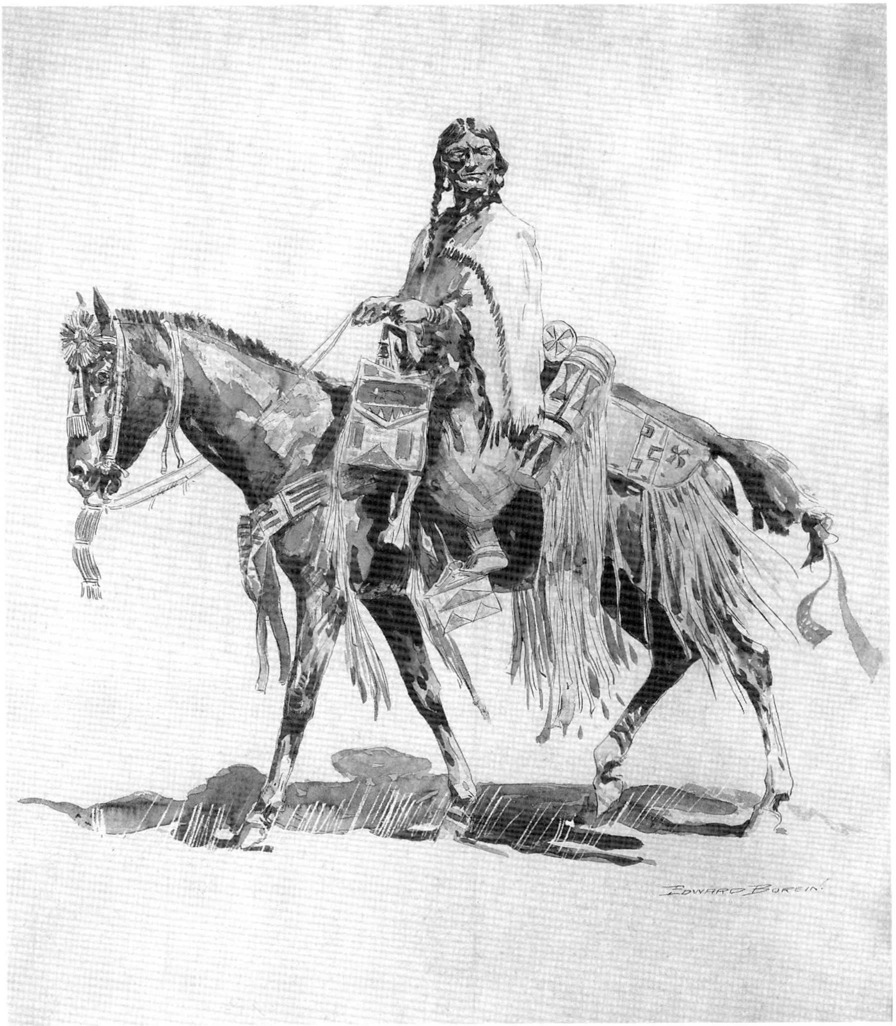

Single Indian Figure on Horseback. Ink and gouache on paper. 18 5/8 x 15 3/4 inches (sight). Signed lower right: *EDWARD BOREIN.*

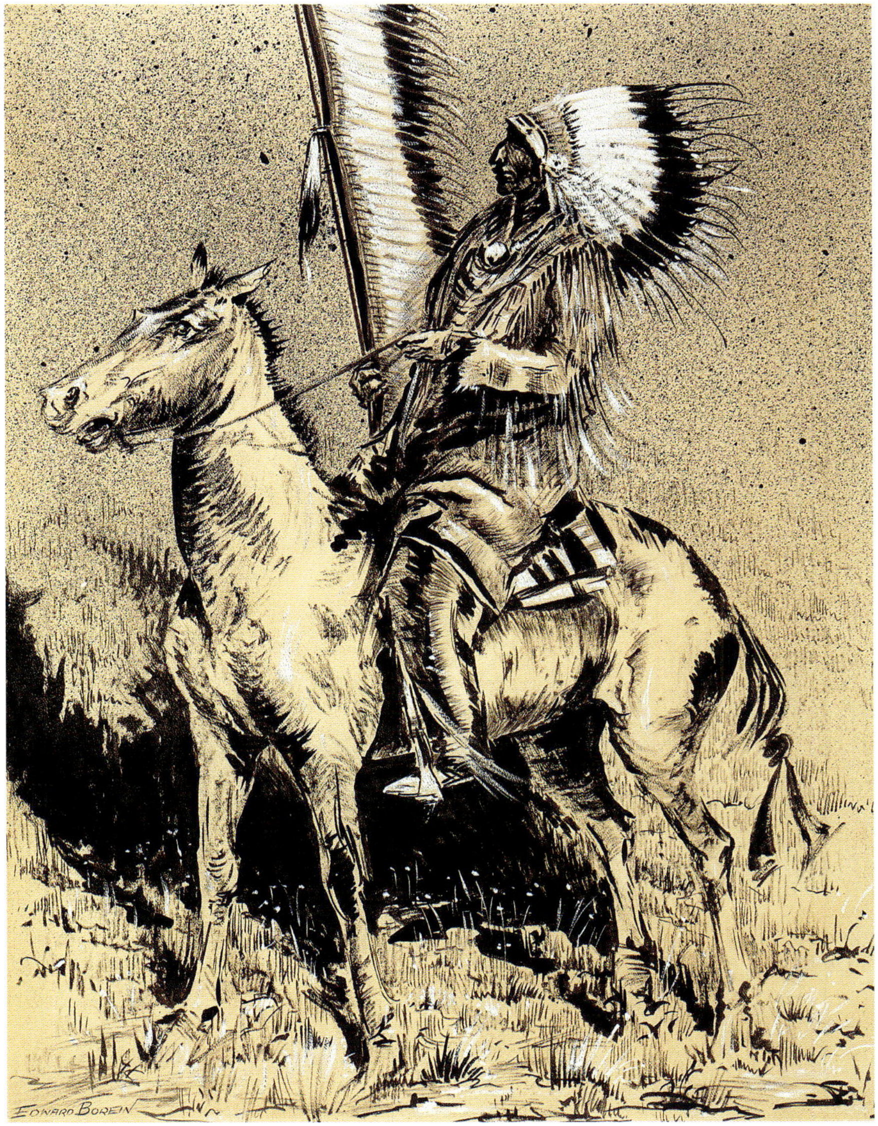

Indian Chief. Ink and gouache on paper. 18 x 13 3/4 inches (sight). Signed lower left: *EDWARD BOREIN*.

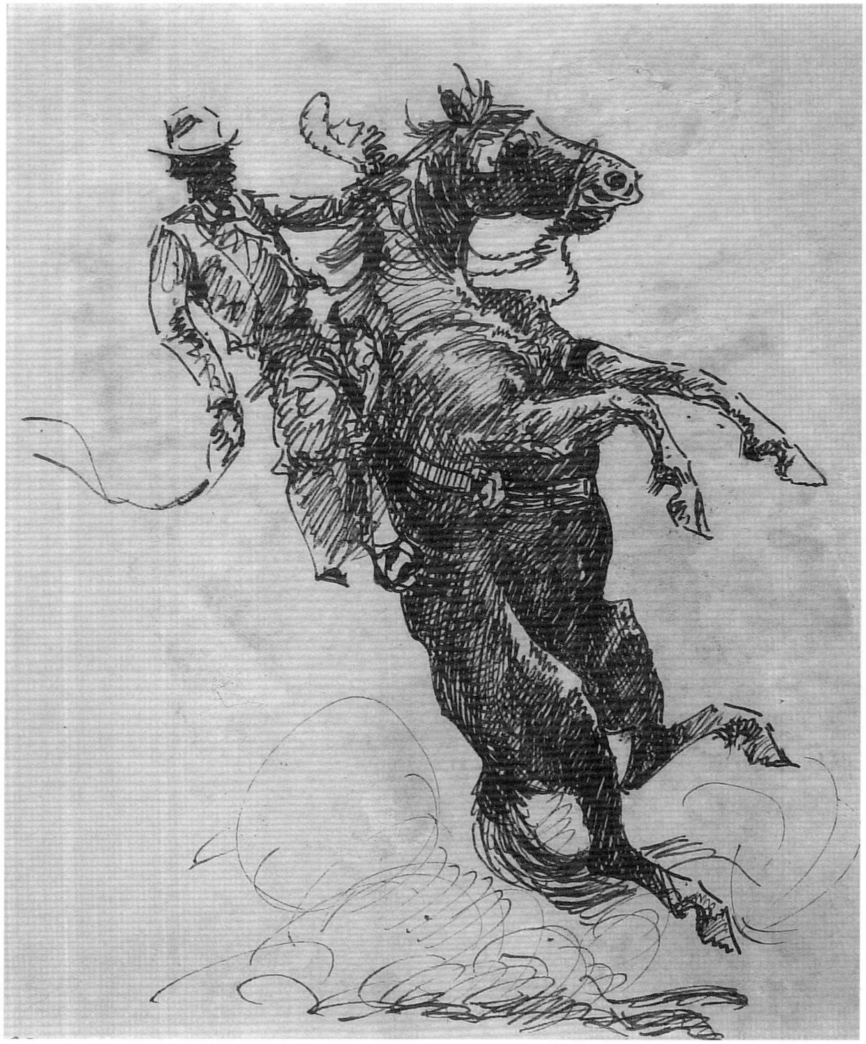

Cinch Binder (Study for Etching). Ink on paper. 7 3/8 x 6 1/4 inches (sheet).

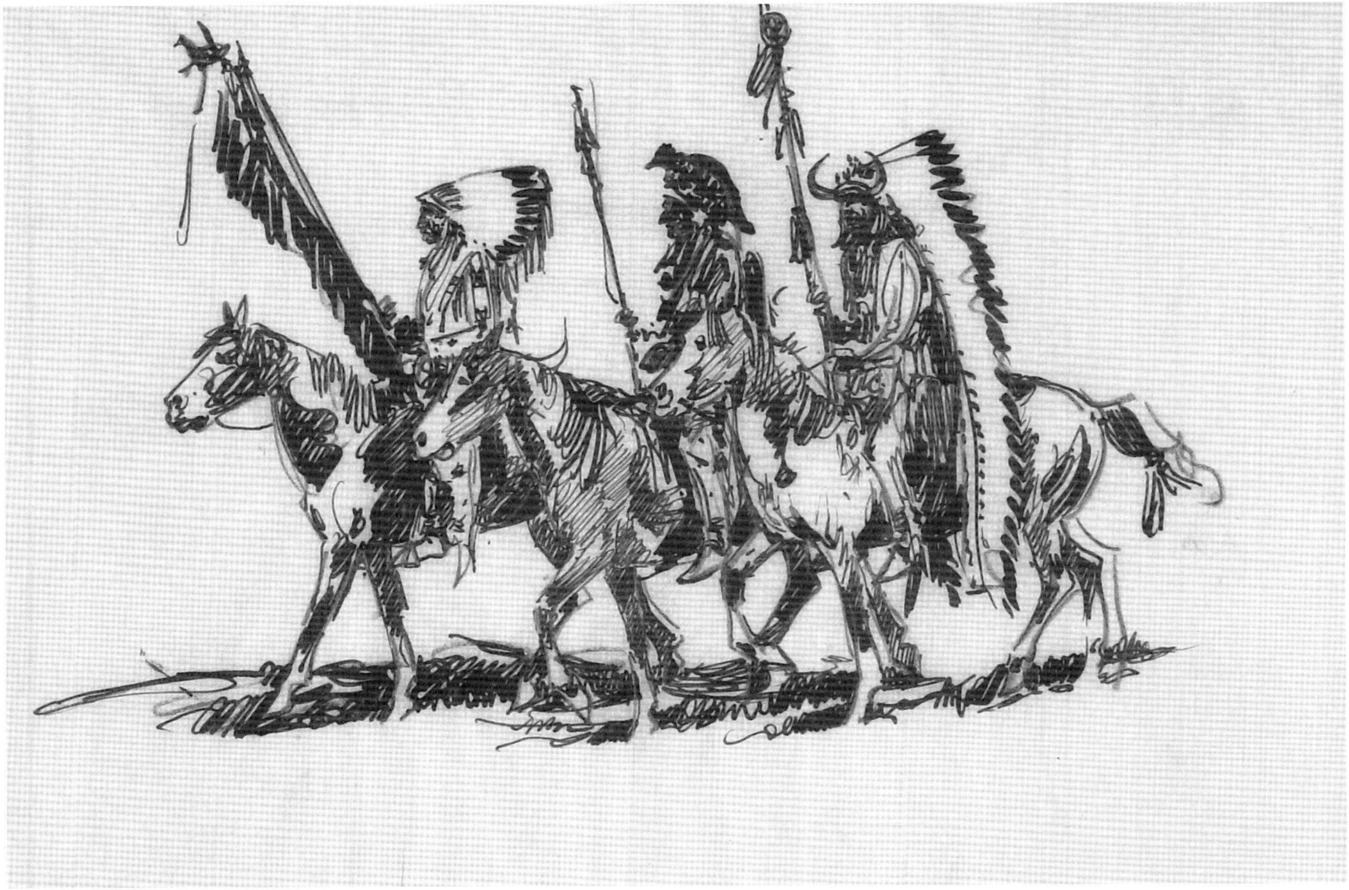

Three Indians on Horseback. Ink and graphite on paper. 6 3/8 x 9 1/2 inches (sight).

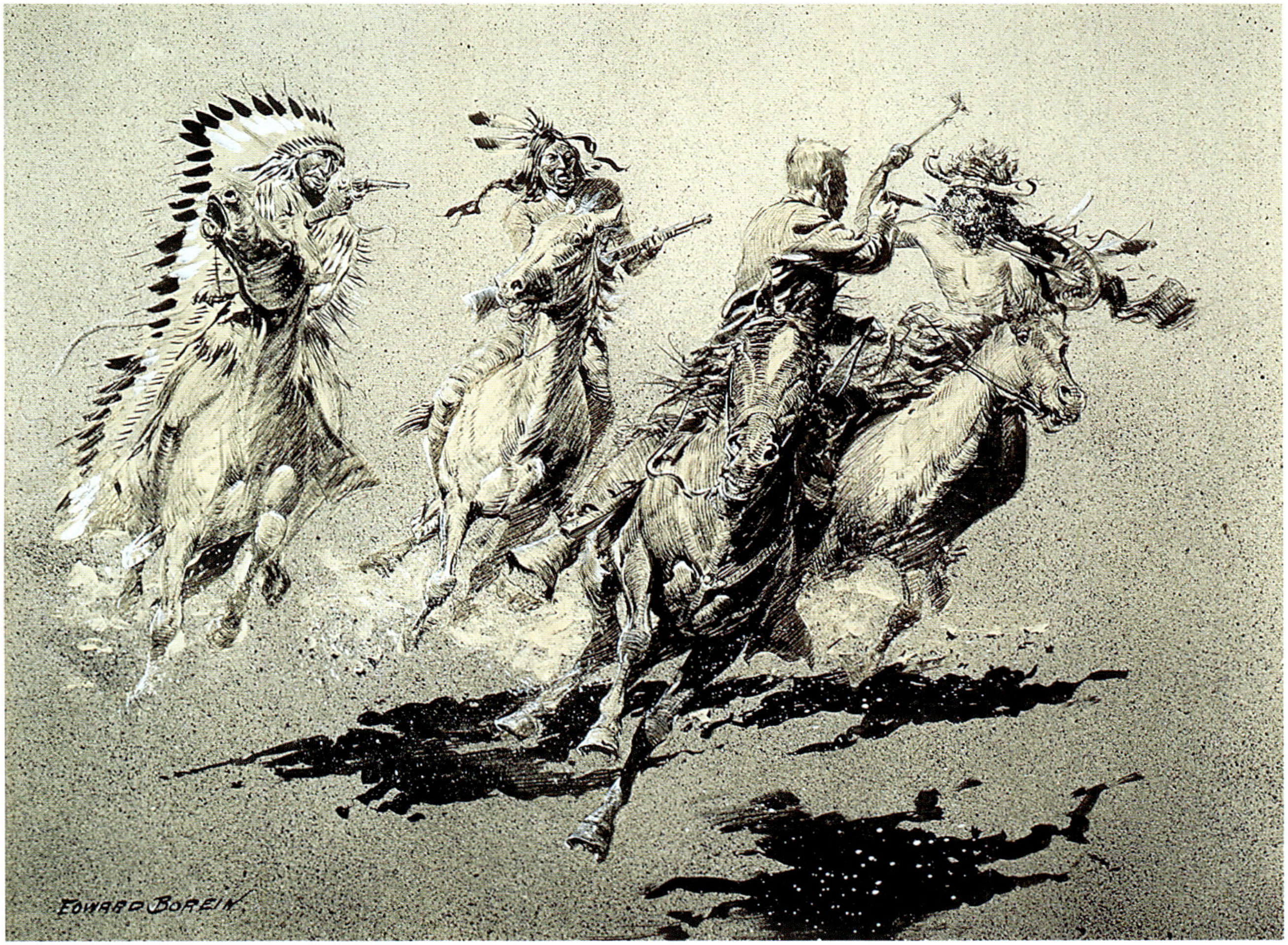

Pony Express on the Plains. Ink and gouache on paper. 20 1/2 x 26 1/2 inches (sight). Signed lower left: *EDWARD BOREIN.*

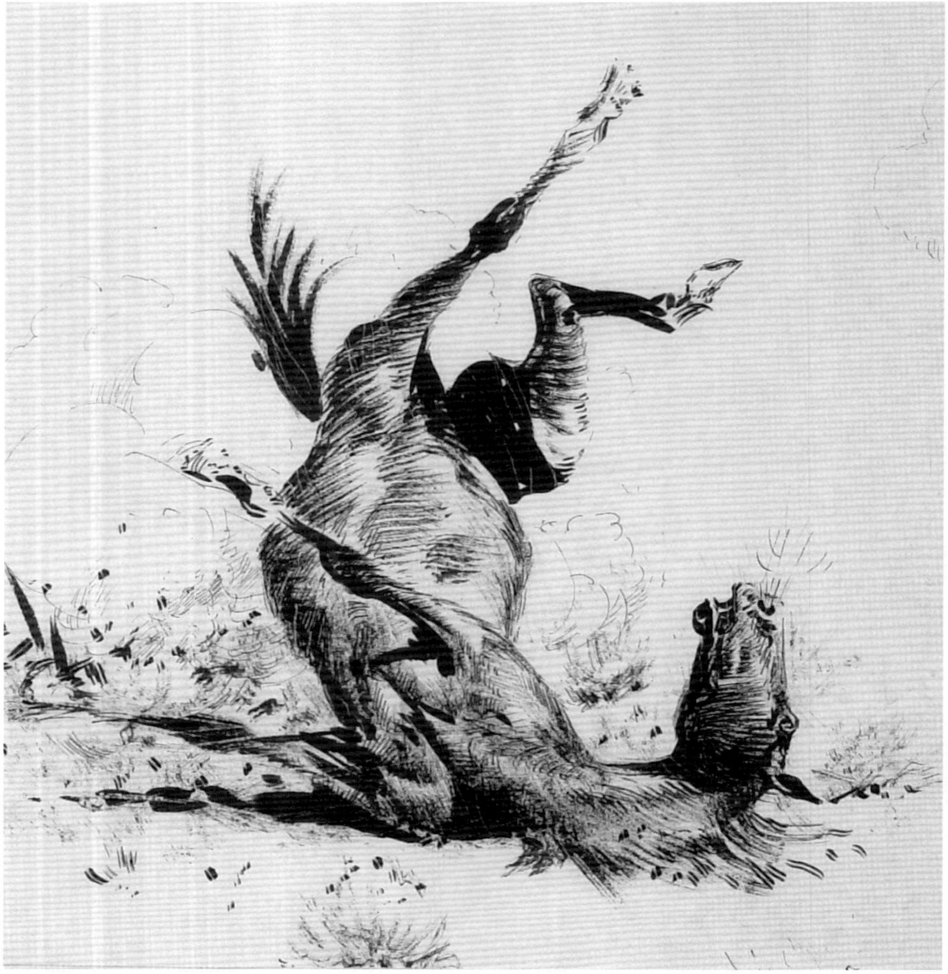

Horse Scratching Its Back. Ink on paper. 7 1/2 x 7 1/8 inches (sheet).

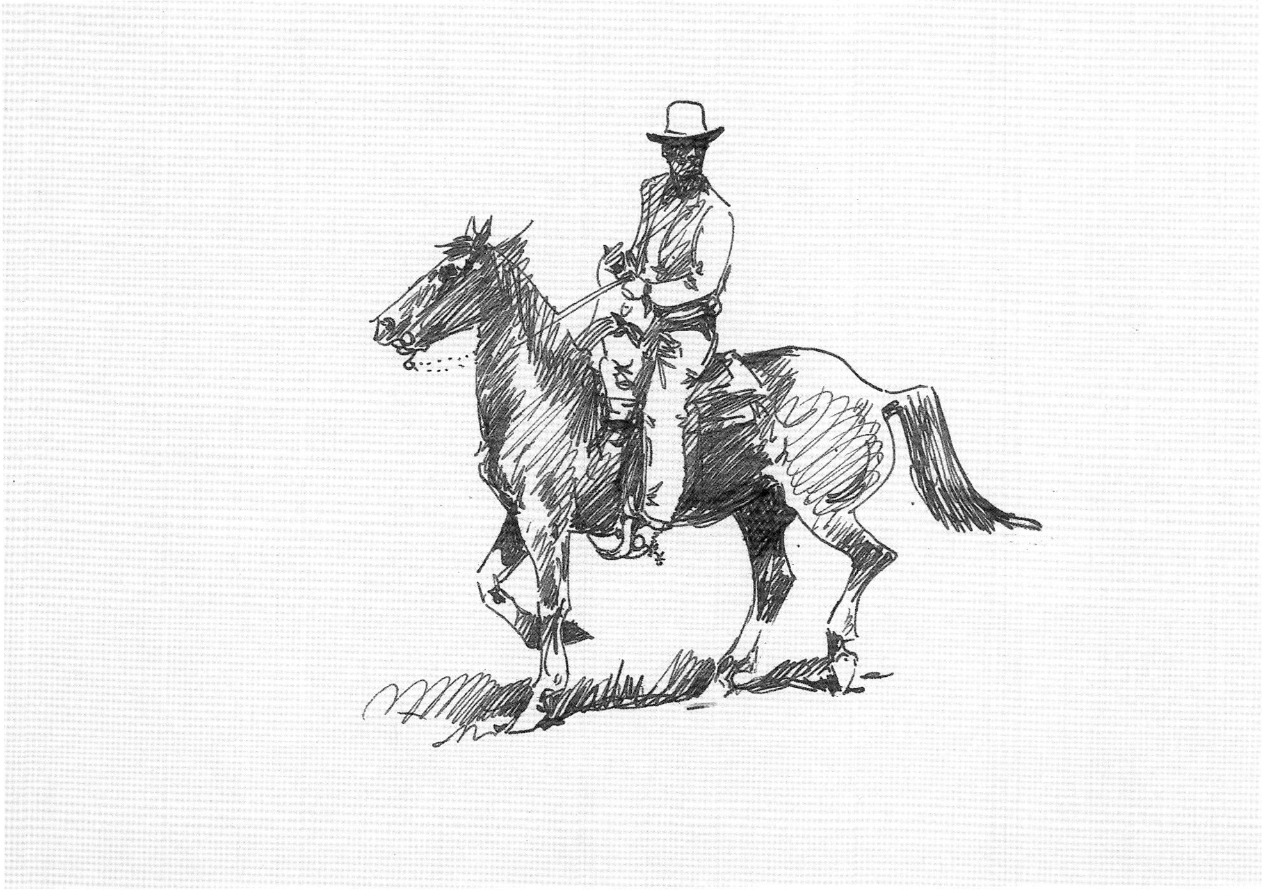

Horse and Rider. Ink on paper. 8 1/2 x 11 inches (sheet).

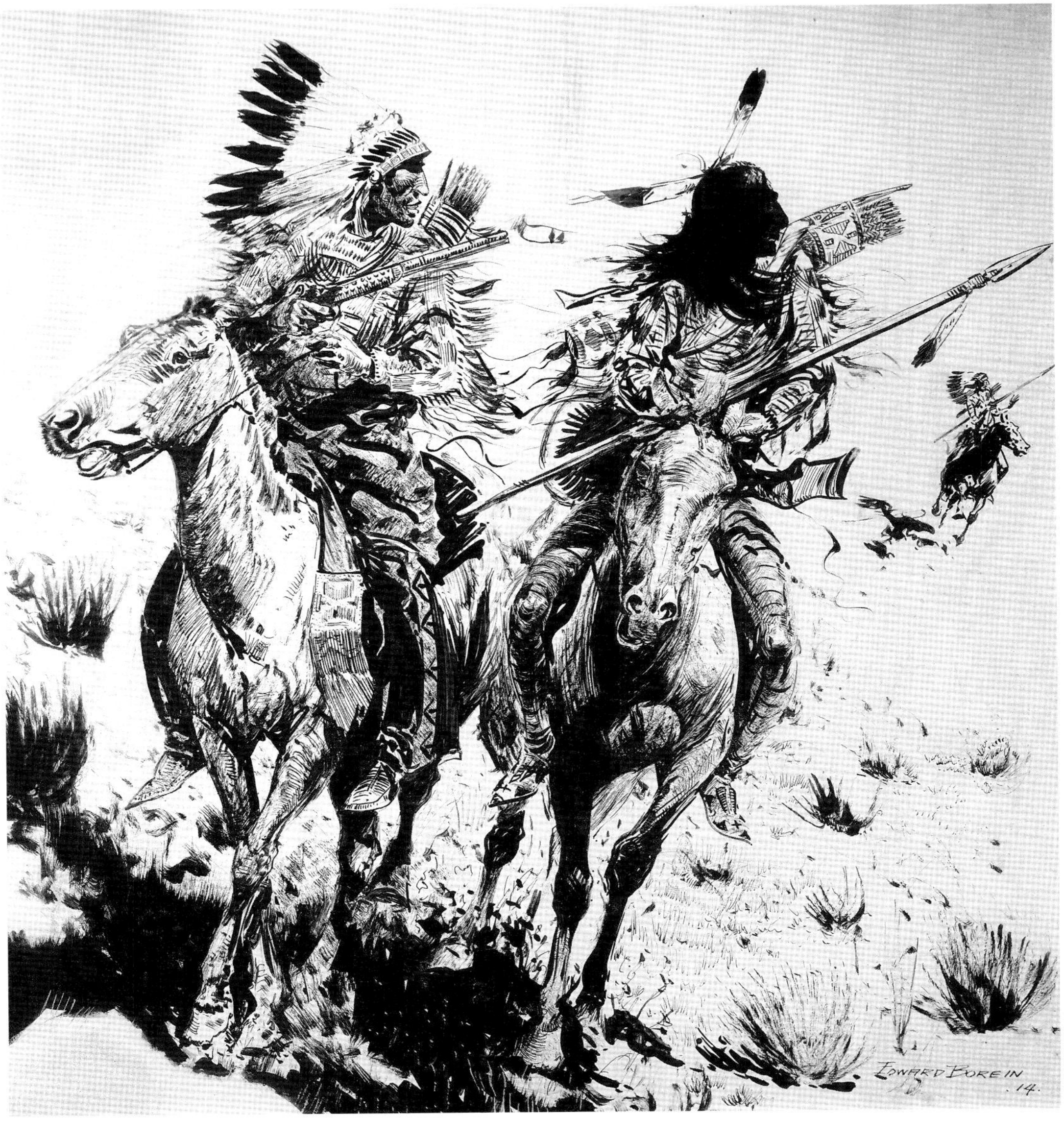

Indian Warriors. India ink on paper. 21 x 19 1/2 inches (sight). Signed and dated lower right: *EDWARD BOREIN / .14.*

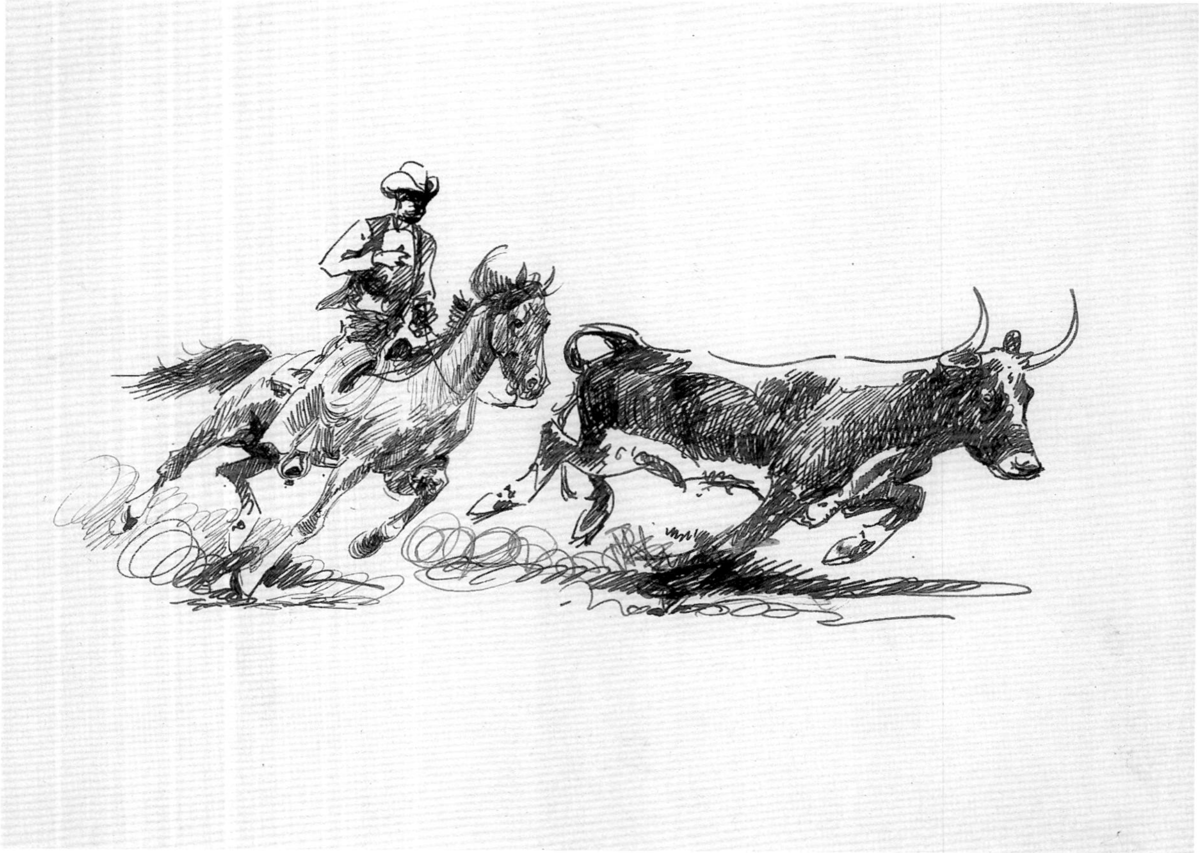

Heading a Steer. Ink on paper. 8 3/8 x 11 inches (sheet).

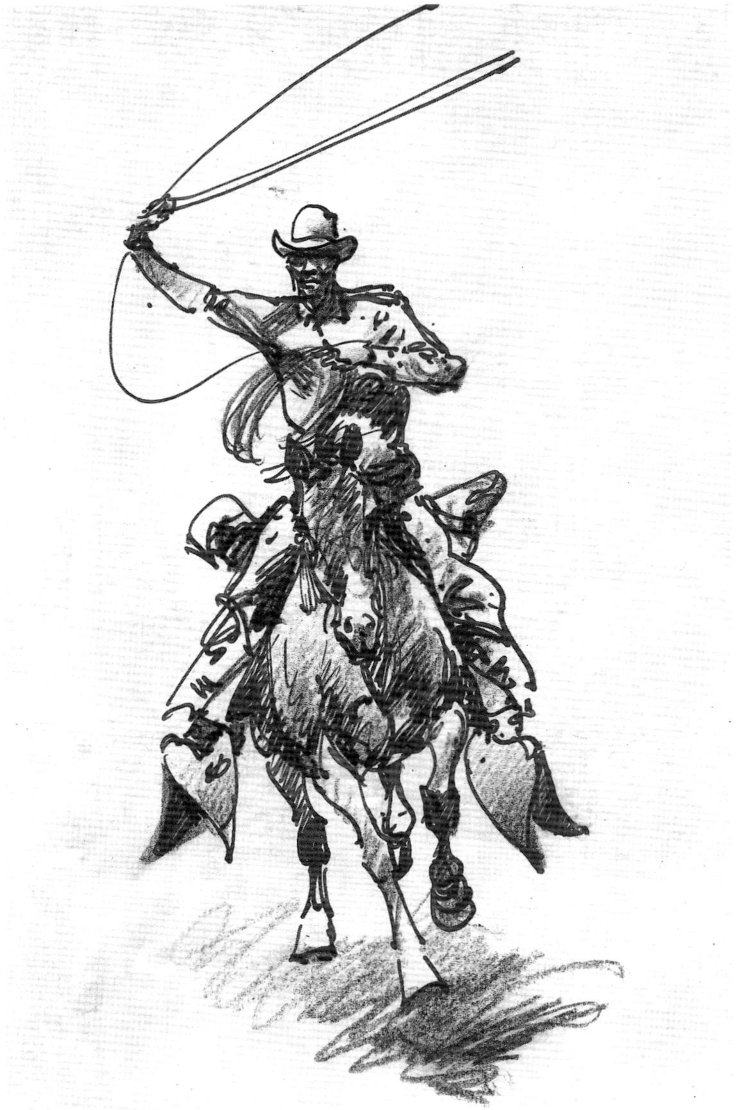

Cowboy Roping. Ink and graphite on paper. 11 1/4 x 7 1/4 inches (sheet).

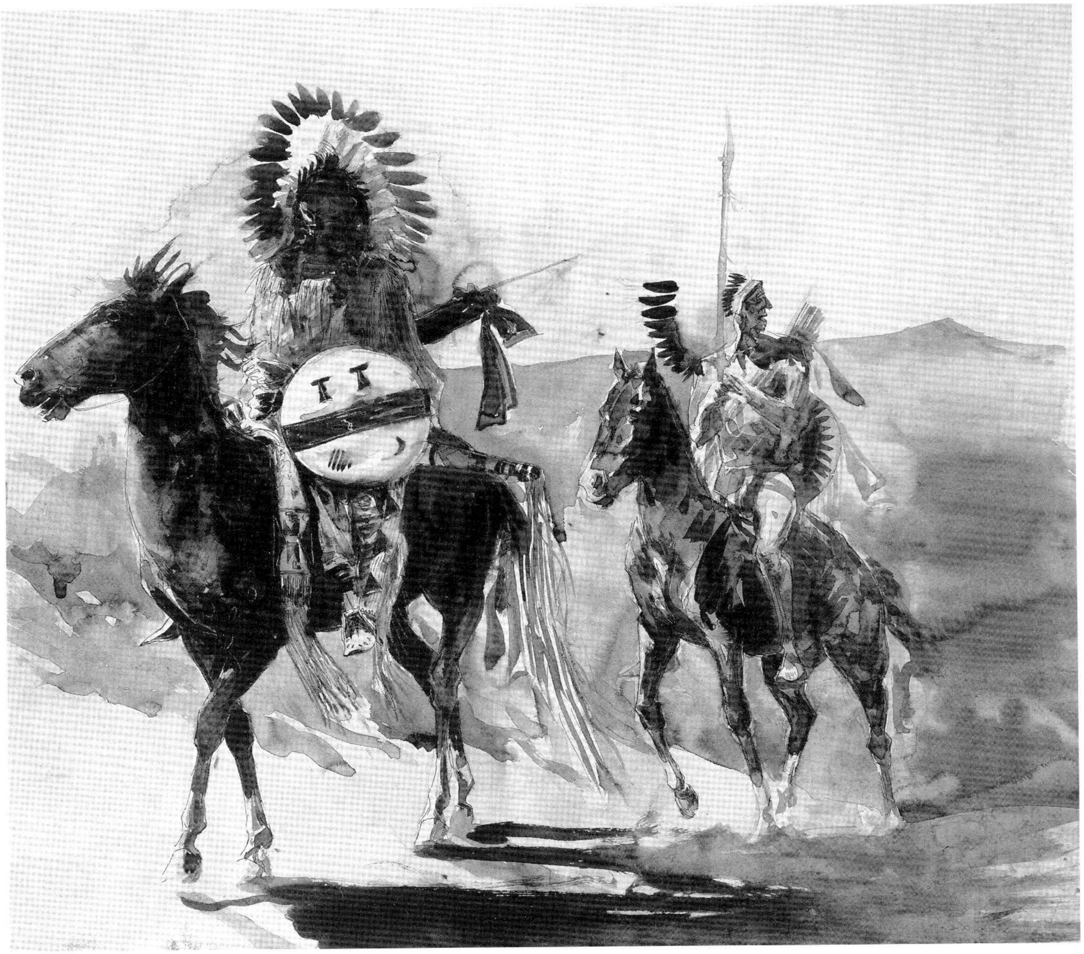

Two Indians on Horseback. Ink and ink wash on paper. 18 1/2 x 20 1/2 inches (sight).

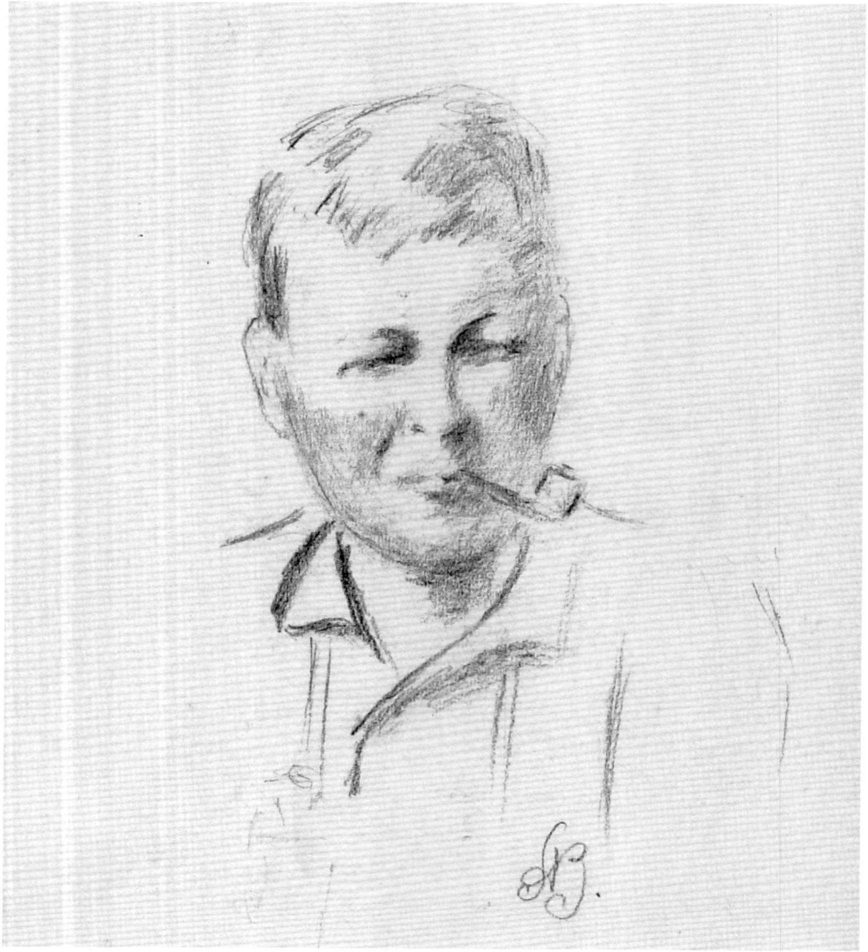

Man with Pipe, ca. 1897. Graphite on paper. 5 7/8 x 4 3/4 inches (sheet). Signed lower right with monogram.

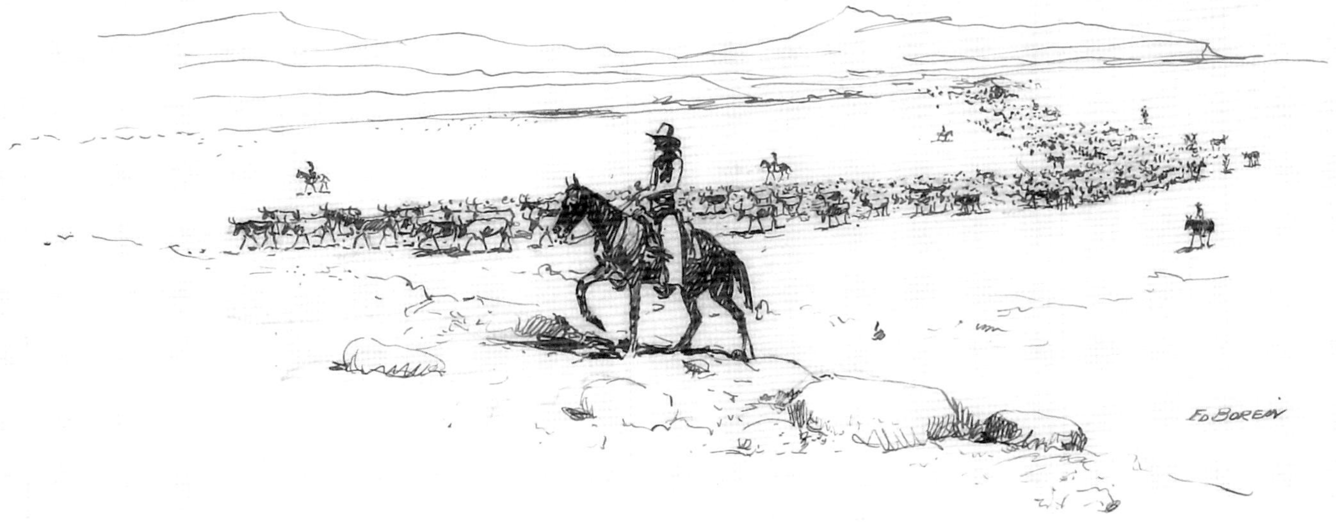

Trail Herd. Ink on paper. 5 3/4 x 11 inches (sight). Signed lower right: *ED BOREIN*.

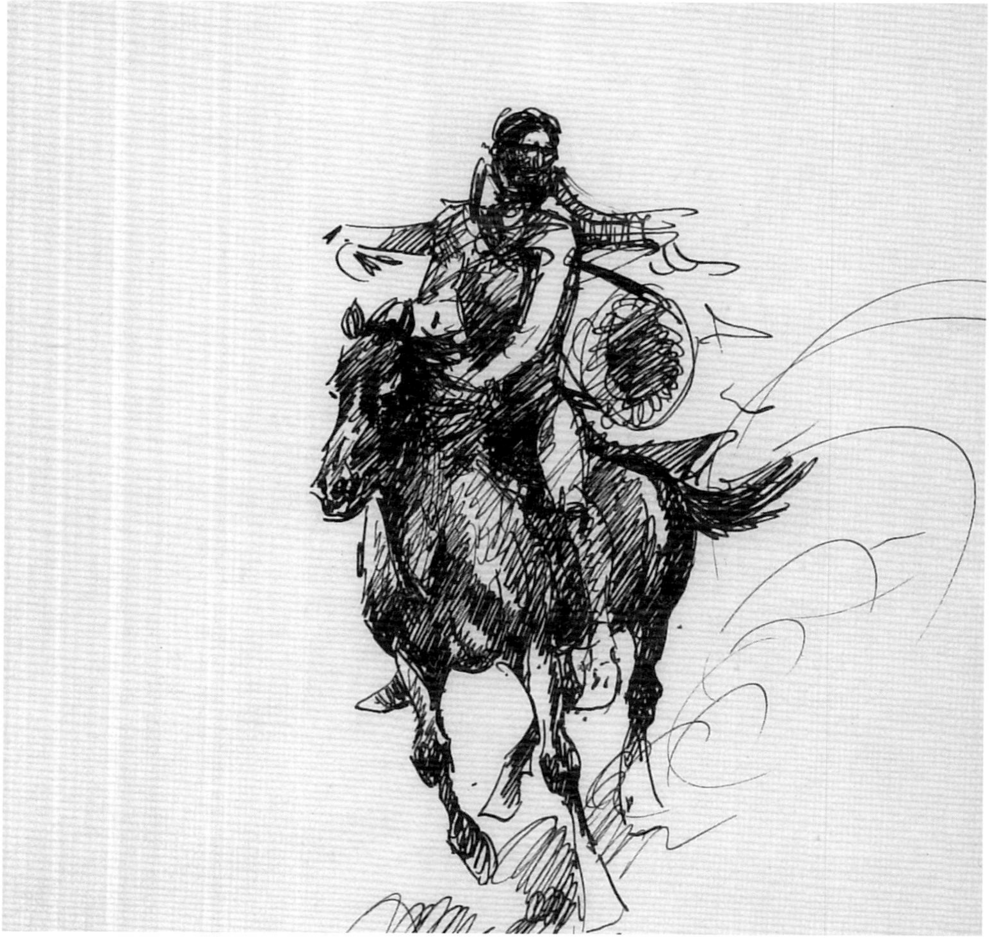

Indian Warrior on Horseback. Ink on paper. 7 x 7 inches (sight).

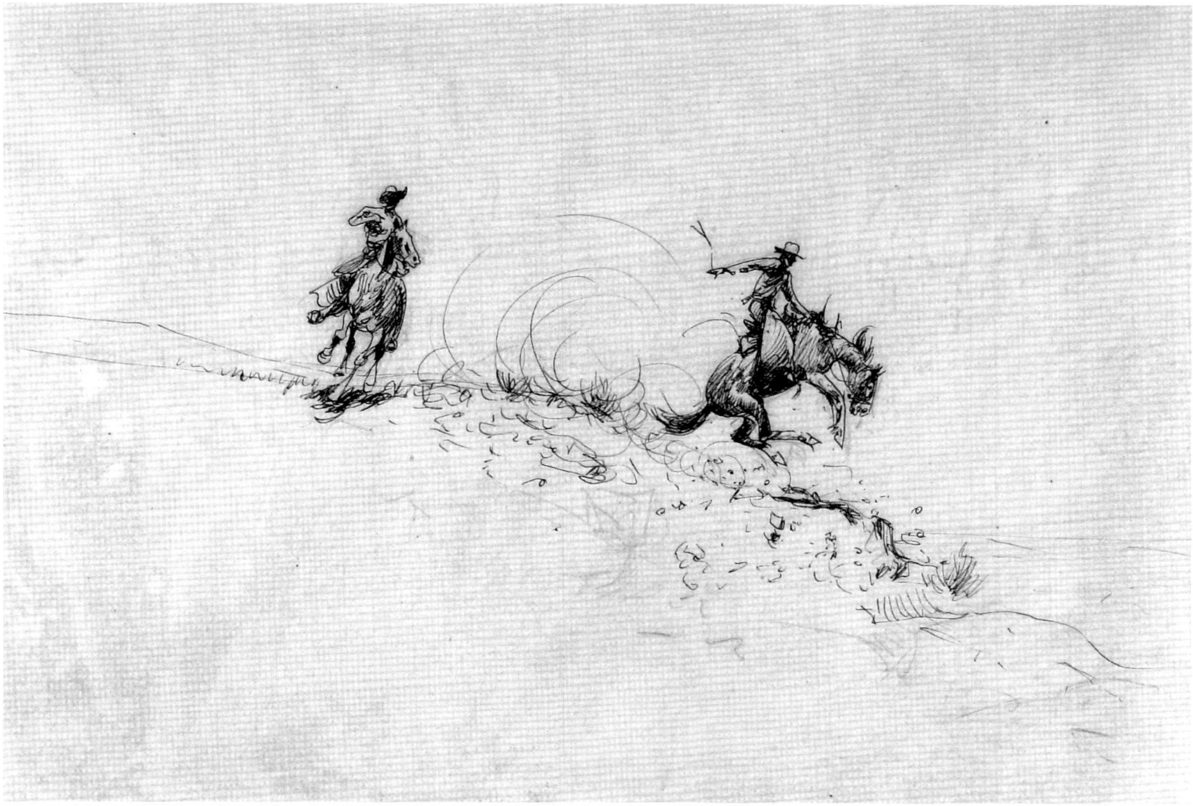

Two Riders. Ink on paper. 8 1/4 x 10 5/8 inches (sheet).

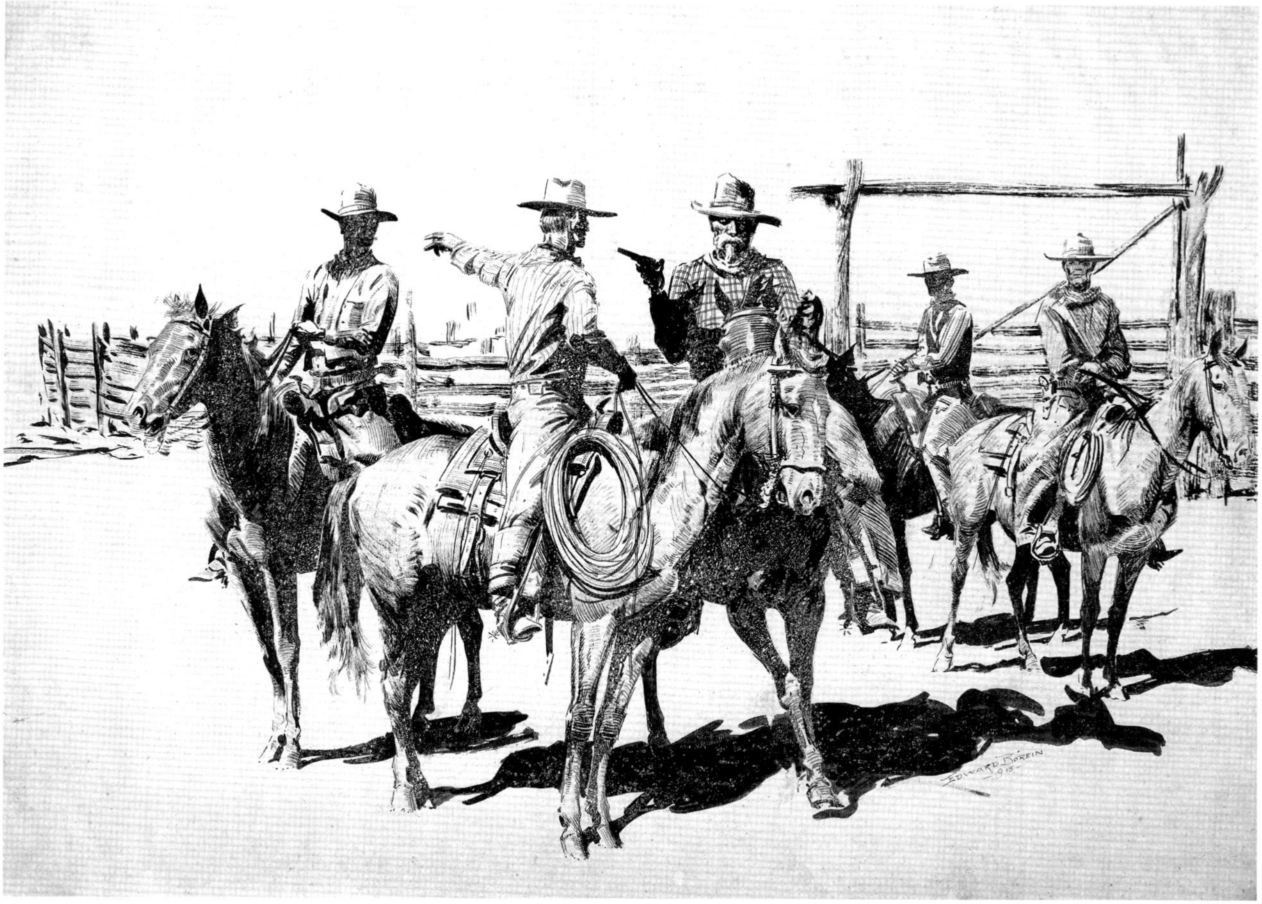

A Confrontation. Ink and gouache on paper. 20 x 27 1/4 inches (sight).
Signed and dated lower right: *EDWARD BOREIN / -1915-.*

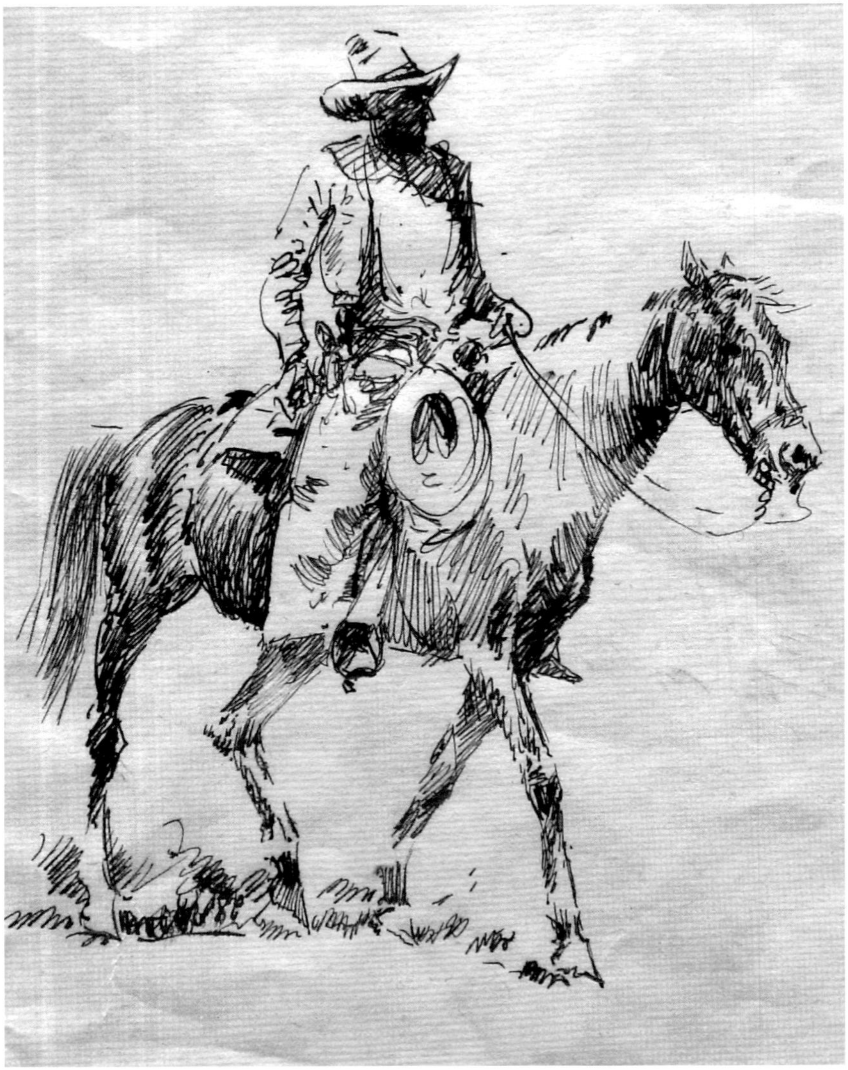

Cowboy on Horseback. Ink on paper. 5 x 4 1/8 inches (sheet).

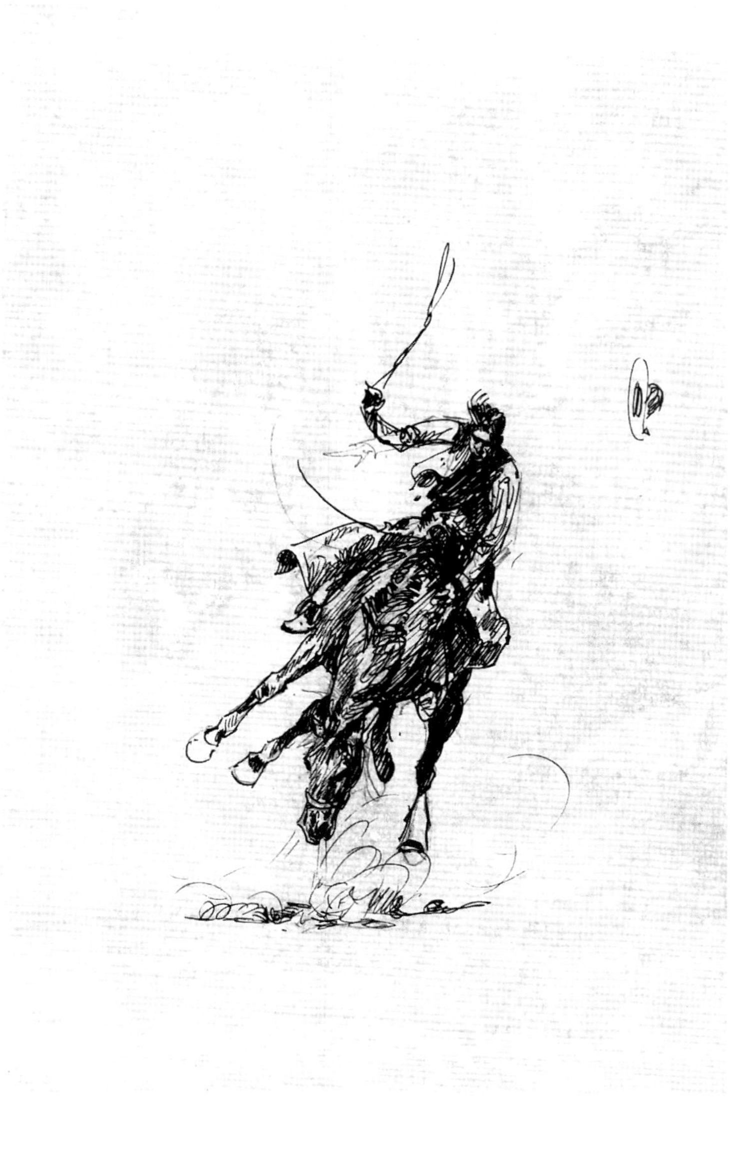

Bucking Horse (Study for Etching). Ink on paper. 11 x 8 inches (sheet).

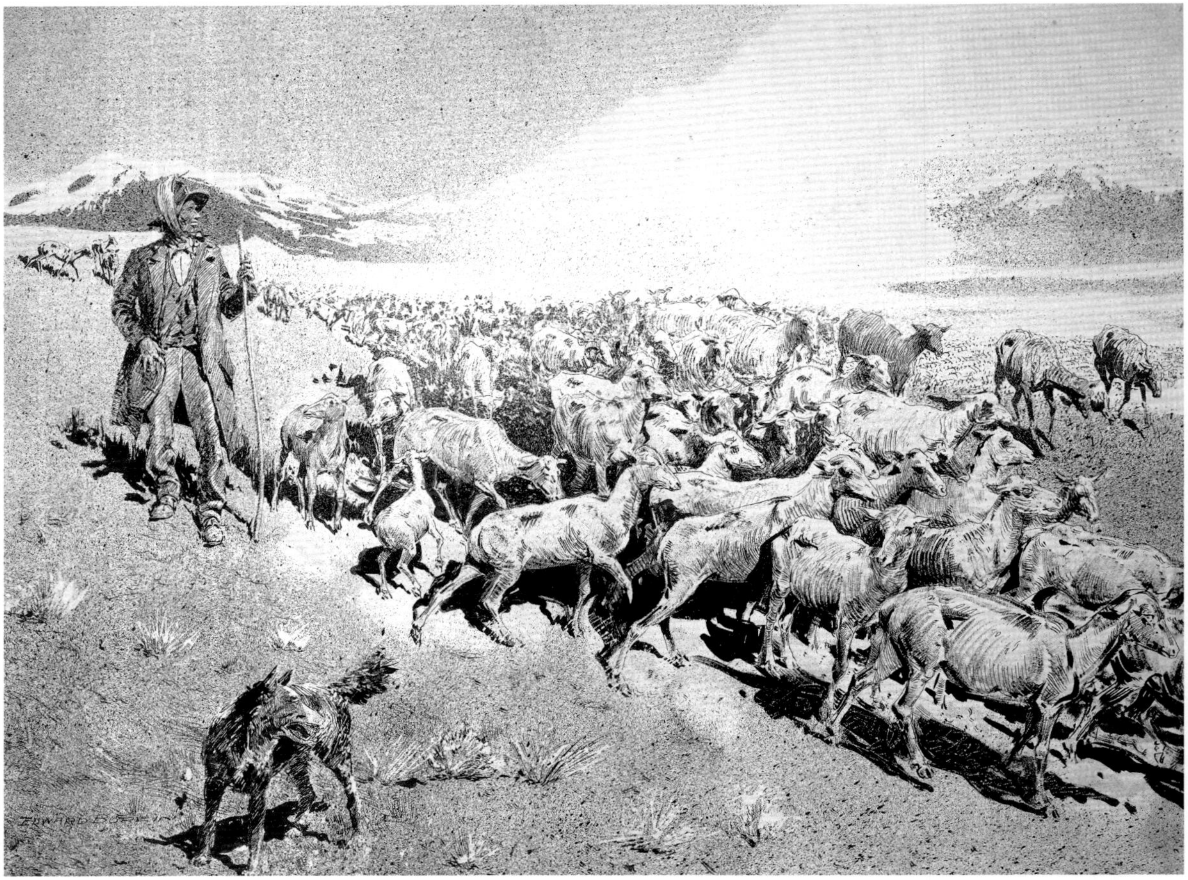

A Goatherder with His Flock. Ink and gouache on paper. 21 x 27 1/4 inches (sight). Signed lower left: *EDWARD BOREIN*.

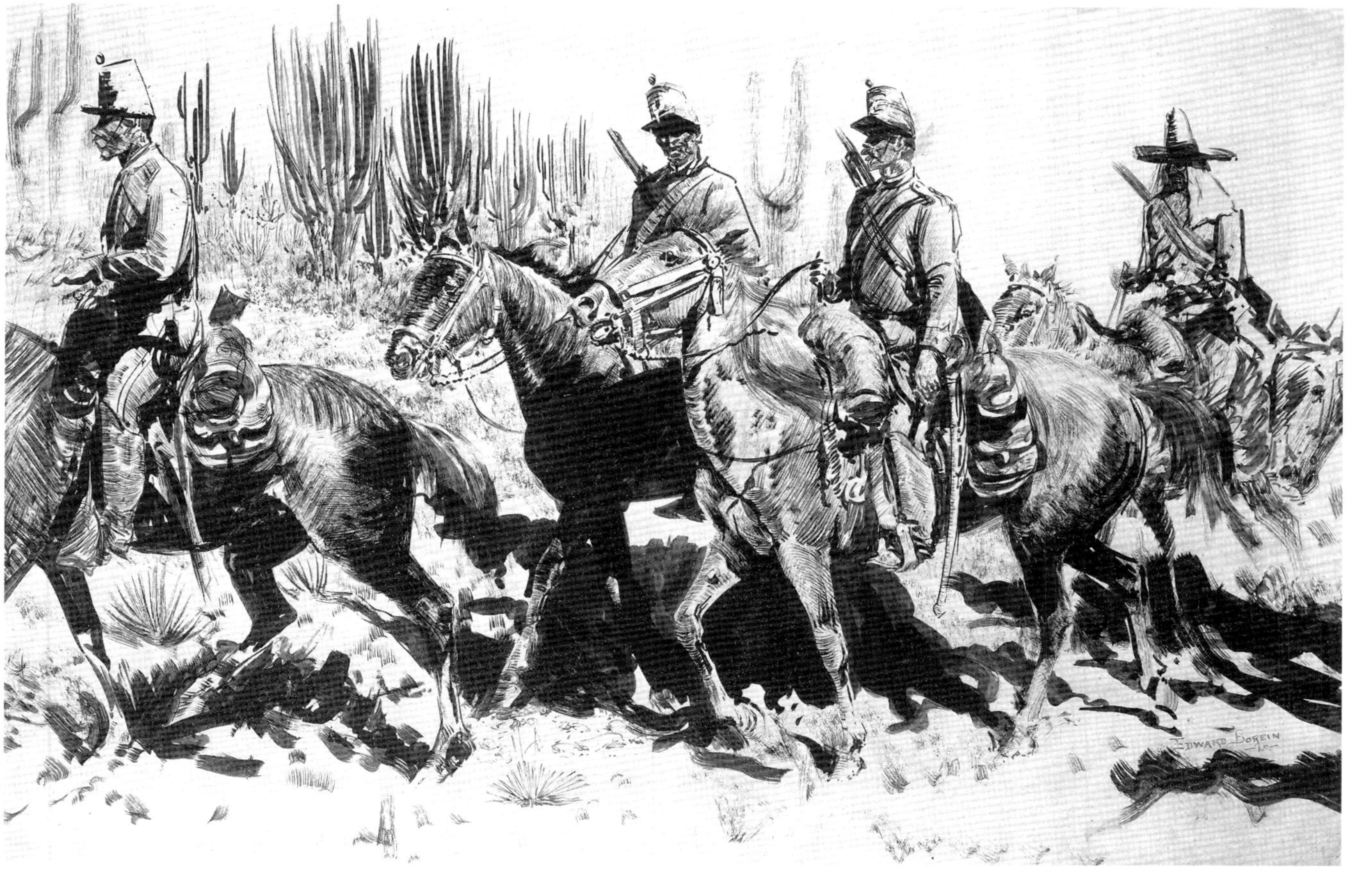

Mexican Rurales in the Desert. Ink and gouache on paper. 18 x 27 1/4 inches.
Signed and dated lower right: *EDWARD BOREIN / -15-.*

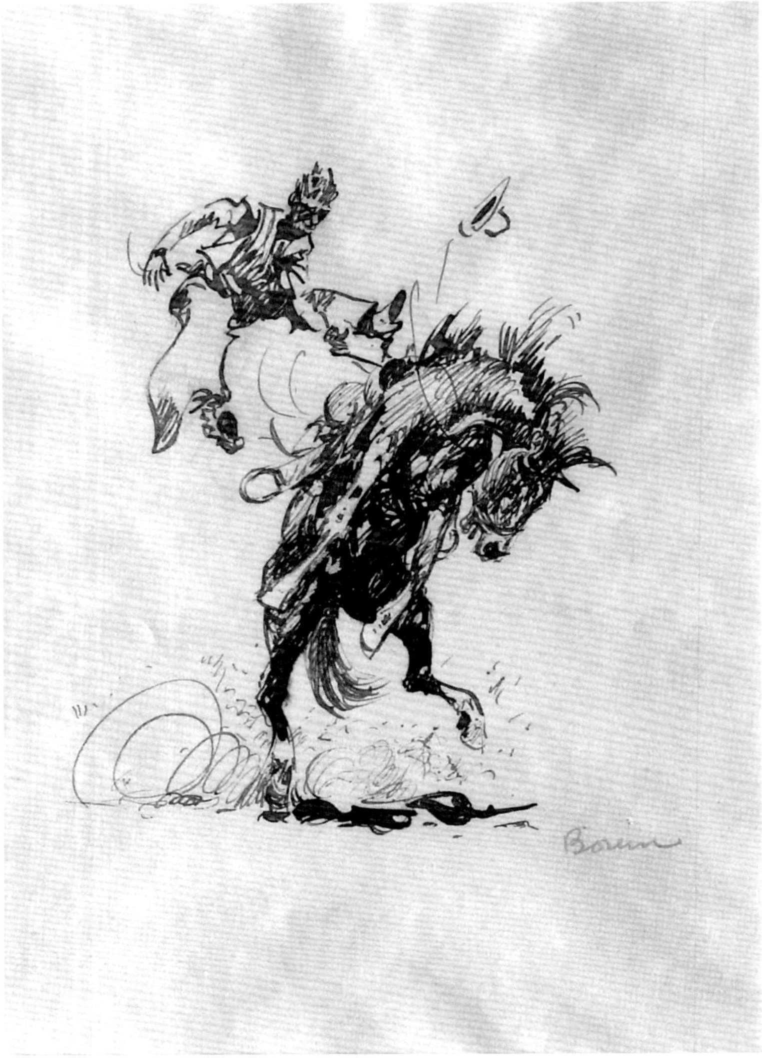

Bucking Horse. Ink on paper. 7 x 5 inches (sight). Signed lower right: *Borein*.

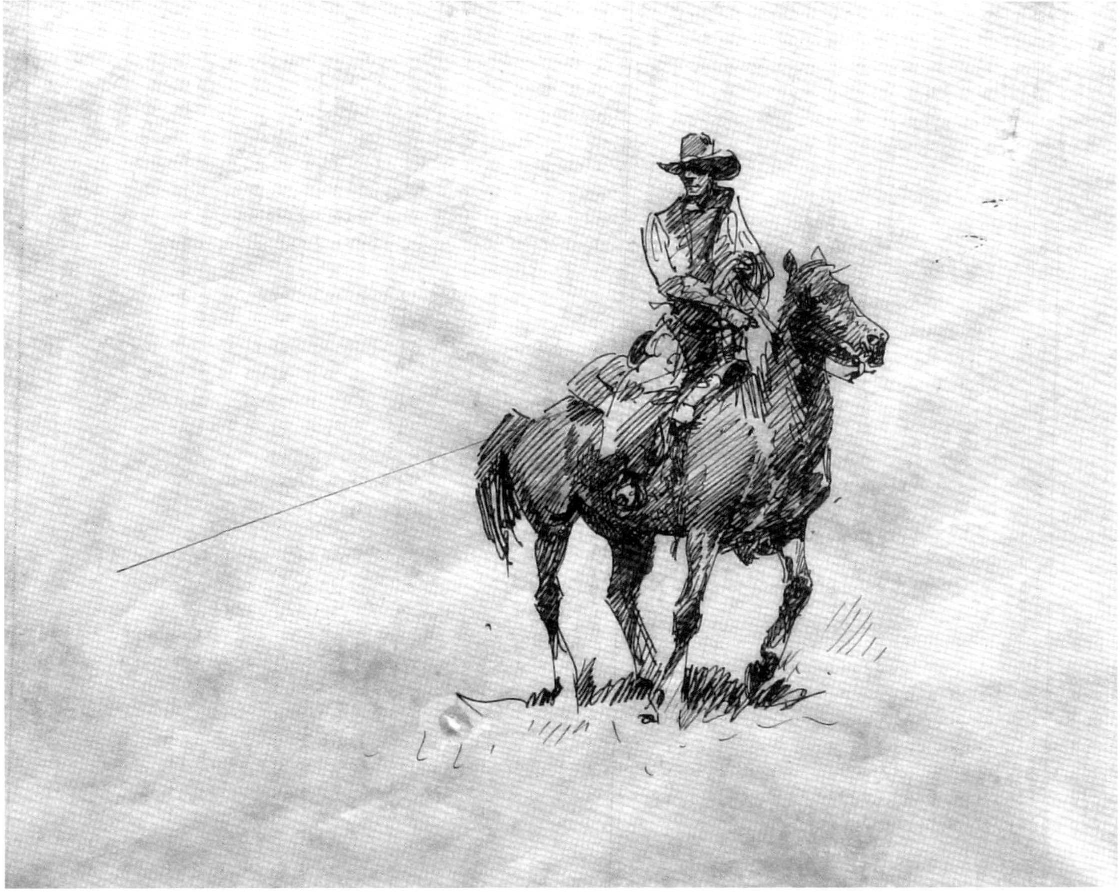

Rider on Horse. Ink on paper. 7 x 8 1/2 inches (sight).

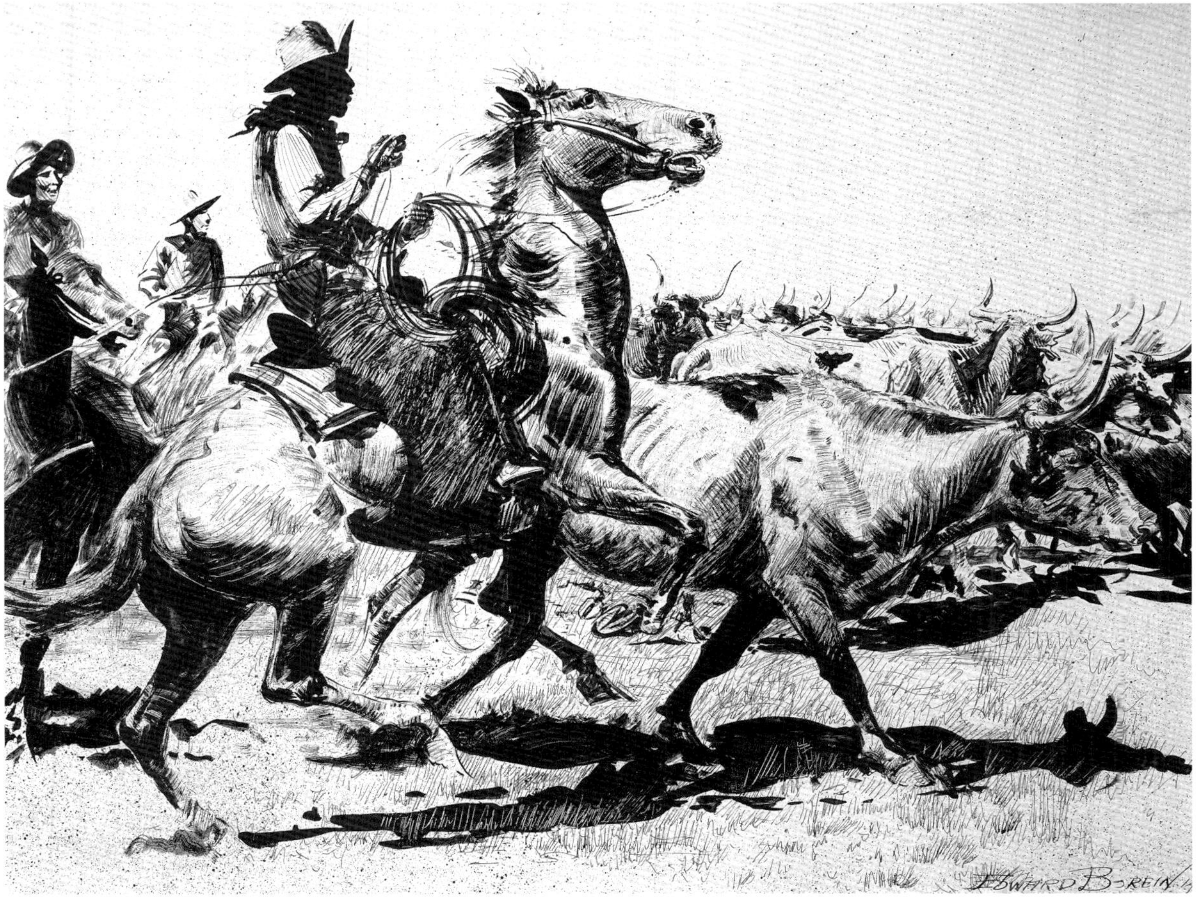

Longhorn Trail Drive. Ink and gouache on paper. 18 x 22 3/4 inches (sight).
Signed and dated lower right: *EDWARD BOREIN 14.*

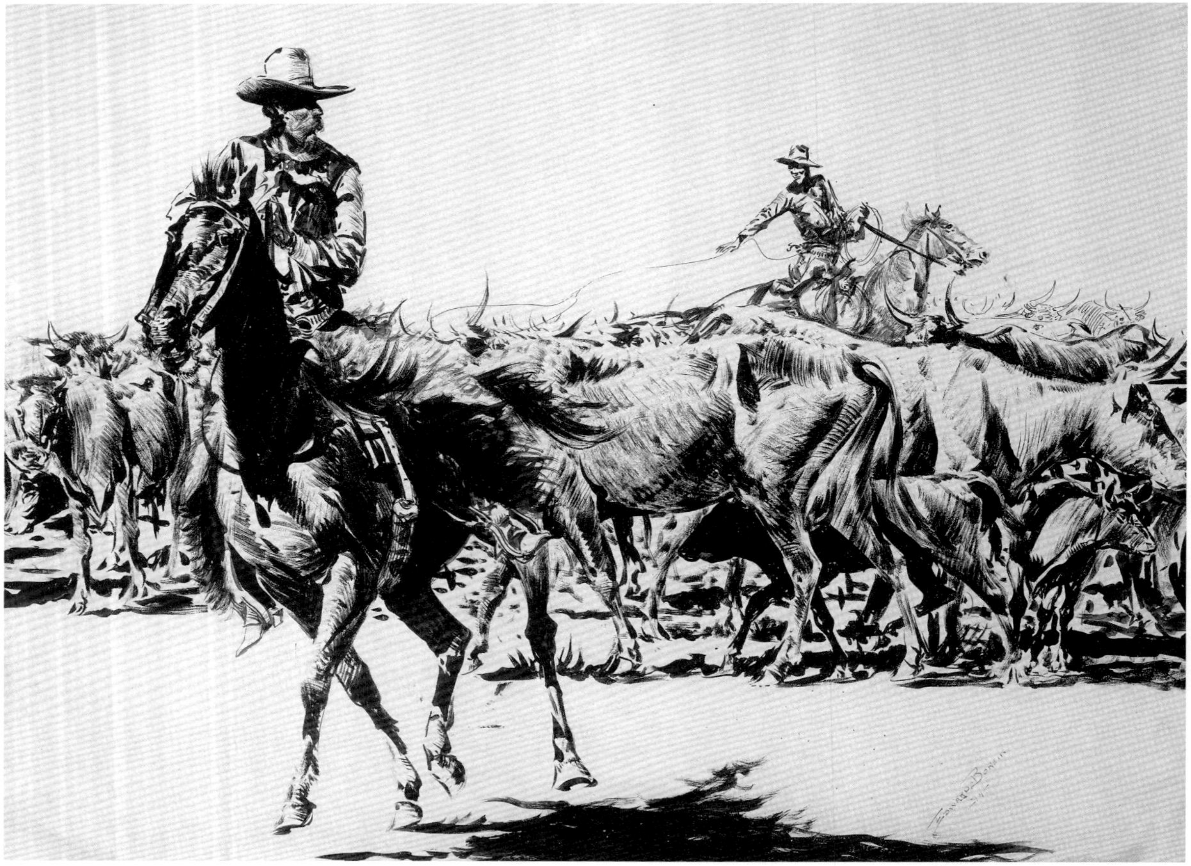

The Roundup. Ink on paper. 20 3/4 x 27 5/8 inches (sight). Signed and dated lower right: *EDWARD BOREIN / -14-*.

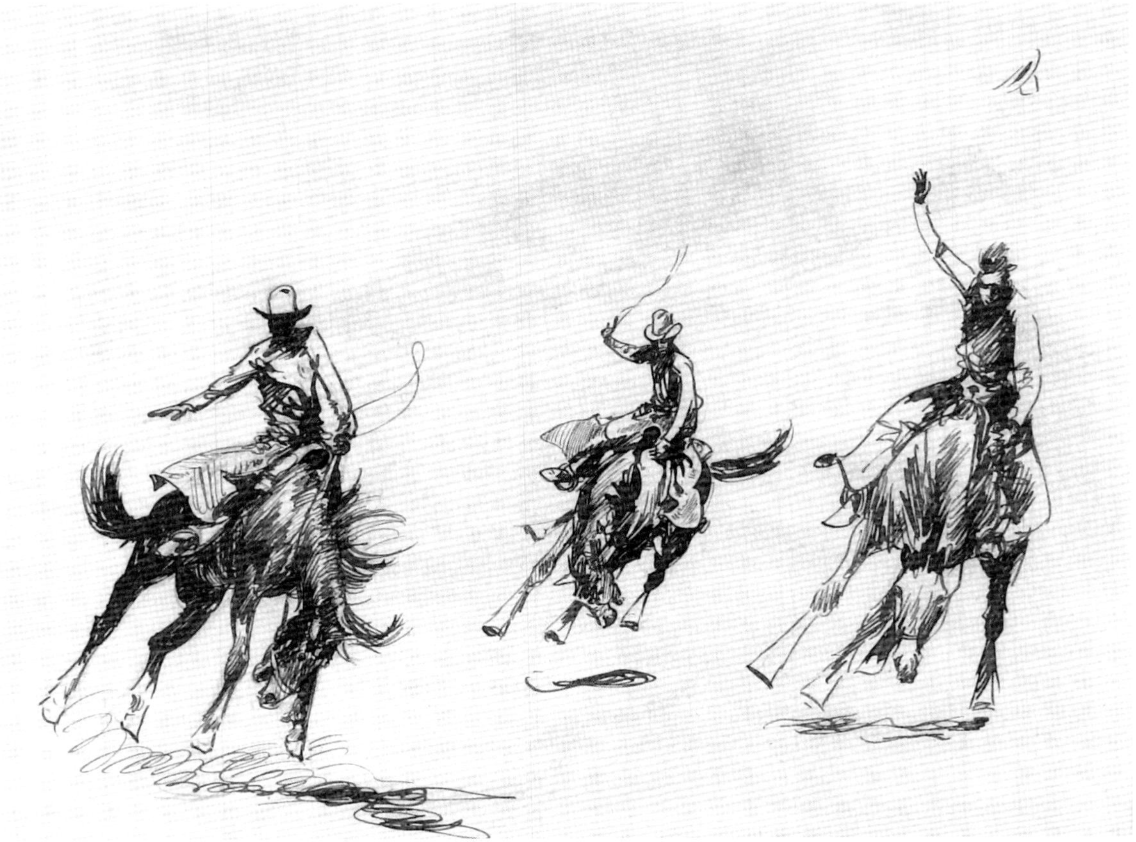

Three Cowboys with Bucking Horse. Ink on paper. 7 1/8 x 9 1/2 inches (sight).

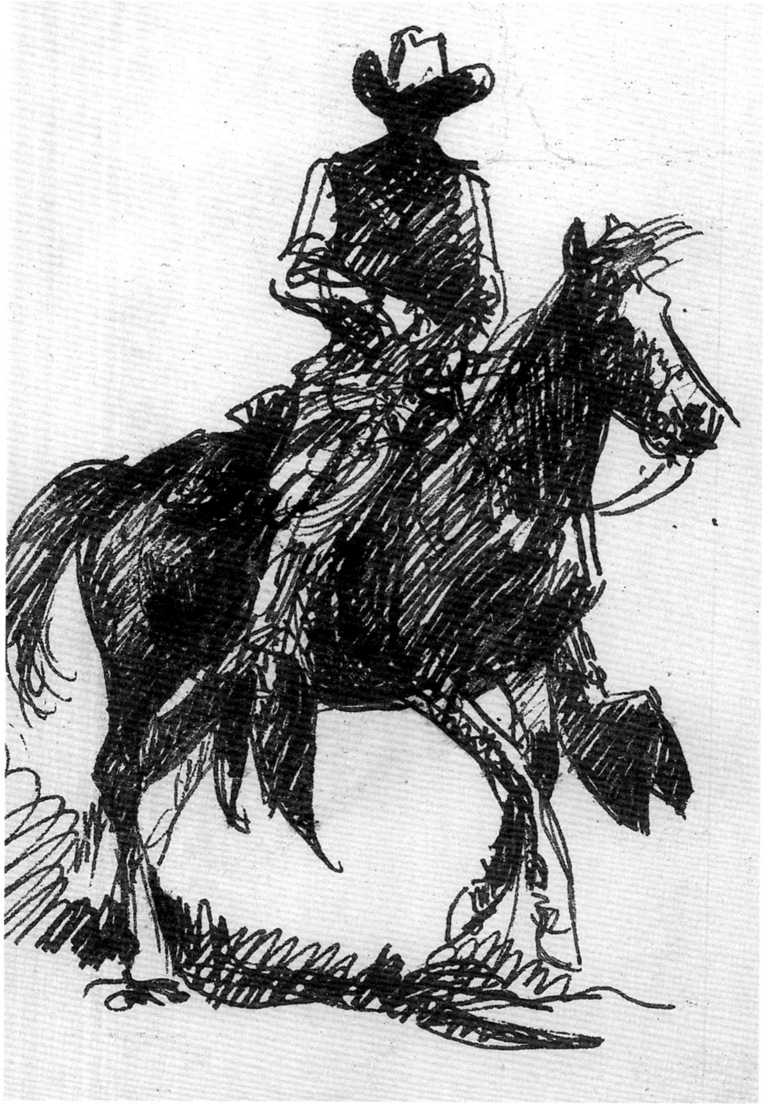

Cowboy on Horseback. Ink on paper. 5 1/8 x 3 1/2 inches (sheet).

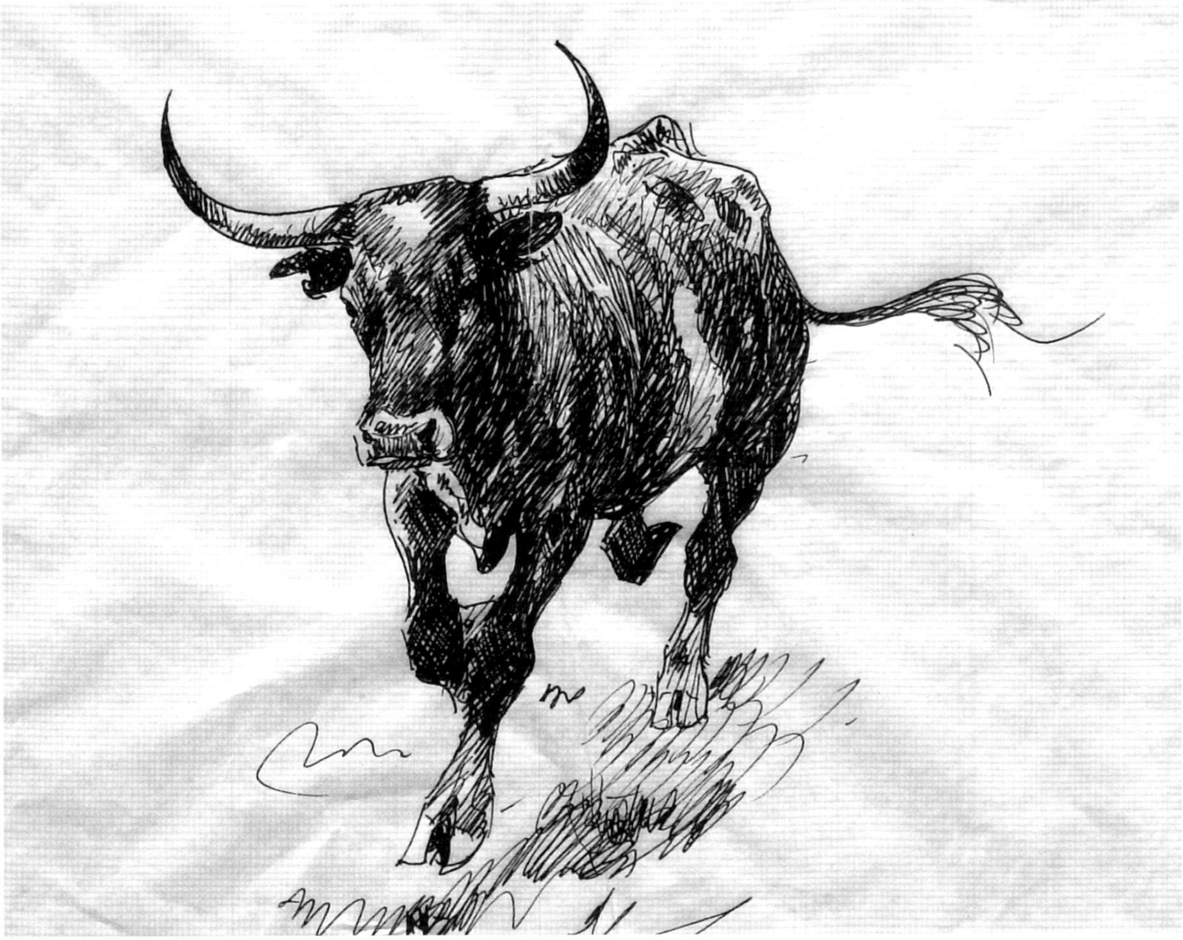

Steer. Ink on paper. 8 1/2 x 11 inches (sheet).

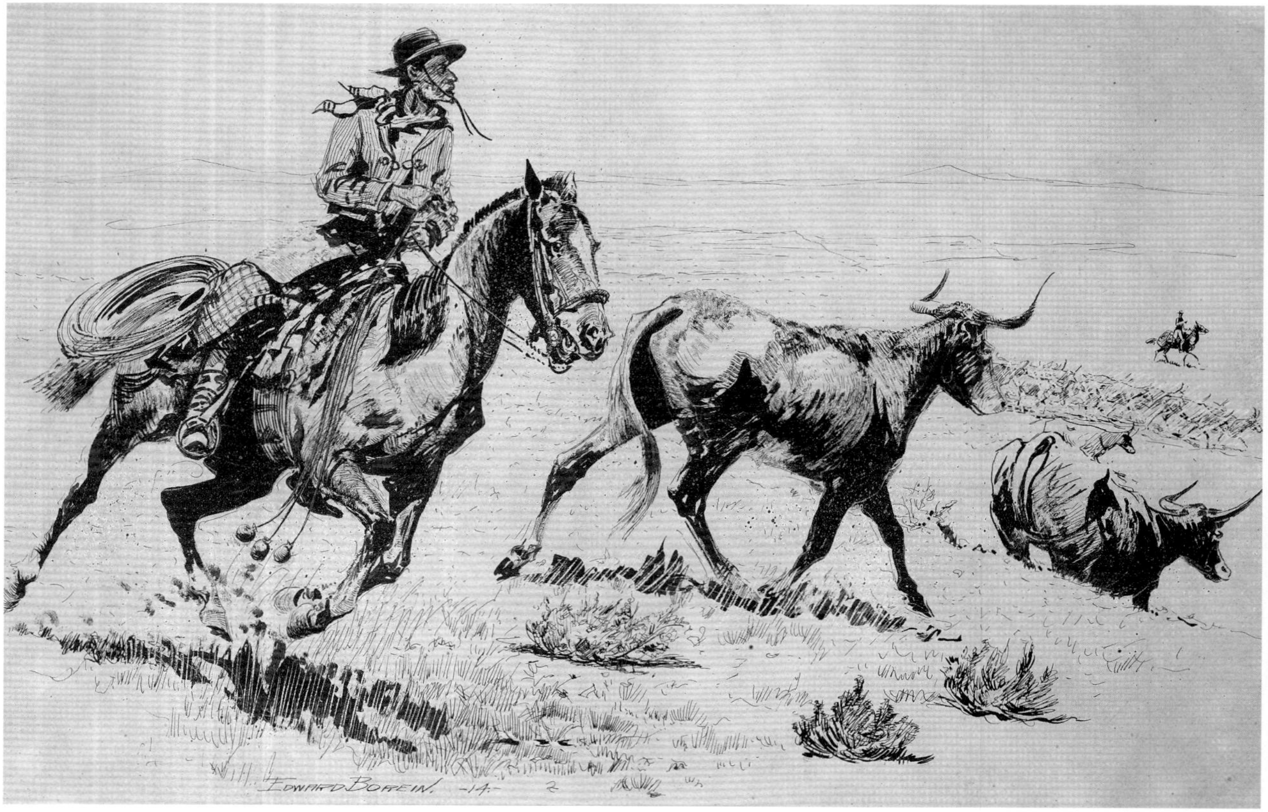

Working a Herd. Ink and gouache on paper. 18 x 27 1/8 inches (sight). Signed and dated lower left: *EDWARD BOREIN -14-*

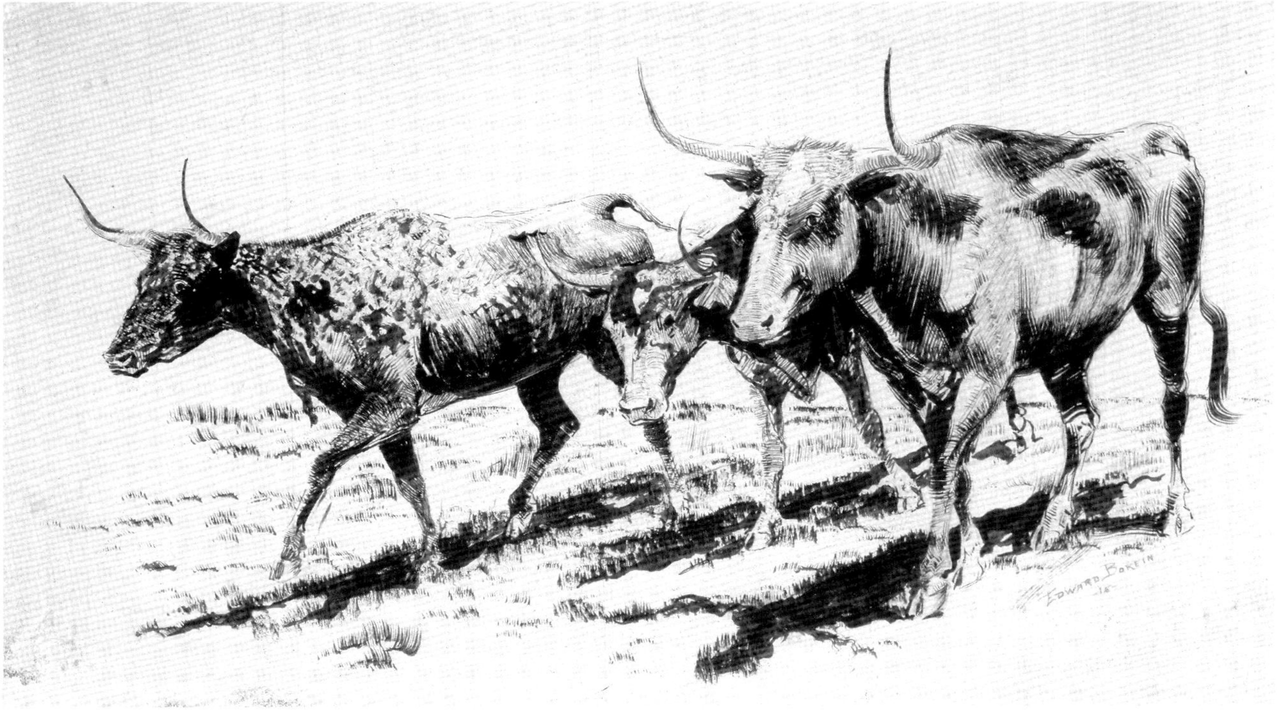

Three Wandering Longhorns. Ink on paper. 11 1/2 x 20 inches (sight). Signed and dated lower right: *EDWARD BOREIN / -15-*.

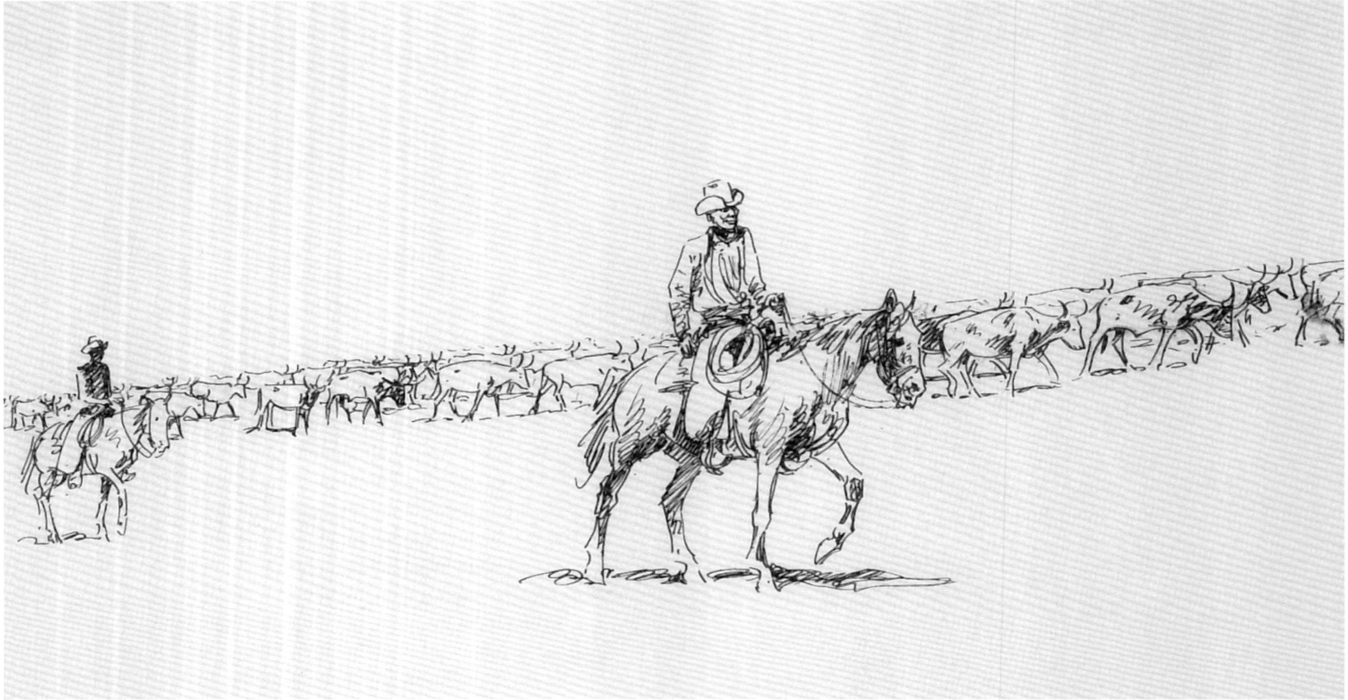

Two Riders and Trail Herd. Ink on paper. 7 1/4 x 13 1/2 inches (sight).

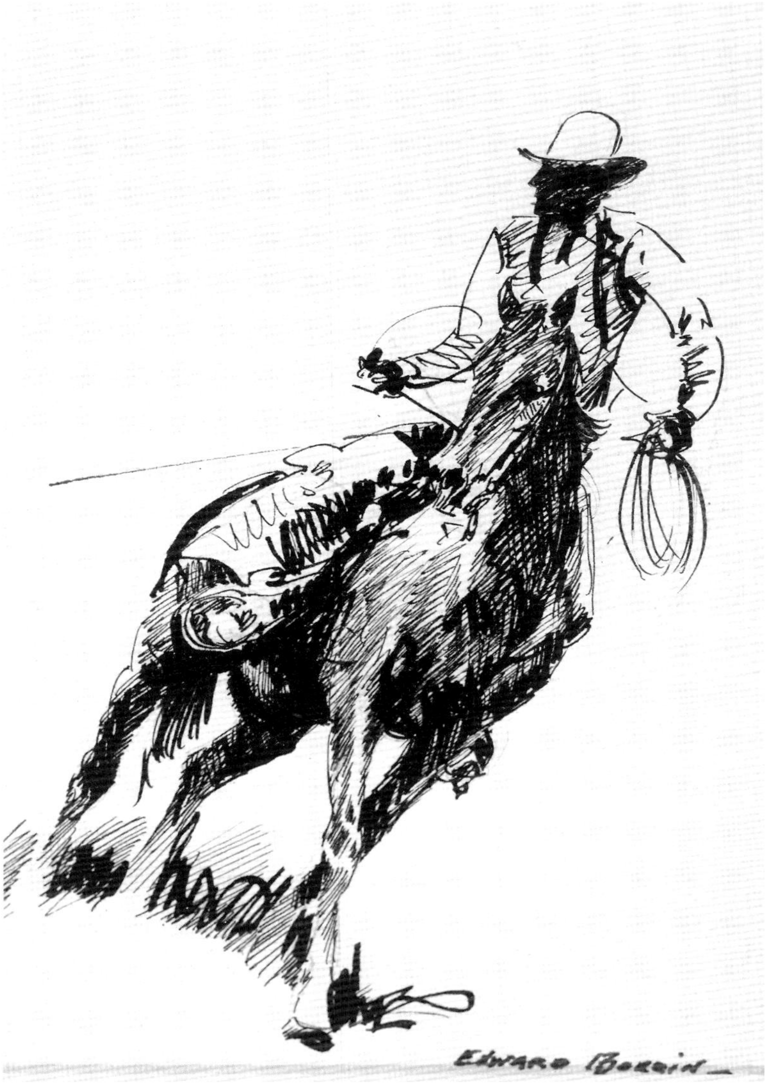

Cowboy Roping. India ink on paper. 6 7/8 x 4 1/2 inches (sight). Signed lower right: *EDWARD BOREIN*.

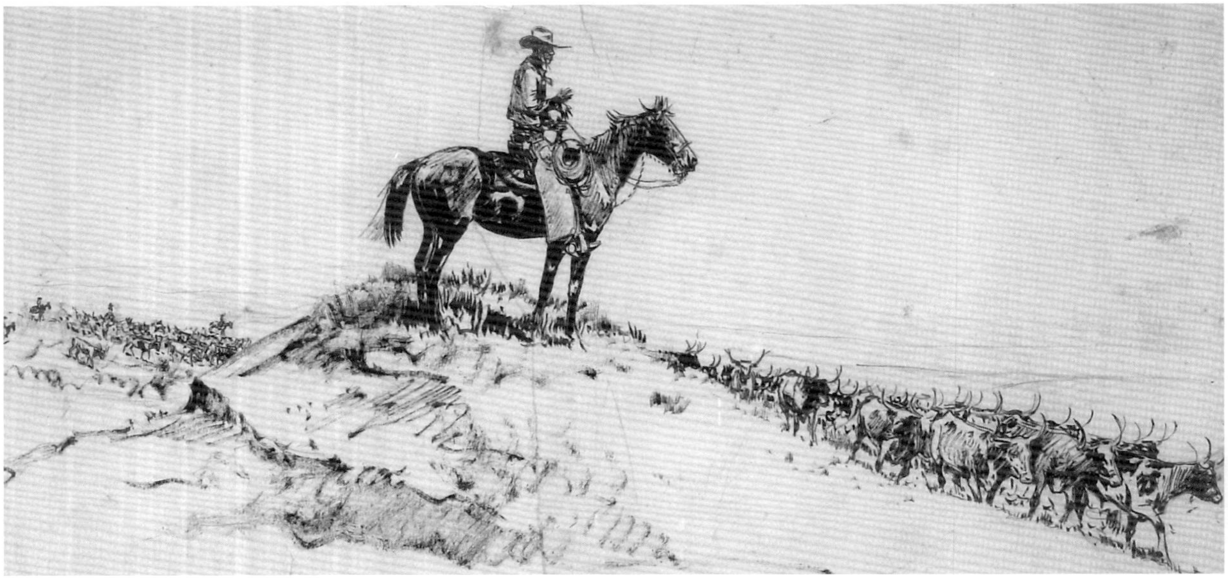

Riding Herd. Ink and graphite on paper. 8 3/4 x 17 inches (sheet).

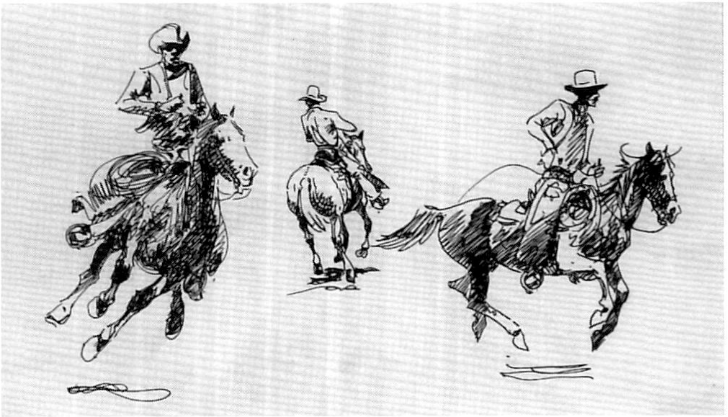

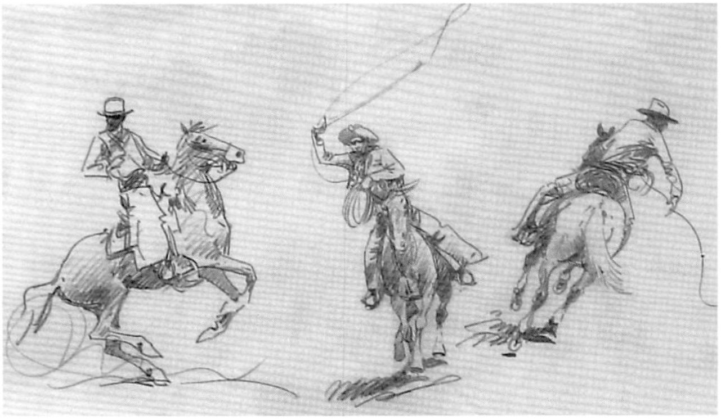

Cowboys. Left: ink on paper. 6 5/8 x 10 3/4 inches (sight). Right: graphite on paper. 6 5/8 x 10 3/4 inches (sight).

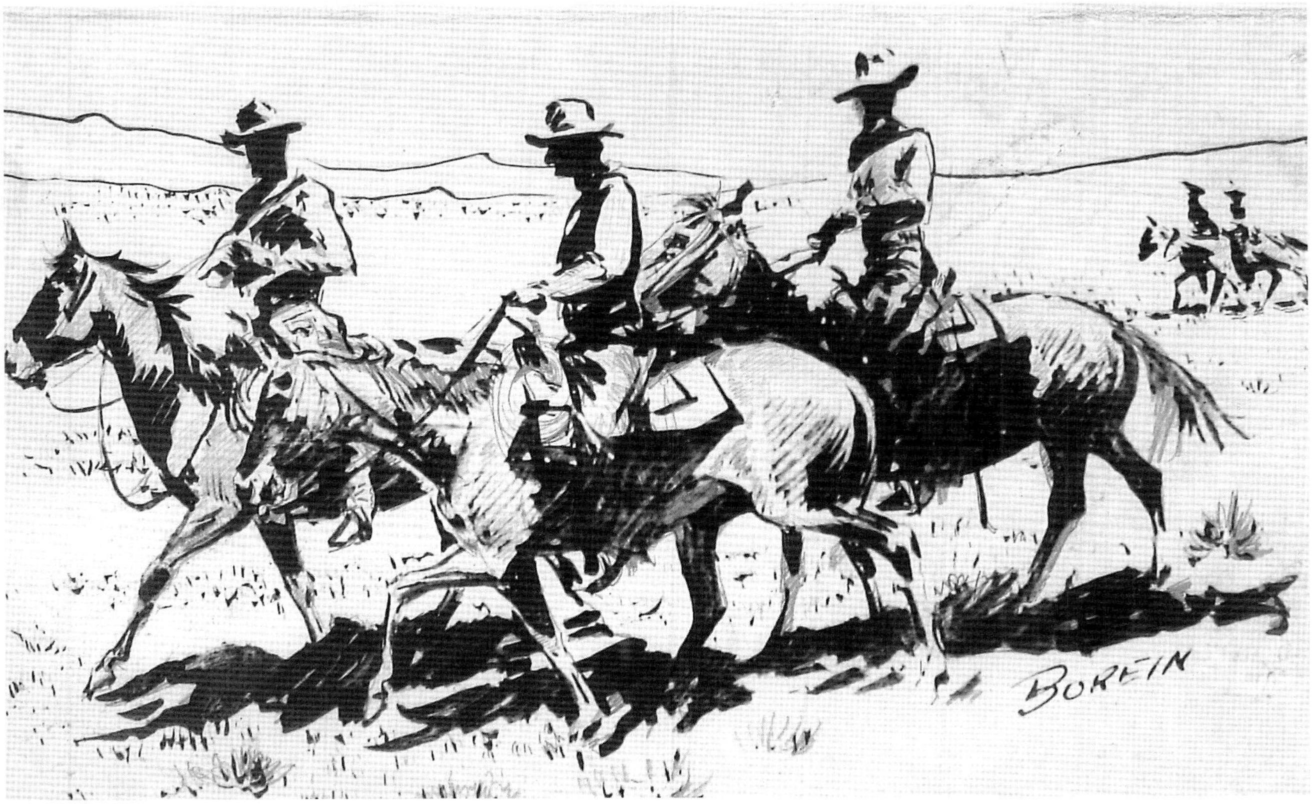

Cowboys on Horseback (recto illustrated). Ink and graphite on paper. 7 1/8 x 11 1/4 inches (sight).
Signed lower right: *BOREIN*.

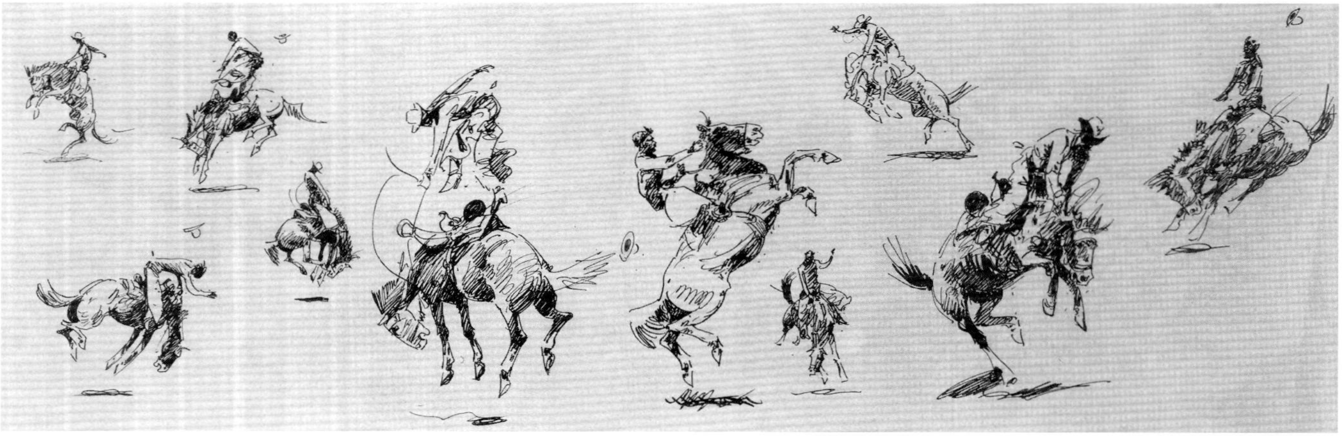

Panel of Mounted Cowboys. Ink on paper. 7 1/2 x 22 3/8 inches (sight).

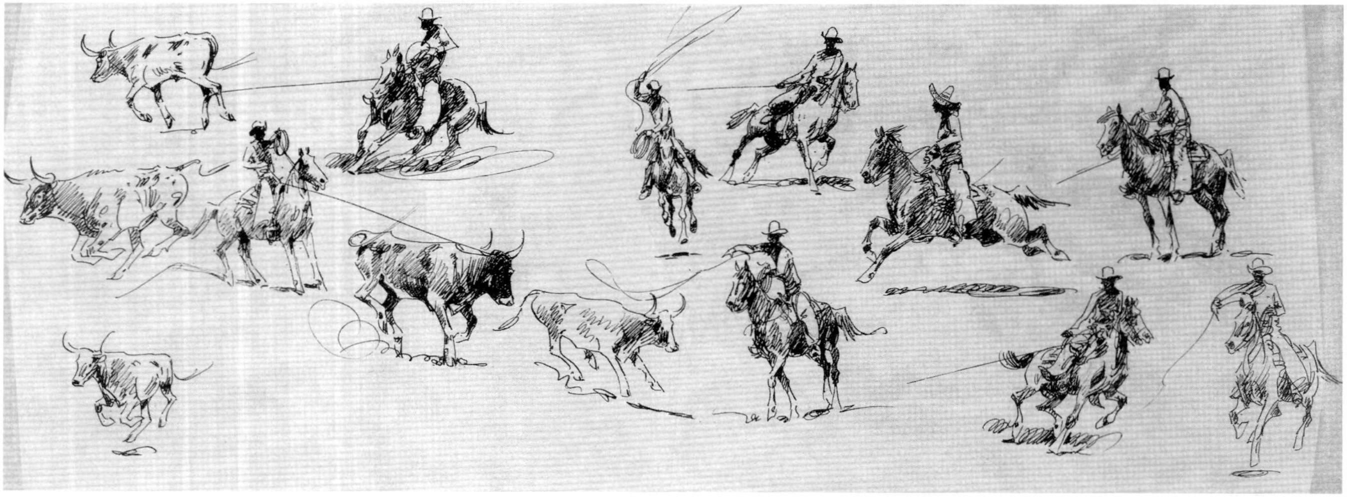

Panel of Nine Mounted Cowboys. Ink on paper. 8 x 22 inches (sight).

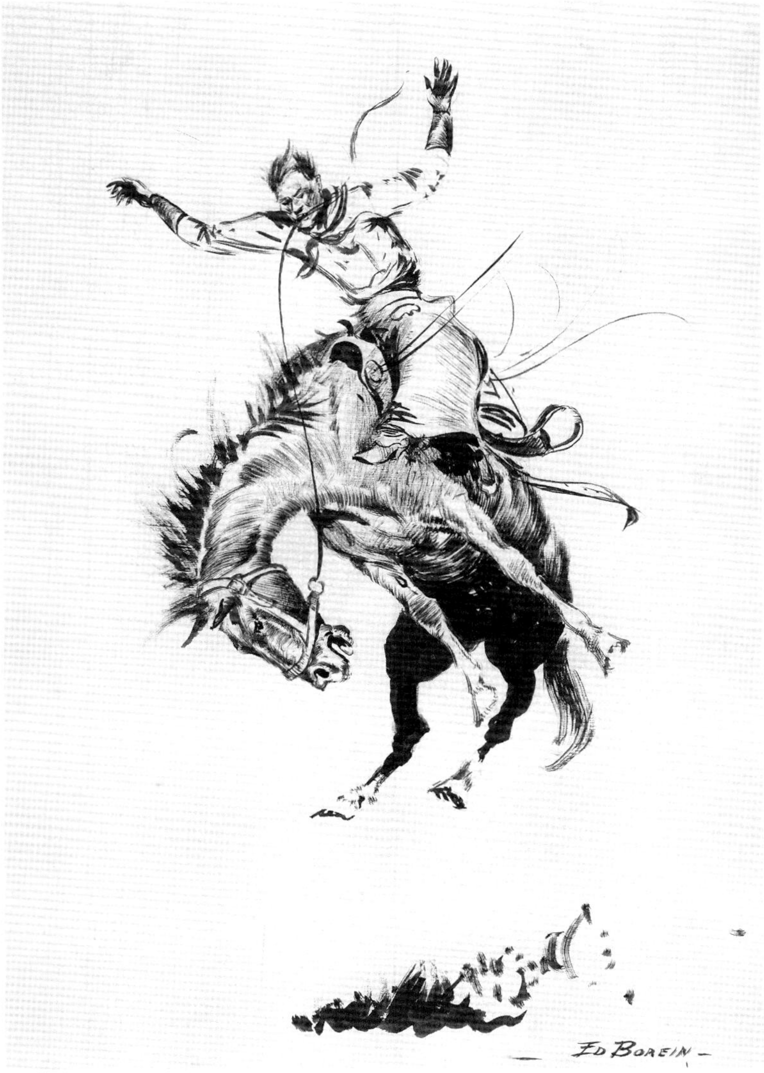

Cowboy on Bucking Horse. Ink on paper. 19 x 13 5/8 inches (sight). Signed lower right: *ED BOREIN*.

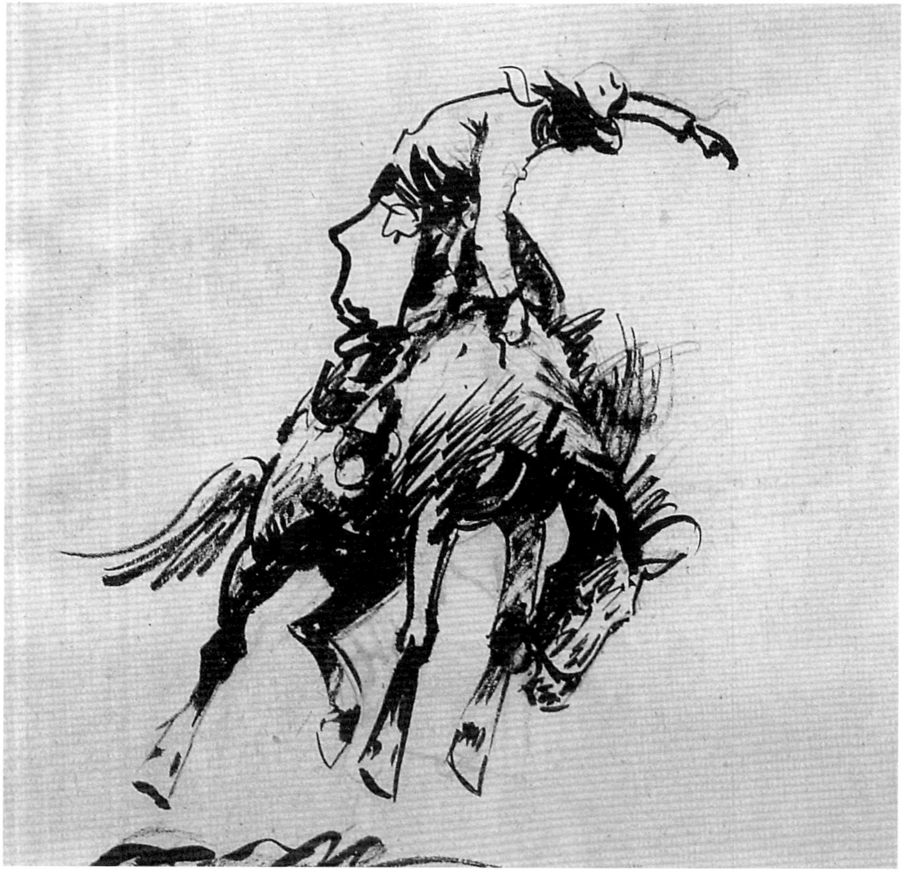

Bronco Buster. Ink and graphite on paper. 7 3/8 x 7 3/8 inches (sight).

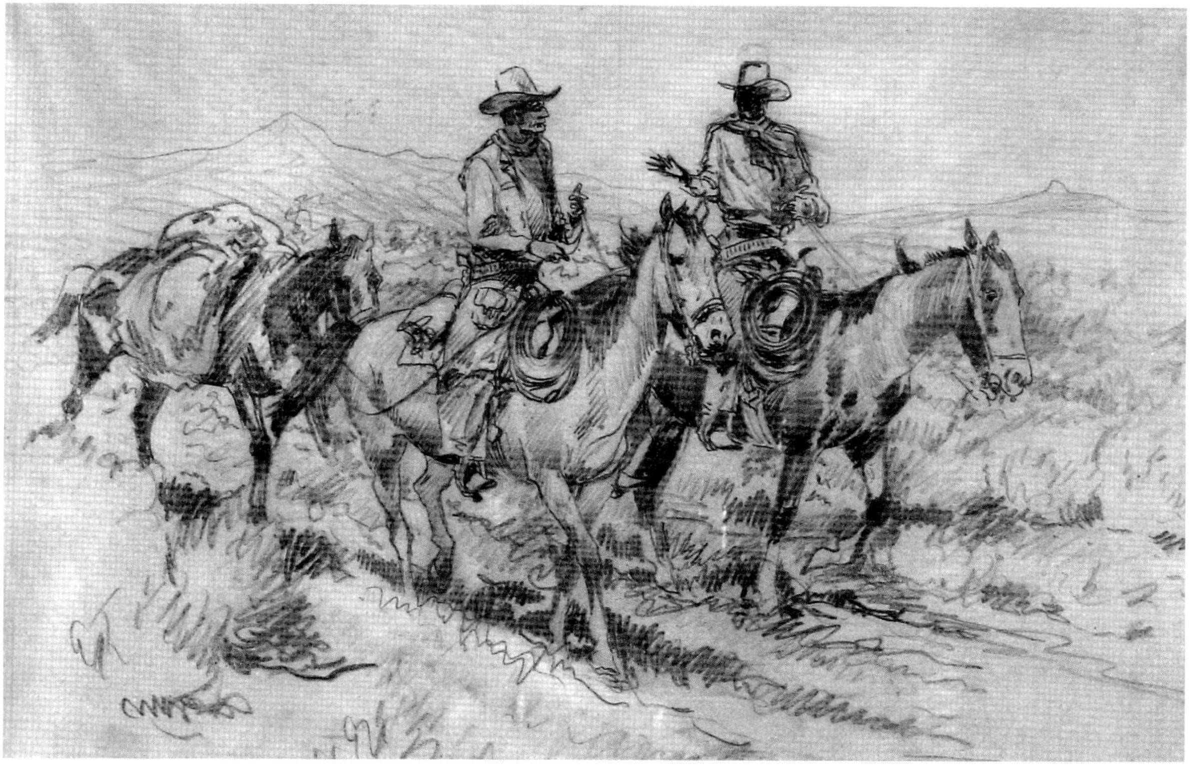

Two Men on Horseback and Packhorse. Graphite on paper. 6 1/4 x 9 1/2 inches (sight).

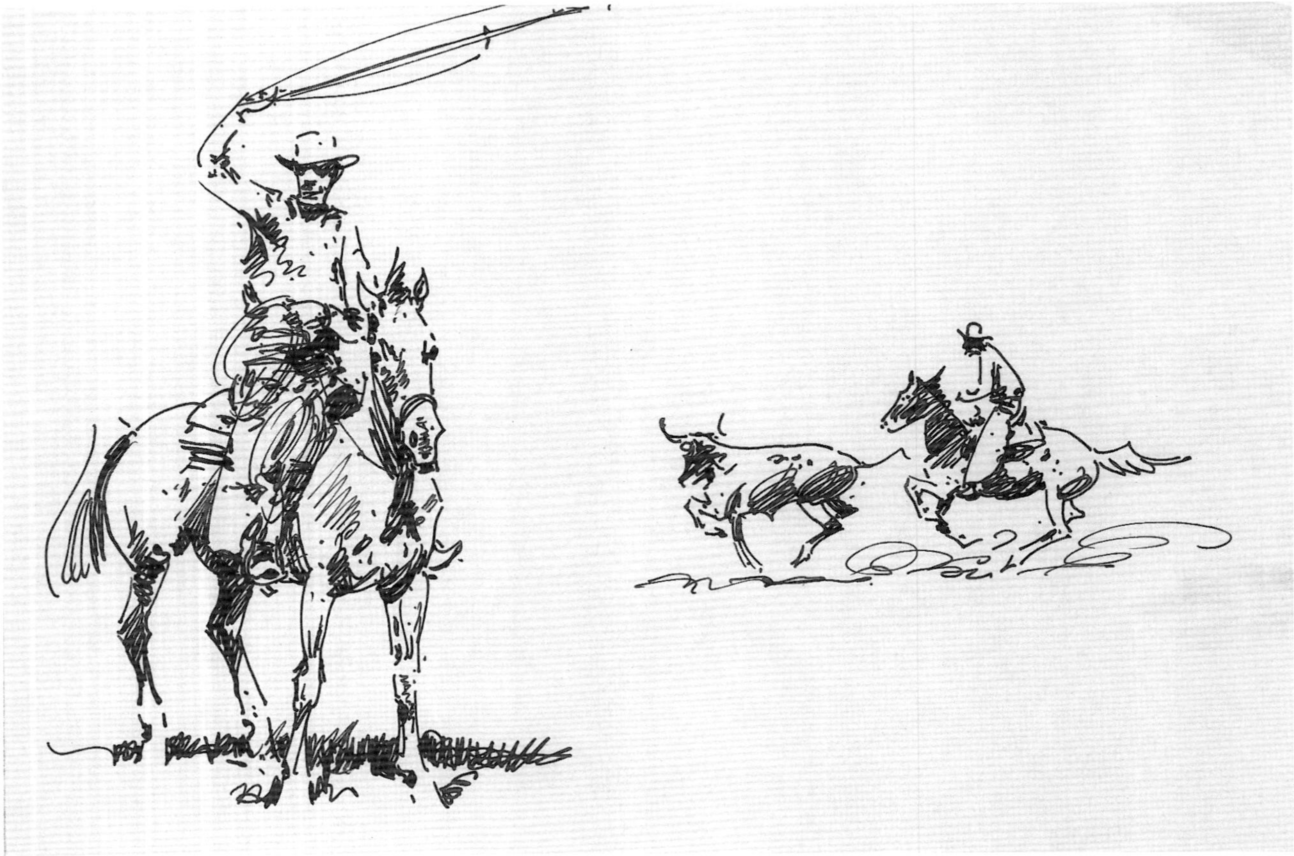

Rounding Up. Ink on paper. 9 3/8 x 12 inches (sheet).

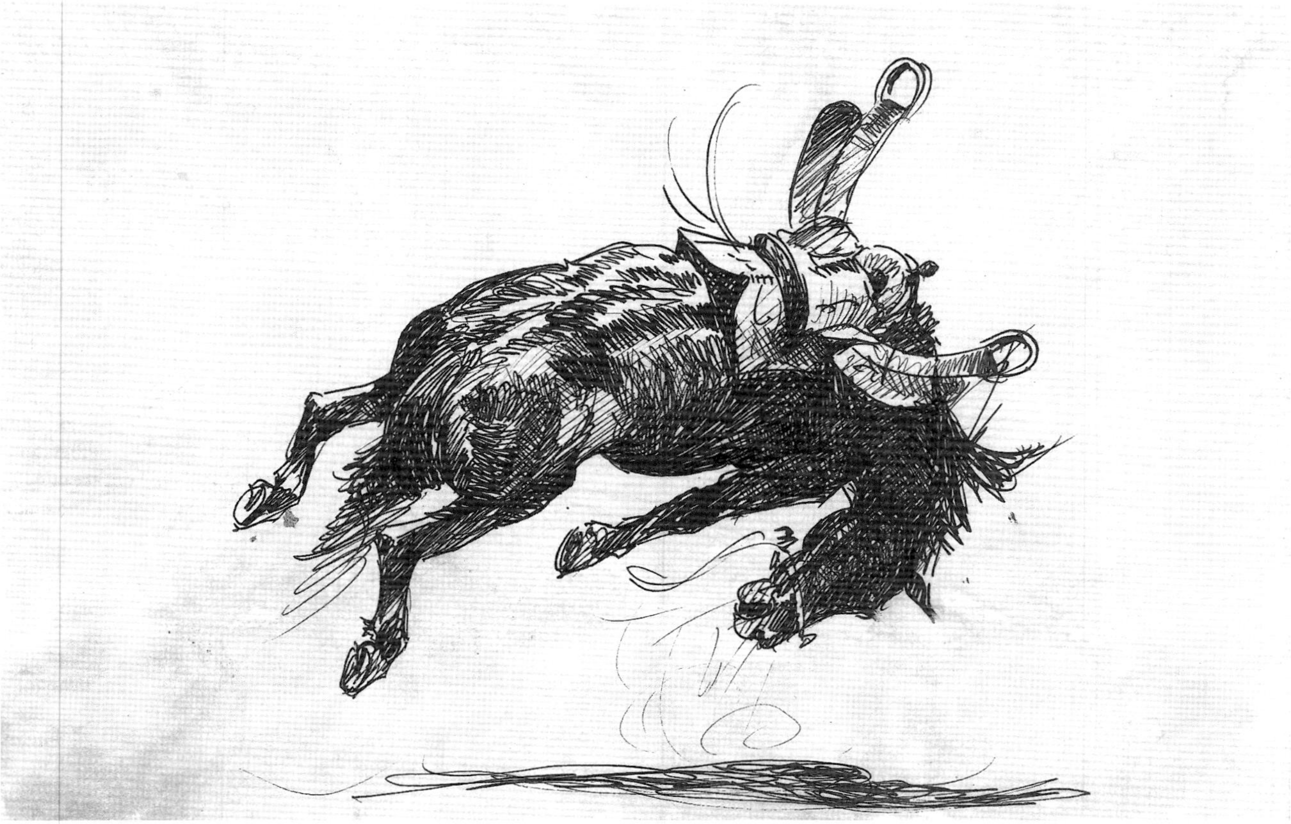

Bucking Bronc. Ink on paper. 7 x 10 3/8 inches (sheet).

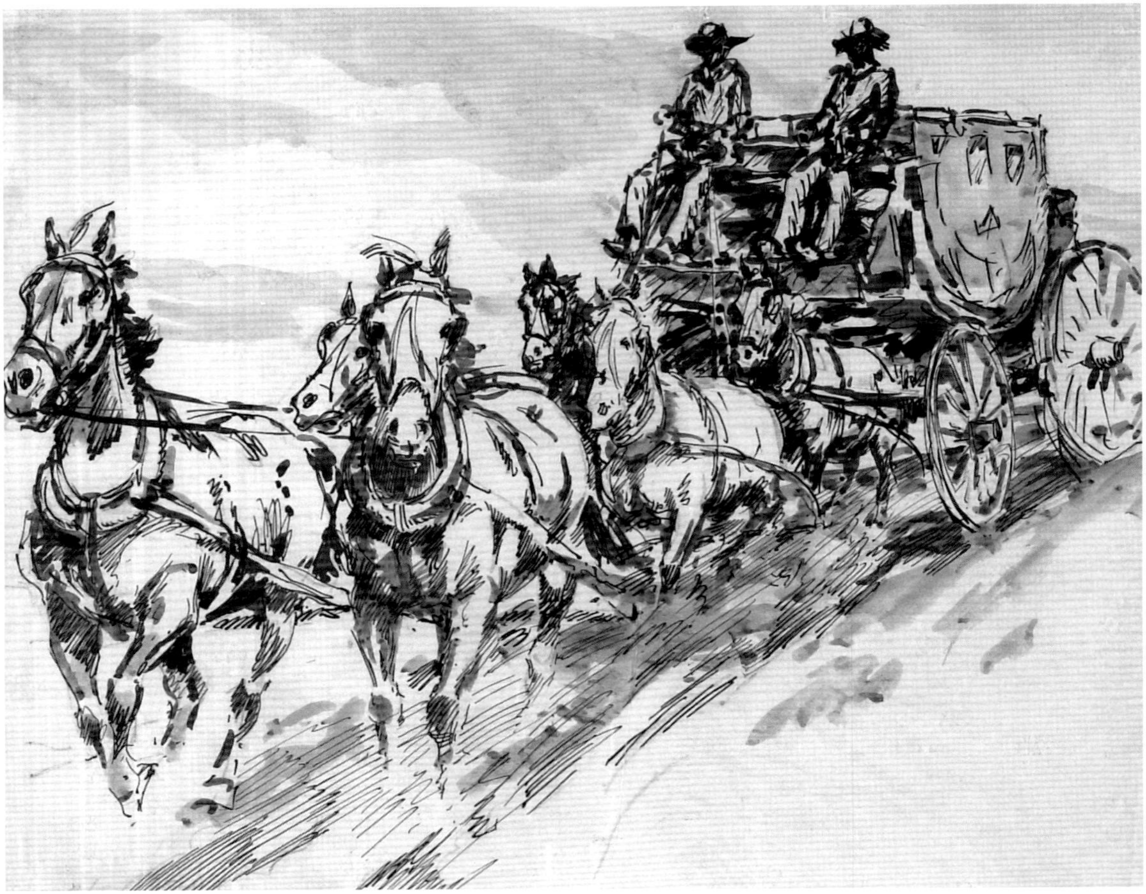

Stagecoach. Ink on paper. 11 x 13 3/4 inches (sight).

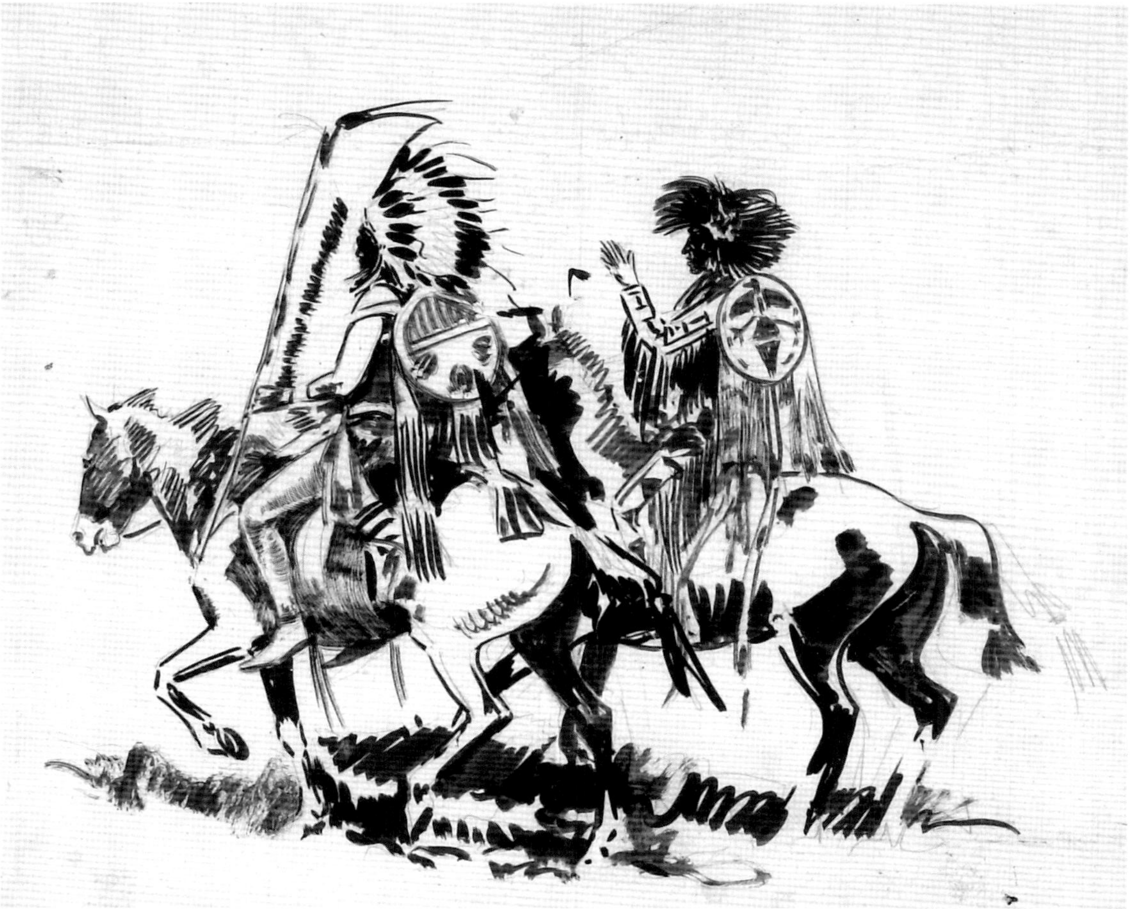

Warriors on Horses. India ink on paper. 14 1/2 x 17 3/4 inches (sight).

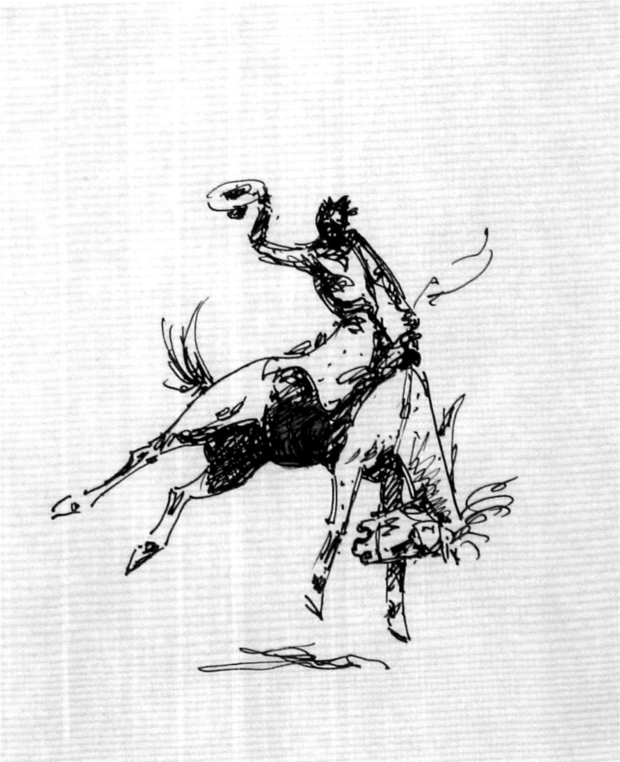

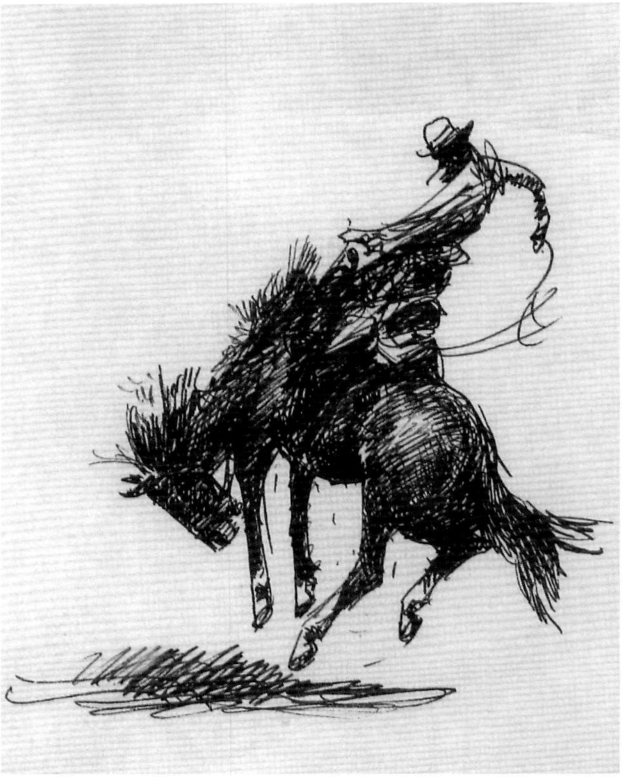

Left: *Bronco Buster.* Ink on paper. 7 1/4 x 5 1/2 inches (sight).

Right: *Bronco Buster.* Ink on paper. 7 1/4 x 5 1/2 inches (sight).

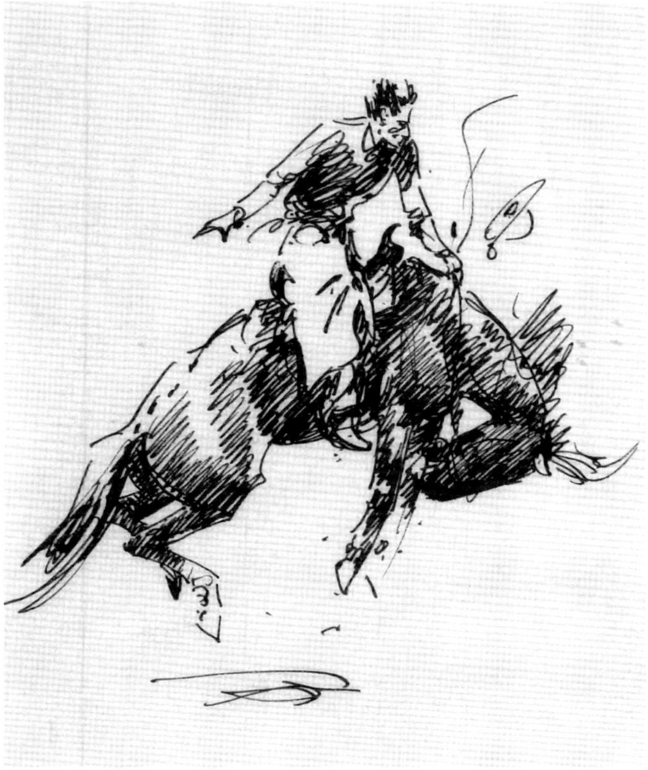 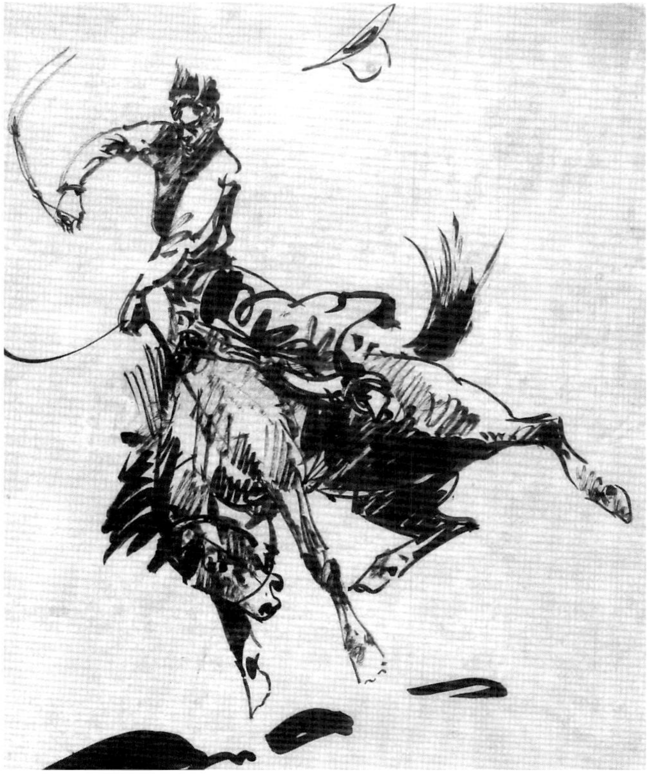

Left: *Bronc Rider.* Ink on paper. 6 1/2 x 5 1/2 inches (sight).

Right: *Bucking Horse.* Ink on paper. 9 3/4 x 7 5/8 inches (sheet).

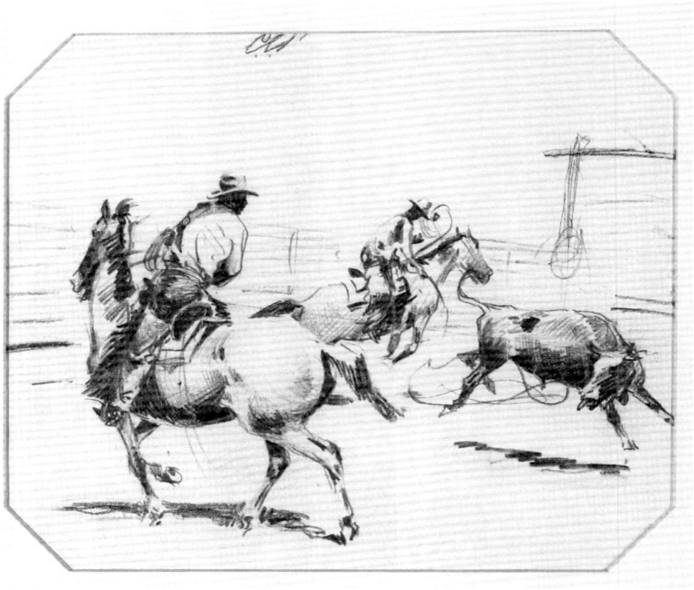

Roping the Steer (recto). Graphite on paper. 6 1/8 x 7 3/8 inches.

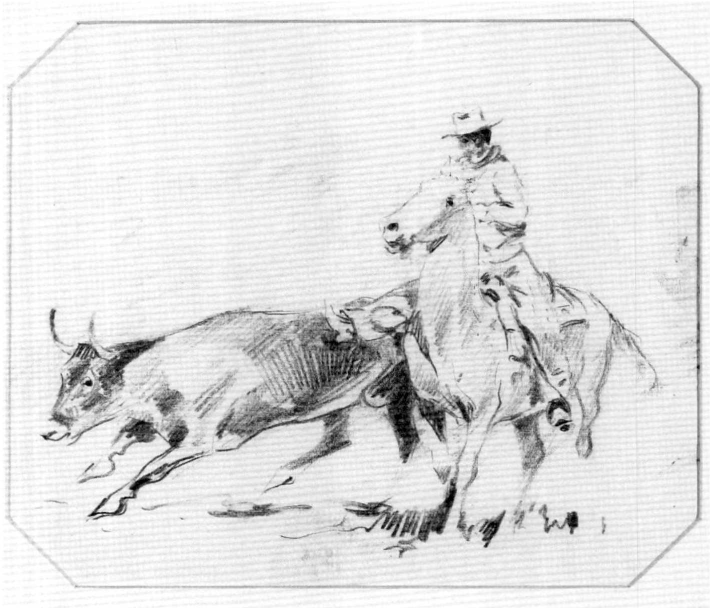

Roping the Steer (verso). Graphite on paper. 6 1/8 x 7 3/8 inches.

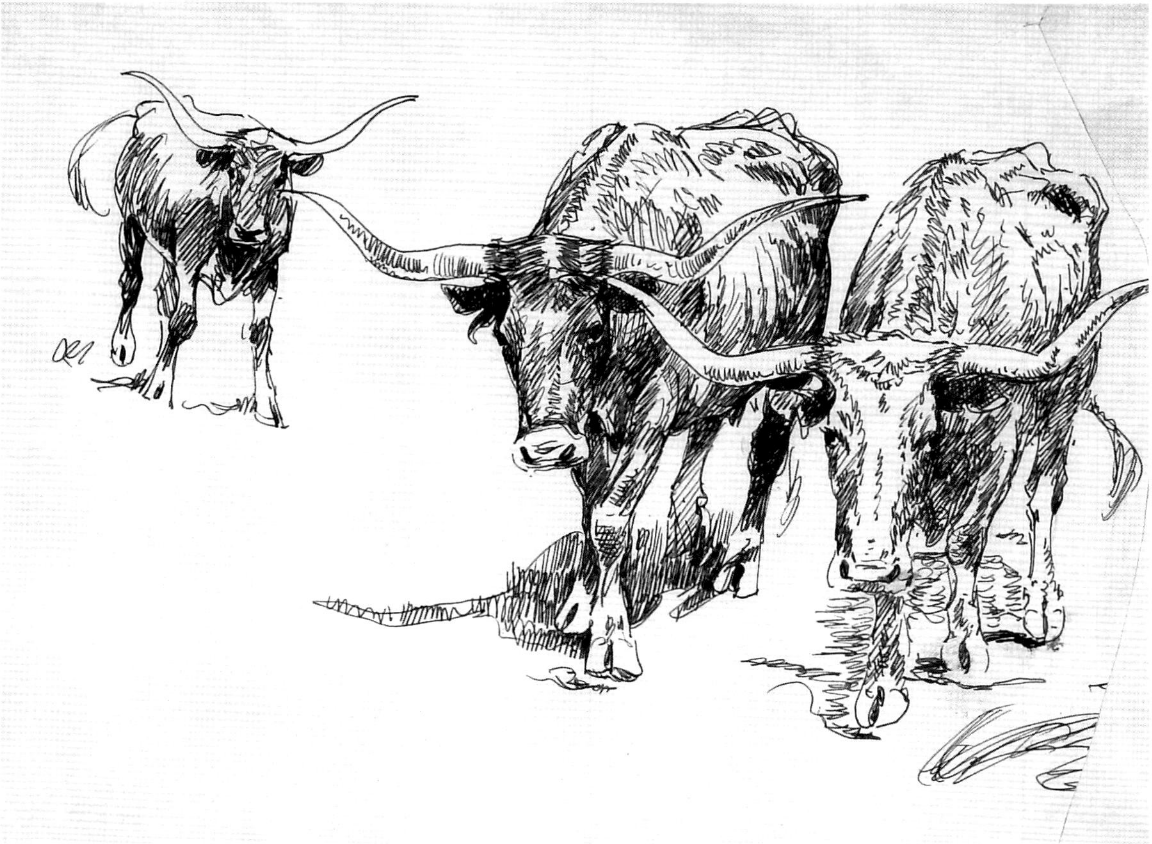

Three Steers. Ink on paper. 8 1/4 x 10 3/4 inches (sight).

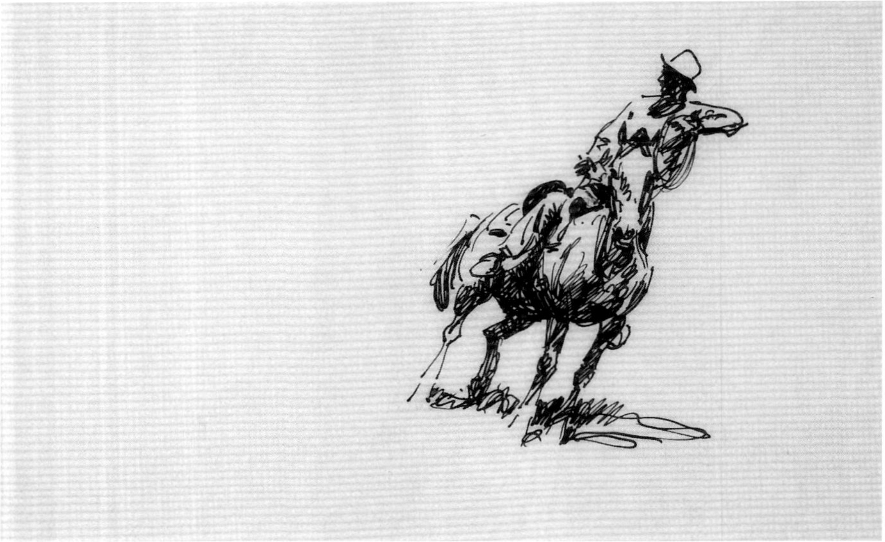

Cowboy on Horse. Ink on paper. 7 x 11 inches (sight).

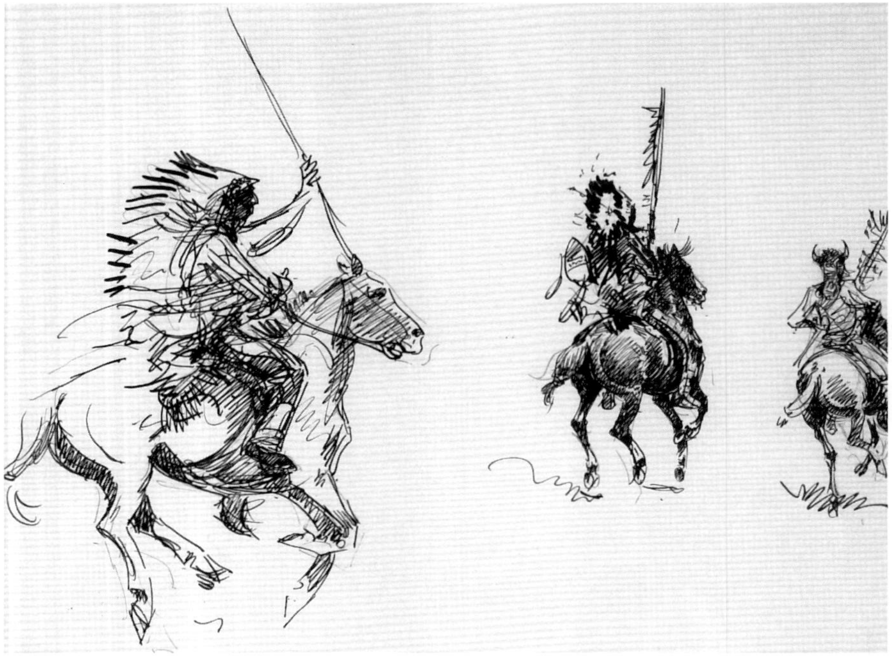

Three Indian Warriors. Ink and graphite on paper. 9 1/2 x 12 1/2 inches (sight).

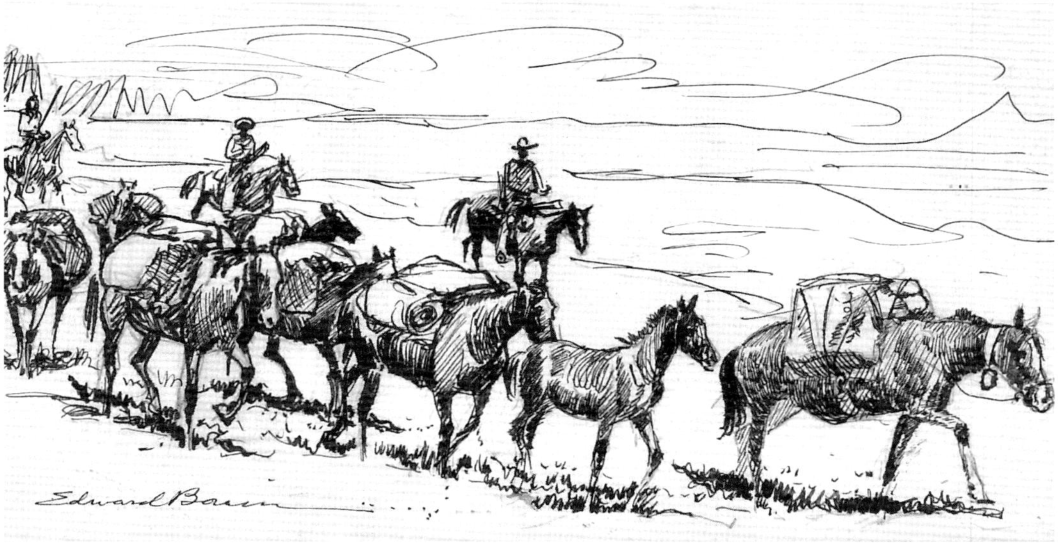

Mule Train. Ink on paper. 3 7/8 x 7 inches (sheet). Signed lower left: *Edward Borein.*

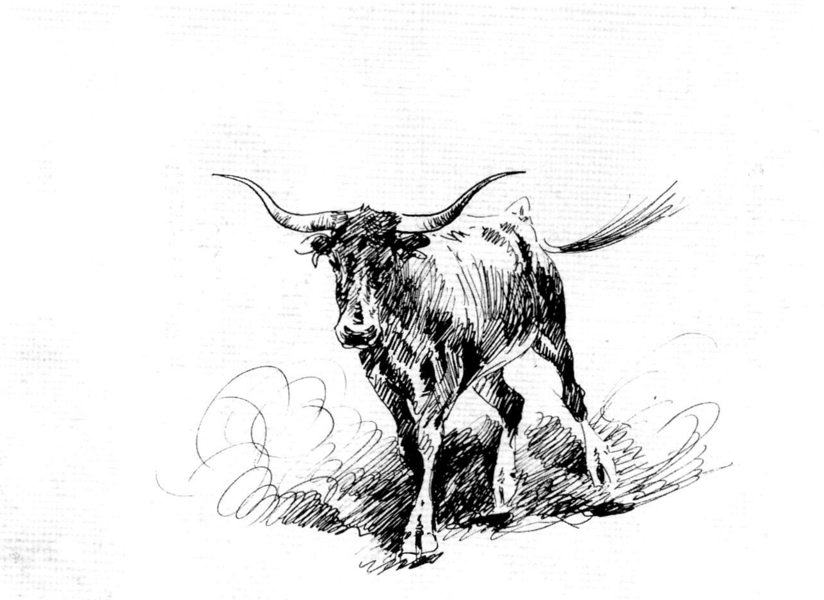

Single Steer. Ink on paper. 8 1/2 x 11 1/4 inches (sheet).

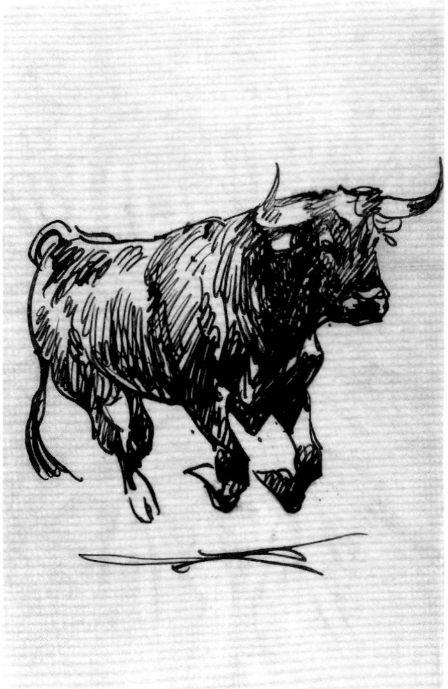

Bull. Ink on paper. 7 3/4 x 4 3/4 inches (sheet).

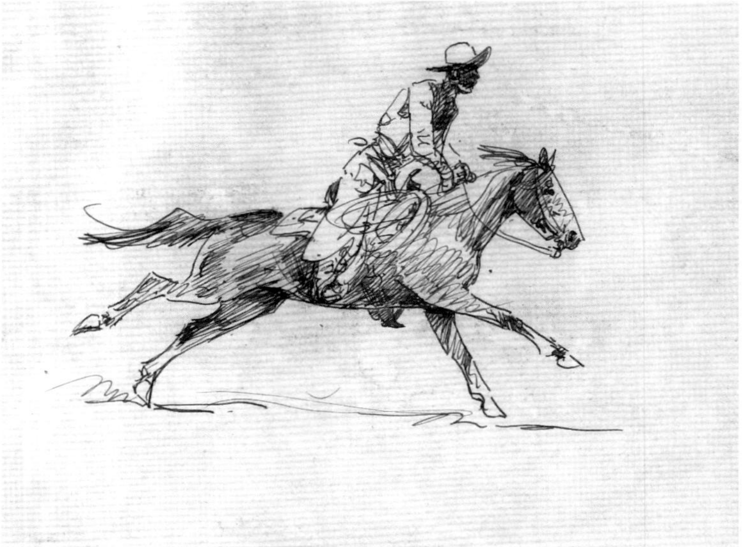

Working a Horse. Ink on paper. 6 x 8 inches (sight).

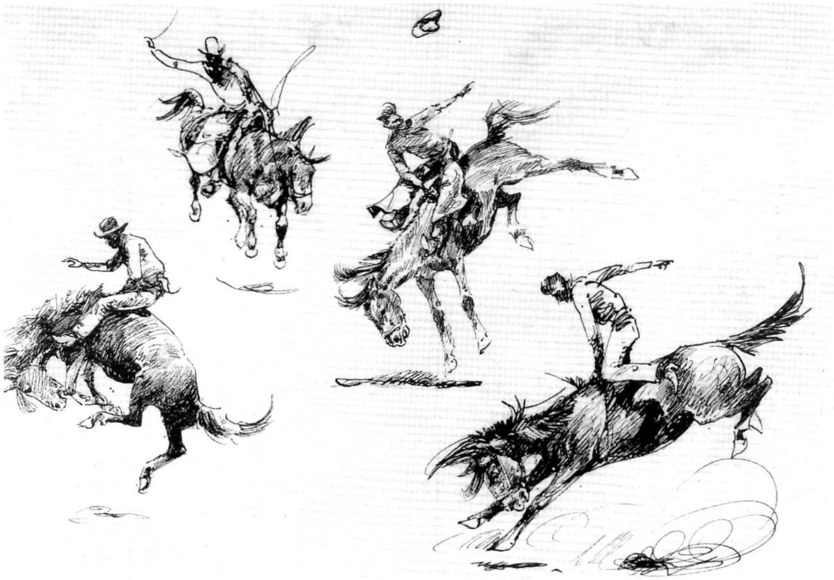

Four Sketches. Ink on paper. 8 3/8 x 11 1/4 inches (sheet).

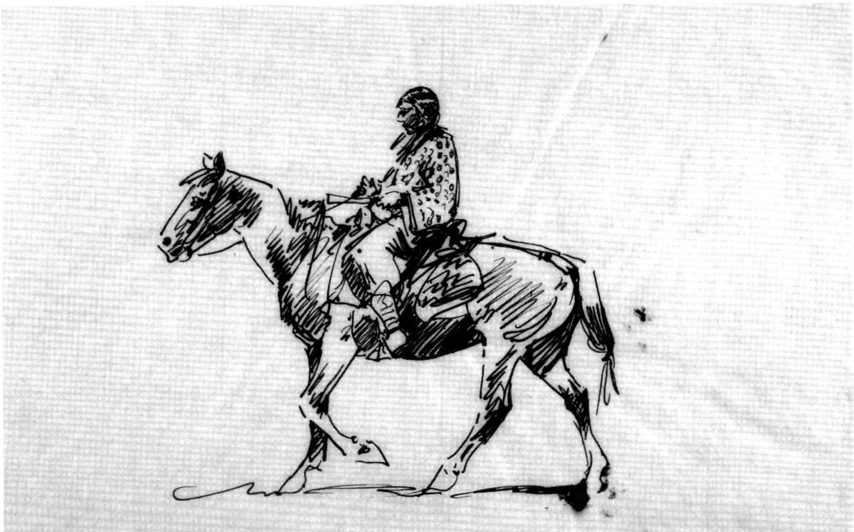

Indian on Horseback. Ink on paper. 9 1/8 x 12 inches (sheet).

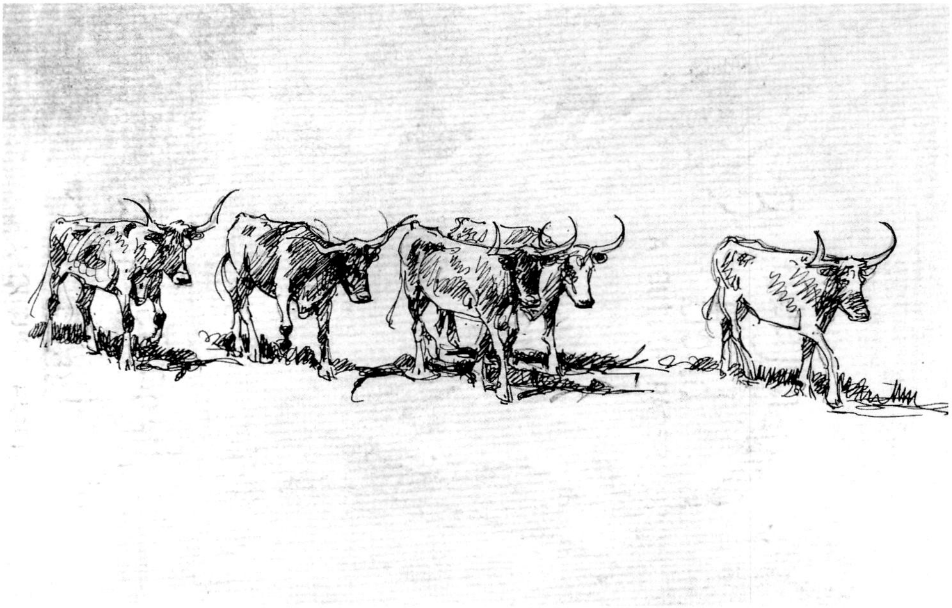

Cattle on the Move. Ink on paper. 8 1/8 x 11 3/4 inches (sheet).

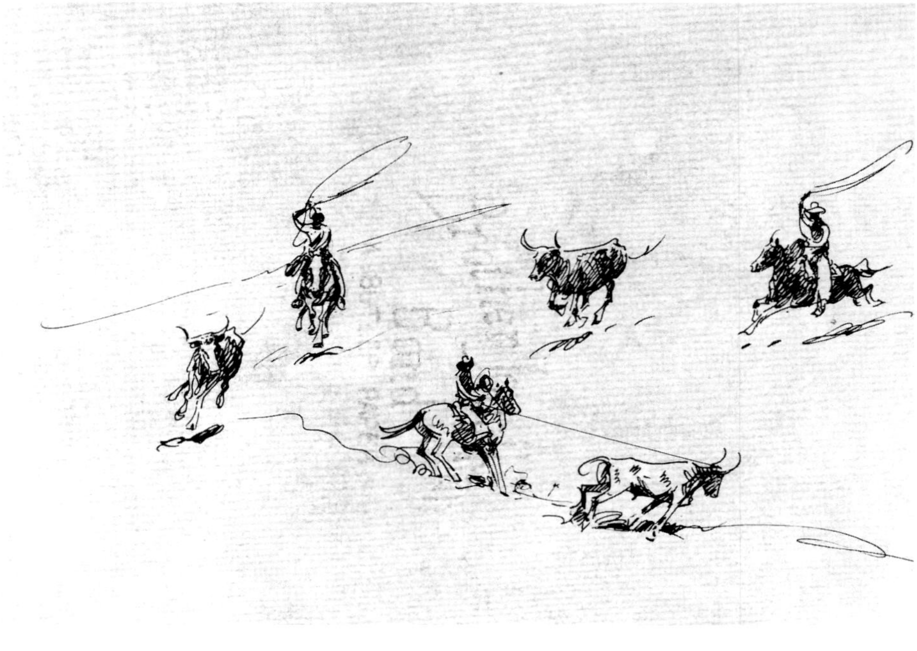

Roping Studies. Ink on paper. 8 x 11 1/2 inches (sheet).

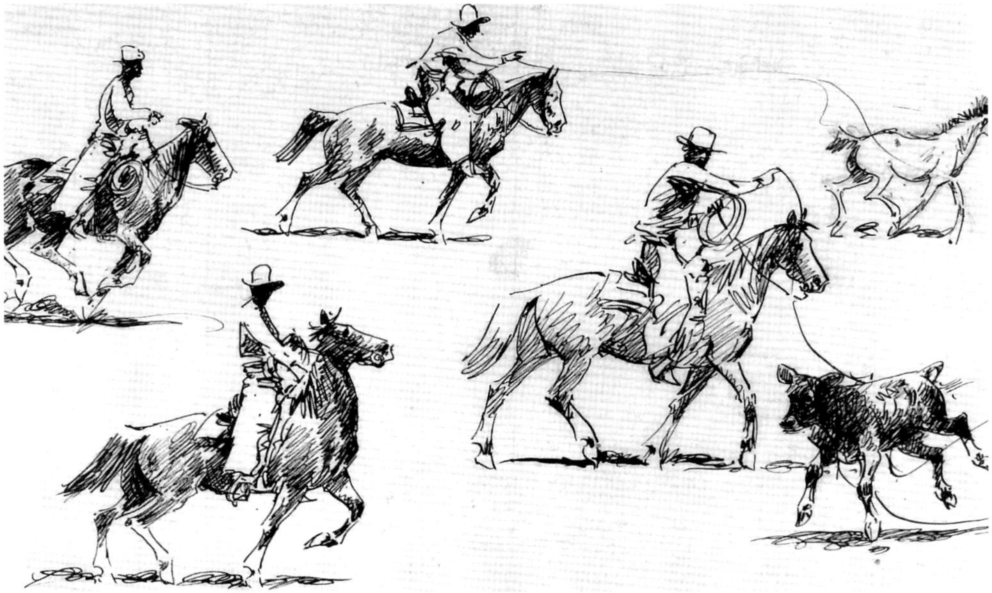

Roping Studies. Ink on paper. 8 3/4 x 11 3/4 inches (sheet).

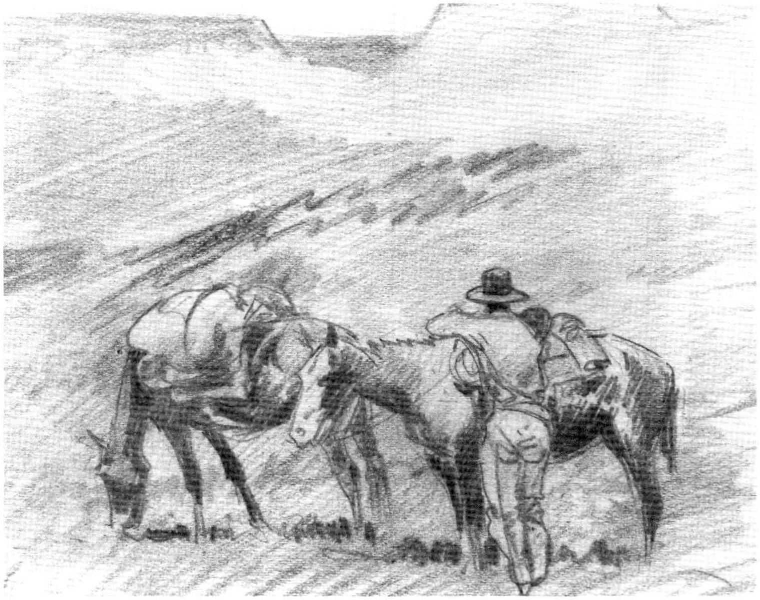

Man with Two Horses. Graphite on paper. 3 3/4 x 4 7/8 inches (sight).

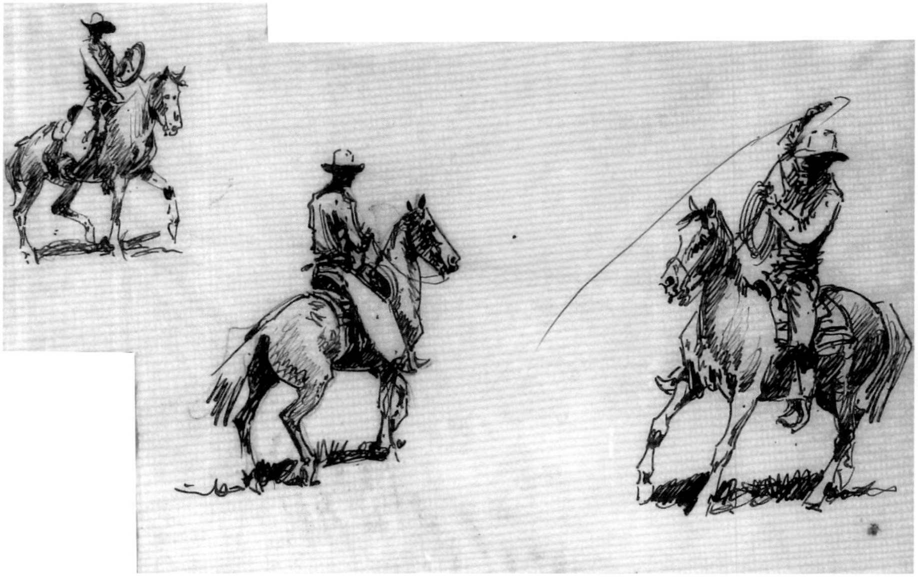

Three Riders Roping. Ink on paper. 5 x 9 inches, irregular (sight).

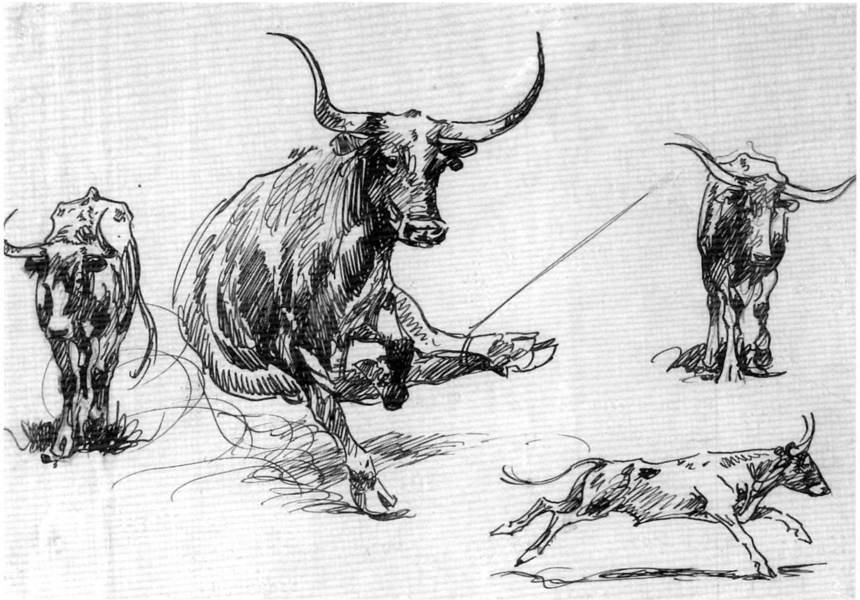

Roping Steers. Ink on paper. 8 x 11 inches (sight).

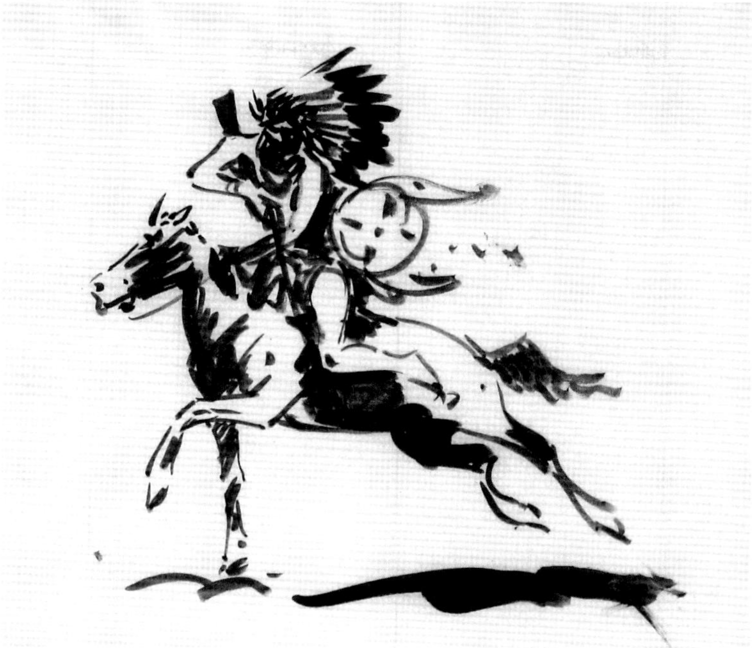

Warrior on Horseback with Gun. Ink on paper. 7 1/2 x 8 1/2 inches (sight).

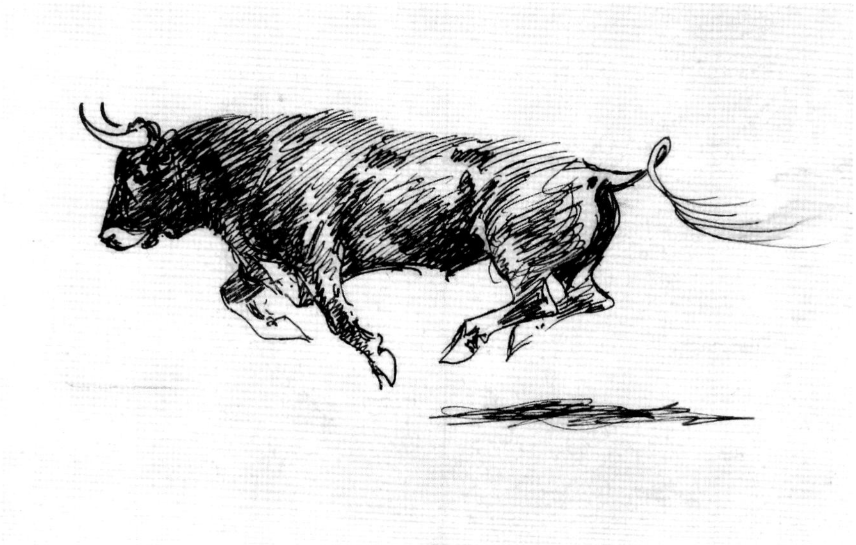

Running Bull. Ink on paper. 8 1/8 x 11 inches (sheet).

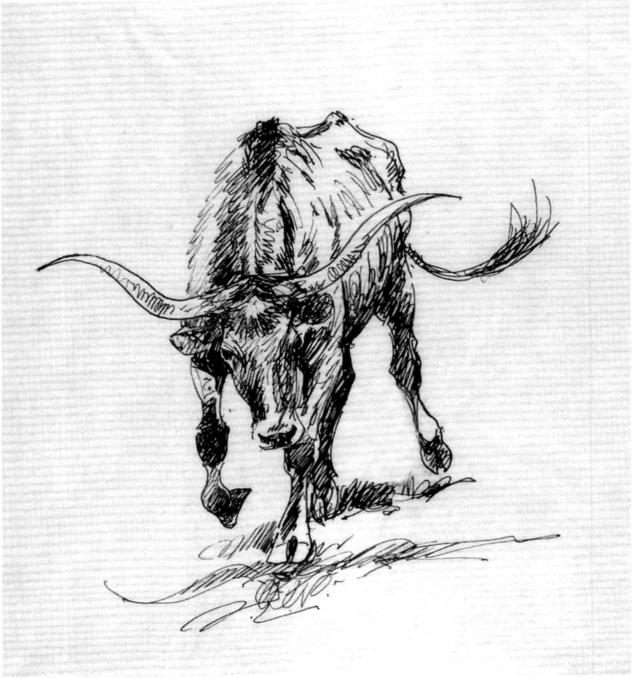

Steer (Head On). Ink on paper. 8 1/2 x 11 inches (sheet).

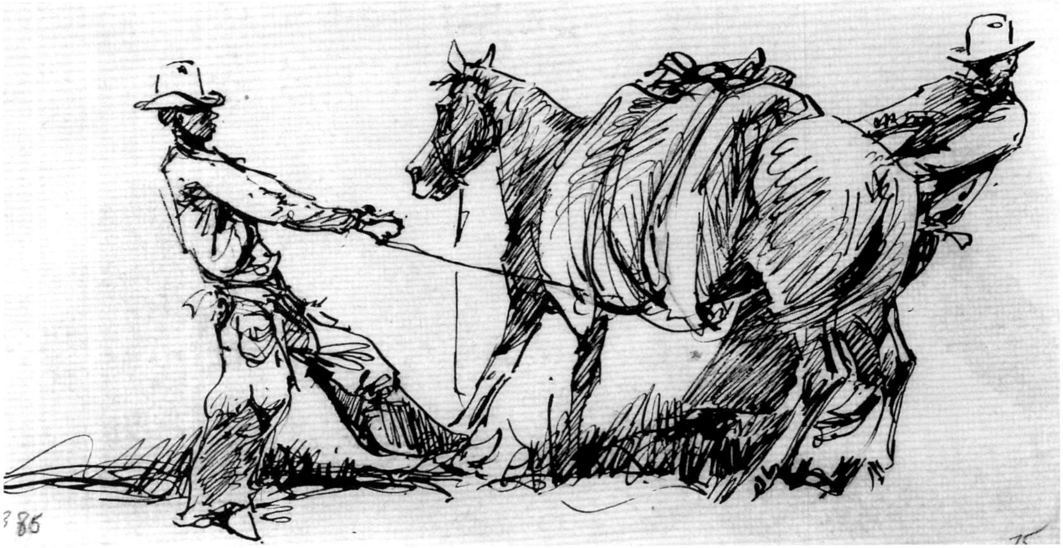

Cinching the Packhorse. Ink on paper. 3 1/2 x 7 3/4 inches (sheet).

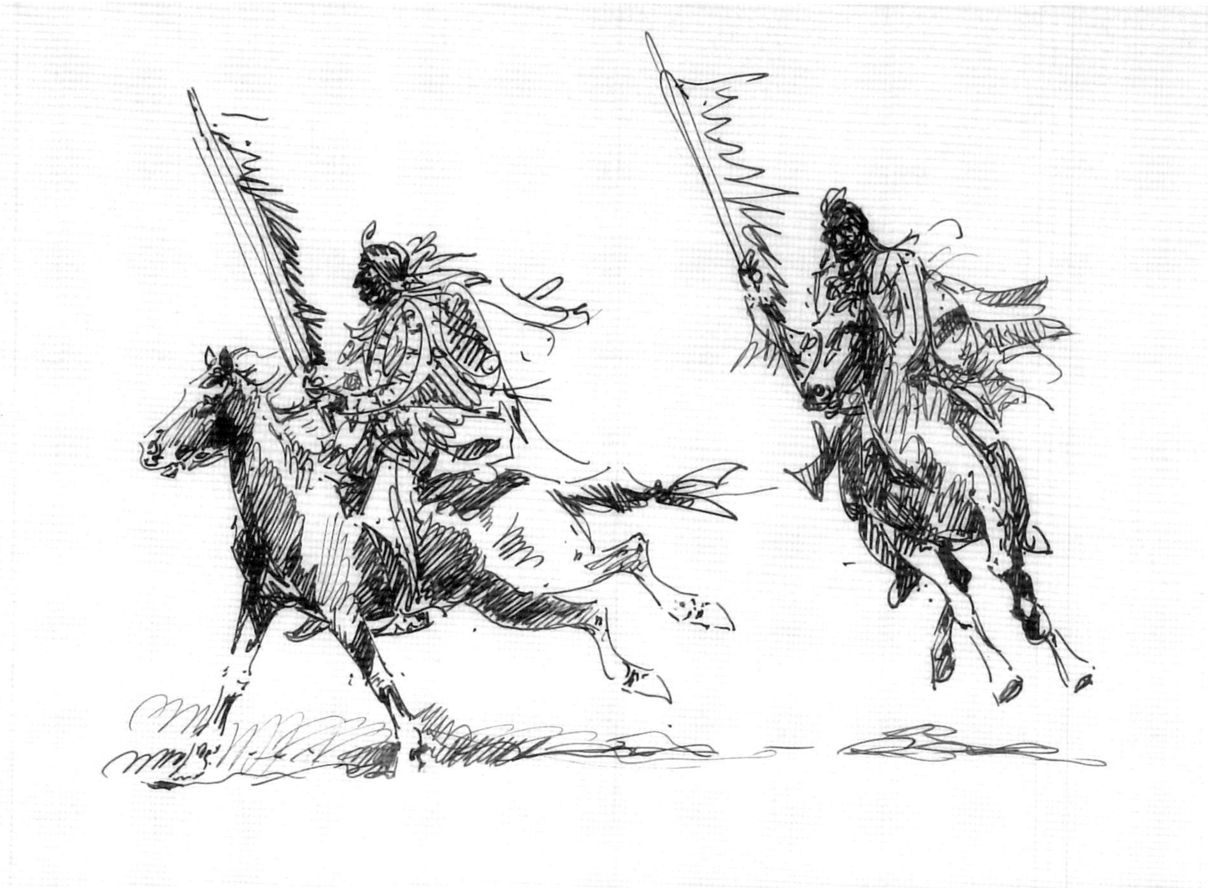

Two Indians on Horseback. Ink on paper. 8 x 10 7/8 inches (sight).

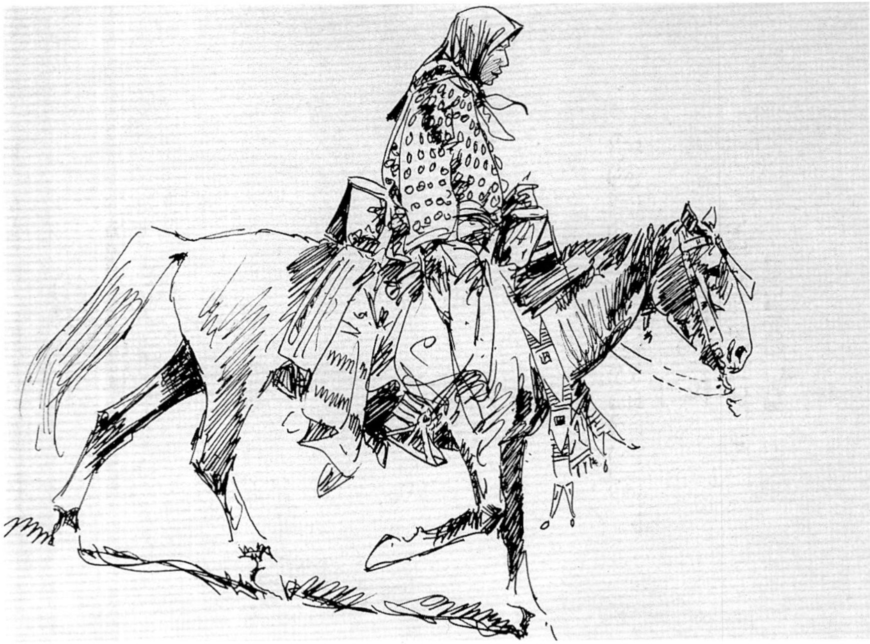

Indian Woman. Ink on paper. 7 7/8 x 10 3/8 inches.

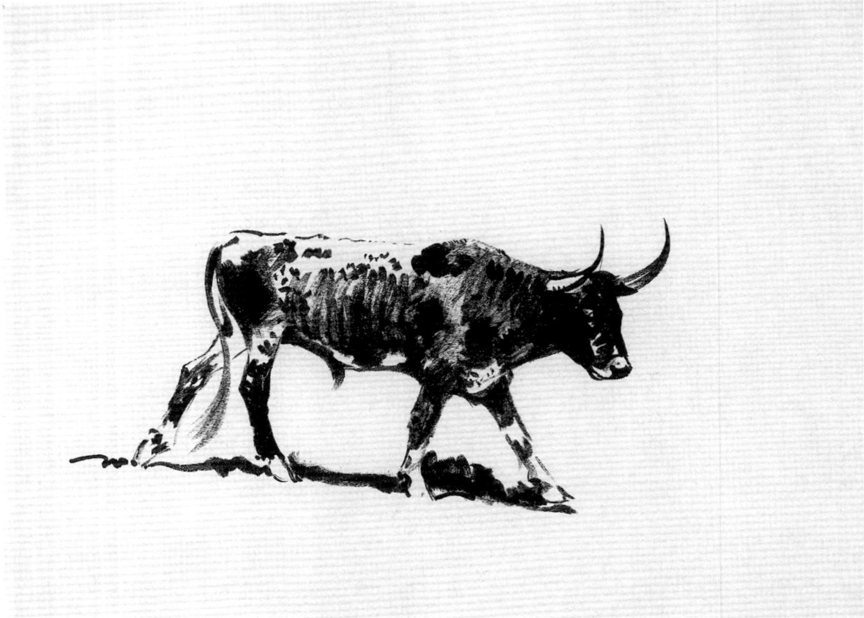

The Steer. Ink on paper. 8 1/2 x 13 inches (sheet).

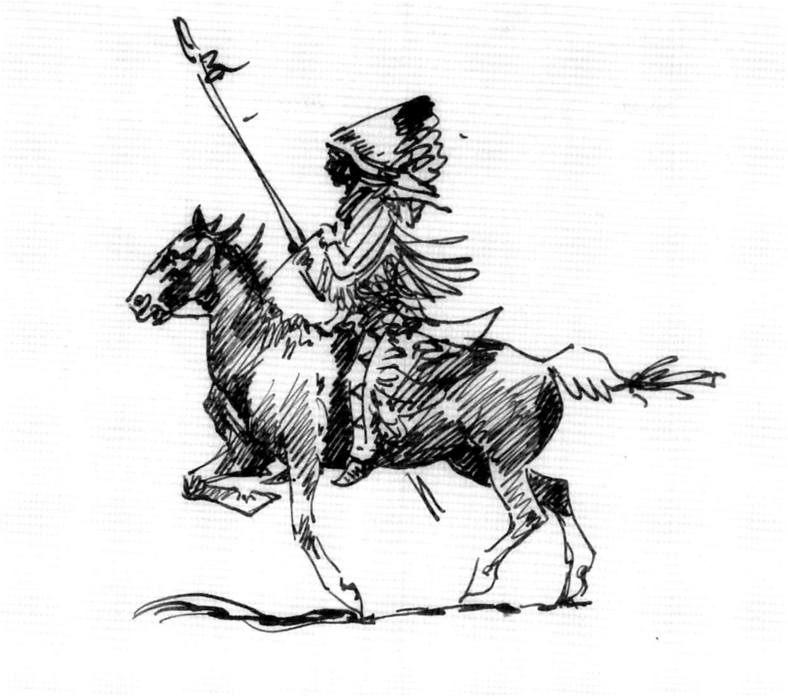

Indian Chief on Horseback. Ink on paper. 8 x 9 inches (sight).

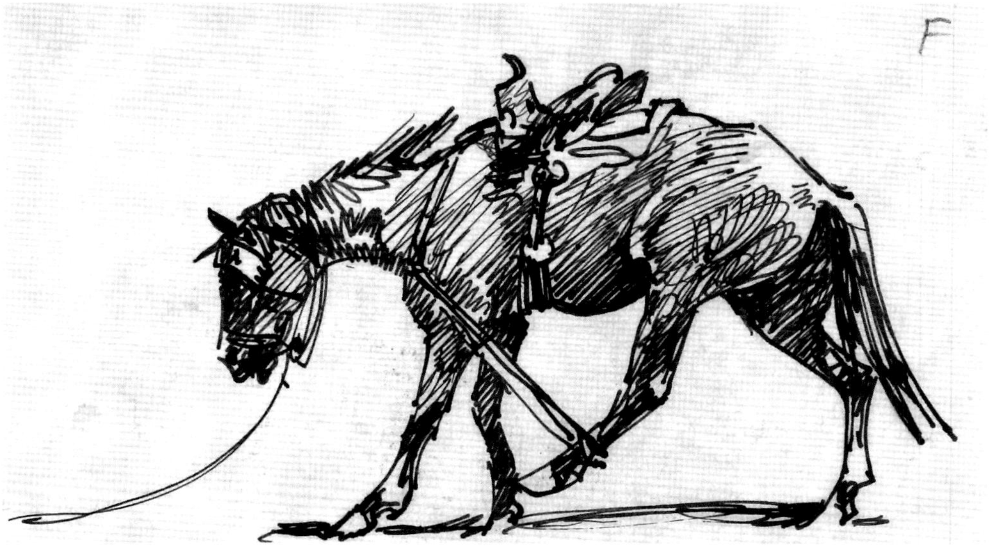

Tethered. Ink on paper. 3 7/8 x 6 5/8 inches (sheet).

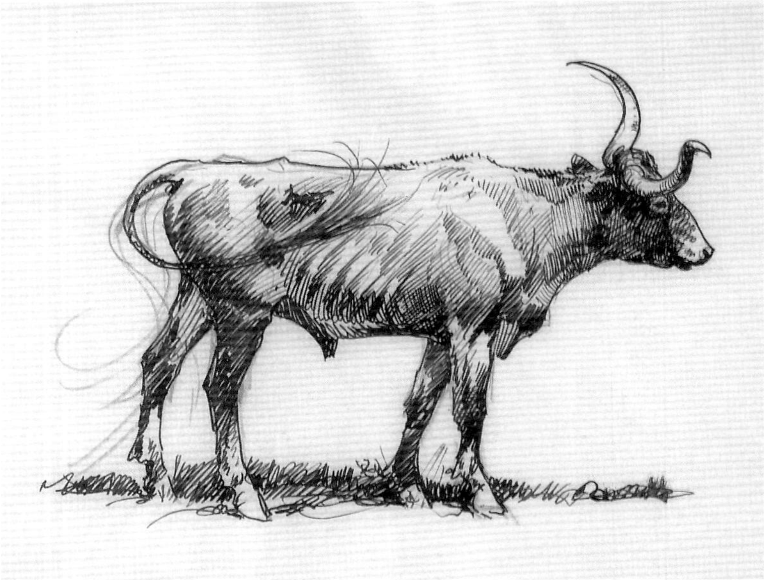

Longhorn Steer. Ink and graphite on paper. 6 1/4 x 8 1/8 inches (sight).

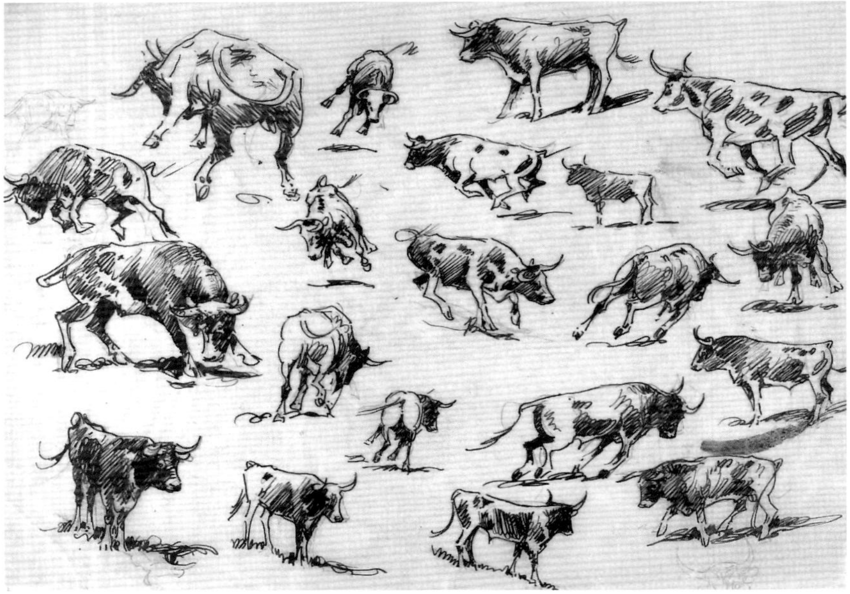

Twenty Steer Studies. Ink on paper. 8 1/8 x 11 1/2 inches (sheet).

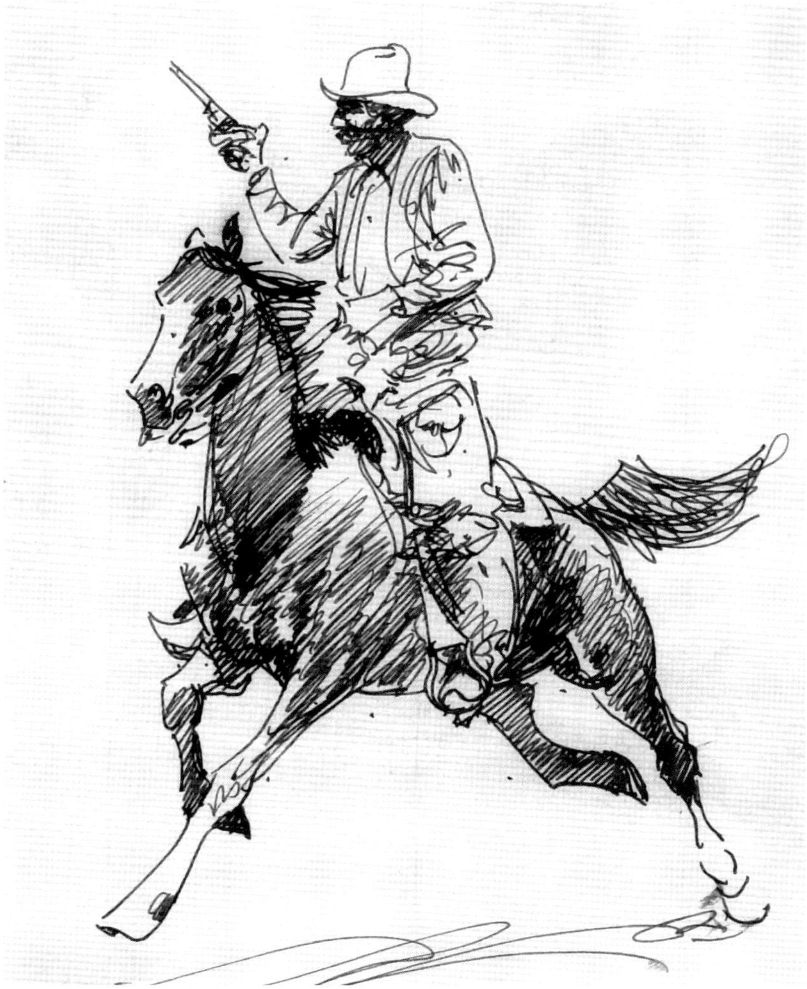

Horse and Gunman. Ink on paper. 7 3/8 x 5 7/8 inches (sight).

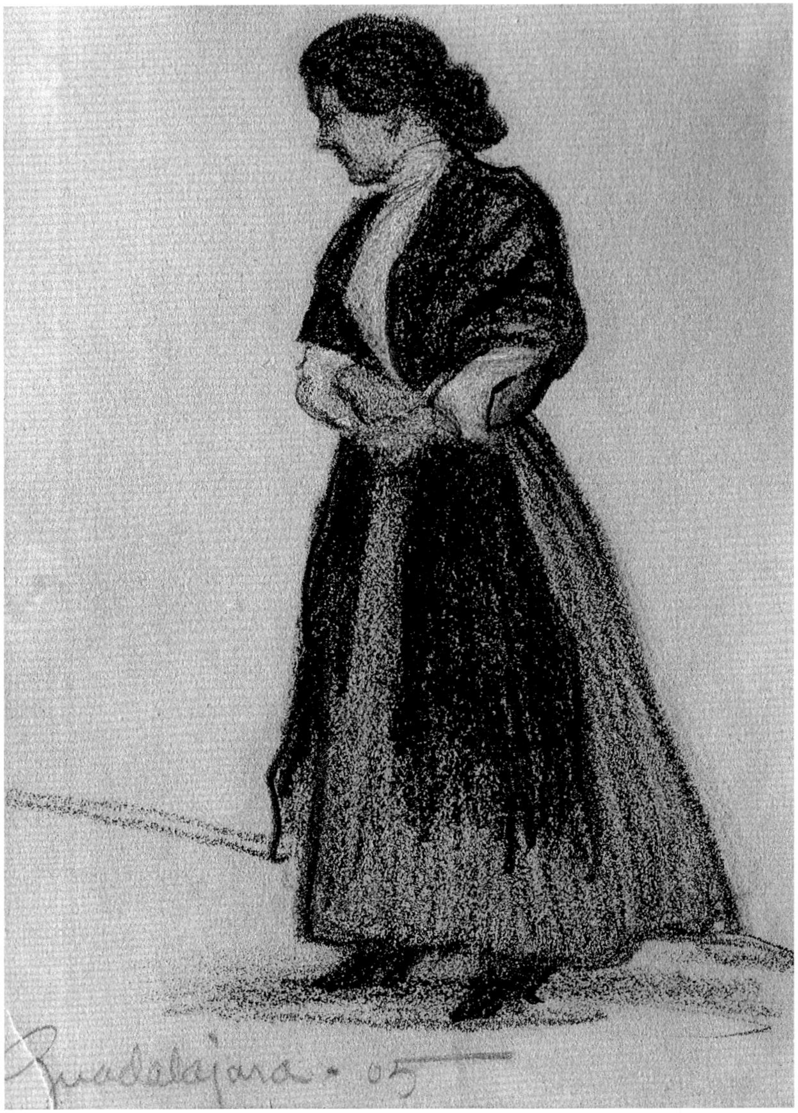

Guadalajara Woman, 1905. Crayon on paper. 7 x 5 1/4 inches (sight). Inscribed lower left: *Guadalajara-05*.

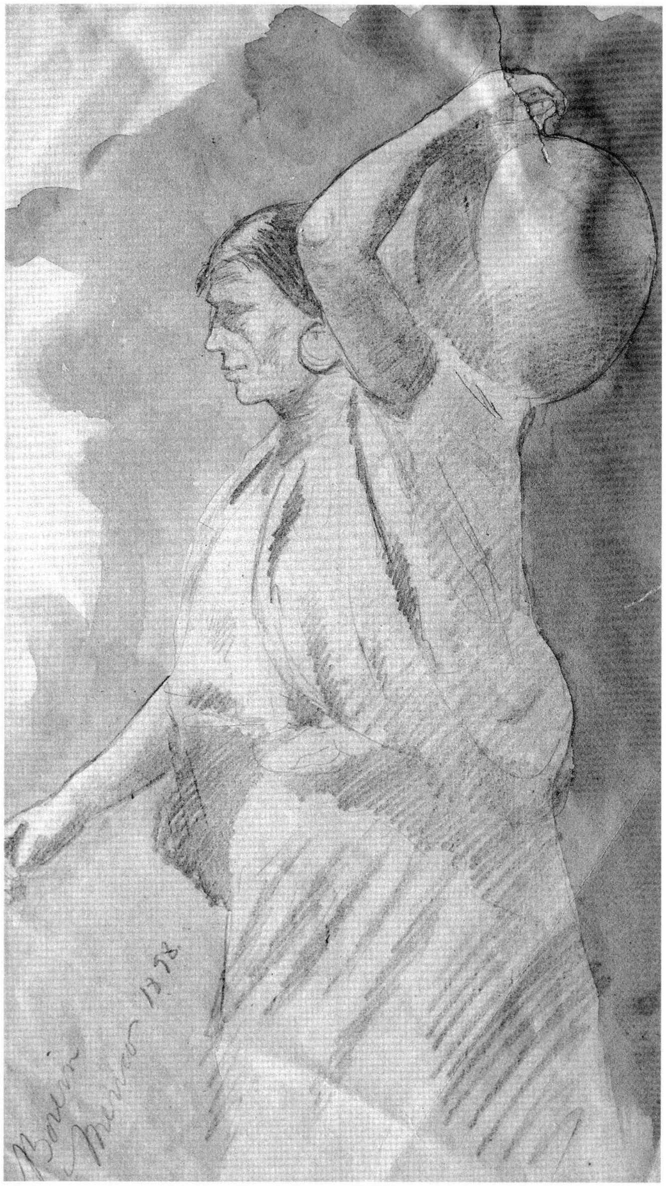

Woman Carrying Jug. Graphite and watercolor on paper. 11 3/4 x 6 5/8 inches.
Signed, inscribed and dated lower left: *Borein / Mexico 1898.*

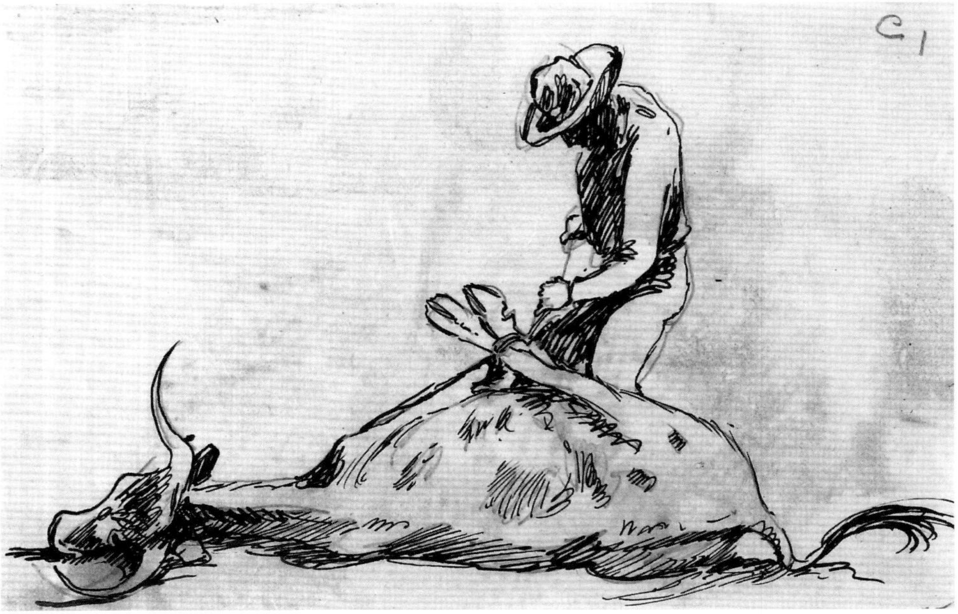

Tied Off. Ink on paper. 4 1/4 x 6 1/4 inches (sheet).

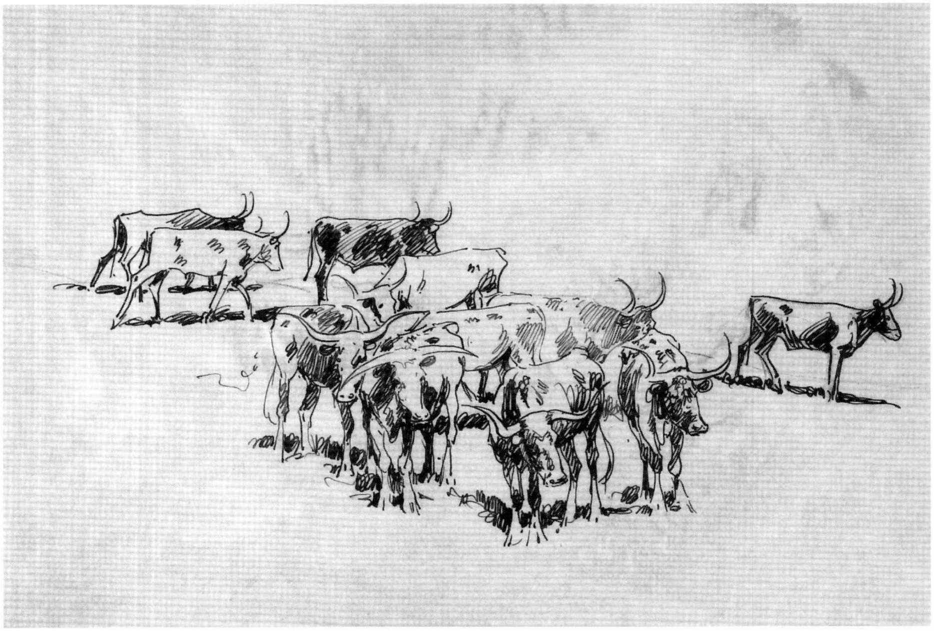

Standing Herd. Ink on paper. 8 x 10 3/4 inches (sheet).

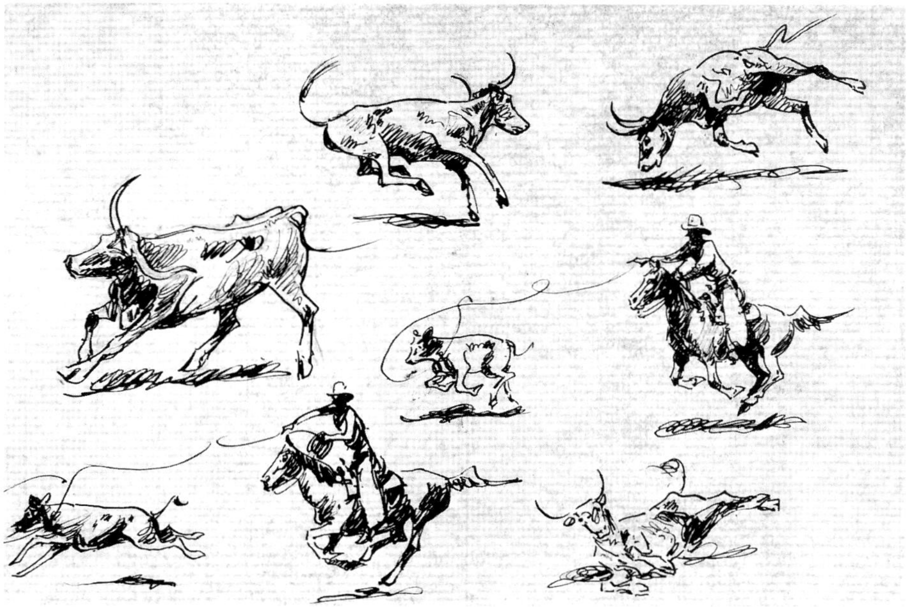

Roping Studies. Ink on paper. 8 x 11 1/2 inches (sheet).

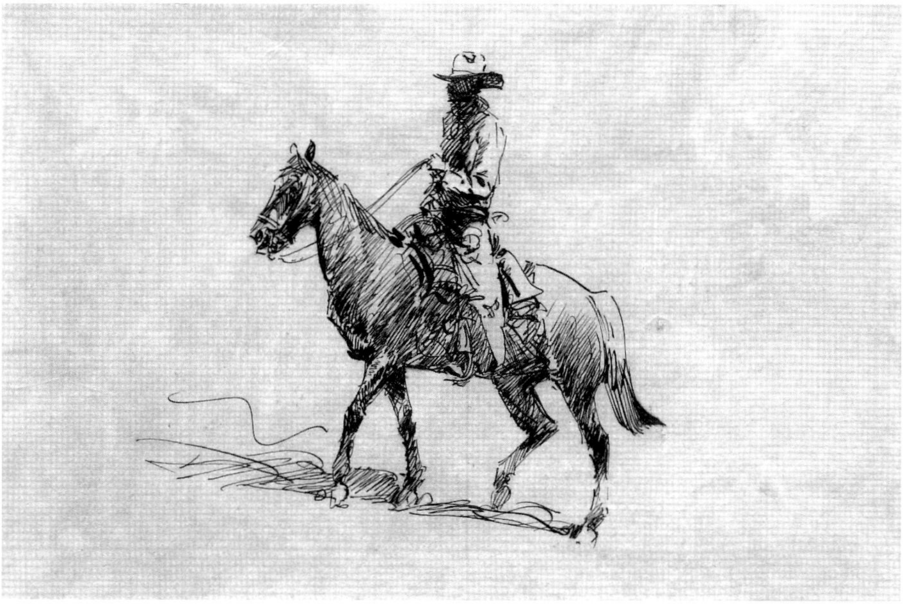

Lone Rider. Ink on paper. 8 1/8 x 11 inches (sheet).

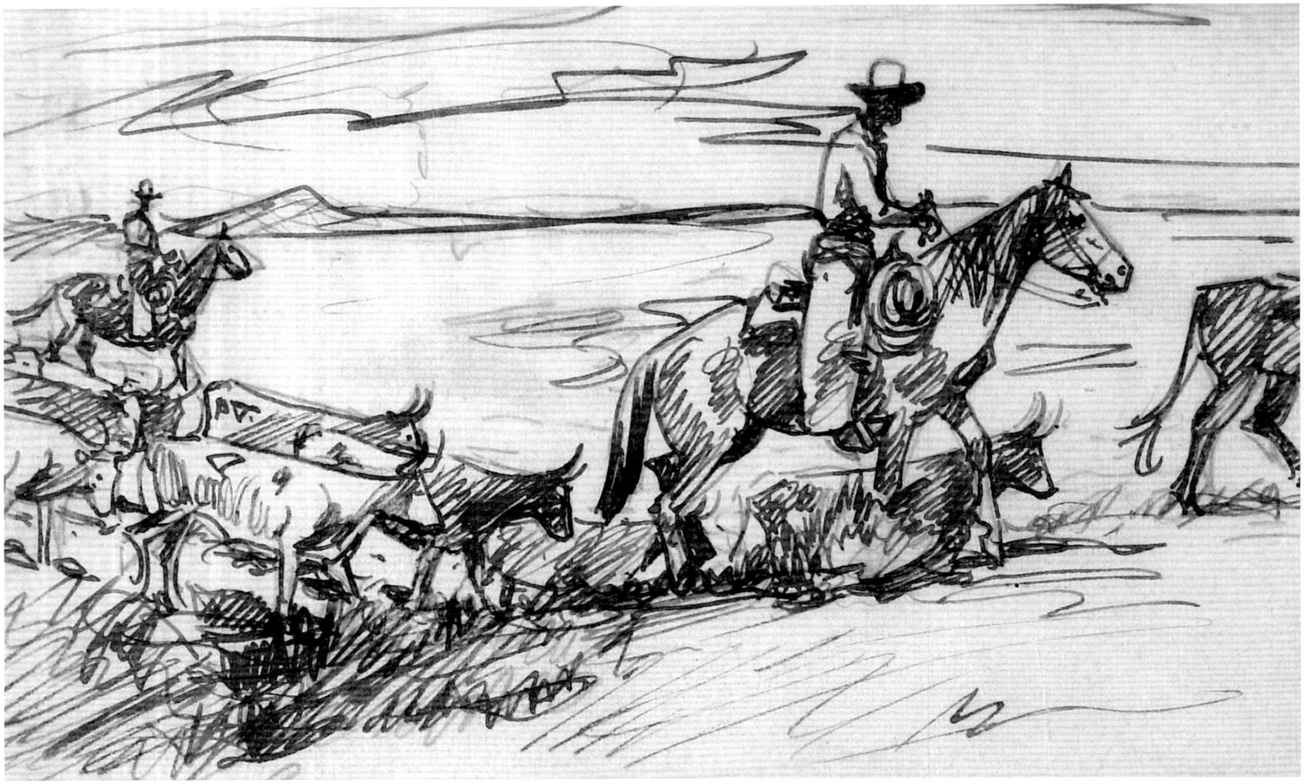

Rounding Up Cattle. Ink and graphite on paper. 4 5/8 x 7 1/4 inches (sheet).

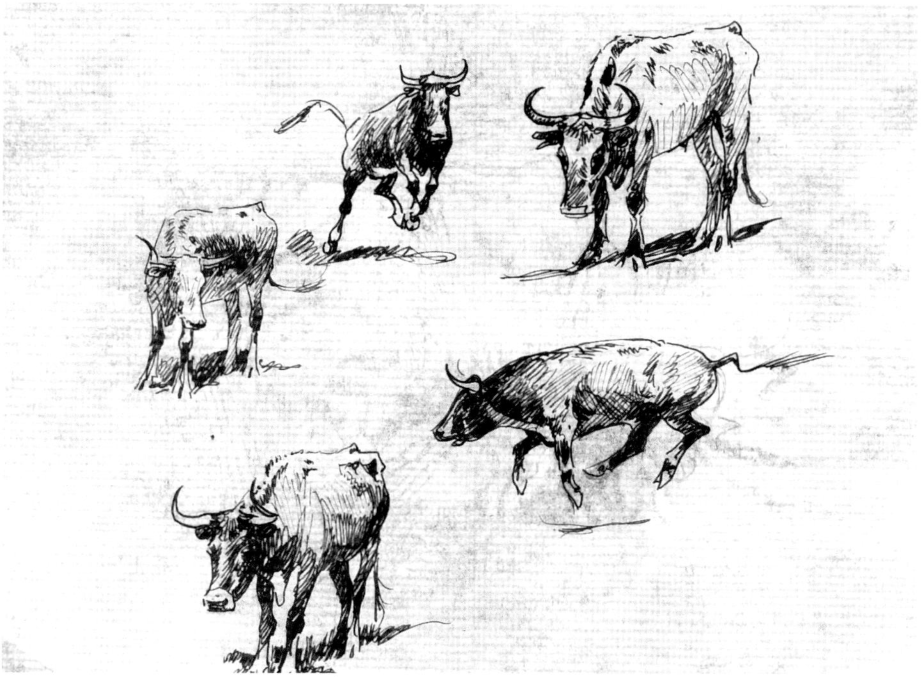

Five Steer Studies. Ink on paper. 8 x 10 7/8 inches (sheet).

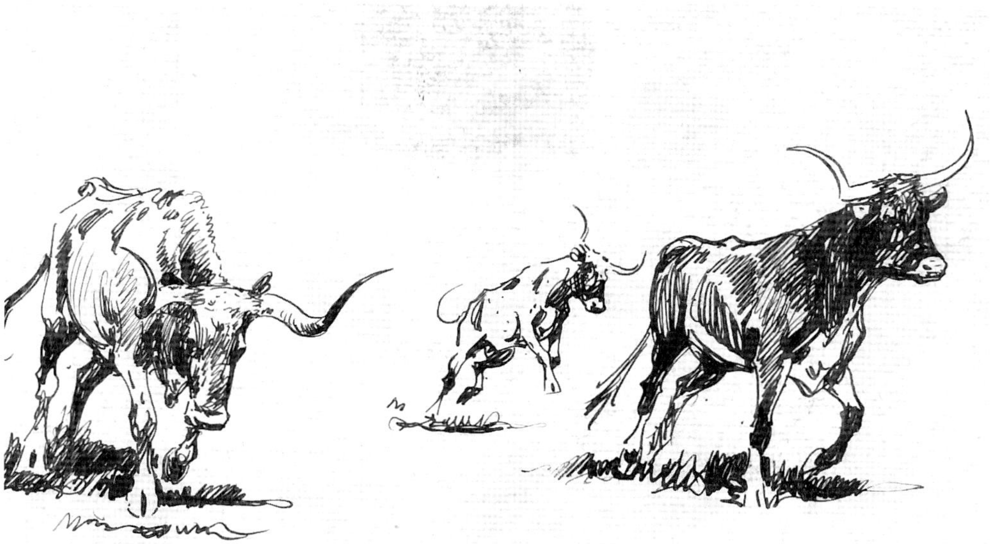

Three Steer Studies. Ink on paper. 8 x 10 7/8 inches (sheet).

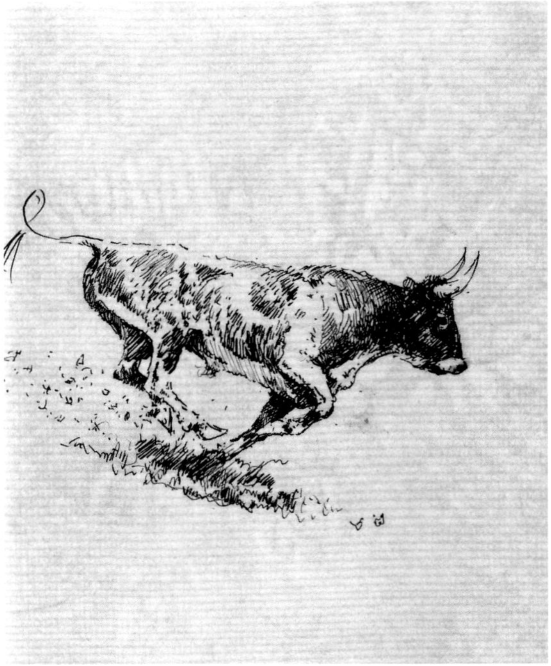

Steer. Ink on paper. 7 3/4 x 6 1/8 inches (sheet).

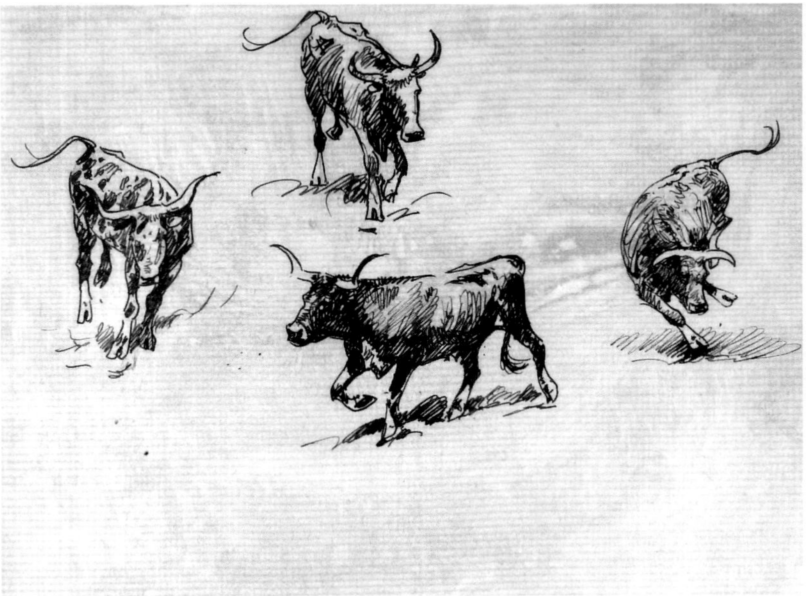

Four Steer Studies. Ink on paper. 8 1/2 x 10 7/8 inches (sheet).

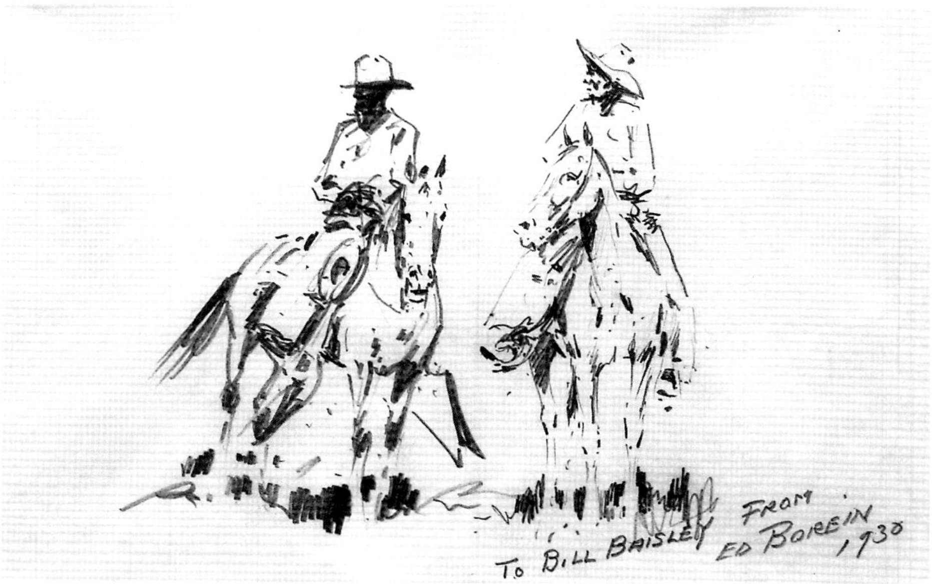

Two Riders on Horseback, 1930. Graphite on paper. 5 1/2 x 8 1/2 inches (sheet).
Signed and dated lower right: *TO BILL BAISLEY FROM / ED BOREIN / 1930*

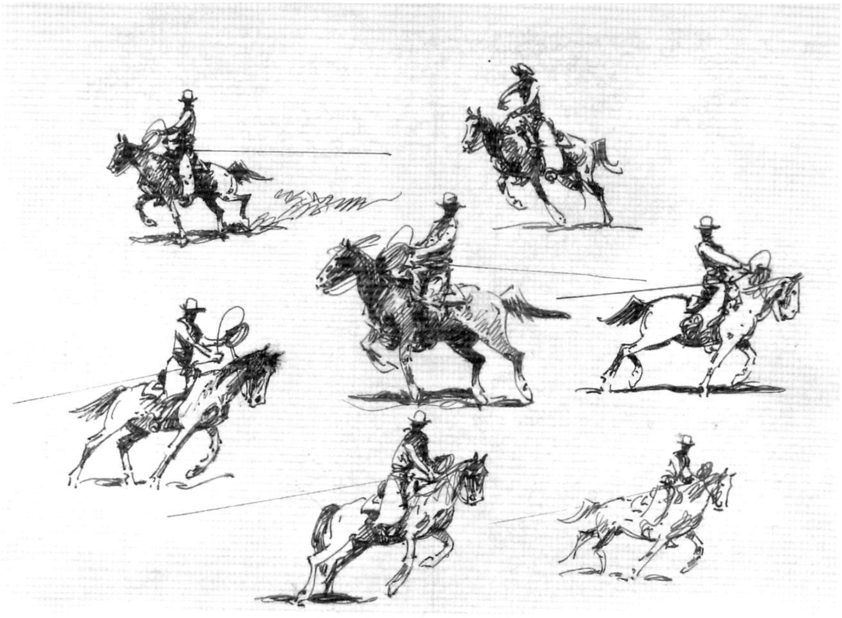

Seven Horse and Rider Studies. Ink on paper. 8 3/8 x 11 inches (sheet).

ETCHINGS

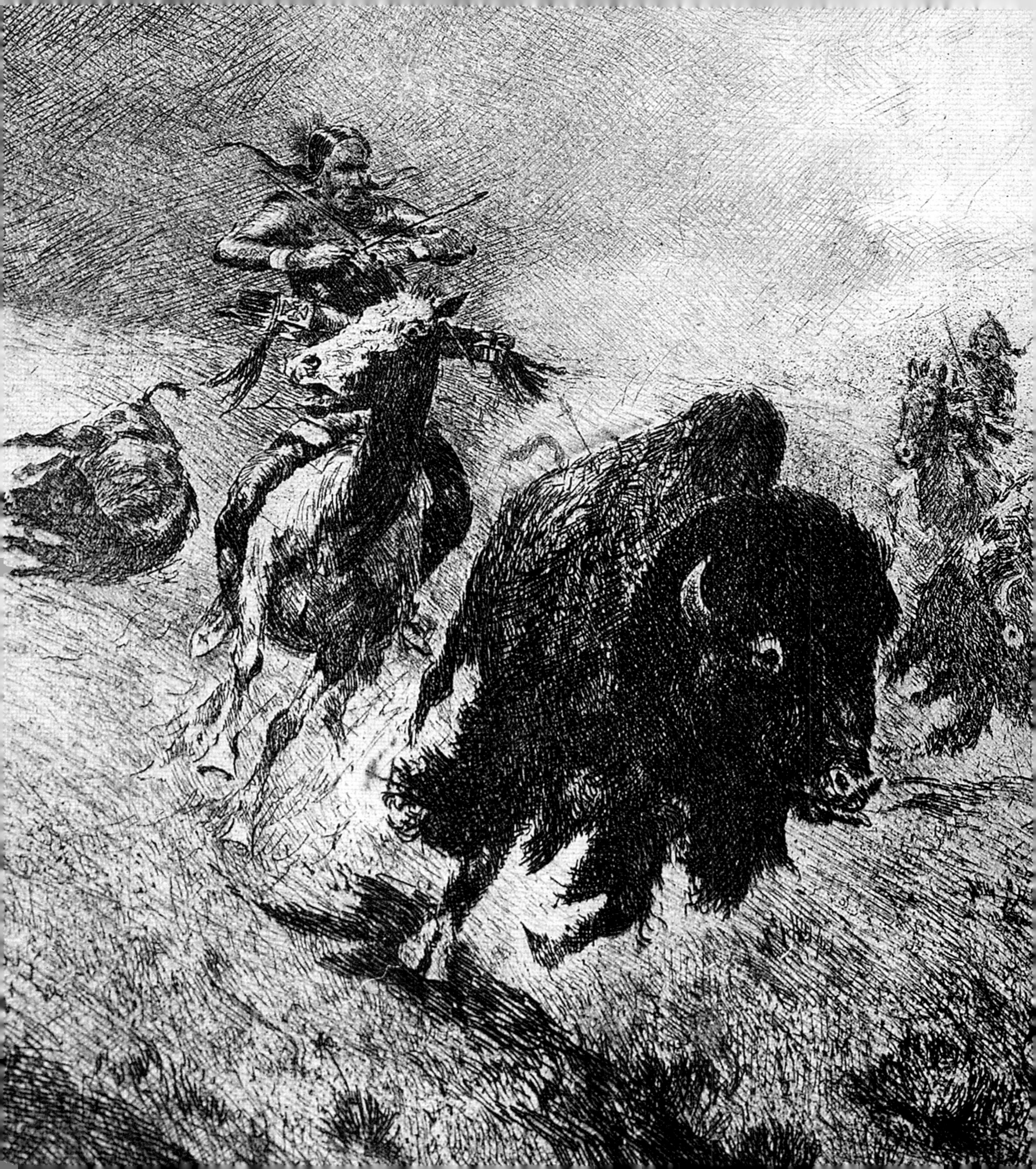

LIFE ON THE RANGE

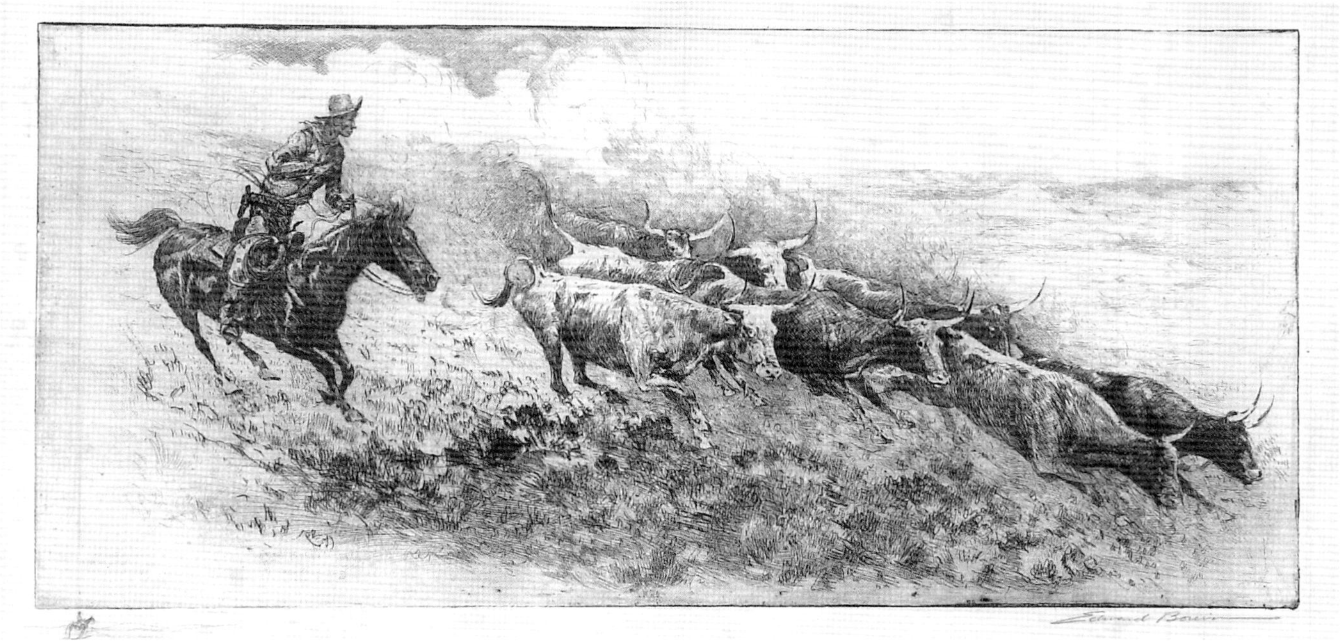

Wild Cattle, No. 2 (G 115). Etching. 5 15/16 x 12 7/16 inches (plate). Signed lower right: *Edward Bcrein*.
Remarqued lower left.

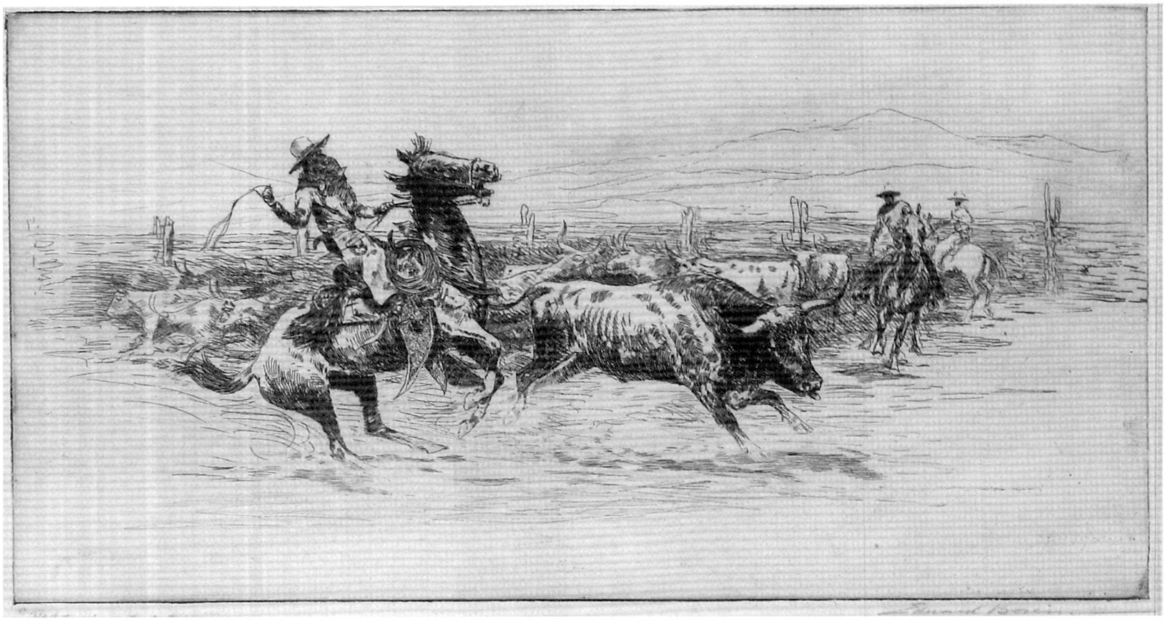

Cutting Out a Bull, No. 1 (G 116). Etching. 5 15/16 x 10 7/8 inches.
Signed lower right: *Edward Borein*. Inscribed lower left: *PARTING OUT A BULL*.

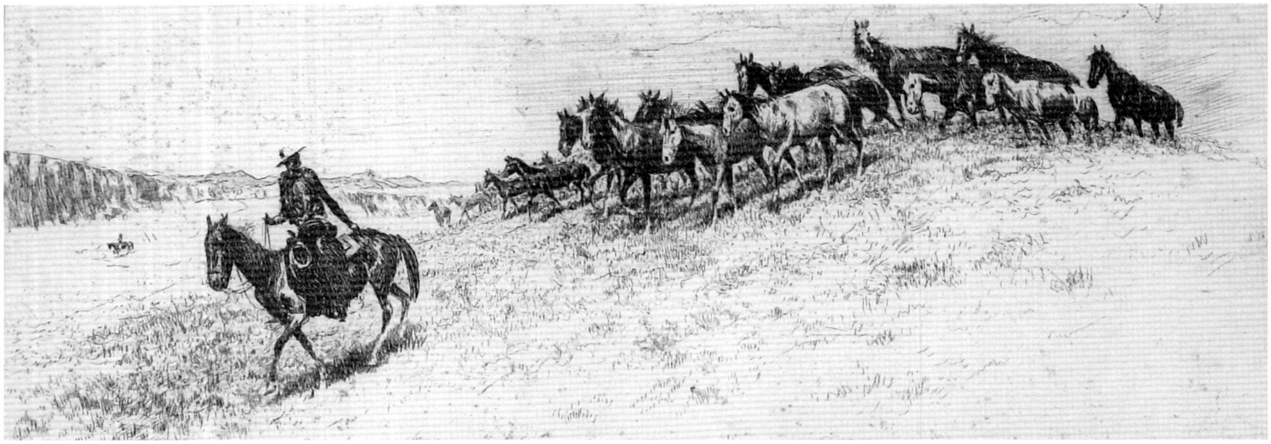

Saddle Bunch (G 51). Etching and drypoint. 3 x 8 1/8 inches (plate). Signed lower right: *Edward Borein*.

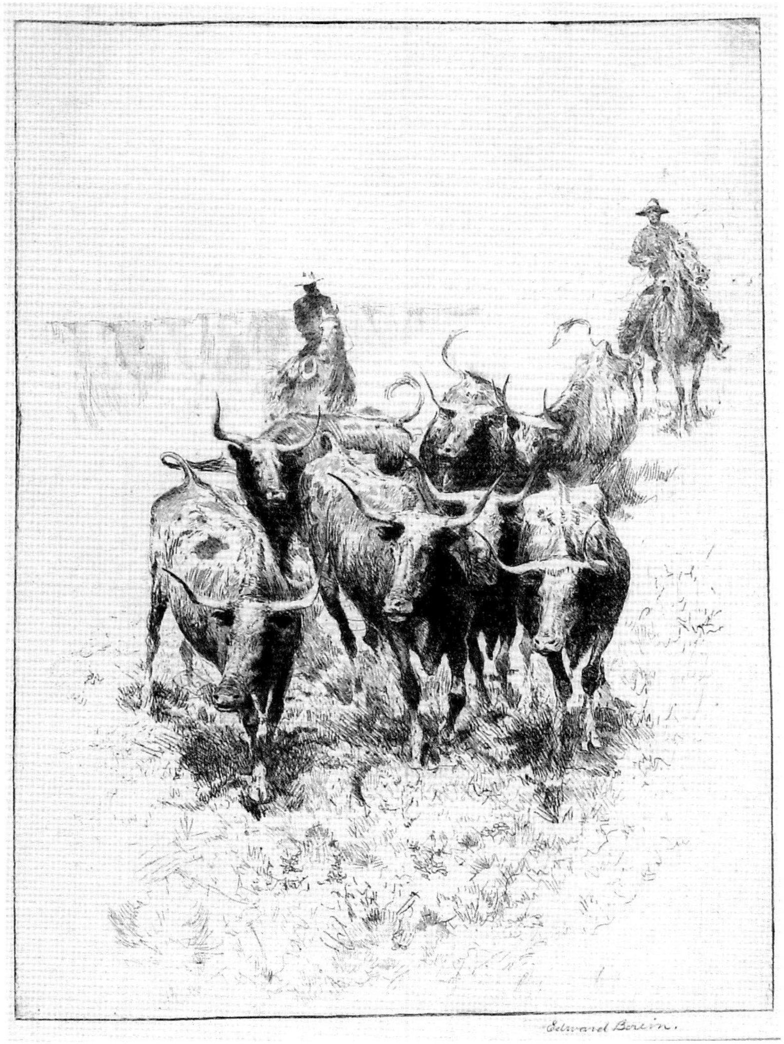

Longhorns, 1st State (G 105). Etching and drypoint. 11 x 8 3/8 inches (plate). Signed lower right: *Edward Borein.*

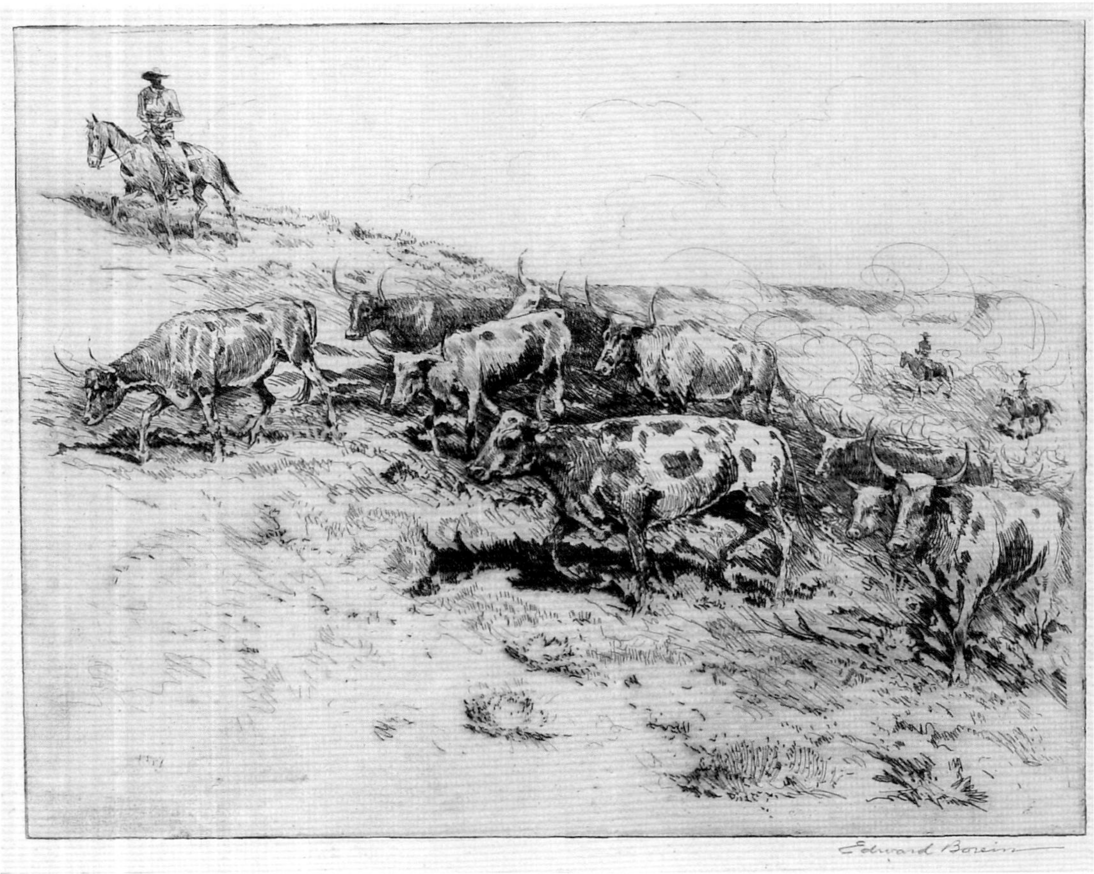

Spring Drive to Grass (G 93). Etching and drypoint. 5 3/4 x 8 5/8 inches (plate).
Signed lower right: *Edward Borein*. Signed lower left in plate: *EDWARD BOREIN*.

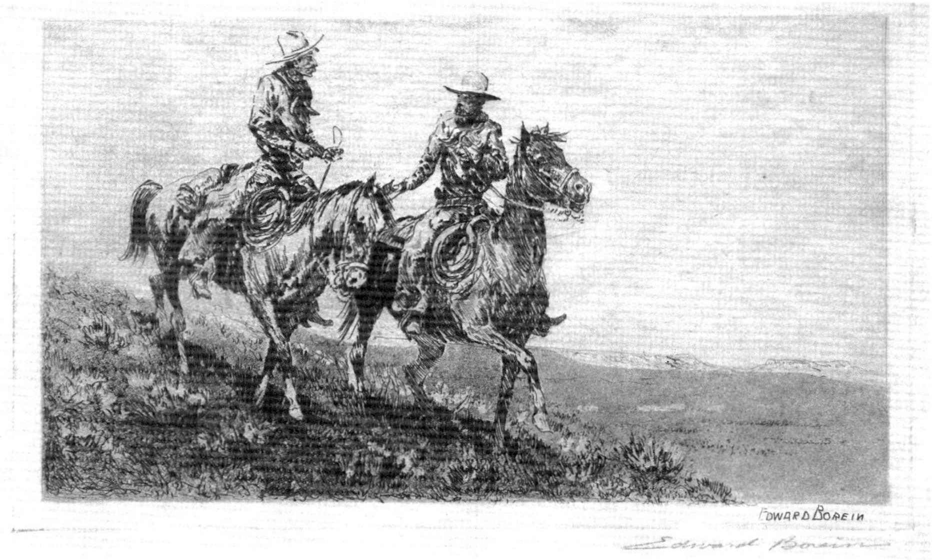

Pals (G 15). Etching and drypoint. 4 7/8 x 7 13/16 inches (plate). Signed lower right: *Edward Borein.* Signed lower right in plate: *EDWARD BOREIN.*

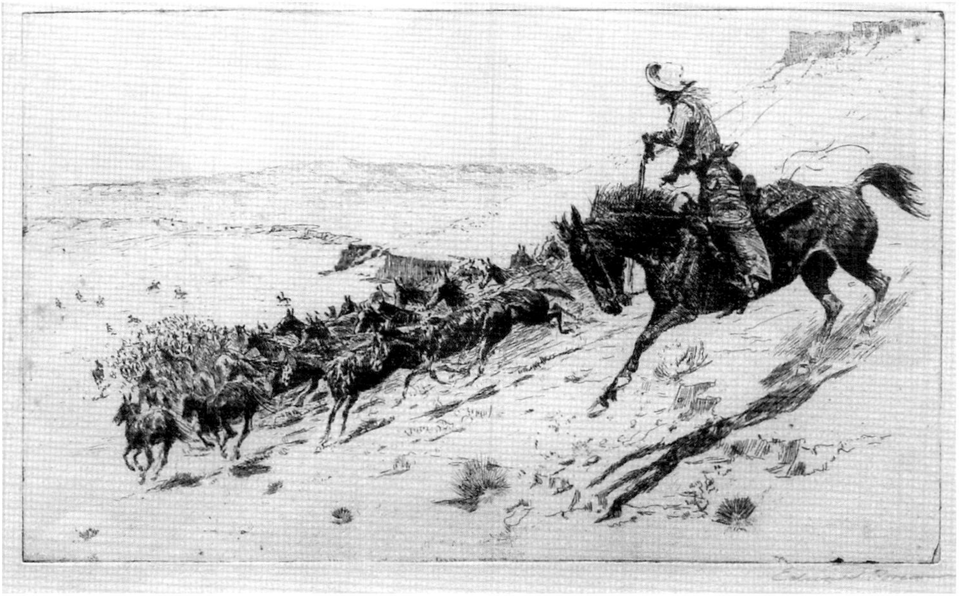

Running Wild Horses (G 49). Etching and drypoint. 6 3/4 x 10 7/8 inches (plate). Signed lower right: *Edward Borein.*

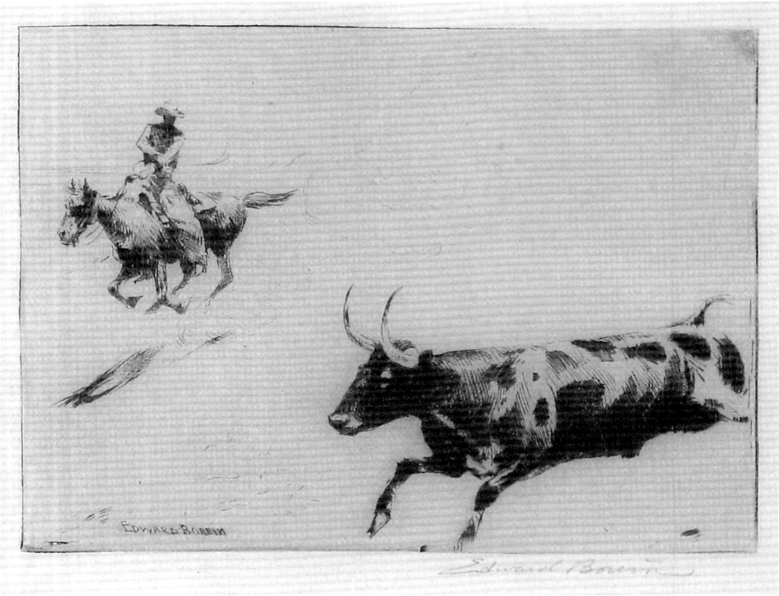

Headin' a Steer, No. 3 (G 120). Drypoint. 3 11/16 x 5 1/16 inches (plate).
Signed lower right: *Edward Borein*. Signed lower left in plate: *EDWARD BOREIN*.

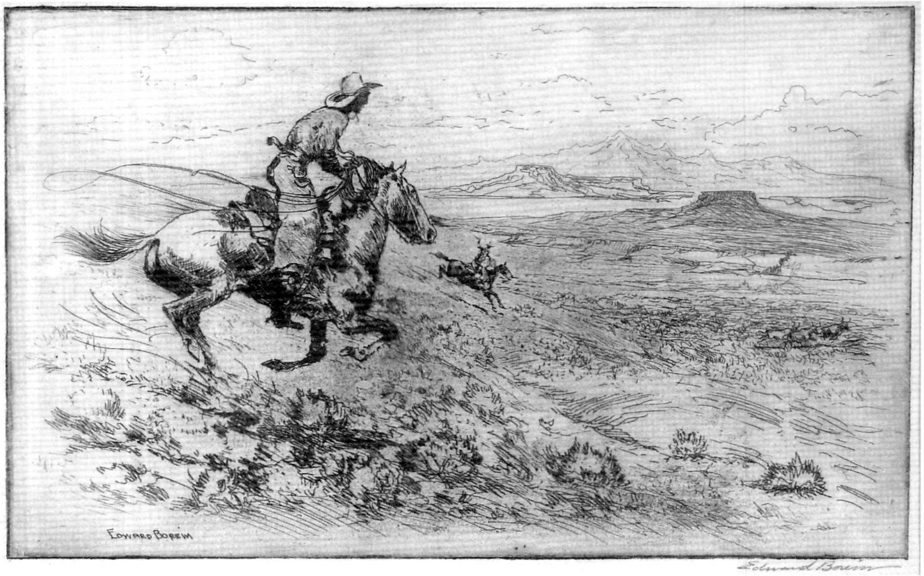

Race to the River (G 86). Etching and drypoint. 6 11/16 x 10 5/8 inches (plate).
Signed lower right: *Edward Borein*. Signed lower left in plate: *EDWARD BOREIN*.

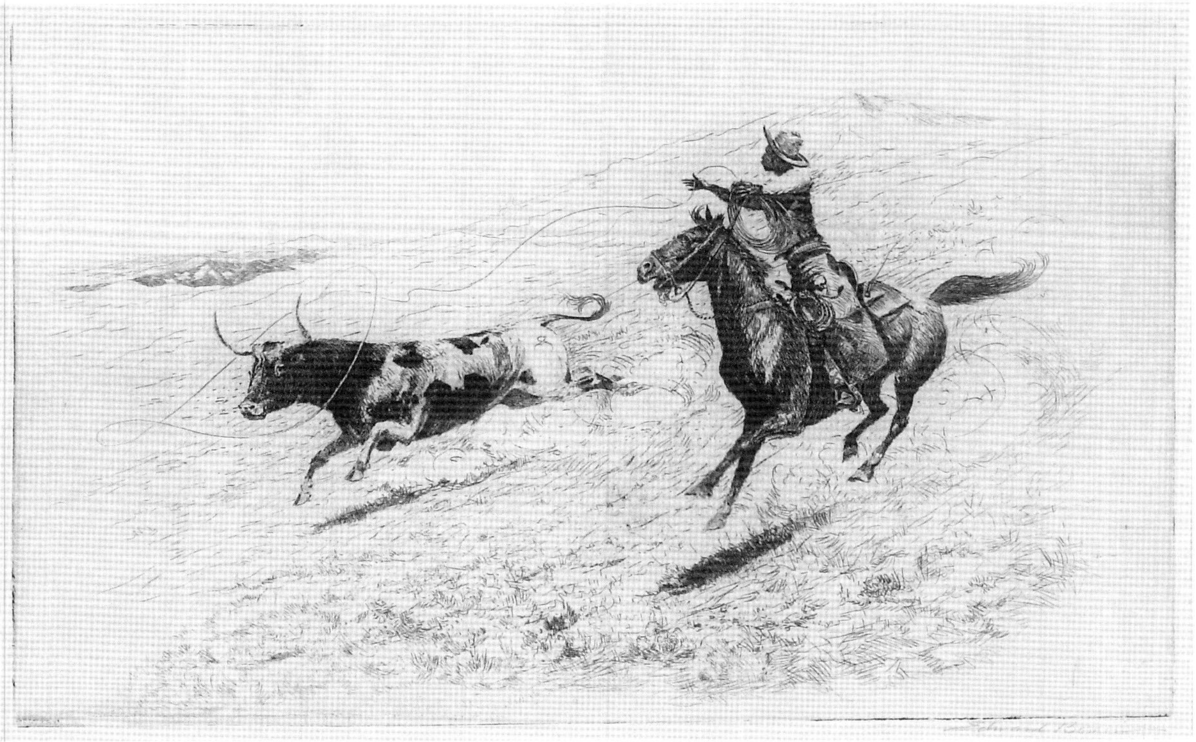

End of the Race, 2nd State (G 131). Etching and drypoint. 7 3/8 x 11 3/4 inches (plate). Signed lower right: *Edward Borein.*

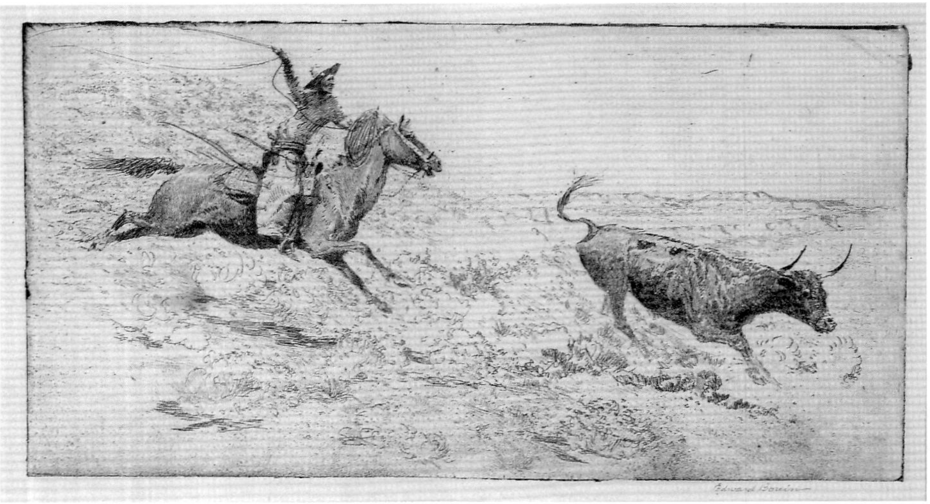

The Long Throw, 2nd State (G 125). Etching and drypoint. 5 9/16 x 10 1/2 inches (plate).
Signed lower right: *Edward Borein.*

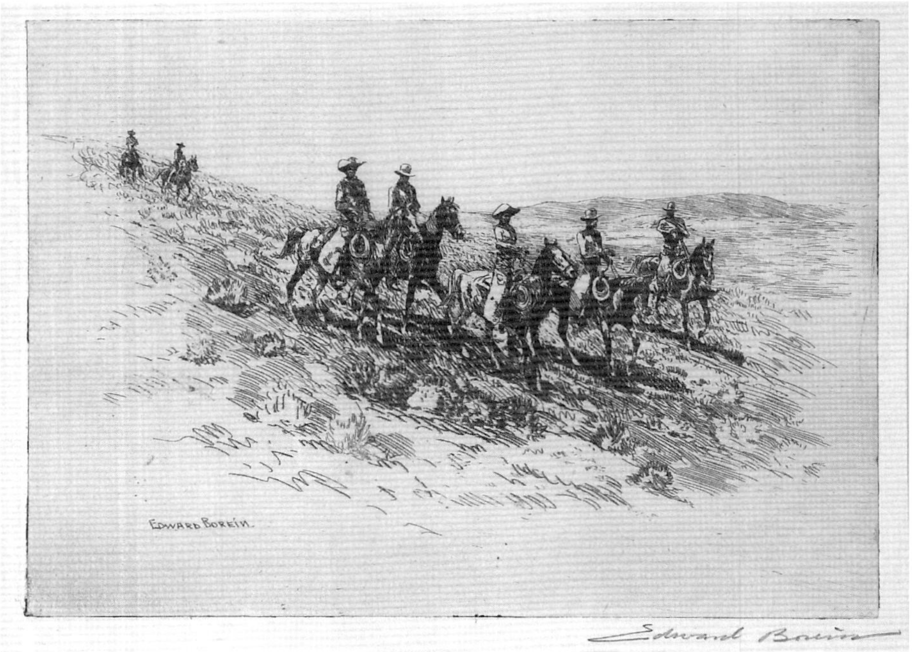

On the Move (G 33). Etching and drypoint. 4 15/16 x 6 13/16 inches (plate).
Signed lower right: *Edward Borein.* Signed lower left in plate: *EDWARD BOREIN.*

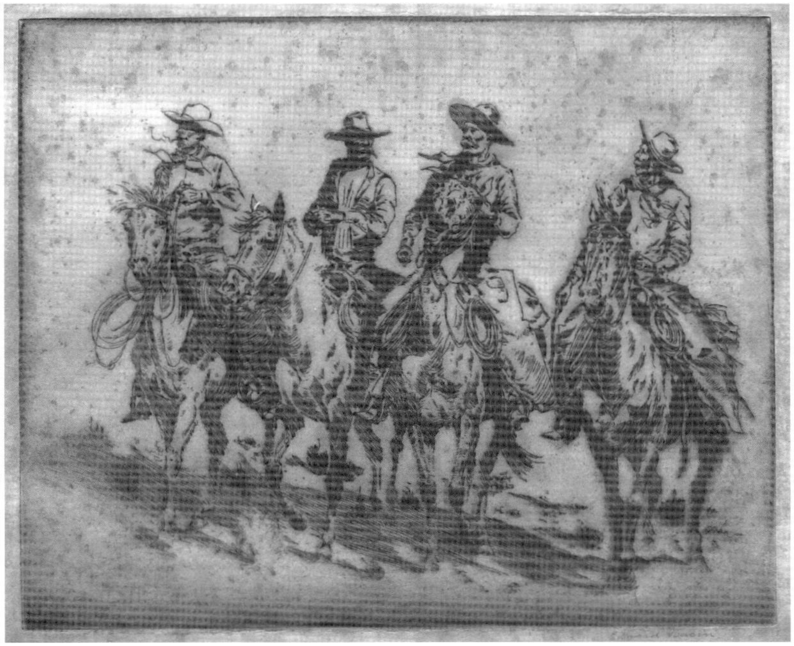

Four Horsemen, No. 2 (G 31), 1915. Etching. 10 x 11 7/8 inches.

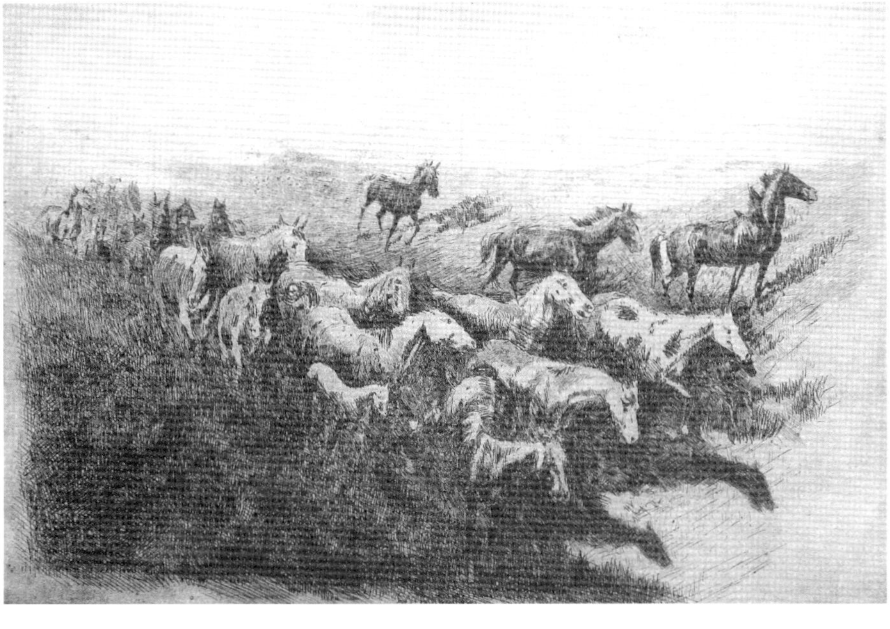

The Horseband (G 291). Etching and drypoint. 7 5/8 x 10 1/2 inches.

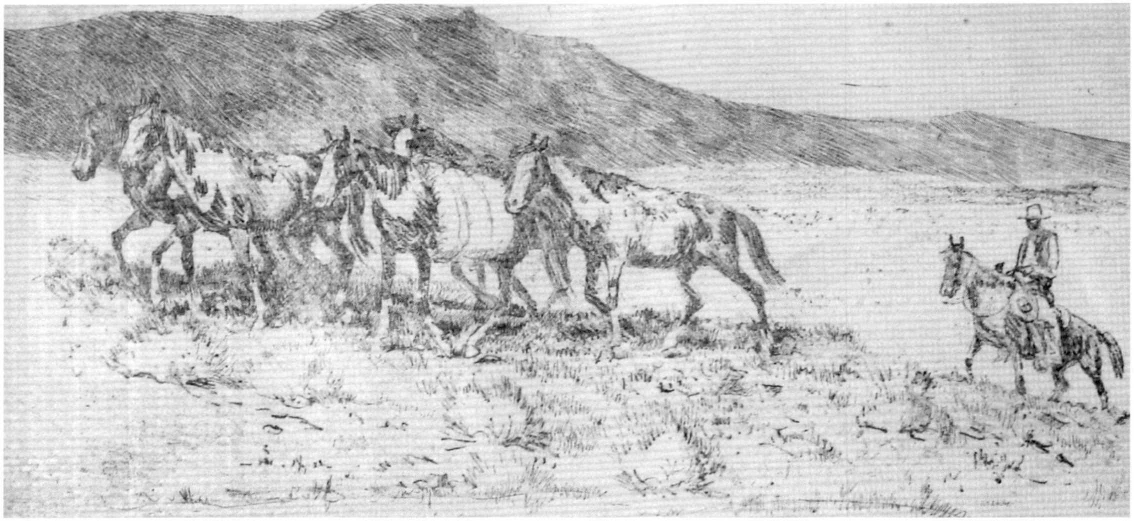

On His Way (G 288). Etching and drypoint. 4 15/16 x 8 7/8 inches (plate).

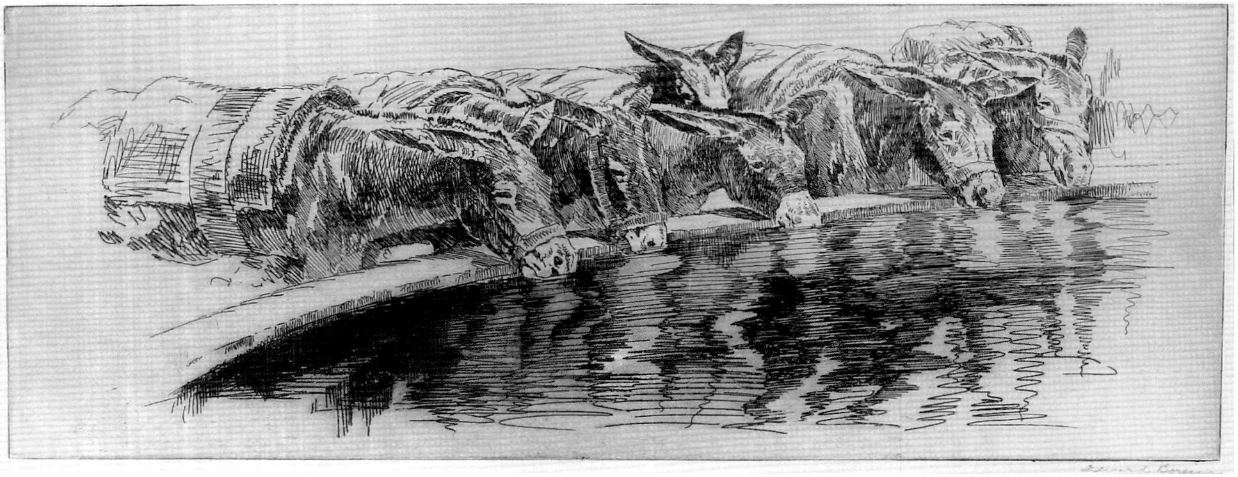

Drink Time (G 283). Etching. 6 7/8 x 17 9/16 inches (plate). Signed lower right: *Edward Borein.*

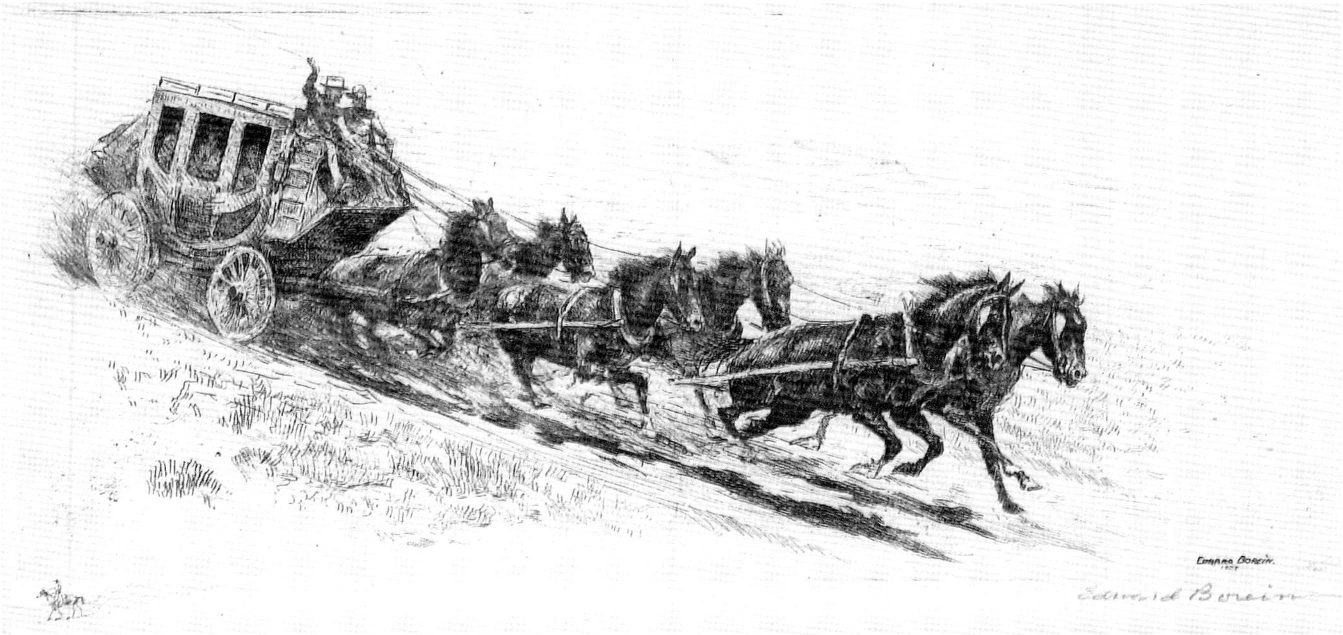

The Overland Mail, 2nd State (G 140), 1922. Etching and drypoint. 4 7/16 x 10 1/8 inches (plate).
Signed lower right: *Edward Borein*. Signed and dated lower right in plate: *EDWARD BOREIN / 1922*. Remarqued lower left.

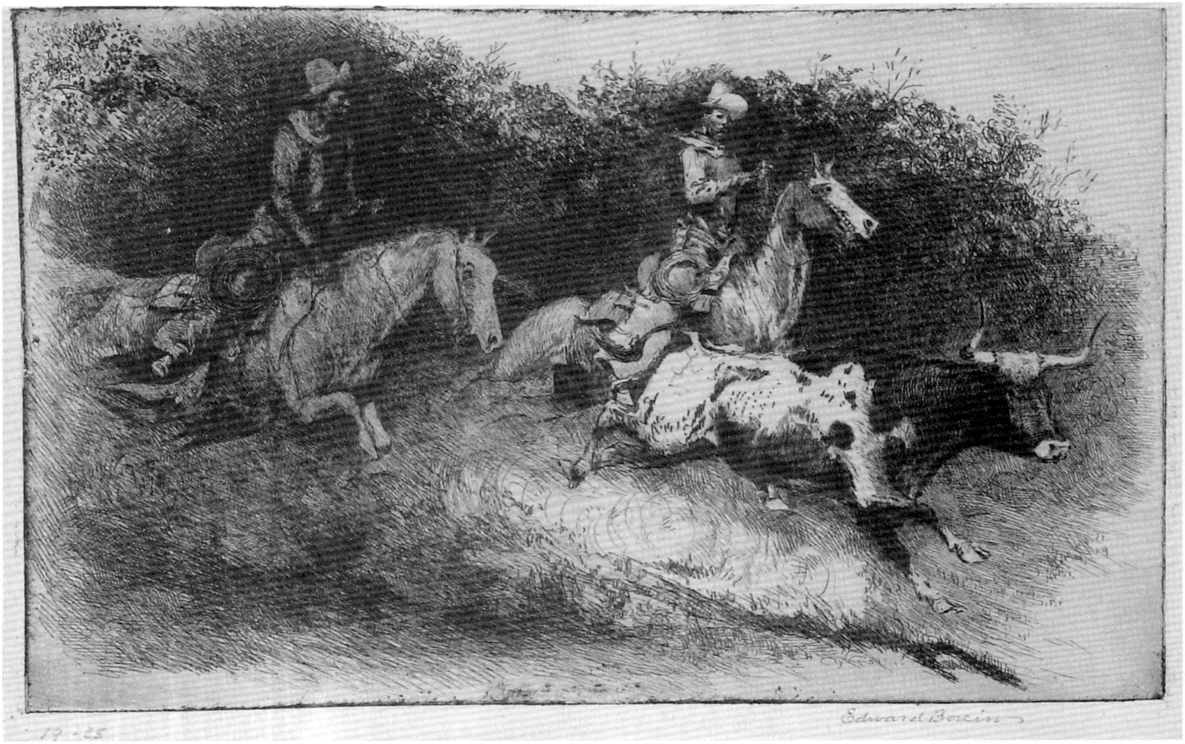

Out of the Mesquite (G 108). Etching and drypoint. 5 1/16 x 8 3/16 inches (plate).
Signed lower right: *Edward Borein*. Dated lower left: *1925*.

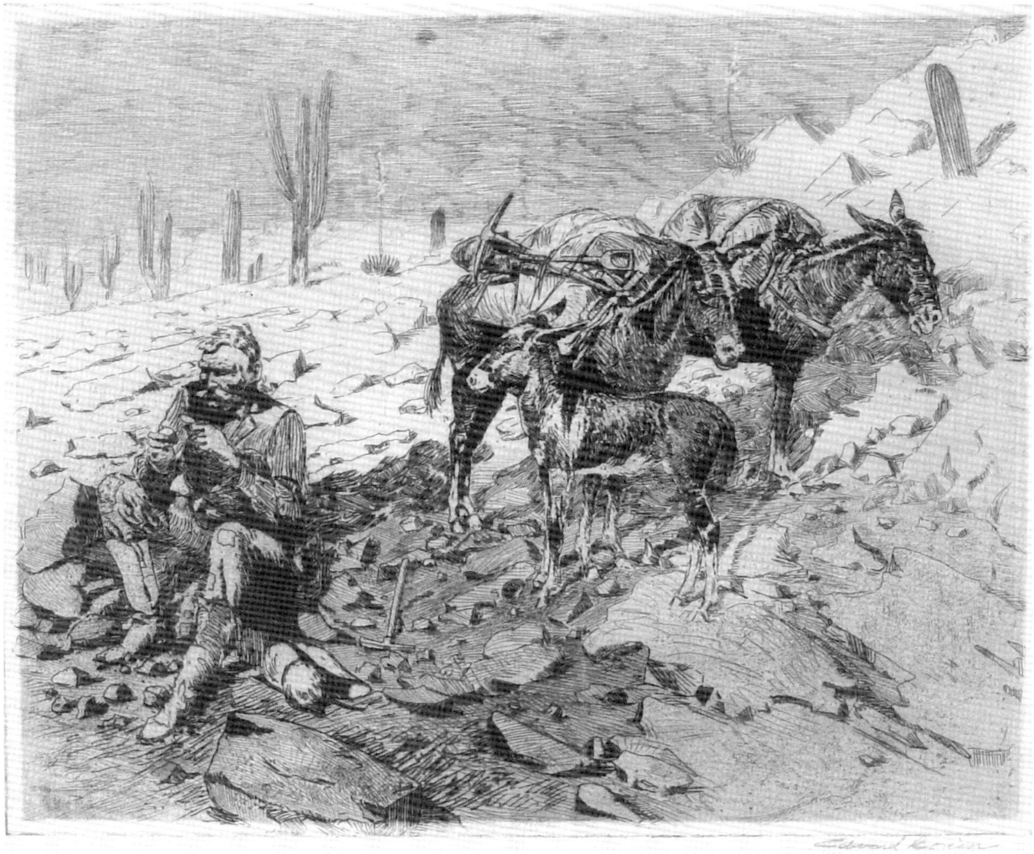

The Prospector (G 279). Etching and drypoint. 9 7/8 x 11 7/8 inches (plate). Signed lower right: *Edward Borein.*

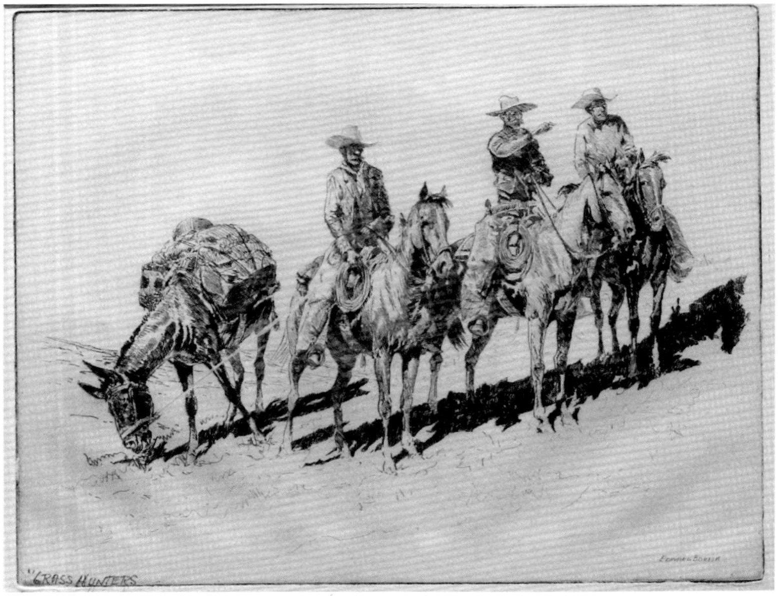

Grass Hunters, No. 1 (G 28). Etching and drypoint. 7 7/8 x 9 7/8 inches (plate).
Signed lower right in plate: *EDWARD BOREIN*. Inscribed lower left: *Grass Hunters*.

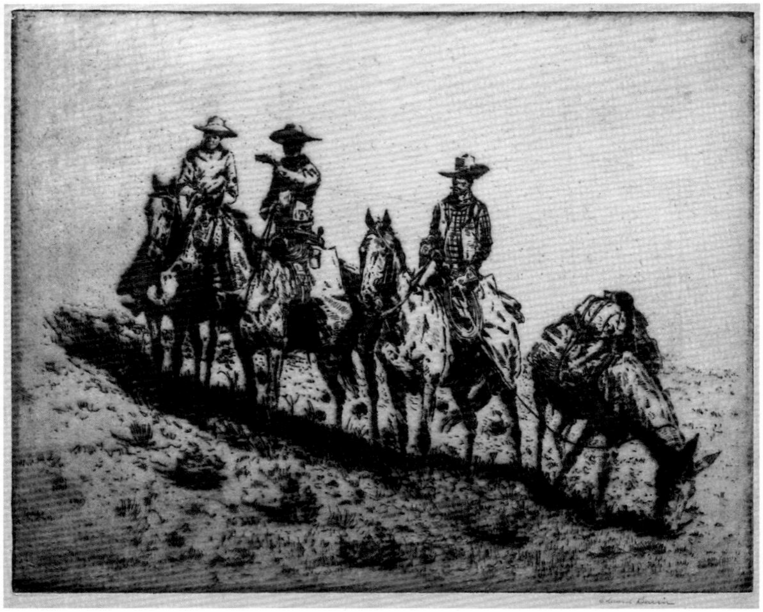

Grass Hunters, No. 2 (G 29). Etching. 7 15/16 x 9 15/16 inches (plate). Signed lower right: *Edward Borein*.

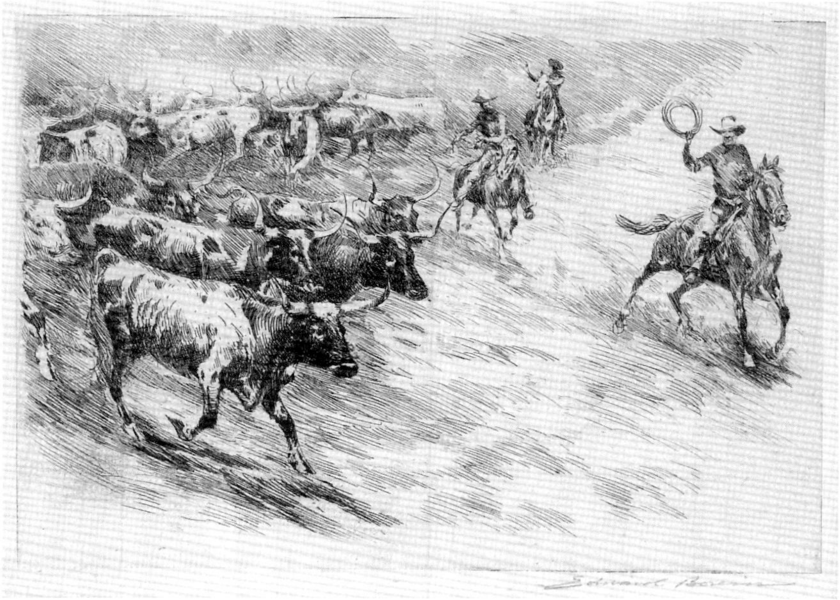

Headin' Em In (G 98). Etching and drypoint. 4 15/16 x 6 15/16 inches (plate). Signed lower right: *Edward Borein.*

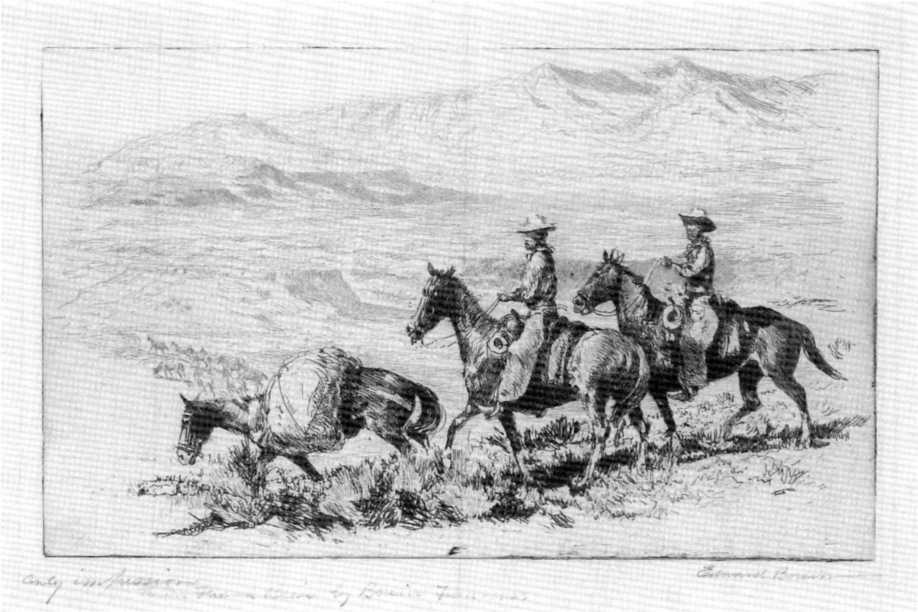

On Their Way (G 11). Etching and drypoint. 4 15/16 x 7 13/16 inches (plate). Signed lower right: *Edward Borein.* Inscribed lower left: *only impression / To Mr Frank Bliss by Borein Feb 10-1925.*

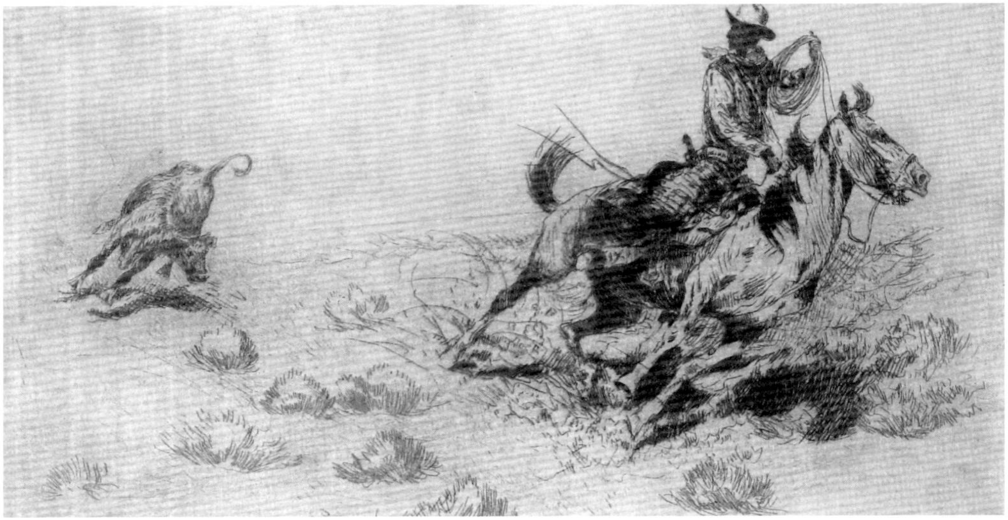

Roped Steer, No. 1 (G 133). Etching and drypoint. 4 3/8 x 7 15/16 inches (plate).

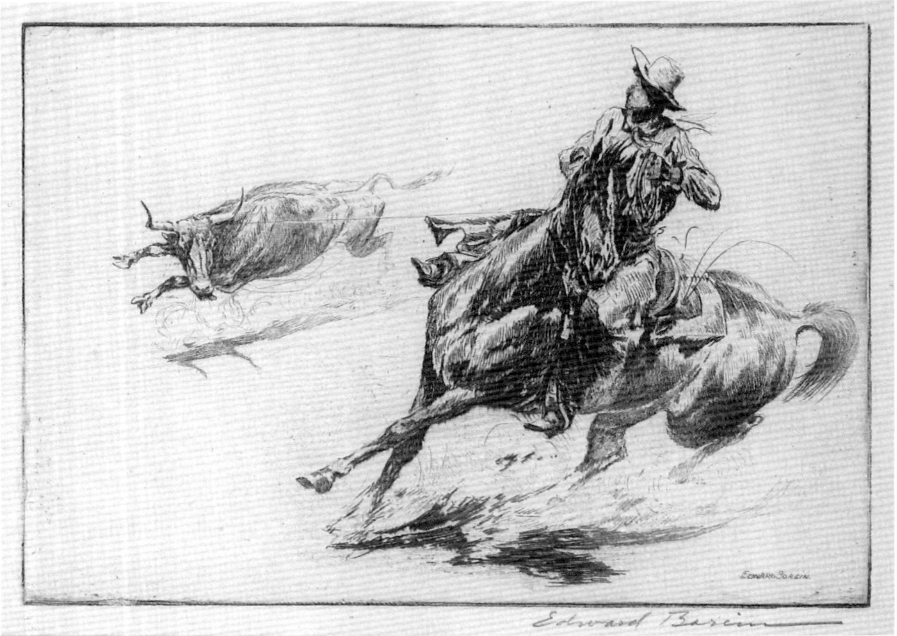

Roped Steer, No. 2 (G 134). Etching and drypoint. 4 15/16 x 6 15/16 inches (plate). Signed lower right: *Edward Borein.* Signed lower right in plate: *EDWARD BOREIN.*

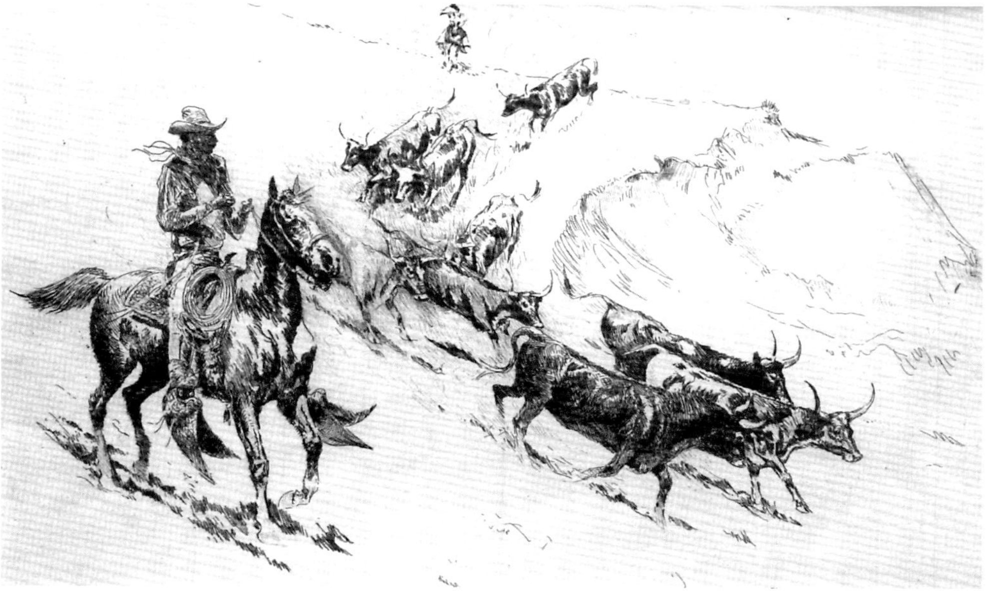

Rounding Up Cattle (D 30). Etching. 7 1/2 x 11 7/8 inches (sight).

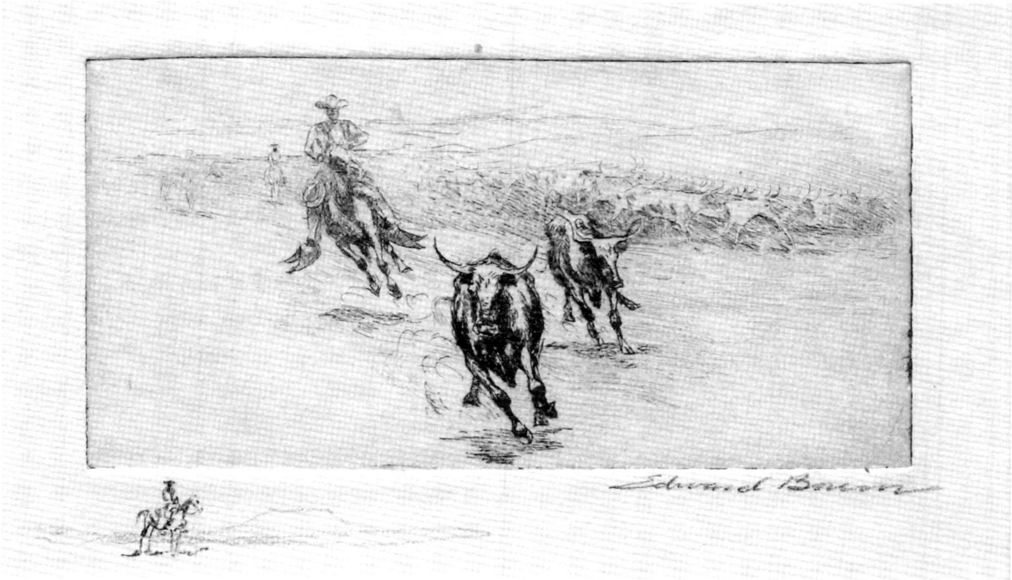

Parting the Herd (G 113). Etching and drypoint. 2 3/8 x 4 5/8 inches (plate). Signed lower right: *Edward Borein.* Remarqued lower left.

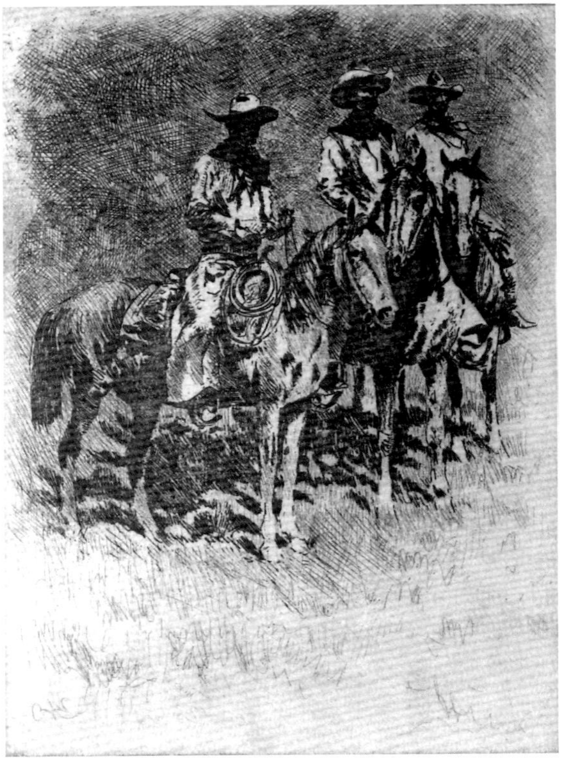

The Meeting (G 287). Etching and drypoint. 7 x 5 inches (plate).

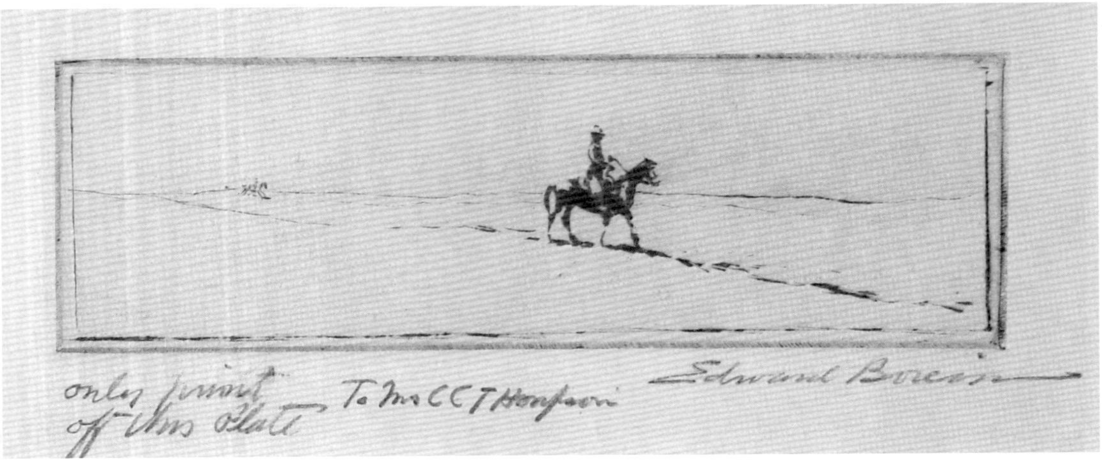

A Presentation (Lone Rider on Plain) (D 12). Etching. 1 1/8 x 3 1/2 inches (plate). Signed lower right: *Edward Borein.* Inscribed lower left: *only print off this plate.* Inscribed lower center: *To Mr CCT Honfson.*

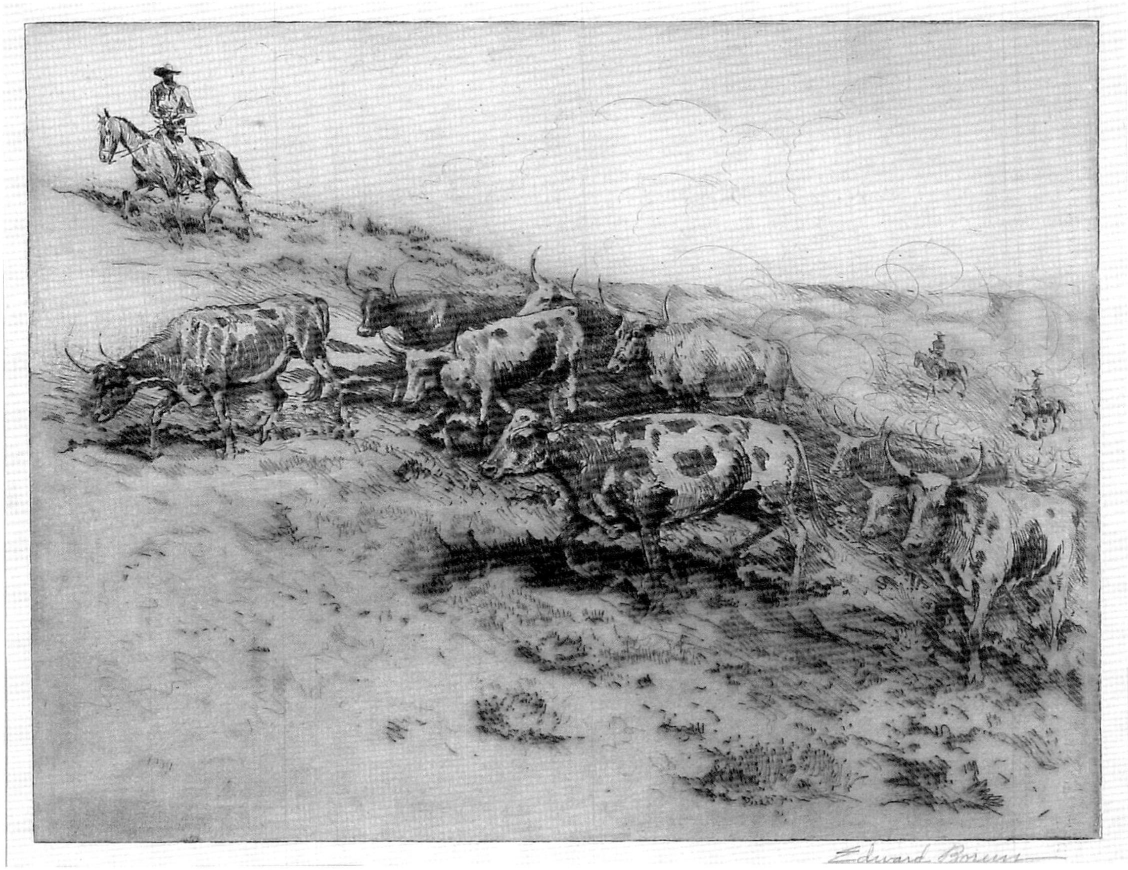

Little Trail Herd (G 94). Etching and drypoint. 7 13/16 x 9 7/8 inches (plate). Signed lower right: *Edward Borein.*

INDIANS

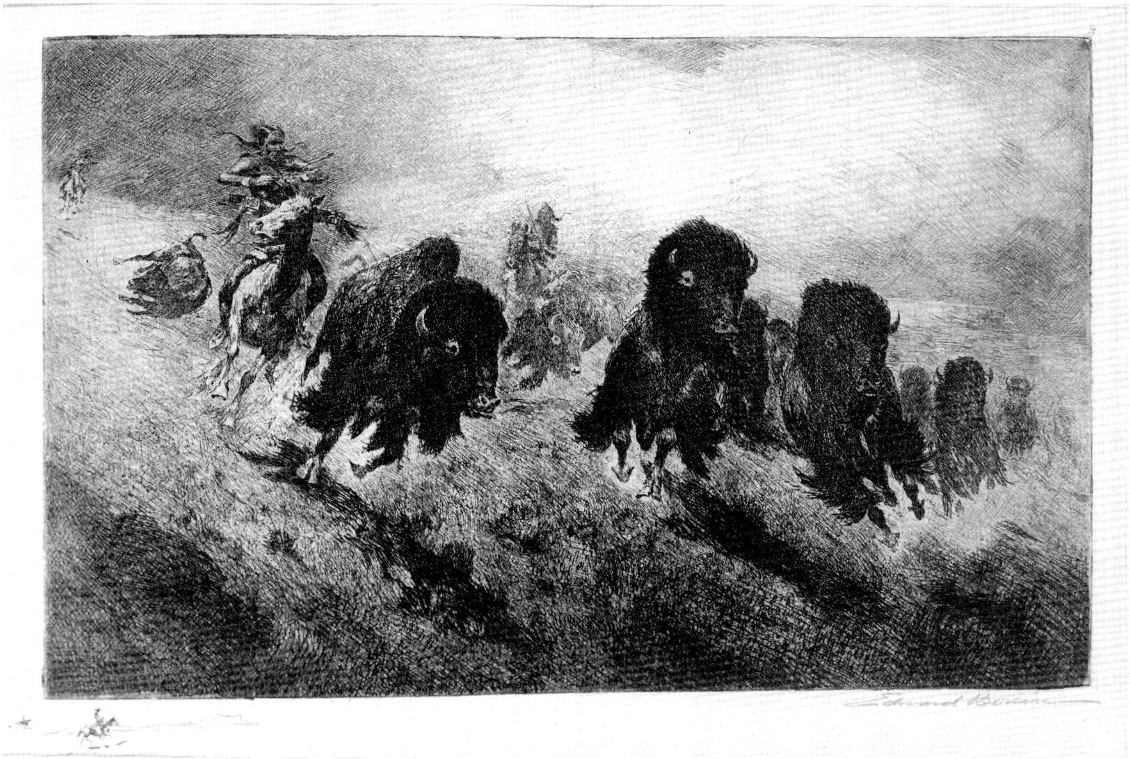

Robes and Meat (G 178). Etching and drypoint. 6 1/8 x 9 7/16 inches (plate).
Signed lower right: *Edward Borein*. Remarqued lower left.

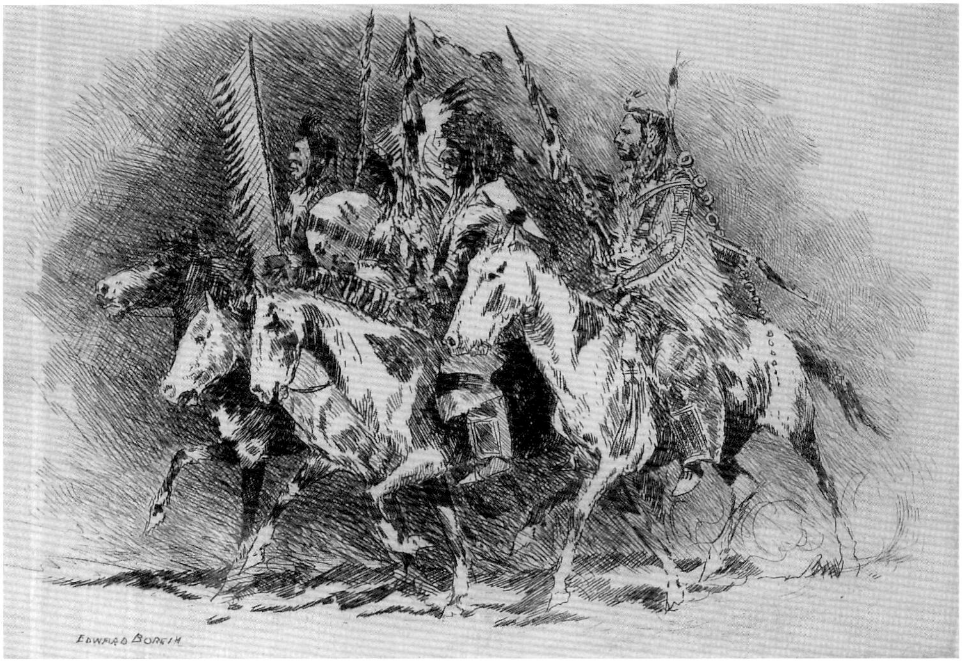

Horse Indians, No. 1 (G 155). Etching and drypoint. 4 15/16 x 7 inches (plate).
Signed lower left in plate: *EDWARD BOREIN.*

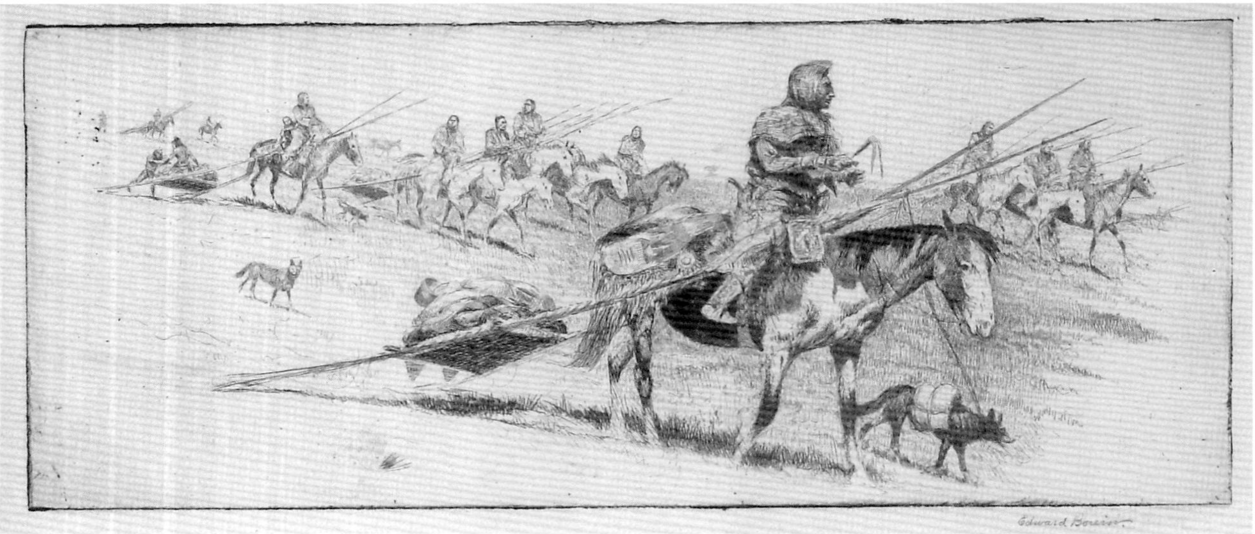

Blackfoot Women Moving Camp, No. 1 (G 168). Etching and drypoint. 3 15/16 x 9 7/16 inches (plate).
Signed lower right: *Edward Borein.*

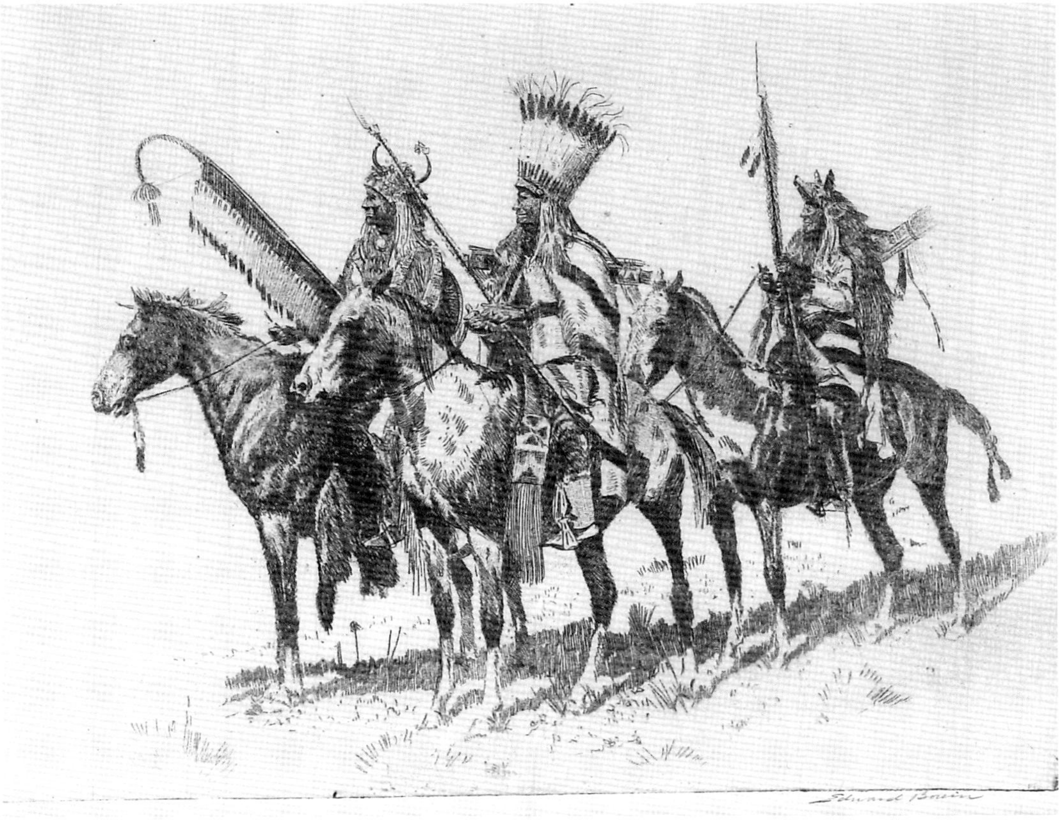

Blackfoot Chief, No. 2 (G 166). Etching and drypoint. 5 5/8 x 11 1/16 inches (plate). Signed lower right: *Edward Borein.*

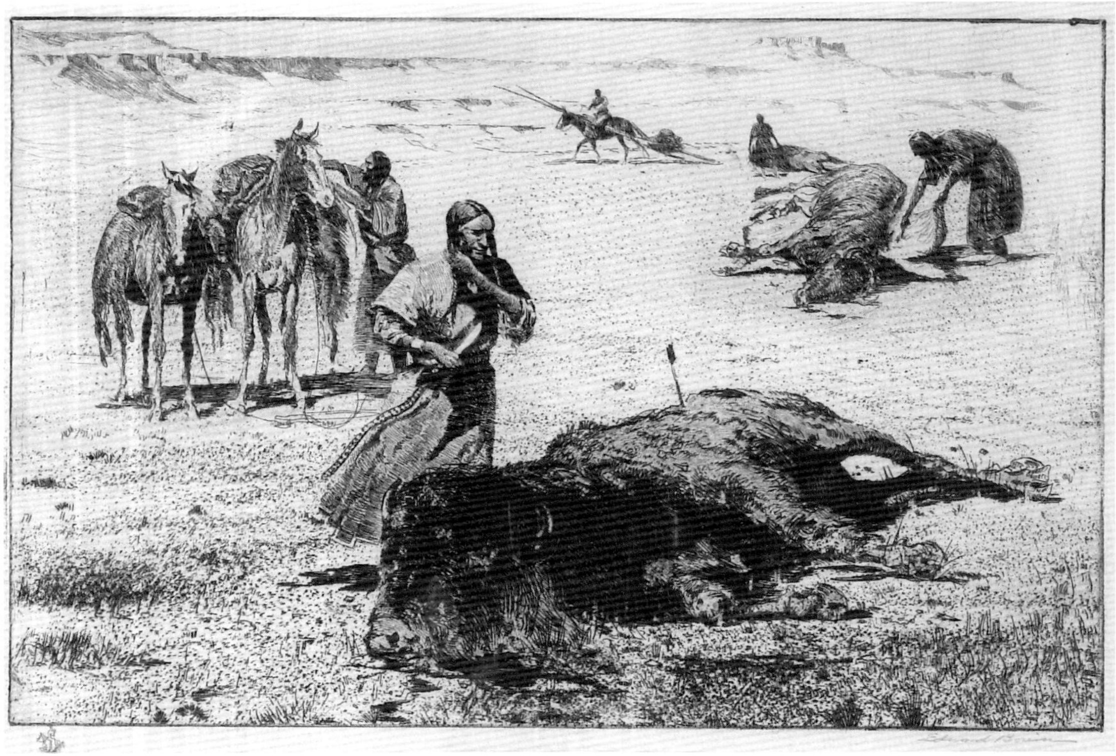

After the Buffalo Hunt (G 180). Etching and drypoint. 7 15/16 x 11 3/4 inches (plate).
Signed lower right: *Edward Borein*. Remarqued lower left.

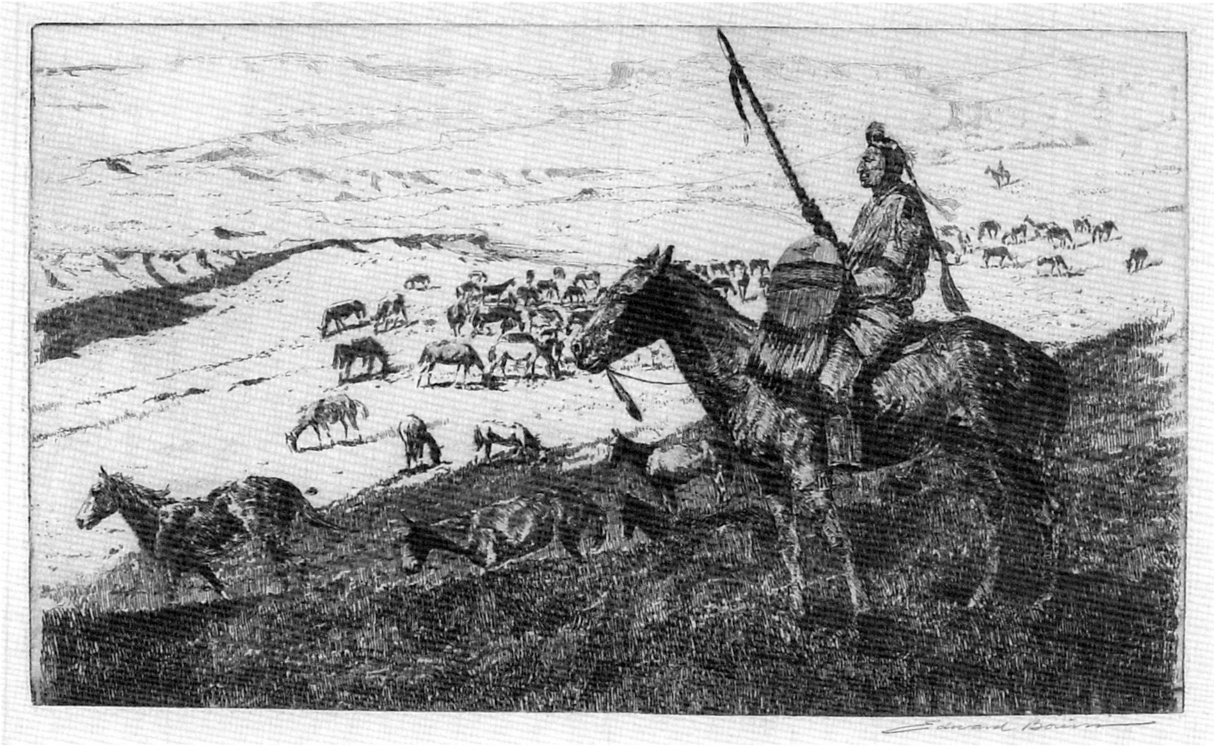

Crow Horse Guard (G 163). Etching and drypoint. 6 11/16 x 10 7/8 inches (plate). Signed lower right: *Edward Borein.*

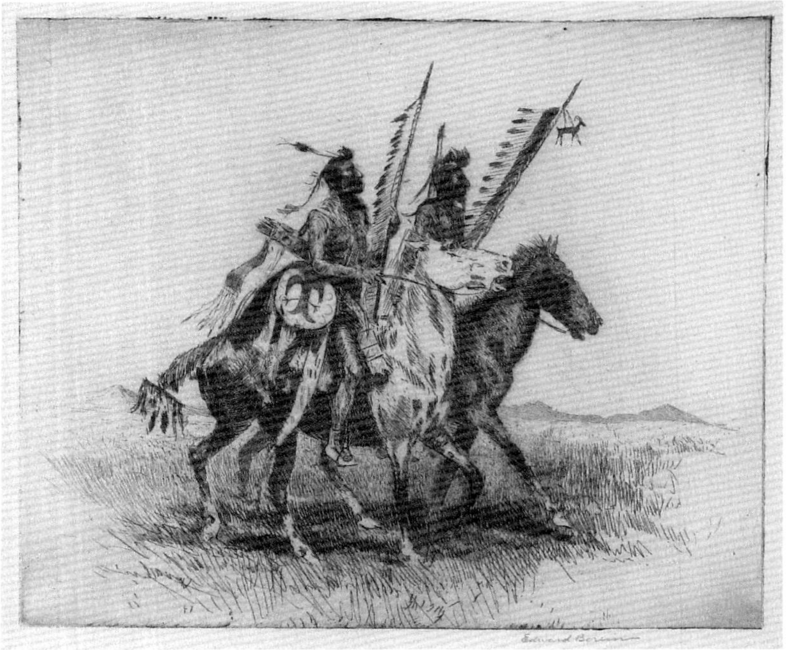

Going to the Dance, No. 2 (G 154). Etching and drypoint. 5 13/16 x 6 15/16 inches (plate).
Signed lower right: *Edward Borein.*

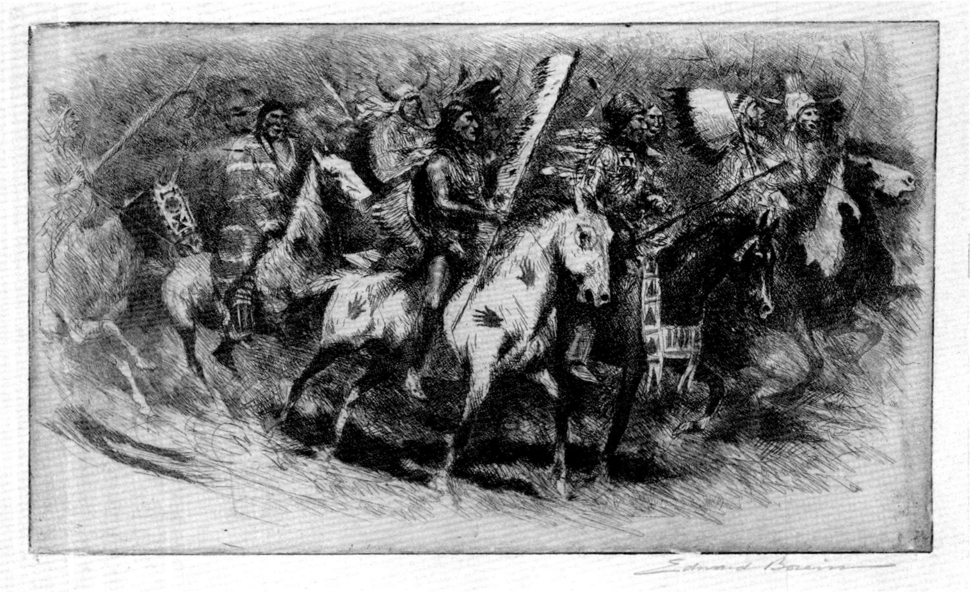

Umatilla Horse Dance (G 164). Etching and drypoint. 5 1/4 x 8 13/16 inches (plate). Signed lower right: *Edward Borein.*

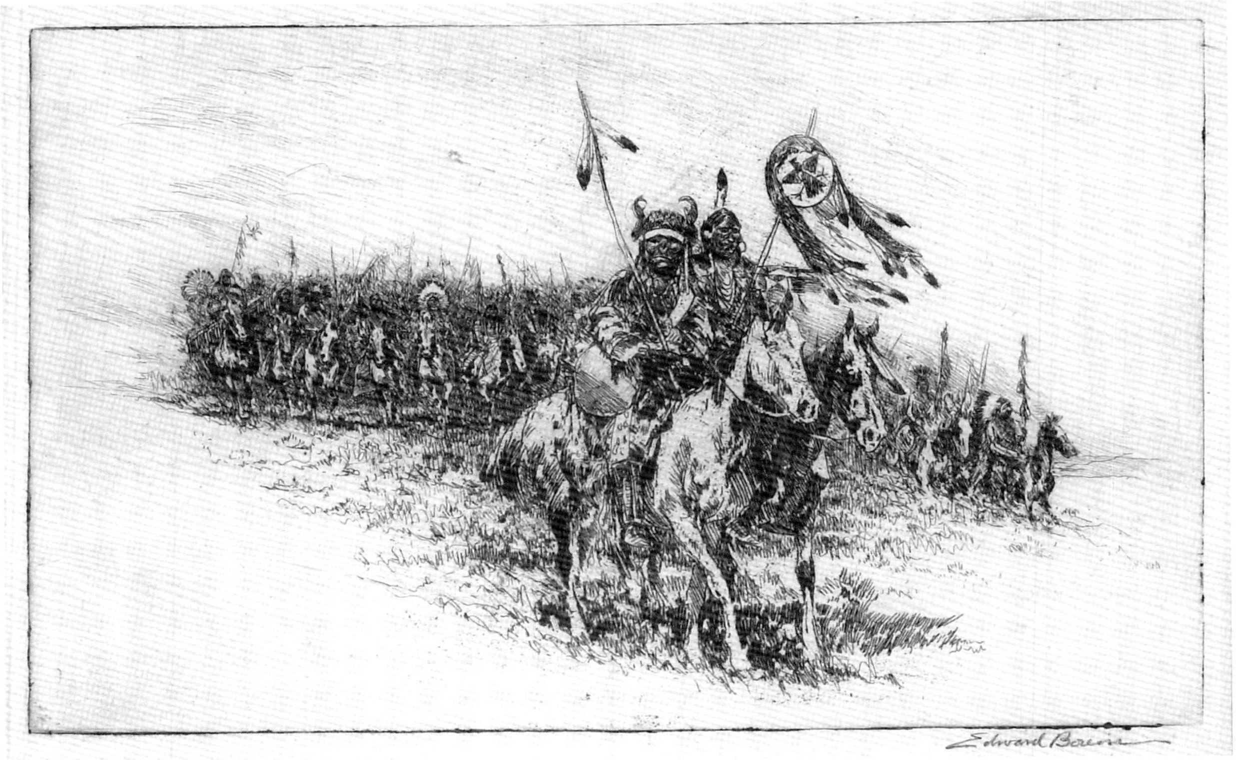

Preparing to Charge (G 310). Etching and drypoint. 6 3/16 x 9 15/16 inches (plate). Signed lower right: *Edward Borein.*

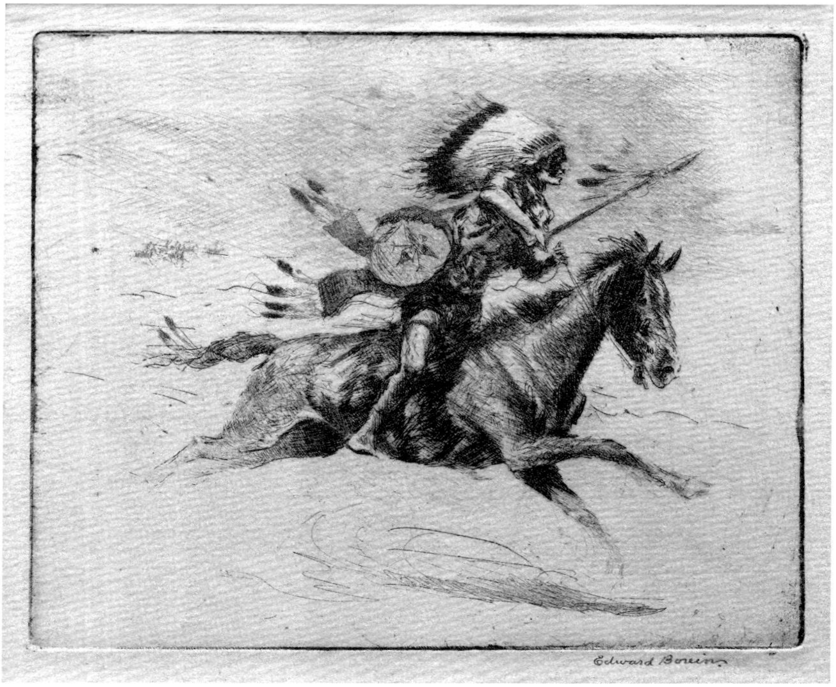

Charging Hawk (G 156). Etching and drypoint. 4 3/8 x 5 3/8 inches (plate). Signed lower right: *Edward Borein.*

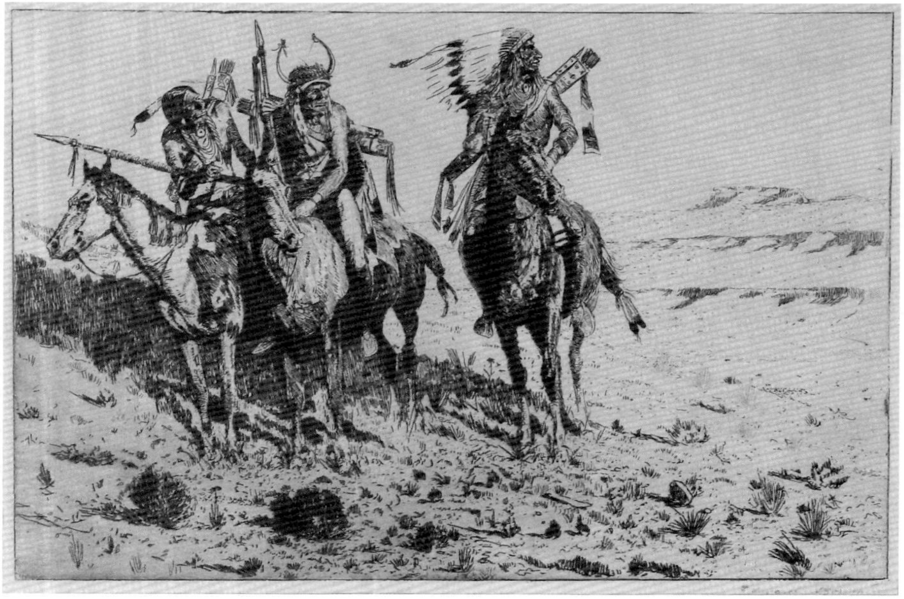

Sioux Chief (G 159). Etching and drypoint. 7 7/8 x 11 7/8 inches (plate). Signed lower right: *Edward Borein.*

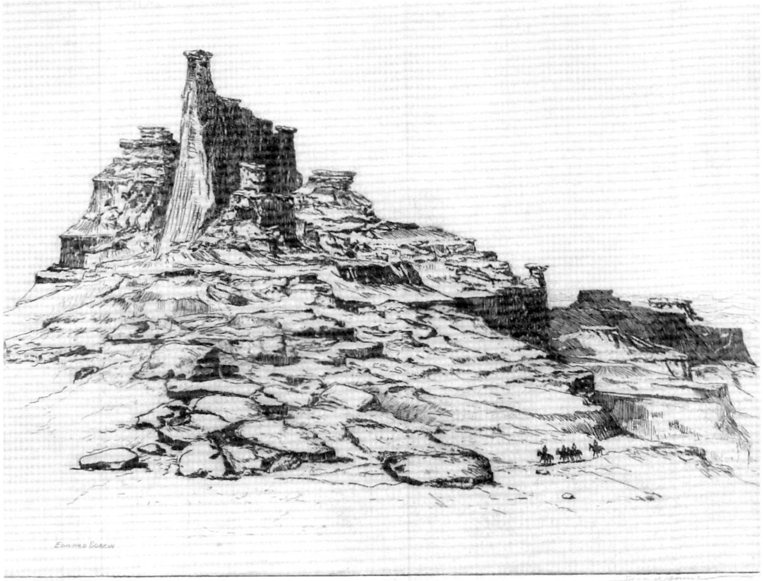

Navajo Land (G 203). Etching and drypoint. 10 7/8 x 13 5/8 inches (plate). Signed lower right: *Edward Borein.* Signed lower left in plate: *EDWARD BOREIN.*

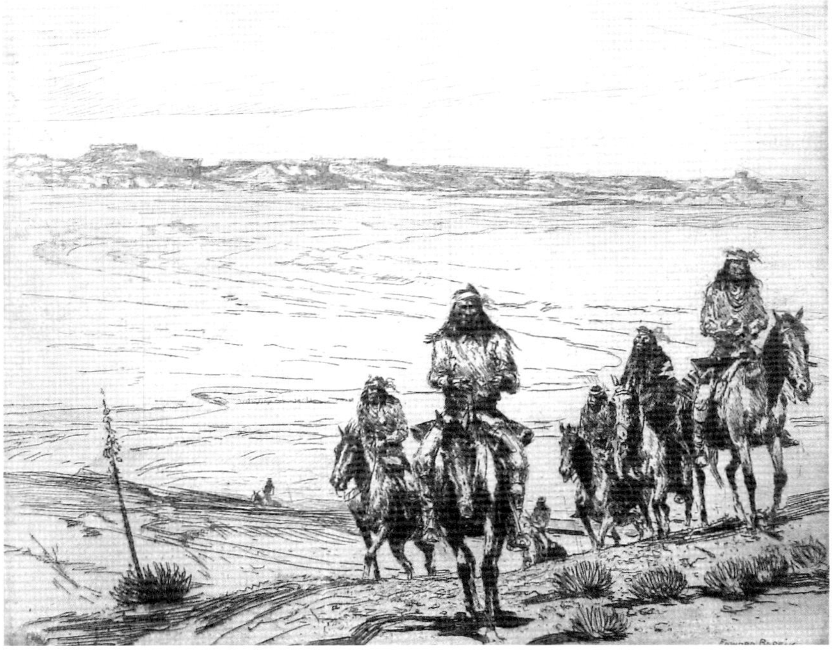

Tonto Apaches (G 172). Etching and drypoint. 5 5/8 x 6 3/4 inches (plate). Signed lower right in plate: *EDWARD BOREIN.*

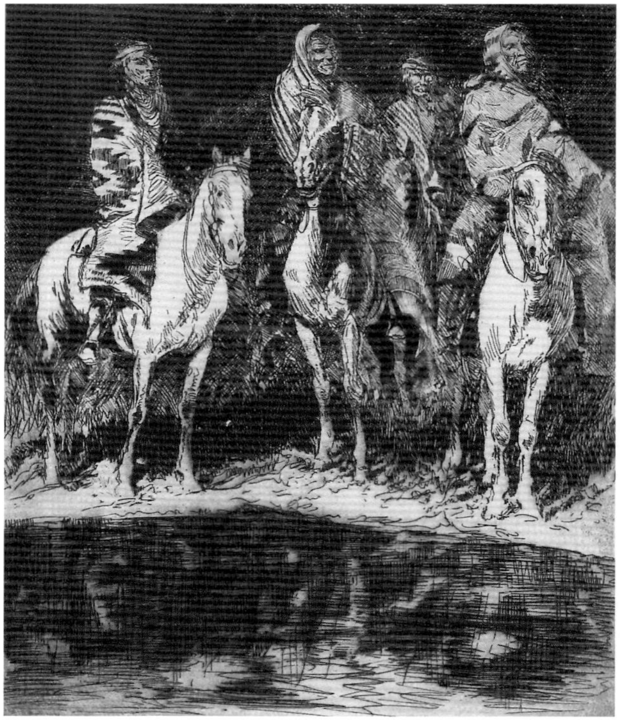

Navajos at the Water Hole, No. 1 (G 181). Etching. 11 15/16 x 9 15/16 inches (plate).

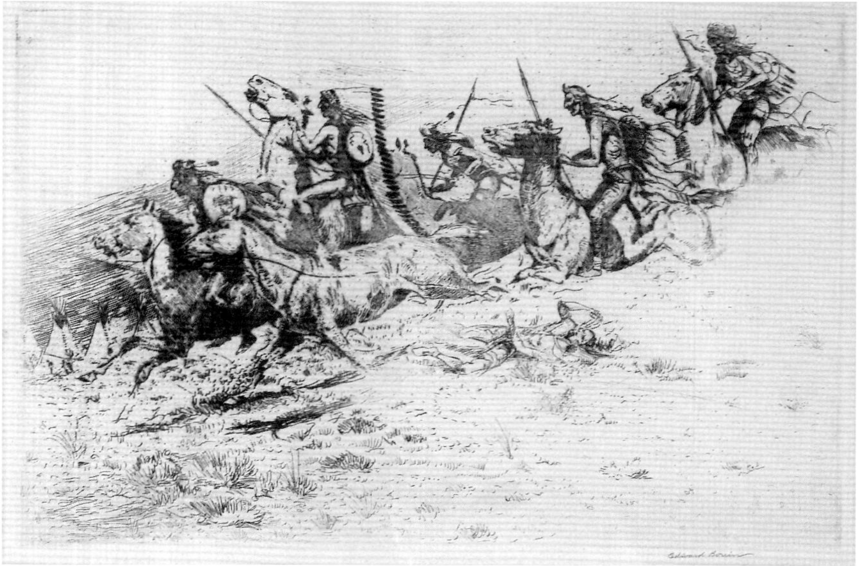

The Cheyenne Raid, 1st State (G 157). Etching and drypoint. 7 7/8 x 11 7/8 inches (plate). Signed lower right: *Edward Borein.*

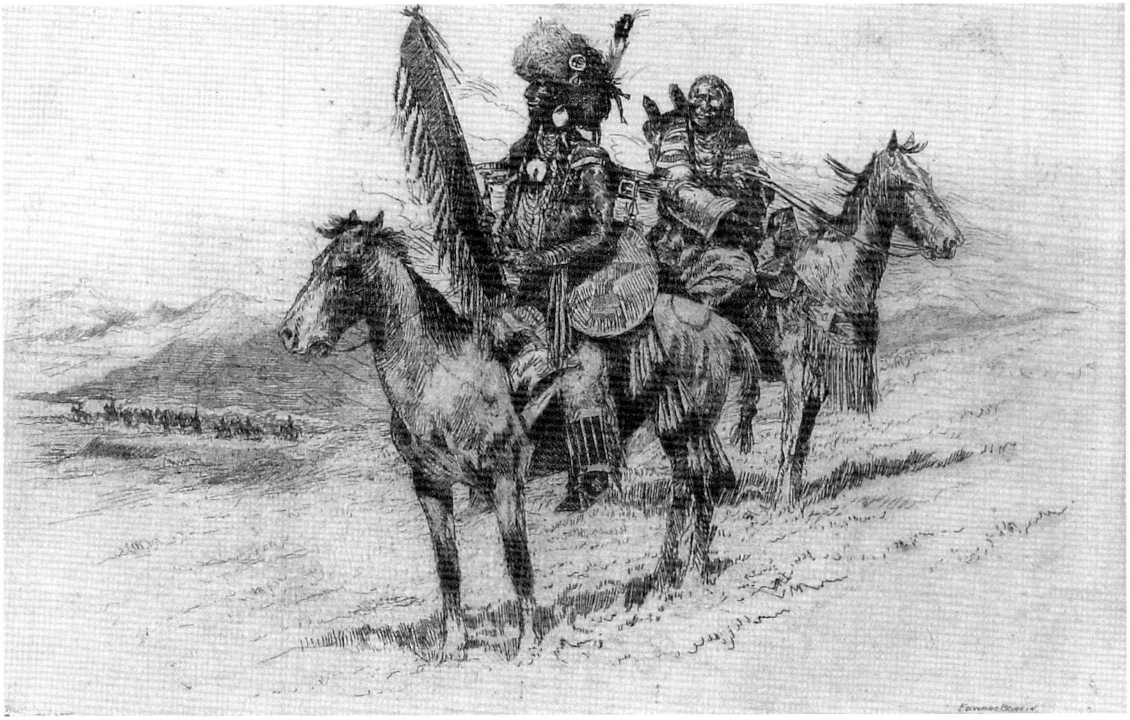

Flathead Indians (G 173). Etching. 5 13/16 x 9 inches (plate). Signed lower right in plate: *EDWARD BOREIN.*

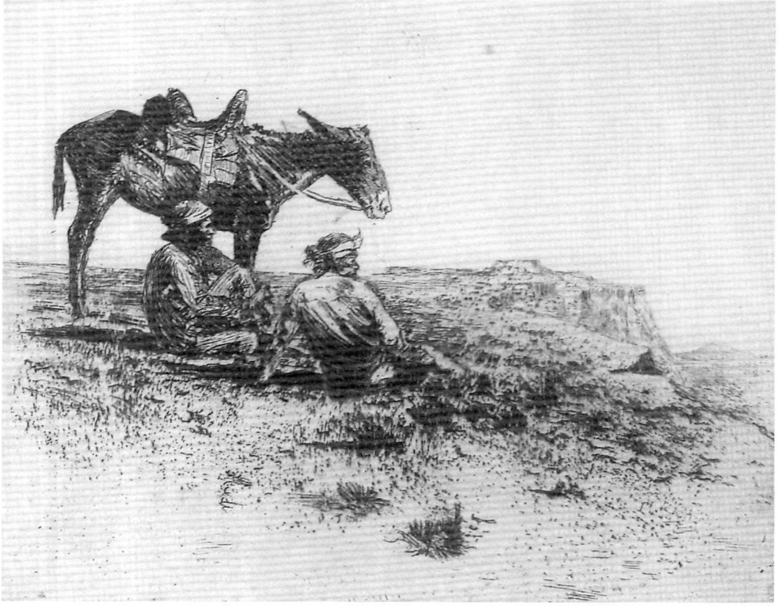

Hopi Boys, 2nd State (G 187). Etching and drypoint. 5 1/2 x 6 7/8 inches (plate).

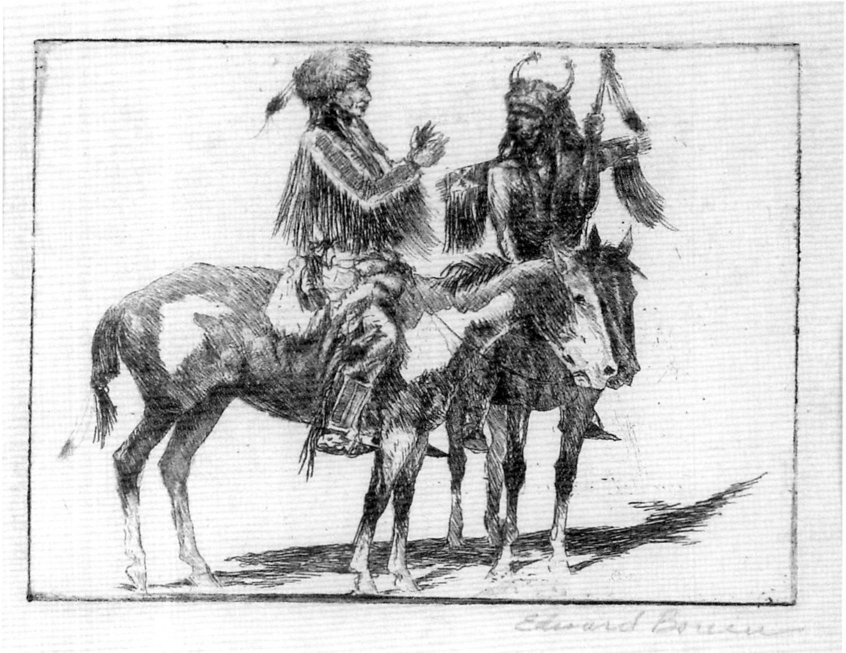

Sign Talk, No. 1 (G 175). Drypoint. 2 9/16 x 3 3/8 inches (plate). Signed lower right: *Edward Borein.*

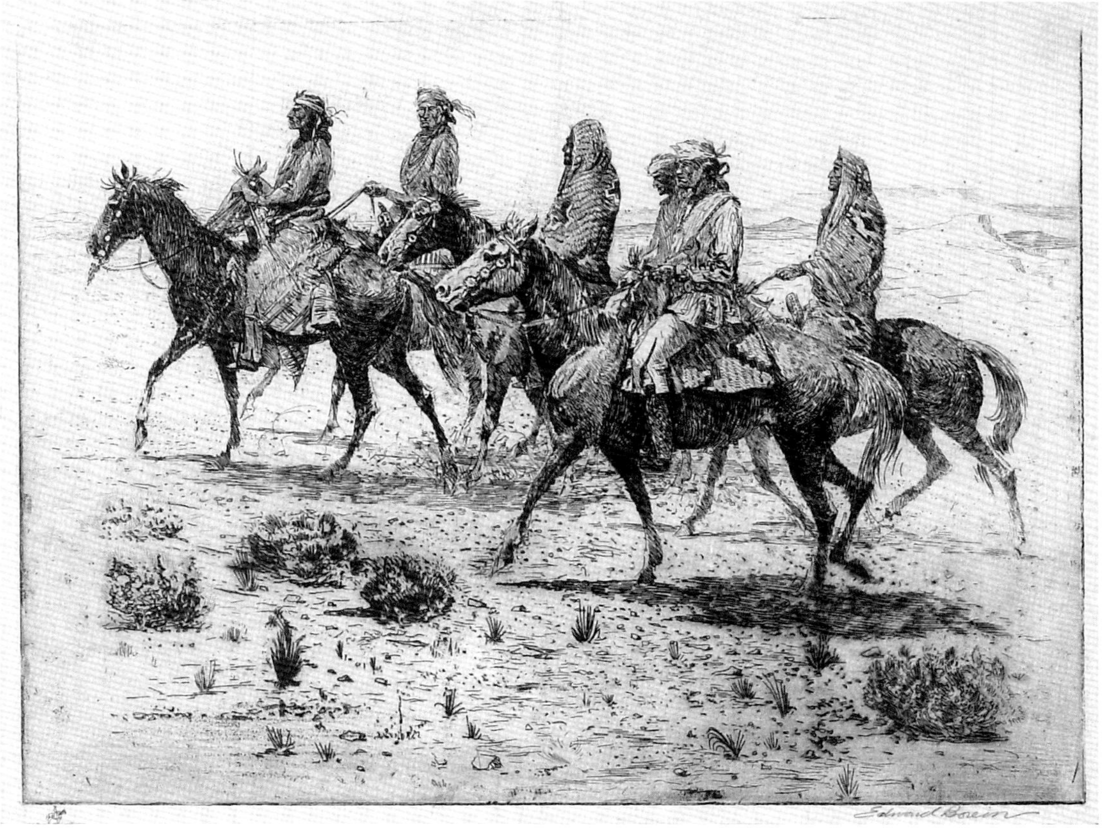

Navajos (G 183). Etching and drypoint. 9 1/4 x 12 1/8 inches (plate). Signed lower right: *Edward Borein*. Remarqued lower left.

COWBOYS

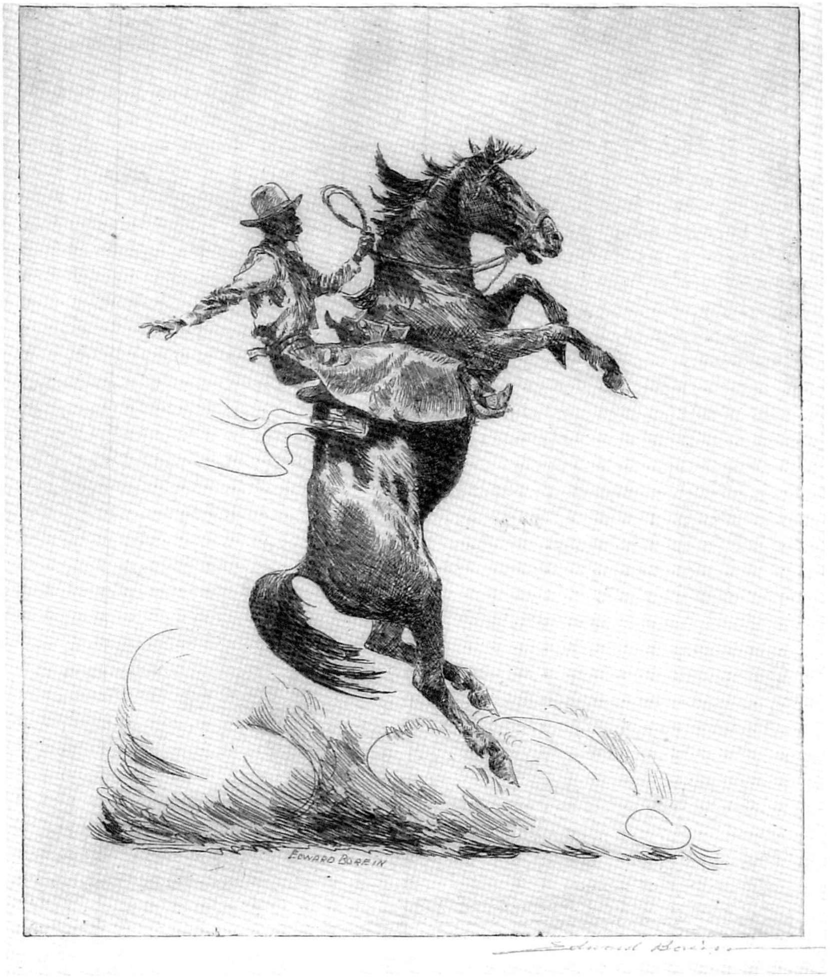

Cinch Binder (G 55). Etching and drypoint. 9 13/16 x 8 inches (plate). Signed lower right: *Edward Borein.* Signed lower left center in plate: *EDWARD BOREIN.*

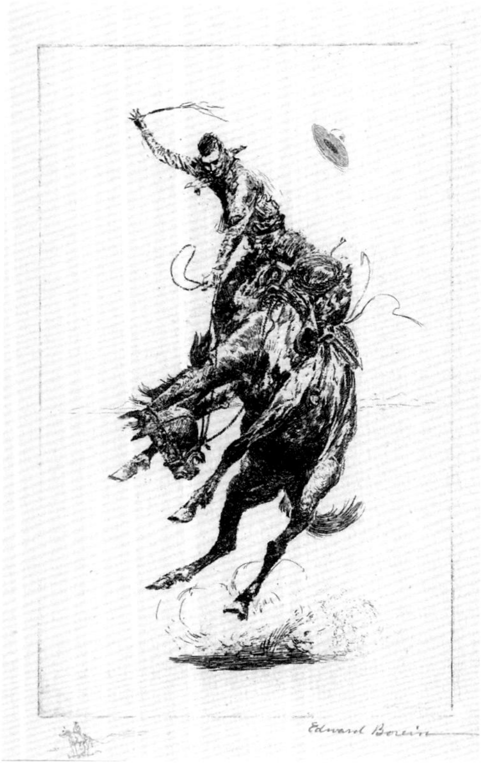

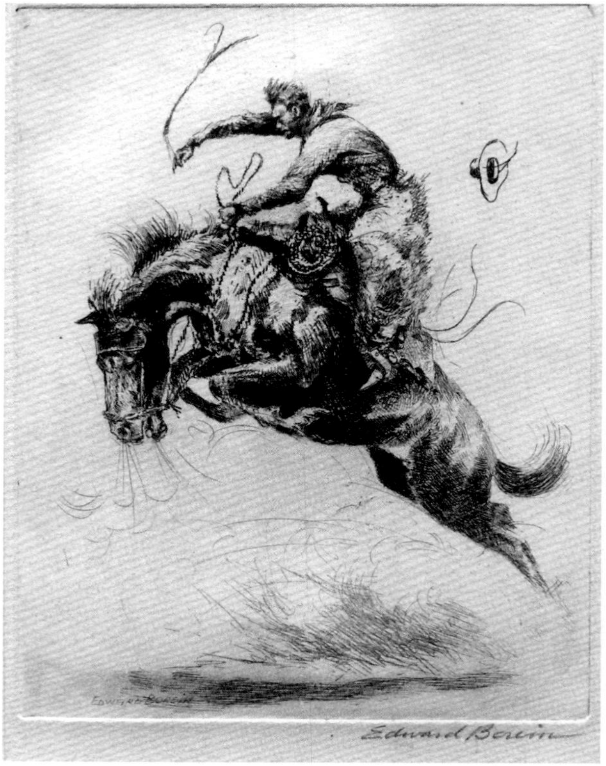

Left: *Scratchin' High* (G 69). Etching and drypoint. 7 7/8 x 4 5/8 inches (plate). Signed lower right: *Edward Borein.* Remarqued lower left.

Right: *Bronc Peeler* (G 75). Etching and drypoint. 5 5/8 x 4 3/8 inches (plate). Signed lower right: *Edward Borein.* Signed lower left in plate: *EDWARD BOREIN.*

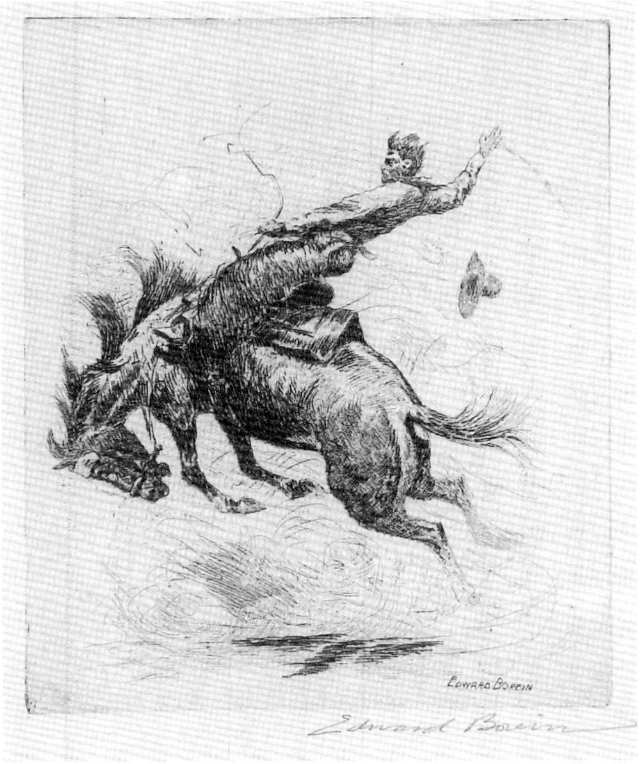

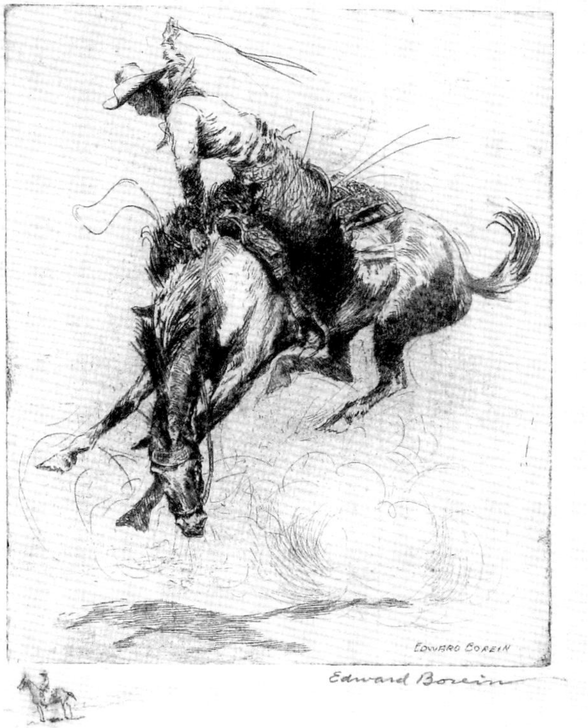

Left: *High Wide and Handsome* (G 76). Etching and drypoint. 4 13/16 x 4 inches (plate). Signed lower right: *Edward Borein*. Signed lower right in plate: *EDWARD BOREIN*.

Right: *Who Wins?* (G 63). Etching and drypoint. 4 15/16 x 4 inches (plate). Signed lower right: *Edward Borein*. Signed lower right in plate: *EDWARD BOREIN*. Remarqued lower left.

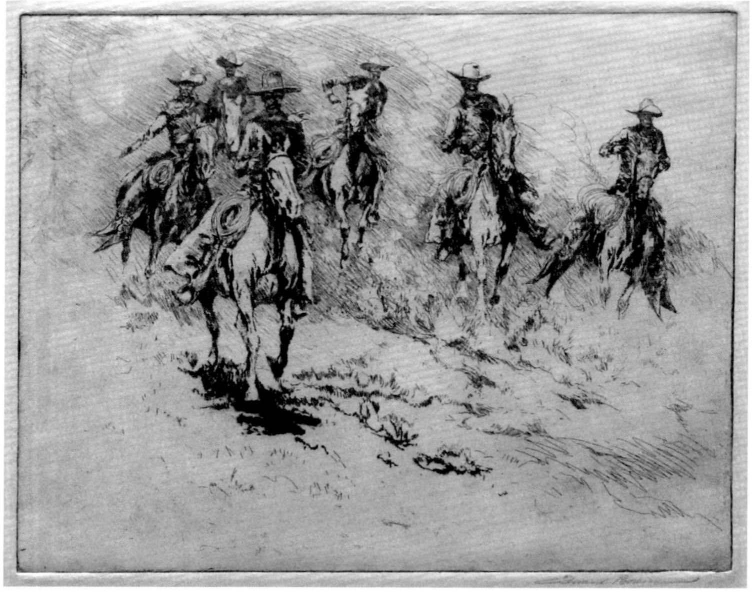

Going to the Wagon, No. 1 (G 44). Etching and drypoint. 7 7/8 x 9 7/8 inches (plate). Signed lower right: *Edward Borein.*

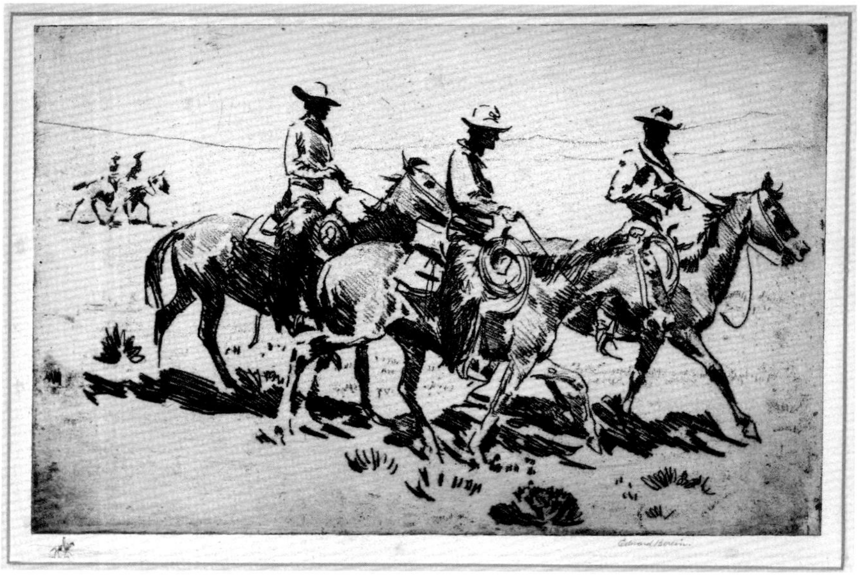

Cowpunchers, No. 2 (G 27), 1914. Soft ground etching. 7 7/8 x 11 3/4 inches (plate). Signed lower right: *Edward Borein.* Remarqued lower left.

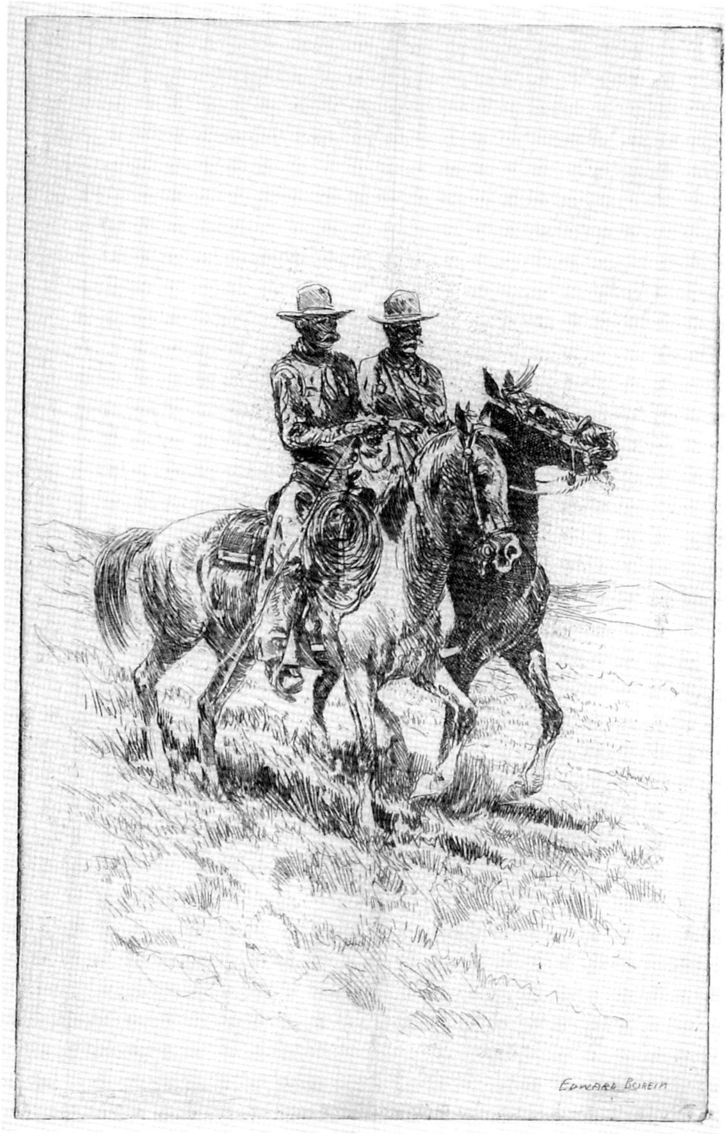

Left: *Pards* (G 18). Etching and drypoint. 7 7/8 x 4 7/8 inches (plate). Signed lower right in plate: *EDWARD BOREIN.*

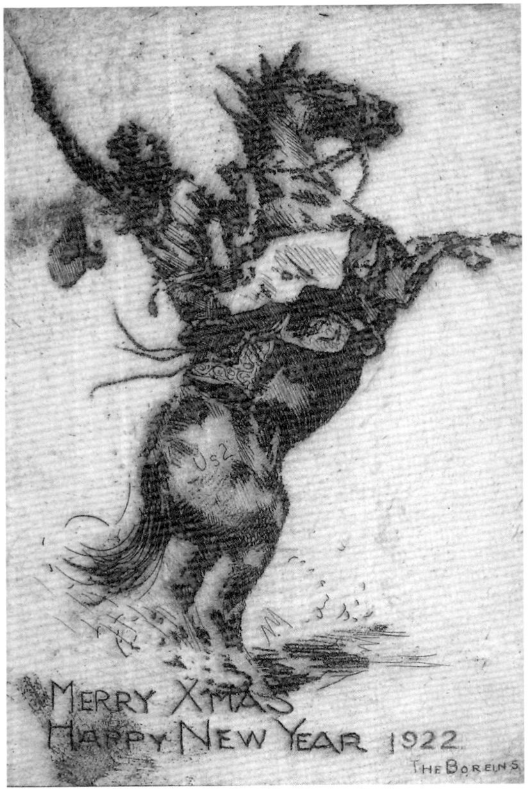

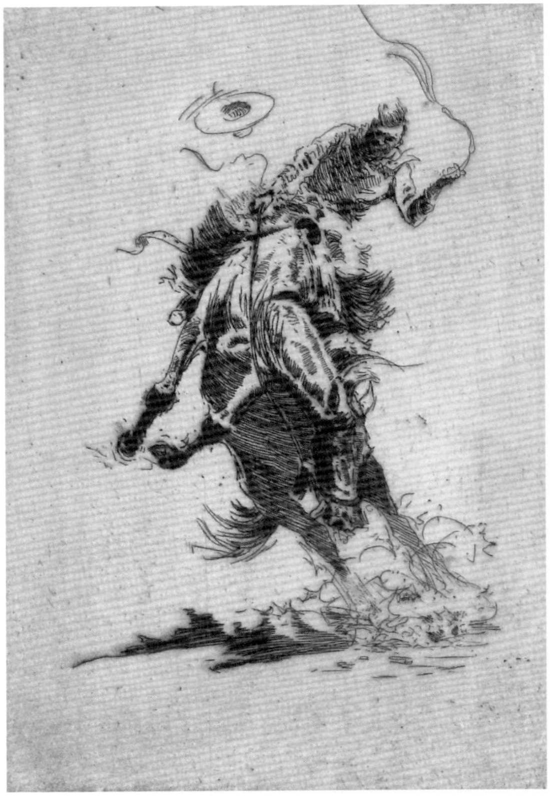

Left: *Holiday Card,* 1922. Etching. 5 7/16 x 3 11/16 inches (plate).
Inscribed in plate: *MERRY XMAS / HAPPY NEW YEAR 1922 / THE BOREINS.*

Right: *The Spinner* (G 71), 1916. Etching. 9 7/8 x 6 7/8 inches (plate).

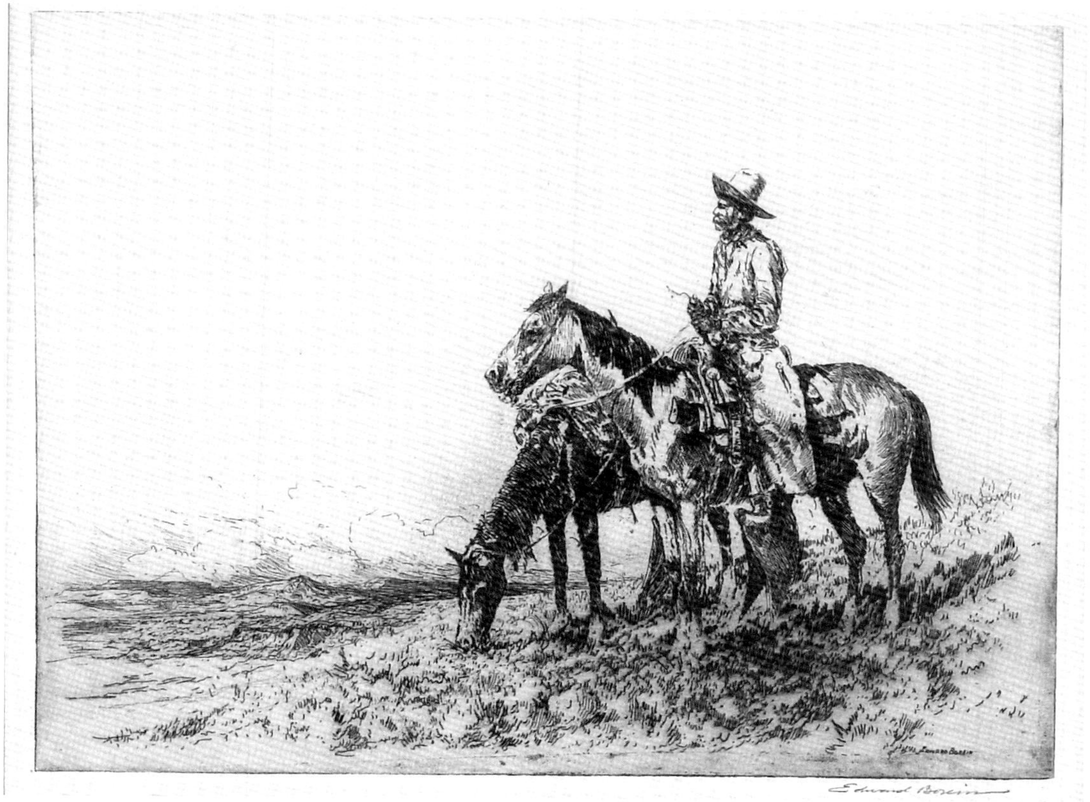

Chuckline Rider (G 9). Etching and drypoint. 8 x 10 11/16 inches (plate). Signed lower right: *Edward Borein.*
Signed lower right in plate: *EDWARD BOREIN.*

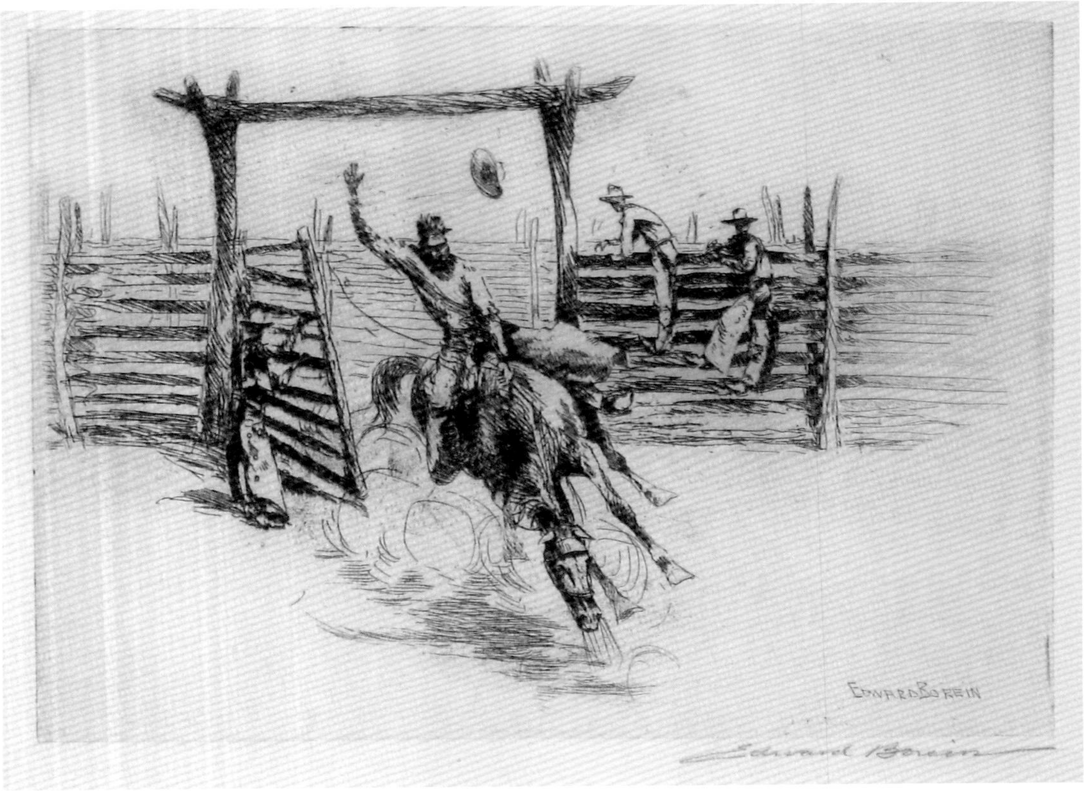

Out of the Gate (G 80). Etching and drypoint. 4 5/16 x 6 15/16 inches (plate). Signed lower right: *Edward Borein*.
Signed lower right in plate: *EDWARD BOREIN*.

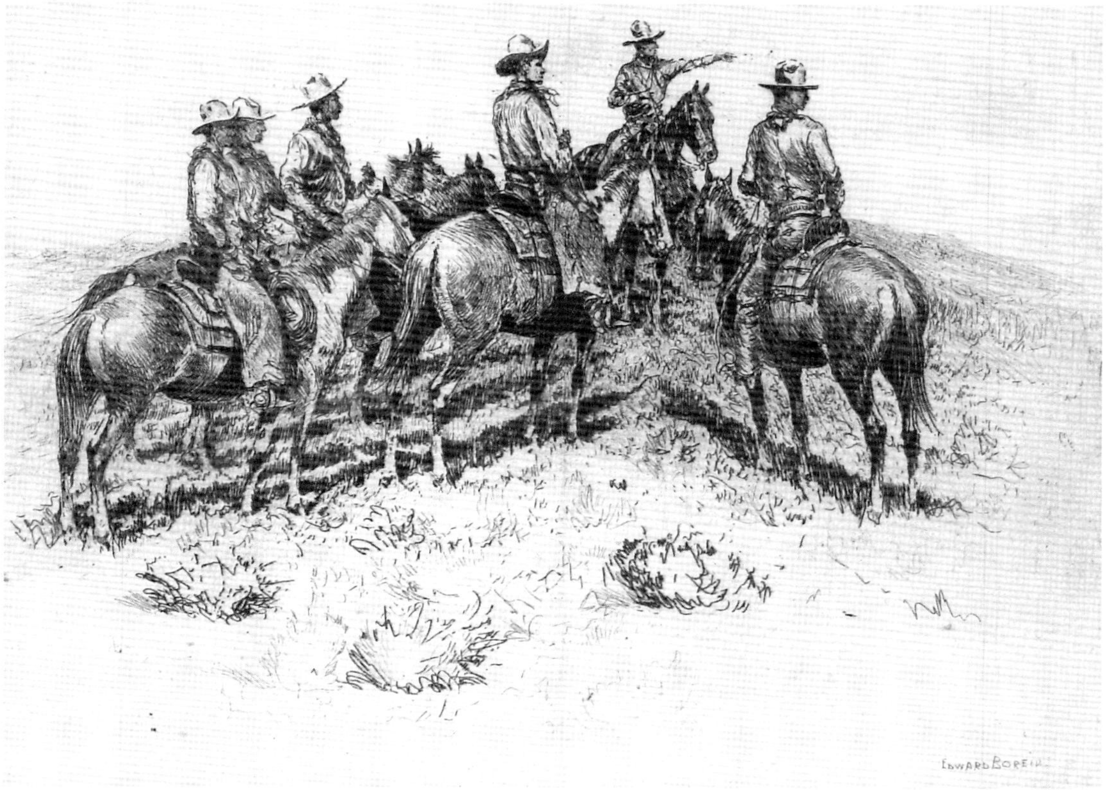

Splitting the Riders (G 35). Etching and drypoint. 5 7/8 x 7 7/8 inches (plate). Signed lower right in plate: *Edward Borein.*

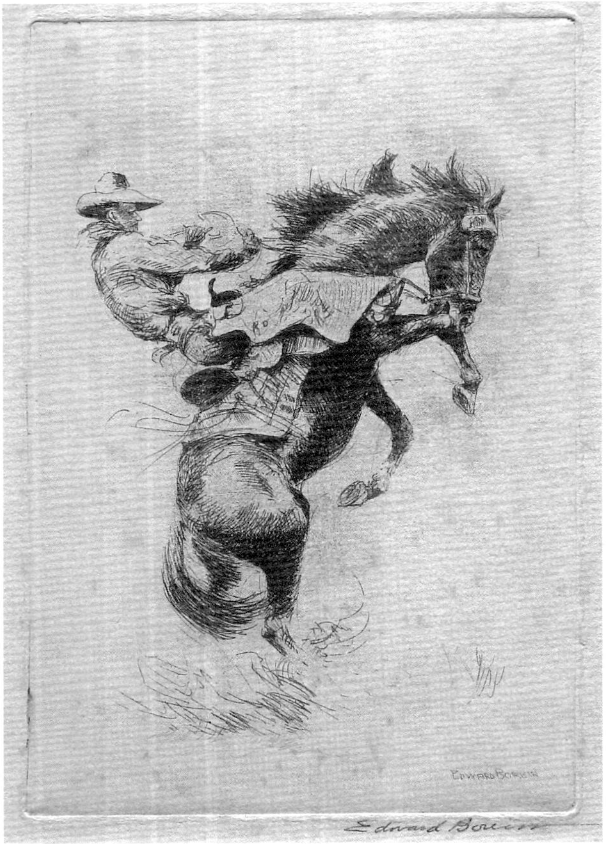

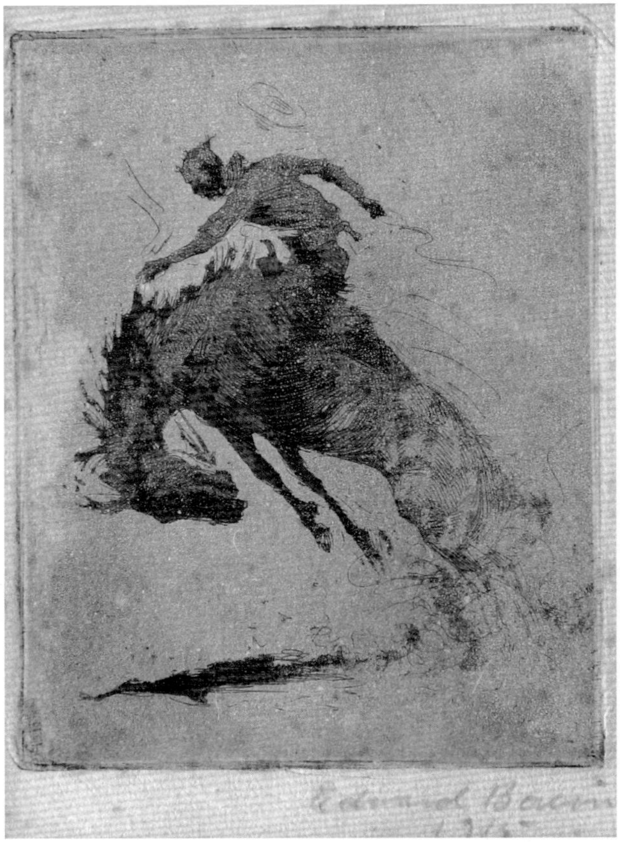

Left: *Bucking Horse, 2nd State* (G 62). Etching. 6 x 4 inches (plate). Signed lower right: *Edward Borein.* Signed lower right in plate: *EDWARD BOREIN.*

Right: *Riding High* (G 77), 1915. Etching and aquatint. 3 15/16 x 3 inches (plate). Signed and dated lower right: *Edward Borein / 1915.*

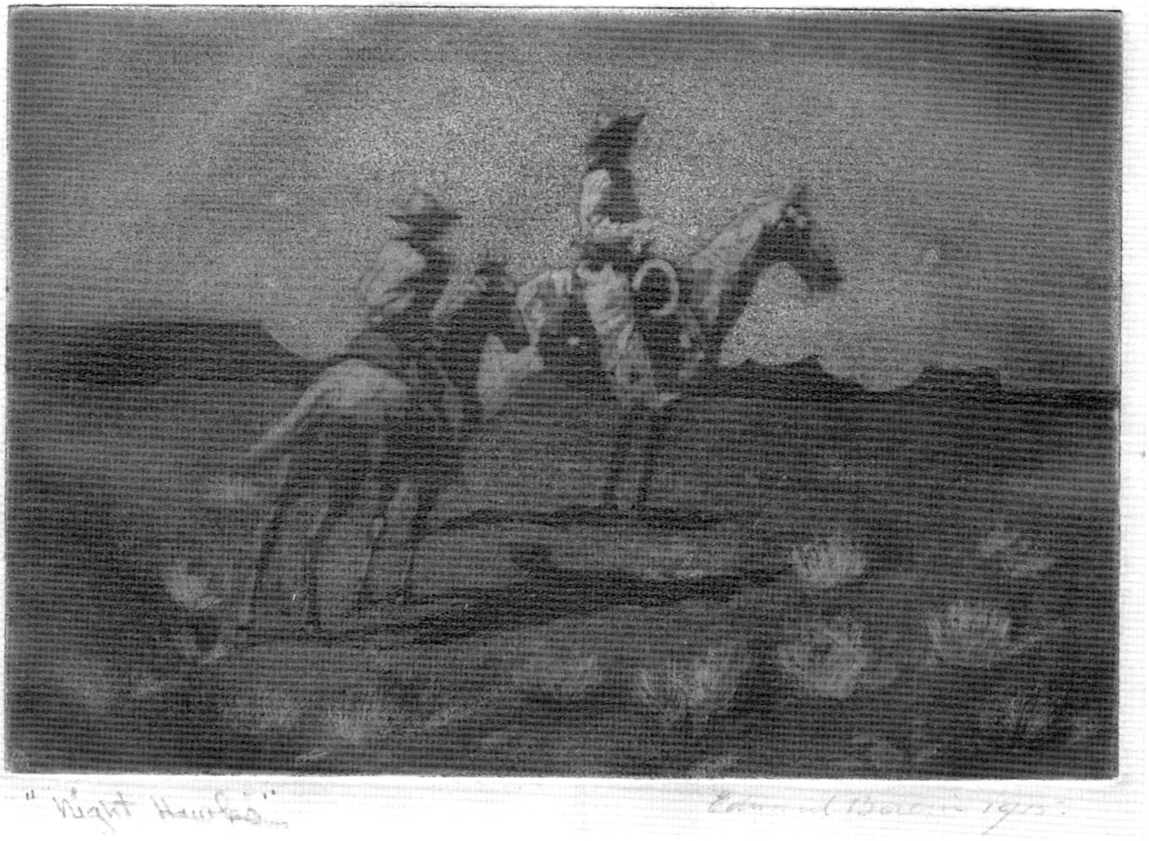

Nighthawks (G 14), 1915. Aquatint (printed in green). 4 15/16 x 6 7/8 inches (plate).
Signed and dated lower right: *Edward Borein 1915*. Titled lower left: *Night Hawks*.

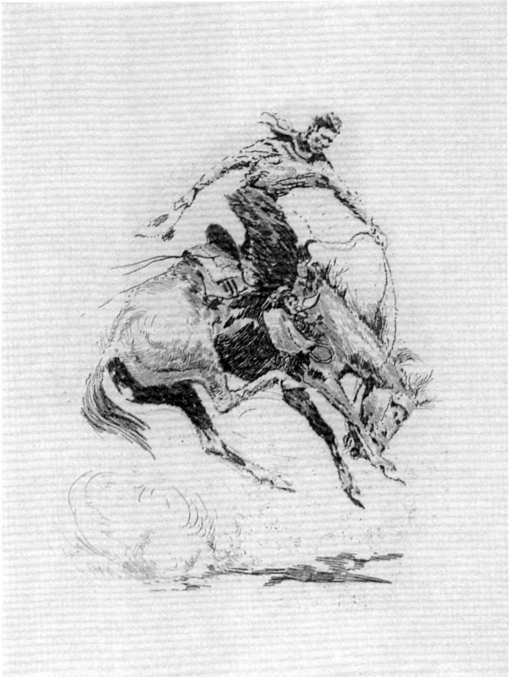

Sitting Pretty, No. 1 (G 65). Etching and drypoint. 6 15/16 x 4 15/16 inches (plate). Signed lower right: *Edward Borein.*

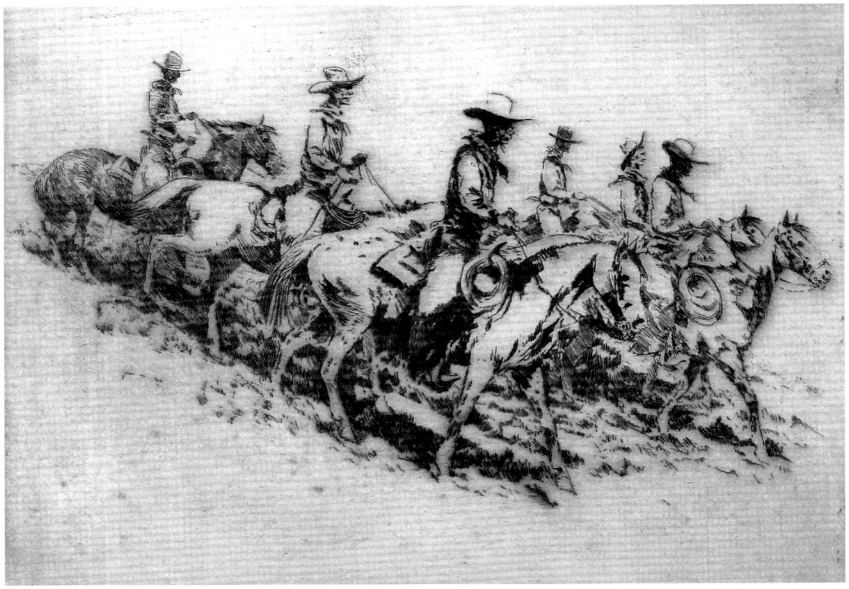

Cowboys (G 34). Etching. 8 11/16 x 11 13/16 inches (plate).

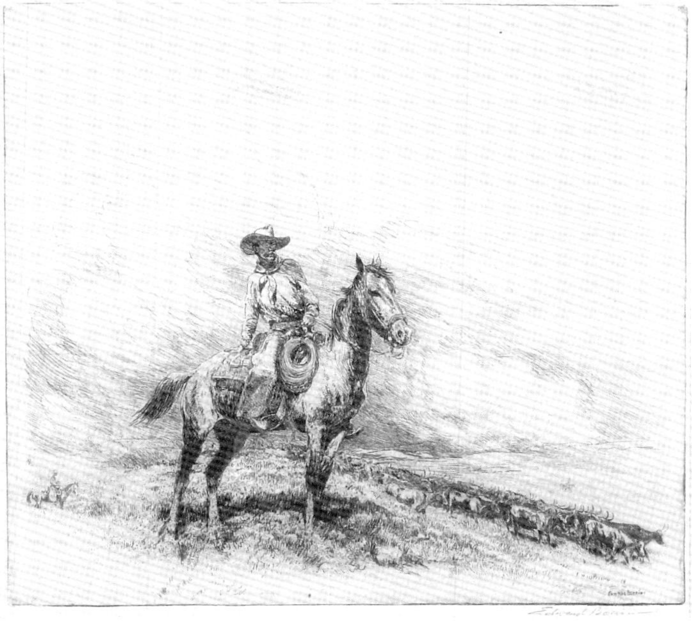

Trail Boss, 1st State (G 85). Etching and drypoint. 7 13/16 x 8 1/2 inches (plate). Signed lower right: *Edward Borein*. Signed lower right in plate: *EDWARD BOREIN*.

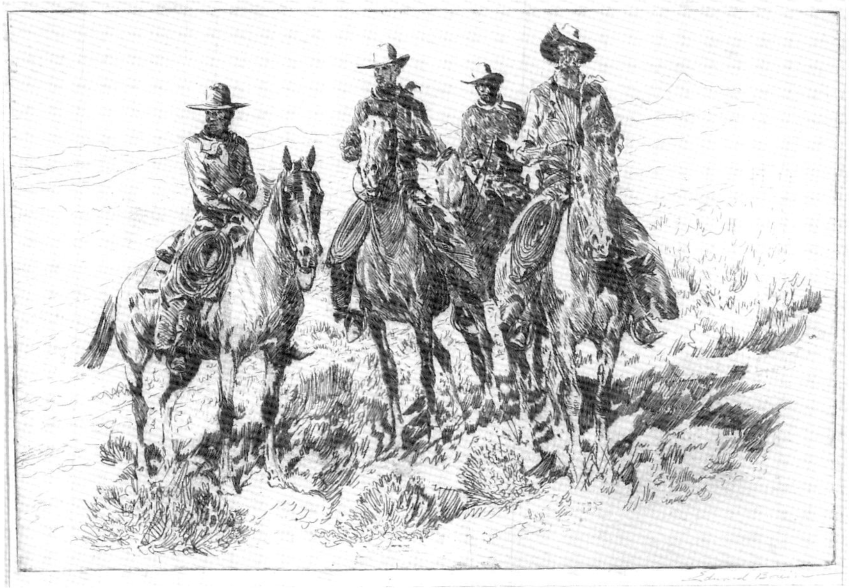

Ranahans (G 32). Etching and drypoint. 8 3/4 x 12 9/16 inches (plate).

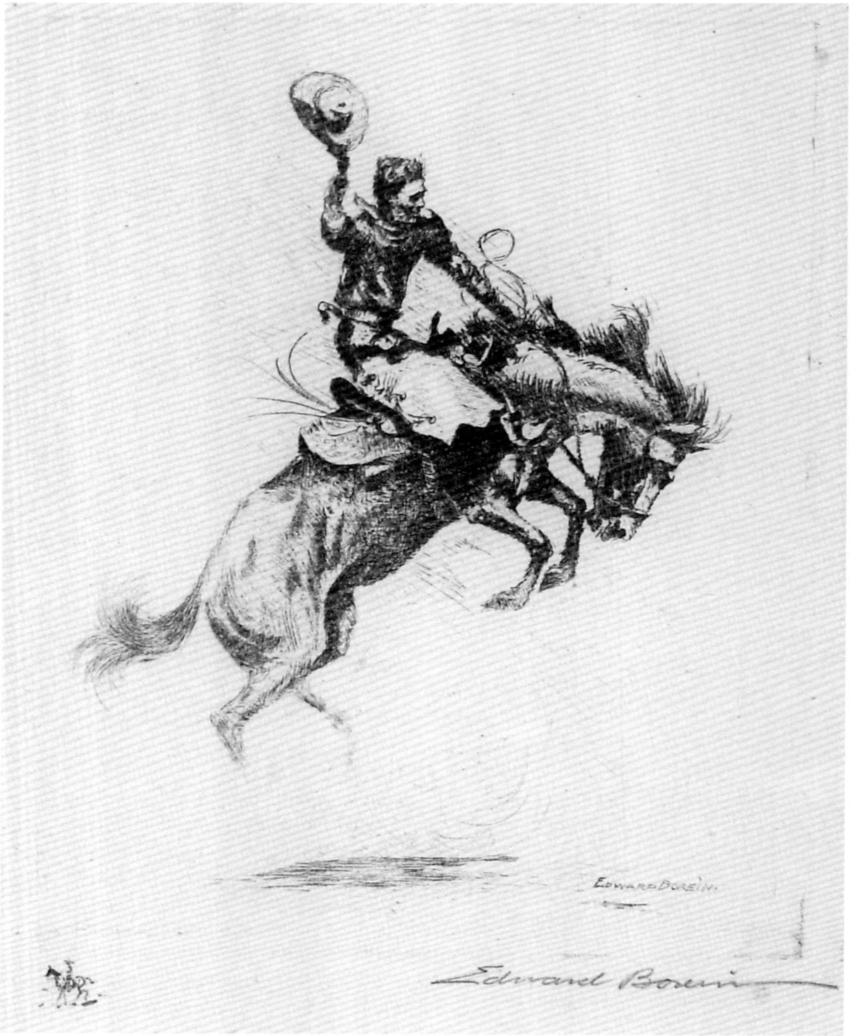

Little Bucking Horse (G 64). Etching and drypoint. 4 7/8 x 3 15/16 inches (plate). Signed lower right: *Edward Borein*. Signed lower right in plate: *EDWARD BOREIN*. Remarqued lower left.

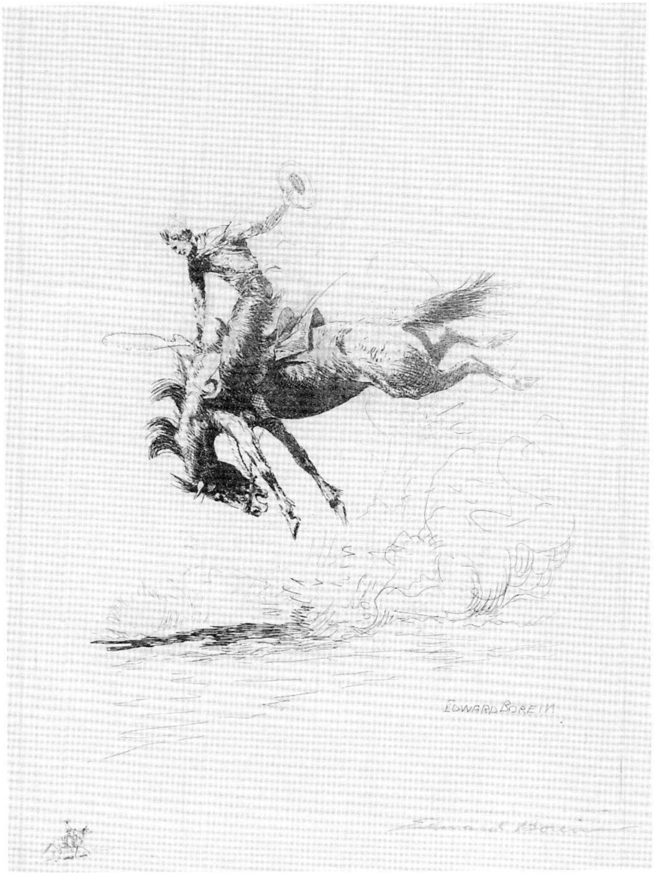

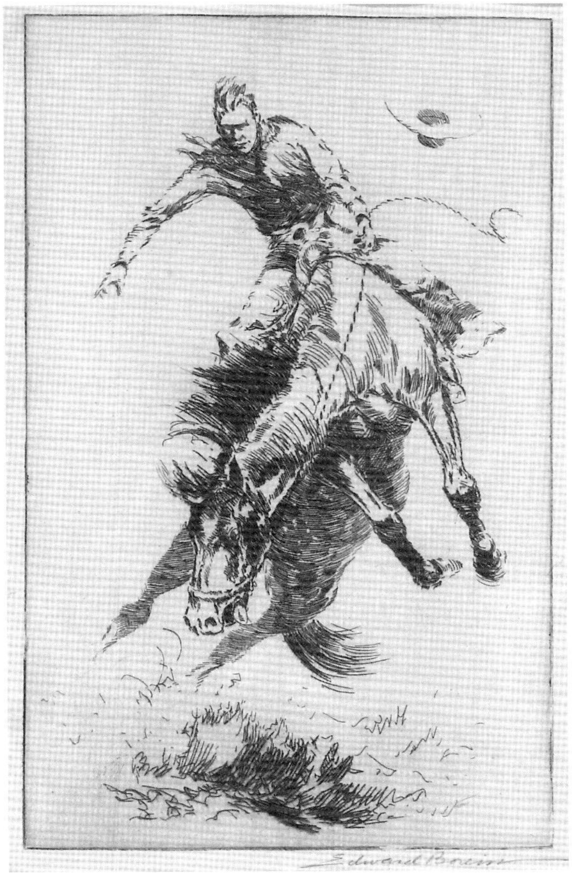

Left: *Ride 'Im Cowboy* (G 67). Etching and drypoint. 6 7/8 x 4 15/16 inches (plate). Signed lower right: *Edward Borein.* Signed lower right in plate: *EDWARD BOREIN.* Remarqued lower left.

Right: *New Bucking Horse* (G 72). Etching. 7 15/16 x 4 15/16 inches (plate). Signed lower right: *Edward Borein.*

MISSIONS

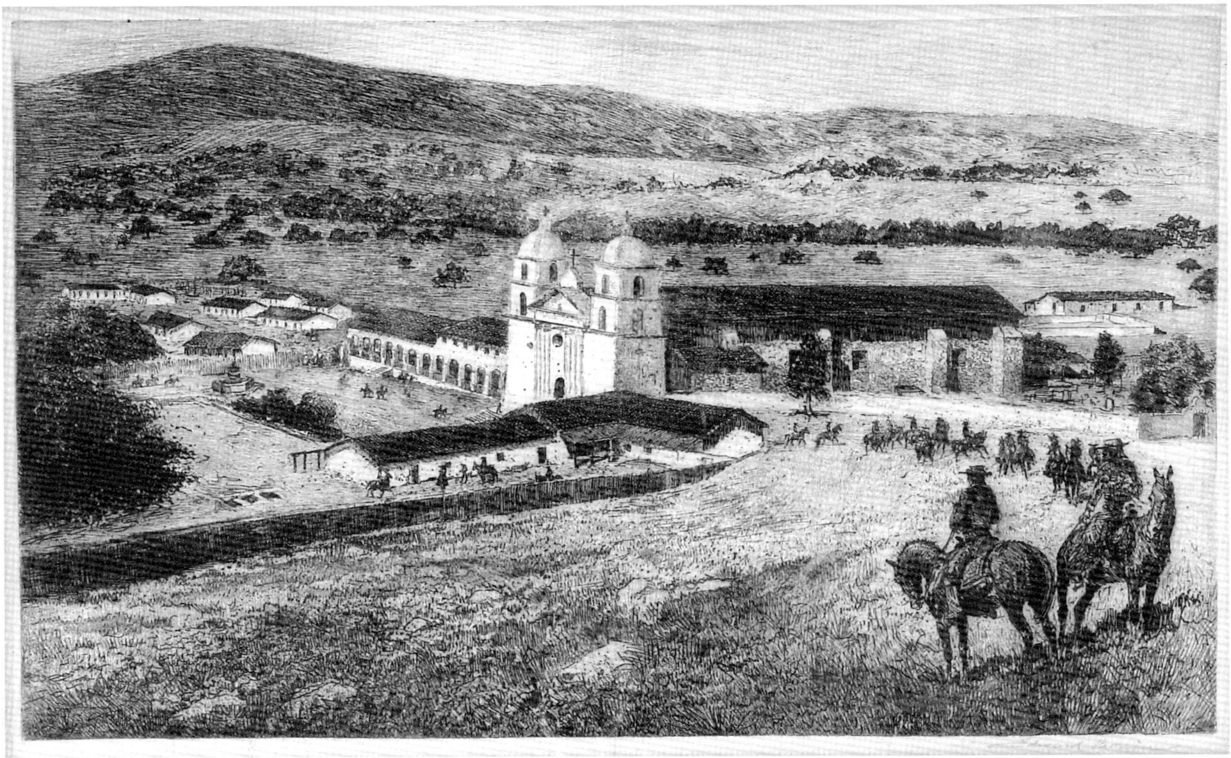

Mission Santa Barbara, No. 1 (G 248). Etching and drypoint. 8 15/16 x 14 3/8 inches (plate).
Signed lower right: *Edward Borein.*

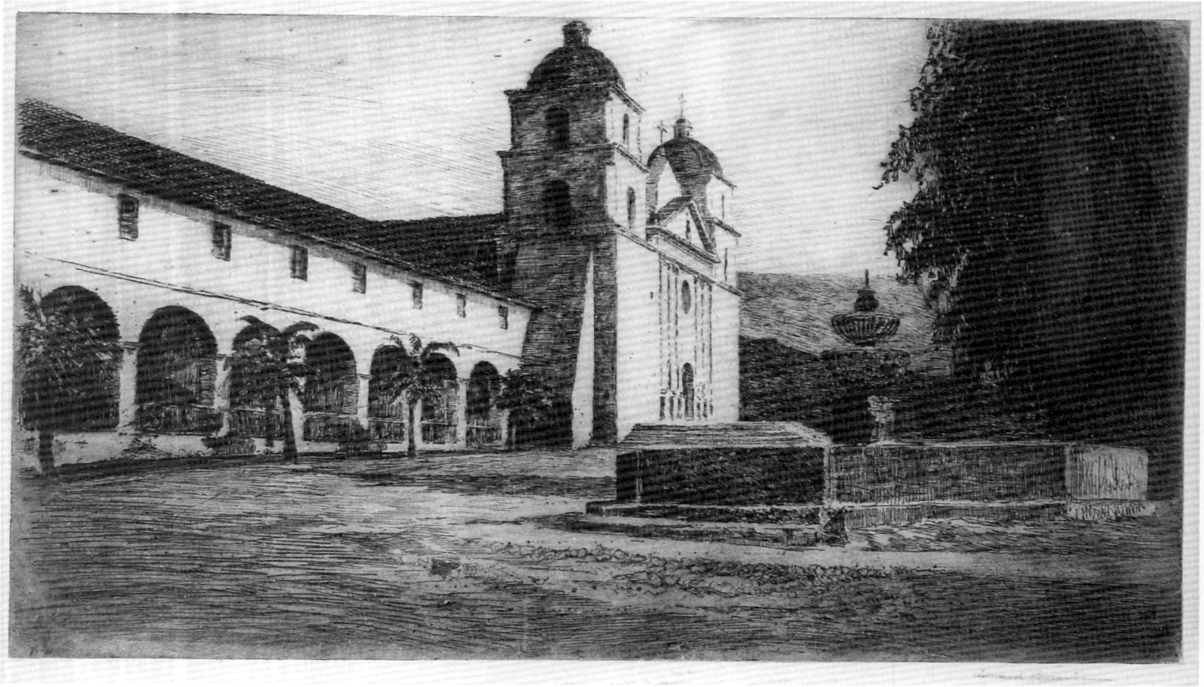

Mission Santa Barbara, No. 3 (G 250). Etching and drypoint. 7 15/16 x 13 7/8 inches (plate).
Signed lower right: *Edward Borein.*

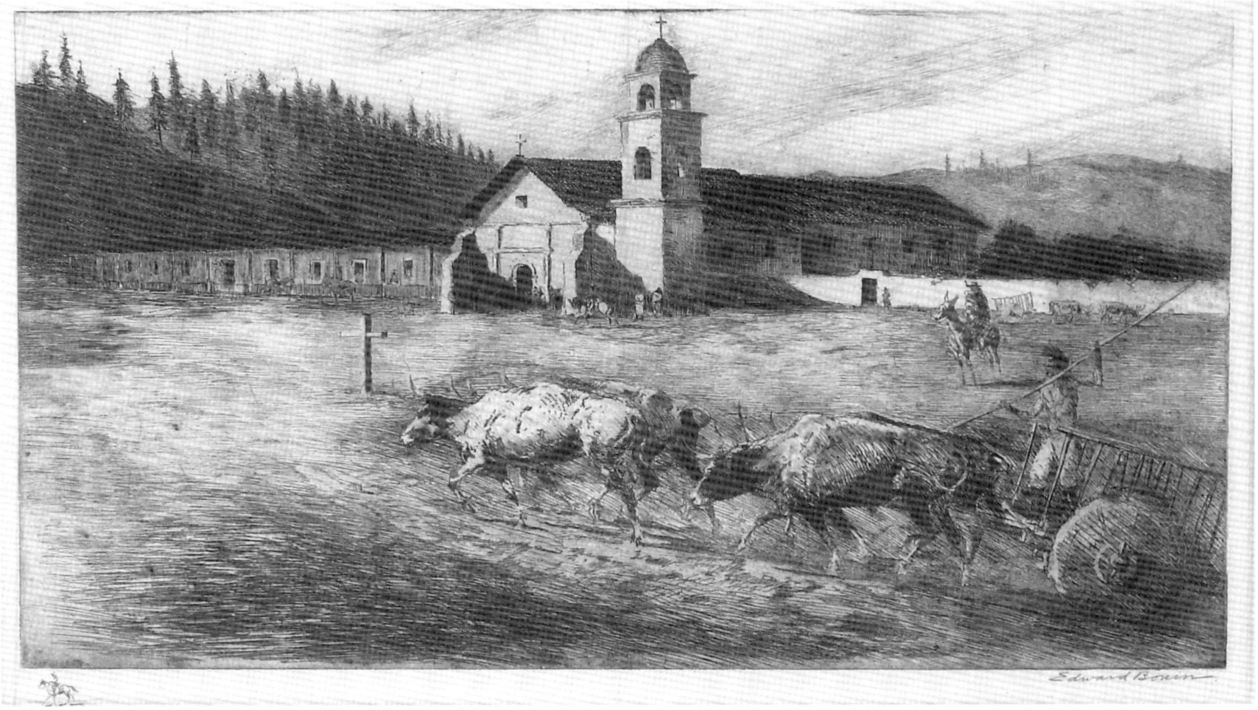

Mission Santa Cruz (G 259). Etching and drypoint. 7 13/16 x 13 7/8 inches (plate). Signed lower right: *Edward Borein*. Remarqued lower left.

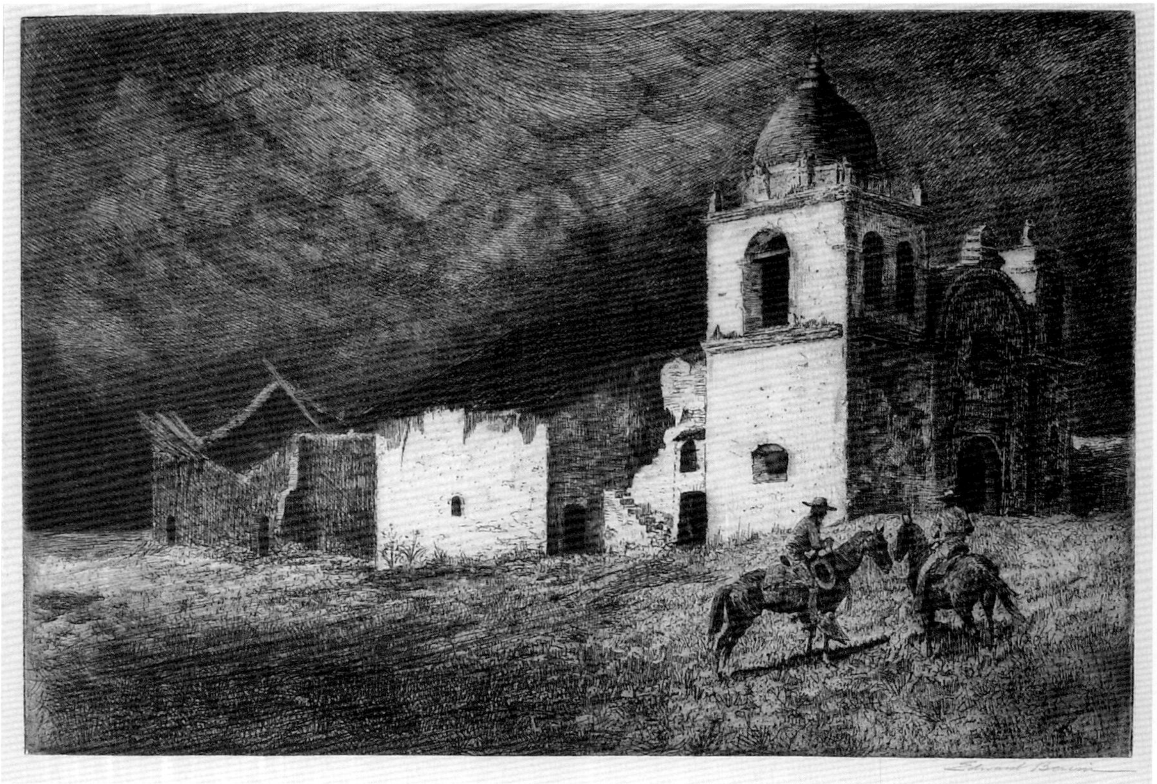

Mission Carmel (G 258). Etching and drypoint. 8 1/2 x 12 3/8 inches (plate). Signed lower right: *Edward Borein.*

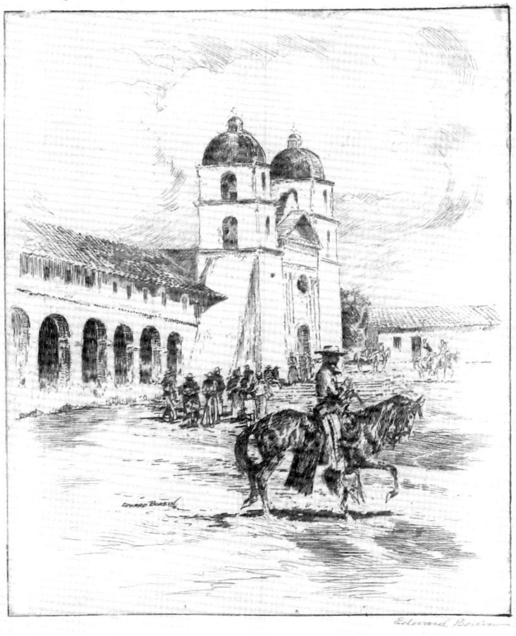

An Old Time Christmas, Mission Santa Barbara. Etching and drypoint. 9 5/8 x 7 5/8 inches (plate).
Signed lower right: *Edward Borein.*

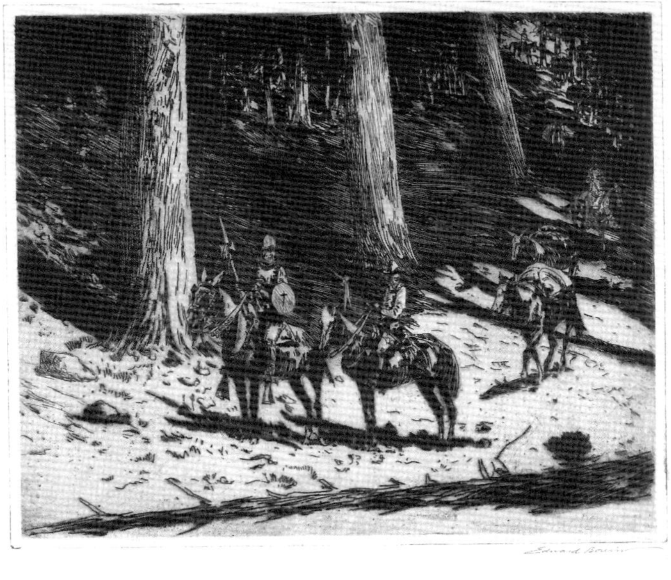

Conquistadores Entering California, 1st State (G 277). Etching. 9 7/8 x 11 13/16 inches (plate).
Signed lower right: *Edward Borein.* Signed lower right in plate: EDWARD BOREIN.

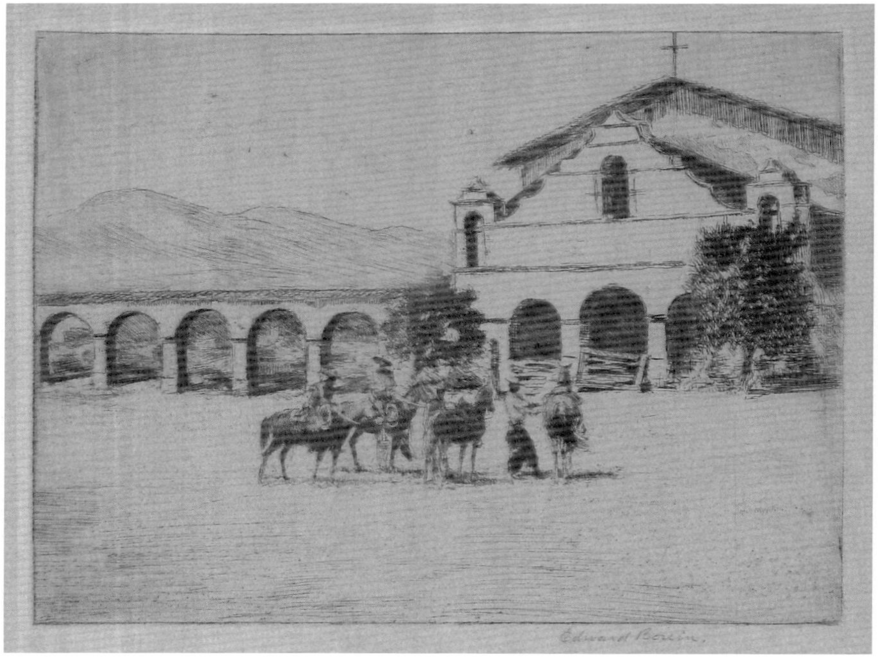

Mission San Antonio de Padua, No. 1, 2nd State (G 256). Etching and drypoint. 5 1/8 x 6 3/4 inches (plate).
Signed lower right: *Edward Borein.*

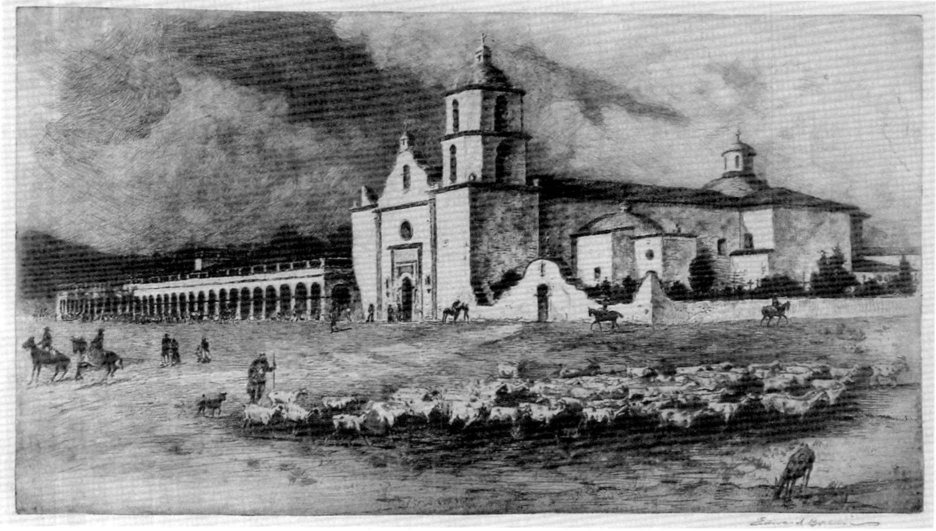

Mission San Luis Rey, No. 1 (G 244). Etching and drypoint. 8 3/4 x 15 5/8 inches (plate).
Signed lower right: *Edward Borein.*

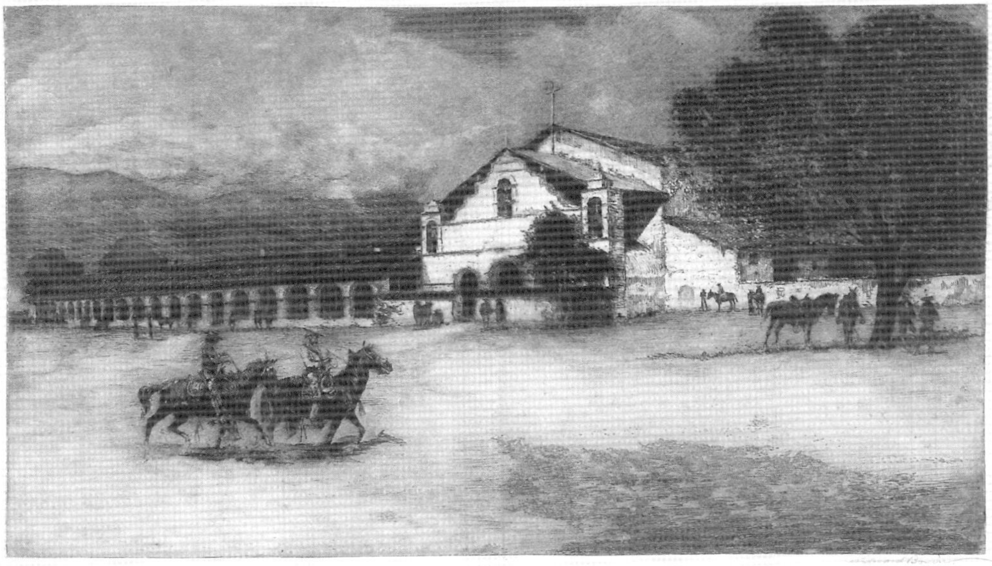

Mission San Antonio de Padua, No. 2, 3rd State (G 257). Etching and drypoint. 8 3/8 x 14 3/8 inches (plate). Signed lower right: *Edward Borein.*

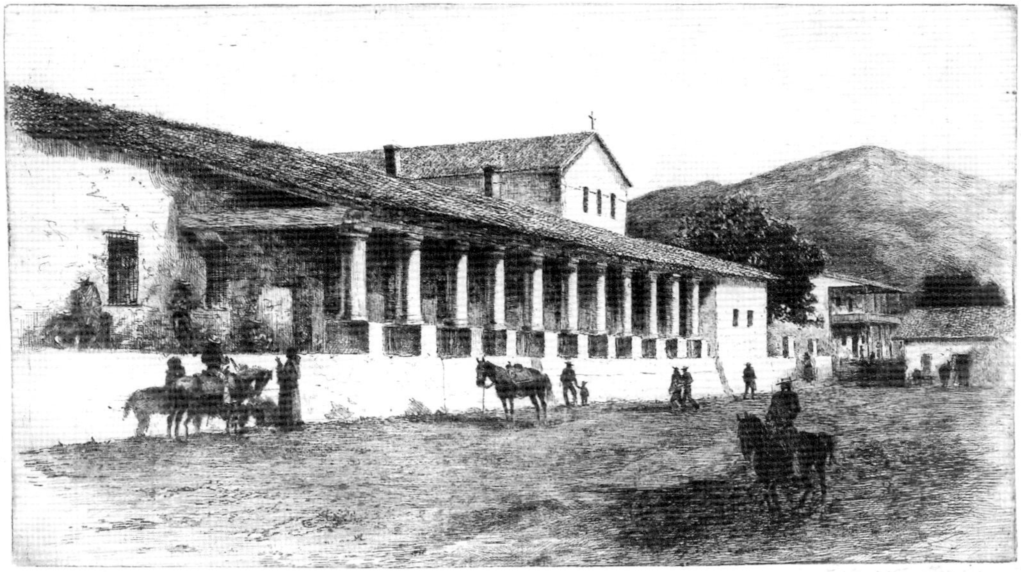

Mission San Luis Obispo (G 255). Etching and drypoint. 7 13/16 x 13 7/8 inches (plate). Signed lower right: *Edward Borein.*

SOUTHWEST

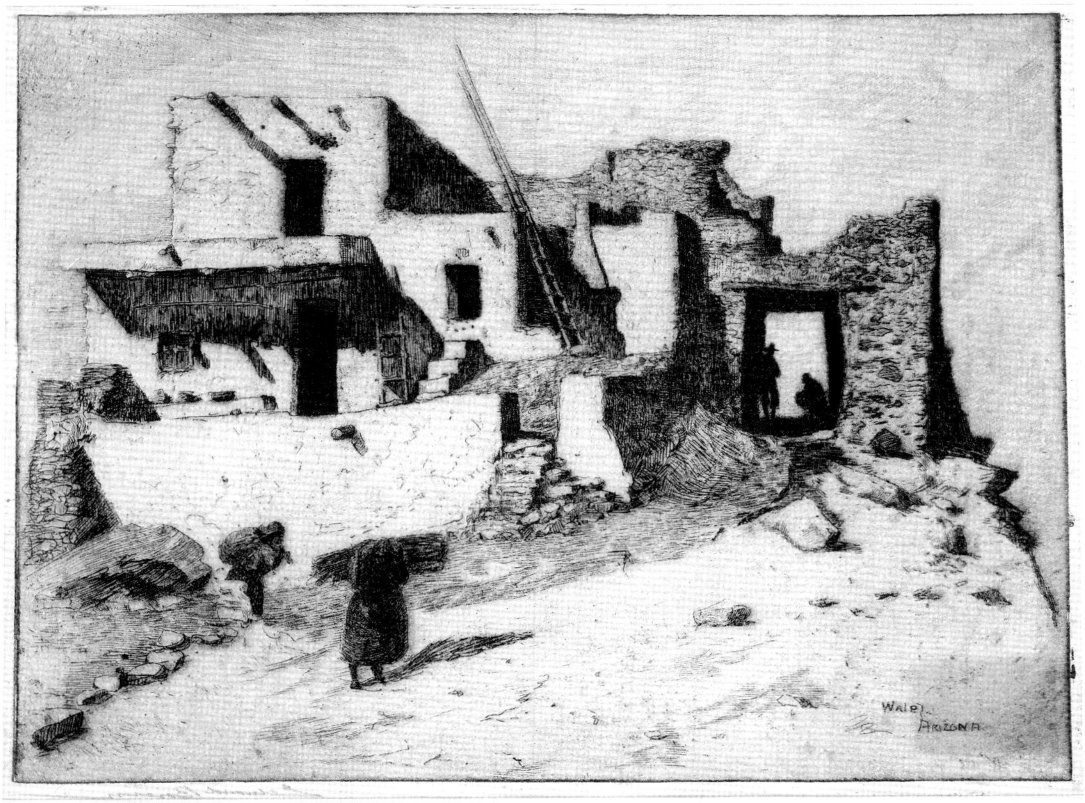

The Last House, Walpi (G 217), 1915. Etching and drypoint. 9 1/2 x 11 7/8 inches (plate).

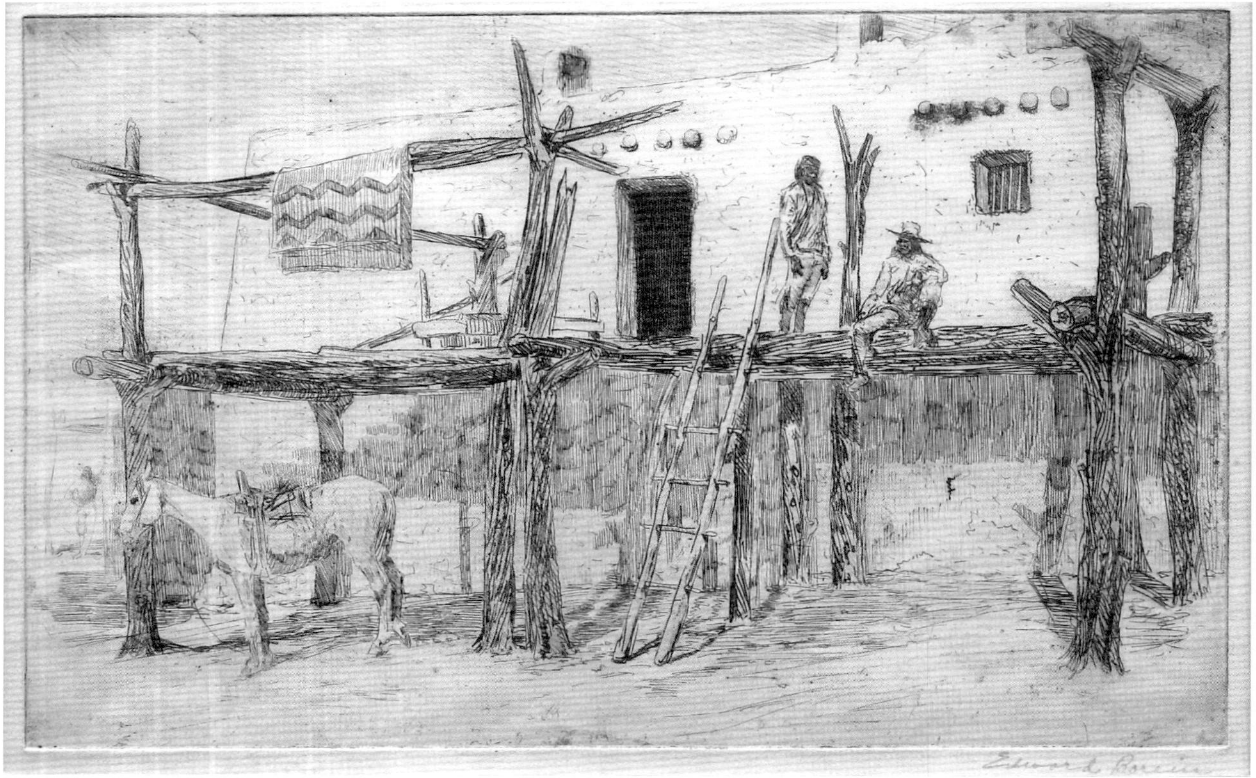

The Ramada (G 238). Etching and drypoint. 6 7/8 x 10 13/16 inches (plate).

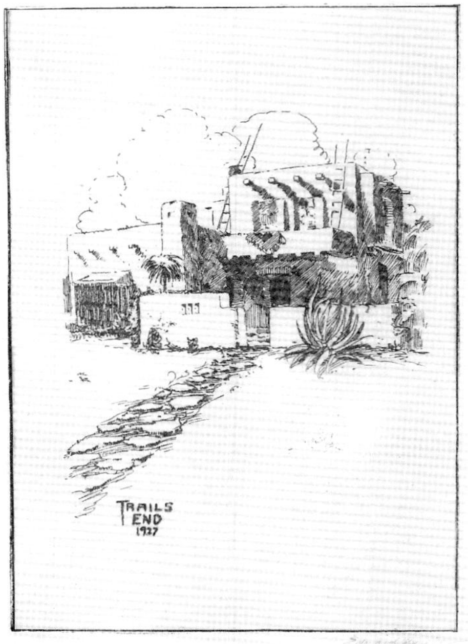

Trails End (G 276), 1927. Etching. 9 3/16 x 6 5/16 inches (plate). Signed lower right: *Edward Borein.*
Titled and dated lower left in plate: *TRAILS / END / 1927.*

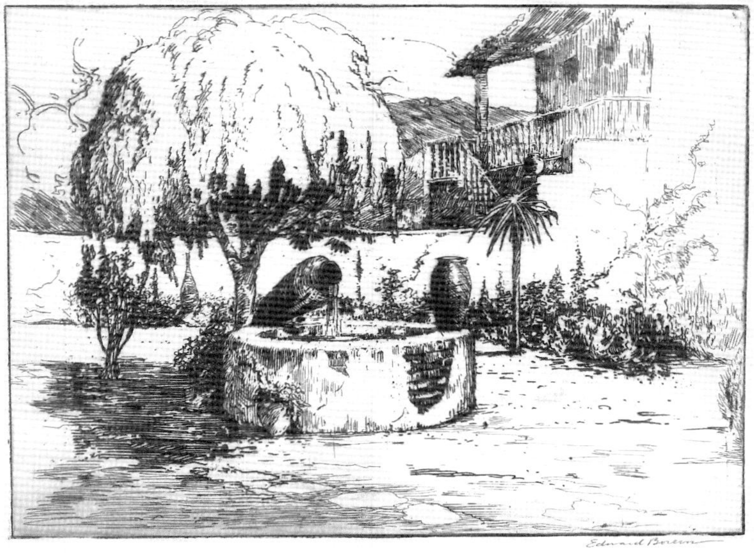

Wishing Well (Charles O. Middleton Home, Beverly Hills) (G 275). Etching. 7 1/4 x 9 7/8 inches (plate).
Signed lower right: *Edward Borein.*

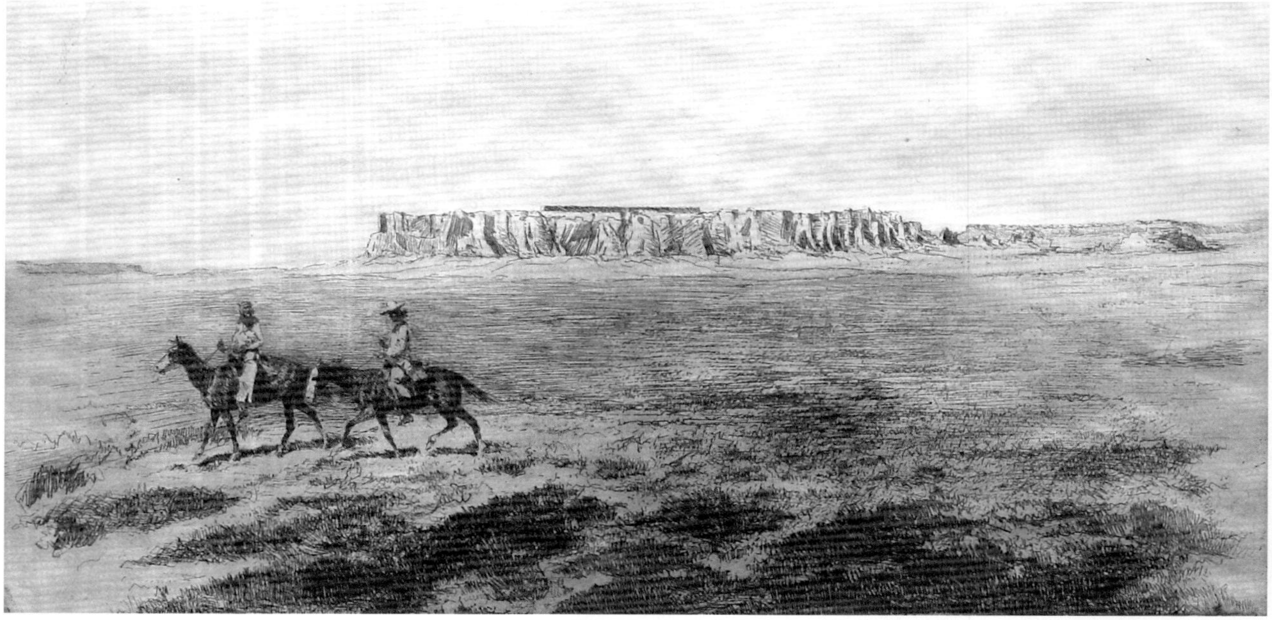

Acoma, New Mexico (G 206). Etching and drypoint. 7 x 13 7/8 inches (plate).

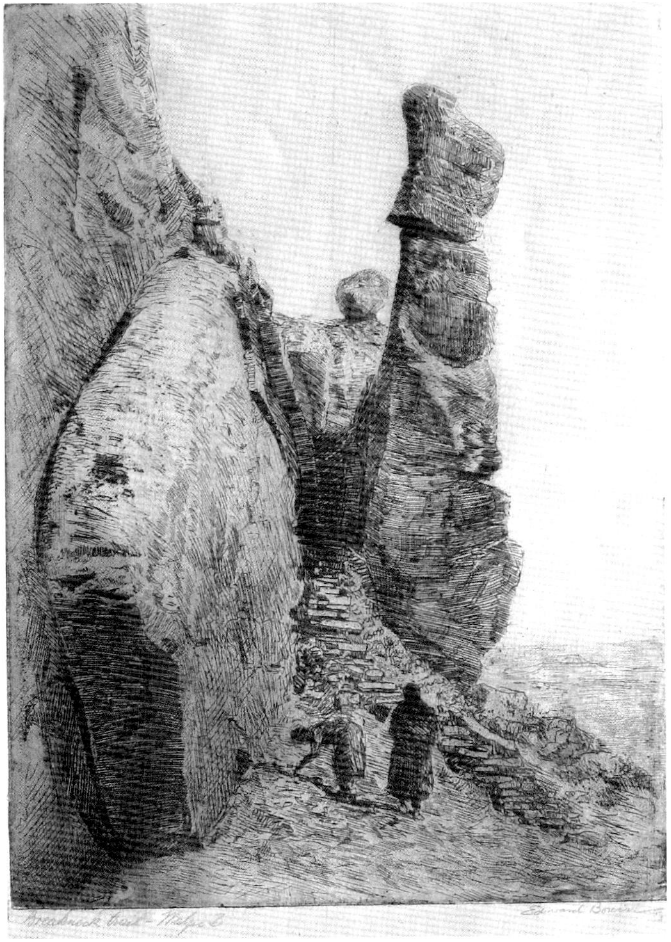

Breakneck Trail to Walpi, No. 2 (G 214). Etching and drypoint. 12 1/2 x 6 7/8 inches (plate).
Signed lower right: *Edward Borein*. Titled lower left: *Breakneck Trail – Walpi 3*.

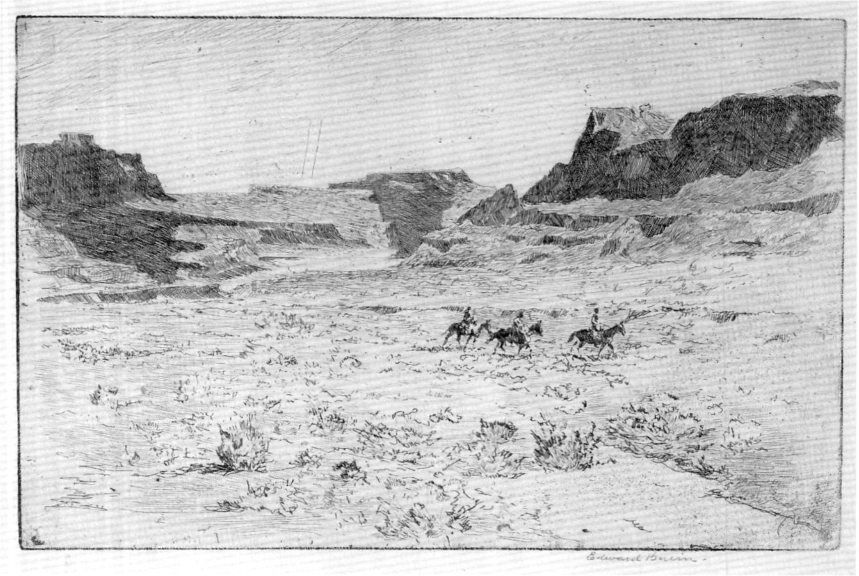

The Edge of the Painted Desert (G 199). Etching and drypoint. 5 15/16 x 8 13/16 inches (plate).
Signed lower right: *Edward Borein*.

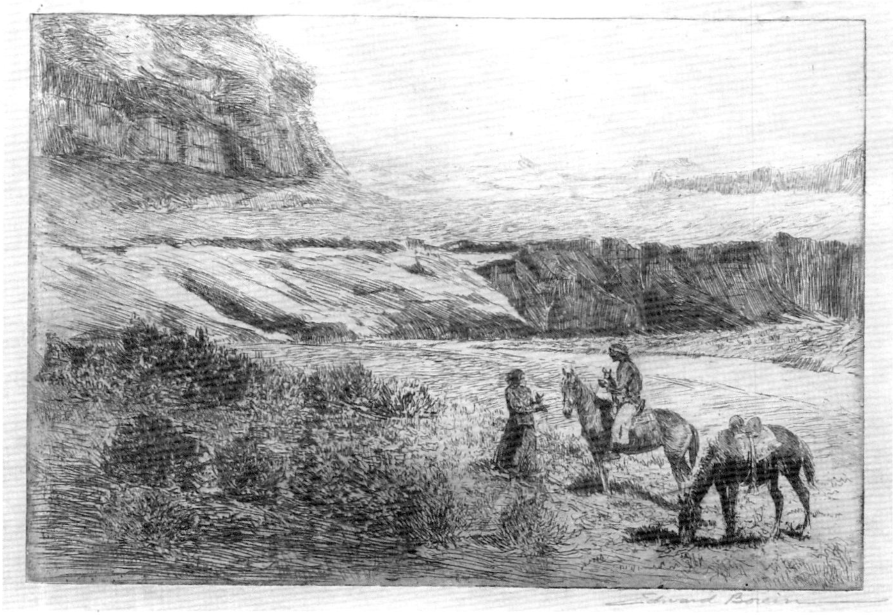

The Gossips, Chinle, Arizona (G 189). Etching and drypoint. 6 11/16 x 9 9/16 inches (plate).
Signed lower right: *Edward Borein*.

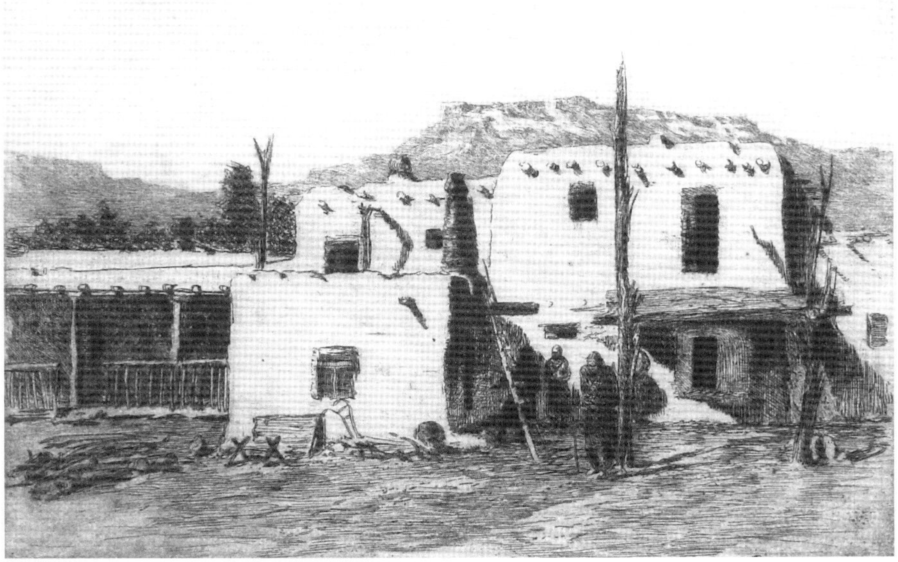

House with High Chimney (G 242). Etching and drypoint. 6 7/8 x 10 1/2 inches (plate).

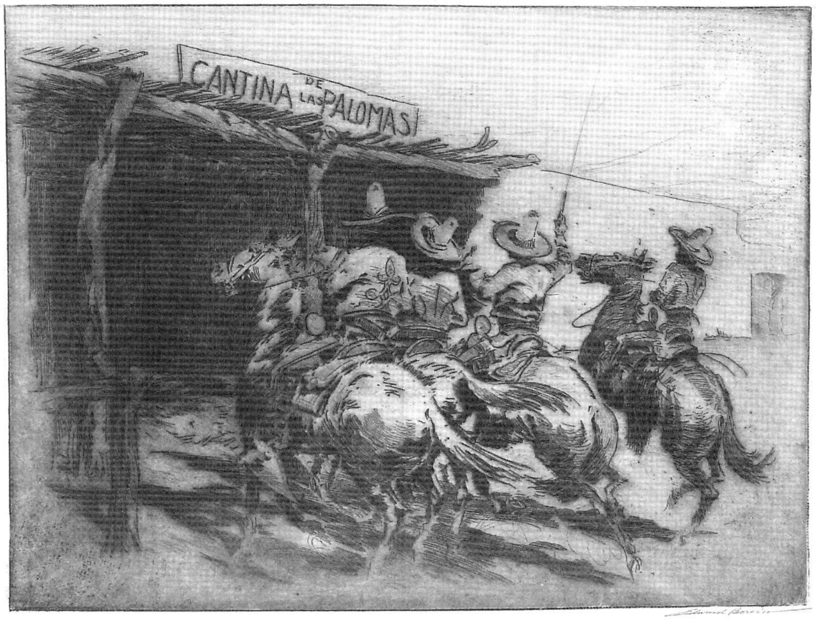

La Cantina de los Palomas, No. 2 (G 271). Etching and drypoint. 9 x 11 7/8 inches (plate).
Signed lower right: *Edward Borein*.

GERALD GP PETERS GALLERY

1011 Paseo de Peralta, Santa Fe NM 87501 Tel 505 954-5700 Fax 505 954-5754
24 East 78th Street, New York NY 10021 Tel 212 628-9760 Fax 212 628-9635
Pillsbury & Peters Fine Art, 2913 Fairmount, Dallas TX 75201 Tel 214 969-9410 Fax 214 969-9023